Reading STREET

Program Authors

Peter Afflerbach	P. David Pearson
Camille Blachowicz	Sam Sebesta
Candy Dawson Boyd	Deborah Simmons
Elena Izquierdo	Alfred Tatum
Connie Juel	Sharon Vaughn
Edward Kame'enui	Susan Watts Taffe
Donald Leu	Karen Kring Wixson
Jeanne R. Paratore	

PEARSON

Glenview, Illinois • Boston, Massachusetts
Chandler, Arizona • Upper Saddle River, New Jersey

We dedicate Reading Street to
Peter Jovanovich.

His wisdom, courage,
and passion for education
are an inspiration to us all.

Accelerated Reader®

ISBN-13: 978-0-328-47049-5
ISBN-10: 0-328-47049-X
2 3 4 5 6 7 8 9 10 V003 14 13 12 11 10
CC1

Any Path, Any Pace

"Welcome to Reading Street! Bienvenidos too."

Find Your Place on Reading Street!

Who said so?

The Leading Researchers,

Practitioners, and Authors.

Consultant

Sharroky Hollie, Ph.D.
Assistant Professor
California State University
Dominguez Hills, CA

Teacher Reviewers

Dr. Bettyann Brugger
Educational Support Coordinator–
Reading Office
Milwaukee Public Schools
Milwaukee, WI

Kathleen Burke
K–12 Reading Coordinator
Peoria Public Schools, Peoria, IL

Darci Burns, M.S.Ed.
University of Oregon

Bridget Cantrell
District Intervention Specialist
Blackburn Elementary School
Independence, MO

Tahira DuPree Chase,
M.A., M.S.Ed.
Administrator of Elementary
English Language Arts
Mount Vernon City School District
Mount Vernon, NY

Michele Conner
Director, Elementary Education
Aiken County School District
Aiken, SC

Georgia Coulombe
K–6 Regional Trainer/
Literacy Specialist
Regional Center for Training and
Learning (RCTL), Reno, NV

Kelly Dalmas
Third Grade Teacher
Avery's Creek Elementary, Arden, NC

Seely Dillard
First Grade Teacher
Laurel Hill Primary School
Mt. Pleasant, SC

Jodi Dodds-Kinner
Director of Elementary Reading
Chicago Public Schools, Chicago, IL

Dr. Ann Wild Evenson
District Instructional Coach
Osseo Area Schools, Maple Grove, MN

Stephanie Fascitelli
Principal
Apache Elementary, Albuquerque
Public Schools, Albuquerque, NM

Alice Franklin
Elementary Coordinator, Language
Arts & Reading
Spokane Public Schools, Spokane, WA

Laureen Fromberg
Assistant Principal
PS 100 Queens, NY

Kimberly Gibson
First Grade Teacher
Edgar B. Davis Community School
Brockton, MA

Kristen Gray
Lead Teacher
A.T. Allen Elementary School
Concord, NC

Mary Ellen Hazen
State Pre-K Teacher
Rockford Public Schools #205
Rockford, IL

Patrick M. Johnson
Elementary Instructional Director
Seattle Public Schools, Seattle, WA

Theresa Jaramillo Jones
Principal
Highland Elementary School
Las Cruces, NM

Sophie Kowzun
Program Supervisor, Reading/
Language Arts, PreK-5
Montgomery County Public Schools
Rockville, MD

David W. Matthews
Sixth Grade Teacher
Easton Area Middle School
Easton, PA

Ana Nuncio
Editor and Independent Publisher
Salem, MA

Joseph Peila
Principal
Chappell Elementary School
Chicago, IL

Ivana Reimer
Literacy Coordinator
PS 100 Queens, NY

Sally Riley
Curriculum Coordinator
Rochester Public Schools
Rochester, NH

Dyan M. Smiley
Independent Educational Consultant

Michael J. Swiatowiec
Lead Literacy Teacher
Graham Elementary School
Chicago, IL

Dr. Helen Taylor
Director of English Education
Portsmouth City Public Schools
Portsmouth, VA

Carol Thompson
Teaching and Learning Coach
Independence School District
Independence, MO

Erinn Zeitlin
Kindergarten Teacher
Carderock Springs Elementary School
Bethesda, MD

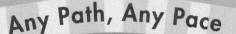
Any Path, Any Pace

UNIT 3

Inventors and Artists

In this Teacher's Edition Unit 3, Volume 1

Table of Contents...vi–xiii
Unit 3 Skills Overview ....xiv–xv
Unit 3 Monitor Progress ....xvi–xvii
Assessment and Grouping ....xviii–xix
Unit 3 Concept Launch .... xx–xxi
Flexible Pacing Plans.. xxii

WEEK 1 · The Fabulous Perpetual Motion Machine Drama...........................324a–353q
The Toy Space Shuttle Is Here! Persuasive Text

Differentiated Instruction **SI OL A ELL** ....DI•1–DI•25

WEEK 2 · Leonardo's Horse
Biography 354a–387q
A Job for Michelangelo Historical Fiction

Differentiated Instruction **SI OL A ELL** ....DI•26–DI•50

WEEK 3 · The Dinosaurs of Waterhouse Hawkins Biography...388a–423q
A Model Scientist Expository Text

Differentiated Instruction **SI OL A ELL** ....DI•51–DI•75

Customize Writing ....CW•1–CW•10
Customize Literacy...CL•1–CL•47
Let's Learn Amazing Words ....OV•1–OV•3

In the **First Stop** on Reading Street

- **Dear Fifth Grade Teacher**
- **Research into Practice on Reading Street**
- **Guide to Reading Street**
- **Assessment on Reading Street**
- **Customize Writing on Reading Street**
- **Differentiate Instruction on Reading Street**

- **ELL on Reading Street**
- **Customize Literacy on Reading Street**
- **Digital Products on Reading Street**
- **Teacher Resources for Grade 5**
- **Index**

GO Digital!

See It!
- Big Question Video
- Concept Talk Video
- Envision It! Animations

Hear It!
- eSelections
- eReaders
- Grammar Jammer
- Leveled Reader Database

Do It!
- Vocabulary Activities
- Story Sort
- 21st Century Skills
- Online Assessment
- Letter Tile Drag and Drop

Meeting Challenges

Table of Contents...vi–xiii

Unit 1 Skills Overview ....xiv–xv

Unit 1 Monitor Progress ....xvi–xvii

Assessment and Grouping ....xviii–xix

Unit 1 Concept Launch .... xx–xxi

Flexible Pacing Plans xxii

Volume 1

WEEK 1 • **Red Kayak** Realistic Fiction...................................20a–49q
What Will I Do in an Emergency? How-to Text

Differentiated Instruction SI OL A ELL ....DI•1–DI•25

WEEK 2 • **Thunder Rose** Tall Tale.......................................50a–81q
Measuring Tornadoes Expository Text

Differentiated Instruction SI OL A ELL ....DI•26–DI•50

WEEK 3 • **Island of the Blue Dolphins** Novel 82a–109q
Seven Survival Questions How-to Text

Differentiated Instruction SI OL A ELL ....DI•51–DI•75

Volume 2

WEEK 4 • **Satchel Paige** Biography 110a–139q
Roberto Clemente: A Baseball Hero Biography

Differentiated Instruction SI OL A ELL ....DI•76–DI•100

WEEK 5 • **Ten Mile Day** Expository Text........................140a–169q
Working on the Railroad E-mail

Differentiated Instruction SI OL A ELL ....DI•101–DI•125

WEEK 6 • **Interactive Review**...................................IR•1–IR•60
What kinds of challenges do people face and
how do they meet them?

Unit 1 Reading Poetry 170–173a

Customize Writing .... CW•1–CW•20
Customize Literacy...CL•1–CL•47
Let's Learn Amazing Words ....OV•1–OV•3

Doing the Right Thing

Key
SI Strategic Intervention
OL On-Level
A Advanced
ELL ELL

Table of Contents...vi–xiii
Unit 2 Skills Overview ....xiv–xv
Unit 2 Monitor Progress ....xvi–xvii
Assessment and Grouping...xviii–xix
Unit 2 Concept Launch ....xx–xxi
Flexible Pacing Plans..xxii

Volume 1

WEEK 1 • **At the Beach** Realistic fiction.............................176a–201q
The Eagle and the Bat Legend

Differentiated Instruction SI OL A ELL ....DI•1–DI•25

WEEK 2 • **Hold the Flag High**
Literary Nonfiction..202a–229q
How to Fold the American Flag Web Site

Differentiated Instruction SI OL A ELL ....DI•26–DI•50

WEEK 3 • **The Ch'i-lin Purse** Folk Tale.........................230a–257q
The Story of Phan Ku Myth

Differentiated Instruction SI OL A ELL ....DI•51–DI•75

Volume 2

WEEK 4 • **A Summer's Trade** Realistic Fiction.............258a–287q
Thunderbird and Killer Whale Myth

Differentiated Instruction SI OL A ELL ....DI•76–DI•100

WEEK 5 • **The Midnight Ride of Paul Revere**
Poem 288a–317q
The Heroic Paul Revere Drama

Differentiated Instruction SI OL A ELL ....DI•101–DI•125

WEEK 6 • **Interactive Review**..IR•1–IR•60
What makes people want to do the right thing?
Unit 2 Reading Poetry 318–321a

Customize Writing ....CW•1–CW•20
Customize Literacy..CL•1–CL•47
Let's Learn Amazing Words ....OV•1–OV•3

UNIT 3

Inventors and Artists

Table of Contents .... vi–xiii

Unit 3 Skills Overview .... xiv–xv

Unit 3 Monitor Progress .... xvi–xvii

Assessment and Grouping .... xviii–xix

Unit 3 Concept Launch .... xx–xxi

Flexible Pacing Plans xxii

Volume 1

WEEK 1 · The Fabulous Perpetual Motion Machine Drama 324a–353q
The Toy Space Shuttle Is Here! Persuasive Text

Differentiated Instruction **SI OL A ELL** .... DI•1–DI•25

WEEK 2 · Leonardo's Horse Biography 354a–387q
A Job for Michelangelo Historical Fiction

Differentiated Instruction **SI OL A ELL** .... DI•26–DI•50

WEEK 3 · The Dinosaurs of Waterhouse Hawkins Biography 388a–423q
A Model Scientist Expository Text

Differentiated Instruction **SI OL A ELL** .... DI•51–DI•75

Volume 2

WEEK 4 · Mahalia Jackson Expository Text 424a–447q
Perfect Harmony Poetry

Differentiated Instruction **SI OL A ELL** .... DI•76–DI•100

WEEK 5 · Special Effects in Film and Television
Expository Text 448a–473q
Searching for Animation Search Engines

Differentiated Instruction **SI OL A ELL** .... DI•101–DI•125

WEEK 6 · Interactive Review .... IR•1–IR•60
What do people gain from the work of inventors and artists?

Unit 3 Reading Poetry 474–477a

Customize Writing .... CW•1–CW•20
Customize Literacy .... CL•1–CL•47
Let's Learn Amazing Words .... OV•1–OV•3

UNIT 4

Adapting

Table of Contents..vi–xiii

Unit 4 Skills Overview ....xiv–xv

Unit 4 Monitor Progress ....xvi–xvii

Assessment and Grouping ....xviii–xix

Unit 4 Concept Launch ....xx–xxi

Flexible Pacing Plans...xxii

Volume 1

WEEK 1 · Weslandia Fiction 20a–45q
Under the Back Porch/Keziah poetry

Differentiated Instruction SI OL A ELL ....DI•1–DI•25

WEEK 2 · Tripping Over the Lunch Lady
Realistic Fiction 46a–75q
Square Dancing Persuasive Text

Differentiated Instruction SI OL A ELL ....DI•26–DI•50

WEEK 3 · Exploding Ants Expository Text 76a–103q
The Art of Mimicry Expository Text

Differentiated Instruction SI OL A ELL ....DI•51–DI•75

Volume 2

WEEK 4 · The Stormi Giovanni Club
Drama..104a–135q
The Extra Credit Club Persuasive Text

Differentiated Instruction SI OL A ELL ....DI•76–DI•100

WEEK 5 · The Gymnast Autobiography....................136a–161q
All About Gymnastics Online Reference Sources

Differentiated Instruction SI OL A ELL ....DI•101–DI•125

WEEK 6 · Interactive Review...............................IR•1–IR•60
How do people and animals adapt to different situations?

Unit 4 Reading Poetry 162–165a

Customize Writing ....CW•1–CW•20
Customize Literacy..CL•1–CL•47
Let's Learn Amazing Words ....OV•1–OV•3

Adventurers

Key
SI Strategic Intervention
OL On-Level
A Advanced
ELL ELL

Table of Contents..vi–xiii
Unit 5 Skills Overview ....xiv–xv
Unit 5 Monitor Progress ....xvi–xvii
Assessment and Grouping ....xviii–xix
Unit 5 Concept Launch .... xx–xxi
Flexible Pacing Plans xxii

Volume 1

WEEK 1 • The Skunk Ladder

Humorous Fiction..168a–197q
Books and Adventure Autobiography

Differentiated Instruction **SI** **OL** **A** **ELL** ....DI•1–DI•25

WEEK 2 • The Unsinkable Wreck of the R.M.S. *Titanic* Expository Text 198a–227q
Shipwreck Season Historical Fiction

Differentiated Instruction **SI** **OL** **A** **ELL** ....DI•26–DI•50

WEEK 3 • Talk with an Astronaut

Expository Text...228a–255q
Women Astronauts Online Directories

Differentiated Instruction **SI** **OL** **A** **ELL** ....DI•51–DI•75

Volume 2

WEEK 4 • Journey to the Center of the Earth

Novel 256a–283q
The Sea Battle Drama

Differentiated Instruction **SI** **OL** **A** **ELL** ....DI•76–DI•100

WEEK 5 • Ghost Towns of the American West

Expository Text...284a–311q
Gold Dreams Historical Fiction

Differentiated Instruction **SI** **OL** **A** **ELL** ....DI•101–DI•125

WEEK 6 • Interactive Review ....IR•1–IR•60
Who goes seeking adventure and why?
Unit 5 Reading Poetry 312–315a

Customize Writing ....CW•1–CW•20
Customize Literacy..CL•1–CL•47
Let's Learn Amazing Words ....OV•1–OV•3

The Unexpected

Table of Contents...vi–xiii
Unit 6 Skills Overview..xiv–xv
Unit 6 Monitor Progress...xvi–xvii
Assessment and Grouping...xviii–xix
Unit 6 Concept Launch..xx–xxi
Flexible Pacing Plans..xxii

Volume 1

WEEK 1 • **The Truth About Austin's Amazing Bats** Expository Text......................318a–343q
The Animals in My Life Autobiography

Differentiated Instruction SI OL A ELL ....DI•1–DI•25

WEEK 2 • **The Mystery of St. Matthew Island**
Expository Text...344a–369q
City Hawks Expository Text

Differentiated Instruction SI OL A ELL ....DI•26–DI•50

WEEK 3 • **King Midas and the Golden Touch**
Myth 370a–401q
Prometheus, the Fire-Bringer Myth

Differentiated Instruction SI OL A ELL ....DI•51–DI•75

Volume 2

WEEK 4 • **The Hindenburg** Expository Text.............402a–433q
The Mystery of the Hindenburg Disaster Web Site

Differentiated Instruction SI OL A ELL ....DI•76–100

WEEK 5 • **Sweet Music in Harlem**
Realistic Fiction 434a–467q
Author's Note Expository Text

Differentiated Instruction SI OL A ELL ....DI•101–DI•125

WEEK 6 • **Interactive Review** ....IR•1–IR•60
What can we learn from encounters with the unexpected?

Unit 6 Reading Poetry..468–471a

Customize Writing ....CW•1–CW•20
Customize Literacy ....CL•1–CL•47
Let's Learn Amazing Words ....OV•1–OV•3

Skills Overview

Key
T Tested Skill
🎯 Target Skill

		WEEK 1	**WEEK 2**
		The Fabulous Perpetual Motion Machine Drama pp. 330–343 **The Toy Space Shuttle Is Here!** Persuasive Text pp. 348–351	**Leonardo's Horse** Biography pp. 360–377 **A Job for Michelangelo** Historical Fiction pp. 382–385
Get Ready to Read	**Question of the Week**	How do inventors inspire our imaginations?	How do artists inspire future generations?
	Amazing Words	*theory, experiment, suggested, device, vehicle, enterprise, improvement, design, entrepreneur, innovation*	*easel, charcoal, canvas, gallery, marble, sculpture, projector, medium, muse, inspire*
	Word Analysis	Shades of Meaning	Greek and Latin Roots
	Literary Terms	Foreshadowing	Tone
	Structure/Features	Rising Action	Conflict and Resolution
Read and Comprehend	**Comprehension**	T 🎯 **Skill** Sequence 🎯 **Strategy** Summarize Review **Skill** Cause and Effect	T 🎯 **Skill** Main Idea and Details 🎯 **Strategy** Visualize Review **Skill** Fact and Opinion
	Vocabulary	T 🎯 **Skill** Multiple-Meaning Words applauds, browsing, fabulous, inspecting, project	T 🎯 **Skill** Greek and Latin Roots achieved, architect, bronze, cannon, depressed, fashioned, midst, philosopher, rival
	Fluency	Expression	Rate
Language Arts	**Writing**	Play Trait: Word Choice	Persuasive Speech Trait: Focus/Ideas
	Conventions	Verb Tenses	Principal Parts of Regular Verbs
	Spelling	Words with Schwa	Compound Words
	Speaking/Listening	Play Review	Media Literacy: Newscast
	Research Skills	Advertisement	Skim and Scan

What do people gain from the work of inventors and artists?

WEEK 3	WEEK 4	WEEK 5	WEEK 6
The Dinosaurs of Waterhouse Hawkins Biography pp. 394–411 **A Model Scientist** Expository Text pp. 416–421	**Mahalia Jackson** Expository Text pp. 430–437 **Perfect Harmony** Poetry pp. 442–445	**Special Effects in Film and Television** Expository Text pp. 454–463 **Searching for Animation** Search Engines pp. 468–471	**Interactive Review**
How can paleontologists help us understand the past?	How does an artist use music to inspire others?	How do artists create special effects to entertain us?	Connect the Question of the Week to the Big Question
fossils, paleontologists, sandstone, uncanny, remains, model, illustration, extinct, replica, archaic	*jam, session, steady, beat, fiddle, symphony, digital, music, harmonize, melody, tempo, movement*	*digital effects, illusion, props, gruesome, realistic, three-dimensional, image, re-create, graphics, simulation*	**Review** Amazing Words for Unit 3
Suffixes *-tion, -sion*	Suffix *-ous*	Compound Words	
Flashback	Imagery	Jargon	
Sequence	Description/Definition	Headings	
T Ⓢ **Skill** Fact and Opinion Ⓢ **Strategy** Predict/Set Purpose **Review** **Skill** Main Idea/Details	T Ⓢ **Skill** Main Idea and Details Ⓢ **Strategy** Text Structure **Review** **Skill** Fact and Opinion	T Ⓢ **Skill** Graphics Sources Ⓢ **Strategy** Important Ideas **Review** **Skill** Author's Purpose	**Review** Sequence, Fact and Opinion, Graphic Sources, Main Idea and Details
T Ⓢ **Skill** Homonyms erected, foundations, mold, occasion, proportion, tidied, workshop	T Ⓢ **Skill** Antonyms appreciate, barber, choir, released, religious, slavery, teenager	T Ⓢ **Skill** Prefixes *pre-, re-* background, landscape, miniature, prehistoric, reassembled	**Review** Multiple-Meaning Words, Greek and Latin Roots, Homonyms, Antonyms, Prefixes *pre-* and *re-*
Appropriate Phrasing	Rate	Accuracy	**Review** Fluency for Unit 3
Advertising Brochure Trait: Word Choice	Description Trait: Word Choice	Expository Text Trait: Organization	Quick Write for Fluency
Principal Parts of Irregular Verbs	Troublesome Verbs	Prepositions and Prepositional Phrases	**Review** Unit 3 Conventions
Consonant Sounds /j/, /ks/, /sk/, and /s/	One Consonant or Two	Prefixes *un-, de-, dis-*	**Review** Unit 3 Spelling Patterns
Making Introductions	Give Directions	Advertisement	
Schedule	Card Catalog/Library Database	Graphics/Symbols	

Don't Wait Until Friday

SUCCESS PREDICTOR	WEEK **1**	WEEK **2**	WEEK **3**	WEEK **4**
Fluency (WCPM)	Expression 115–122 WCPM	Rate 115–122 WCPM	Appropriate Phrasing 115–122 WCPM	Rate 115–122 WCPM
Oral Vocabulary/ Concept Development (assessed informally) (Vocabulary)	theory experiment suggested device vehicle enterprise improvement design entrepreneur innovation	easel charcoal canvas gallery marble sculpture projector medium muse inspire	fossils paleontologists sandstone uncanny remains model illustration extinct replica archaic	jam session steady beat fiddle symphony digital music harmonize melody tempo movement
Lesson Vocabulary	T applauds T browsing T fabulous T inspecting T project	T achieved T architect T bronze T cannon T depressed T fashioned T midst T philosopher T rival	T erected T foundations T mold T occasion T proportion T tidied T workshop	T appreciate T barber T choir T released T religious T slavery T teenager
Text Comprehension (Retelling)	T **Skill** Sequence **Strategy** Summarize	T **Skill** Main Idea and Details **Strategy** Visualize	T **Skill** Fact and Opinion **Strategy** Predict and Set Purpose	T **Skill** Main Idea and Details **Strategy** Text Structure

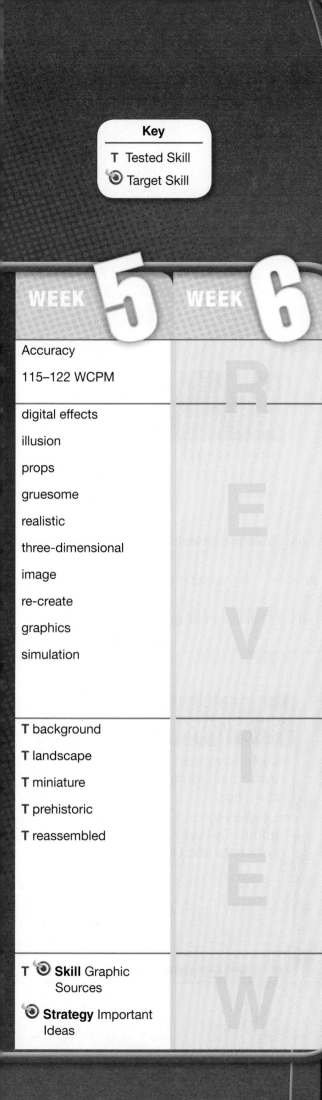

WEEK **5**	WEEK **6**
Accuracy	R
115–122 WCPM	E
digital effects	V
illusion	I
props	E
gruesome	W
realistic	
three-dimensional	
image	
re-create	
graphics	
simulation	
T background	
T landscape	
T miniature	
T prehistoric	
T reassembled	
T Skill Graphic Sources	
Strategy Important Ideas	

Online ASSESSMENT
ReadingStreet.com

Online Classroom

Manage Data

- Assign the Unit 3 Benchmark Test for students to take online.

- Online Assessment records results and generates reports by school, grade, classroom, or student.

- Use reports to disaggregate and aggregate Unit 3 skills and standards data to monitor progress.

- Based on class lists created to support the categories important for AYP (gender, ethnicity, migrant education, English proficiency, disabilities, economic status), reports let you track adequate yearly progress every six weeks.

Group

- Use results from Unit 3 Benchmark Tests taken online through Online Assessment to measure whether students have mastered the English-Language Arts Content Standards taught in this unit.

- Reports in Online Assessment suggest whether students need Extra Support or Intervention.

Individualized Instruction

- Assessments are correlated to Unit 3 tested skills and standards so that prescriptions for individual teaching and learning plans can be created.

- Individualized prescriptions target instruction and accelerate student progress toward learning outcome goals.

- Prescriptions include remediation activities and resources to reteach Unit 3 skills and standards.

UNIT 3

Assessment and Grouping
for Data-Driven Instruction

4-Step Plan for Assessment
1 Diagnose and Differentiate
2 Monitor Progress
3 Assess and Regroup
4 Summative Assessment

STEP 1 Diagnose and Differentiate

Scott Foresman Teacher's Manual
Baseline Group Tests
• Assess vocabulary, comprehension, and fluency
• Guidelines for grouping—strategic intervention, on-level, and advanced

Reading STREET
Grade 4-6

Baseline Group Tests

Diagnose

To make initial grouping decisions, use the Baseline Group Test, the *Texas Primary Reading Inventory (TPRI),* or another initial placement test. Depending on student's ability levels, you may have more than one of each group.

Differentiate

If... student performance is **SI** **then...** use the regular instruction and the daily Strategic Intervention small group lessons.

If... student performance is **OL** **then...** use the regular instruction and the daily On-Level small group lessons.

If... student performance is **A** **then...** use the regular instruction and the daily Advanced small group lessons.

Small Group Time

SI Strategic Intervention

- Daily small group lessons provide more intensive instruction, more scaffolding, more practice, and more opportunities to respond.
- Reteach lessons in the *First Stop on Reading Street* provide more instruction with target skills.
- Leveled readers build background and provide practice for target skills and vocabulary.

OL On-Level

- Explicit instructional routines teach core skills and strategies.
- Daily On-Level lessons provide more practice and more opportunities to respond.
- Independent activities provide practice for core skills and extension and enrichment options.
- Leveled readers provide additional reading and practice for core skills and vocabulary.

A Advanced

- Daily Advanced lessons provide instruction for accelerated learning.
- Leveled readers provide additional reading tied to lesson concepts and skills.

Additional Differentiated Learning Options

Reading Street Response to Intervention Kit

- Focused intervention lessons on the five critical areas of reading: phonemic awareness, phonics, vocabulary, comprehension, and fluency

My Sidewalks on Reading Street

- Intensive intervention for struggling readers

STEP 2 Monitor Progress

Use these tools during lesson teaching to **monitor student progress.**

- **Skill and Strategy** instruction during reading

- **Don't Wait Until Friday** boxes to check retelling, fluency, and oral vocabulary

- **Weekly Assessment** on Day 5 checks comprehension and fluency

- **Reader's and Writer's Notebook** pages at point of use

- **Weekly Tests** assess target skills for the week

- **Fresh Reads** for Fluency and Comprehension

Weekly Tests

Fresh Reads for Fluency and Comprehension

STEP 3 Assess and Regroup

Use these tools during lesson teaching to **assess and regroup.**

- **Weekly Assessments** Record results of weekly assessments in retelling, comprehension, and fluency to track student progress.

- **Unit Benchmark Tests** Administer this assessment to check mastery of unit skills.

- **Regroup** We recommend the first regrouping to be at the end of Unit 2. Use weekly assessment information and Unit Benchmark Test performance to inform regrouping decisions. Then regroup at the end of each subsequent unit.

Unit Assessment Charts in First Stop

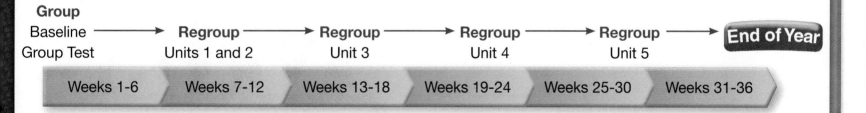

Group

Baseline ⟶ Regroup ⟶ Regroup ⟶ Regroup ⟶ Regroup ⟶ End of Year
Group Test   Units 1 and 2   Unit 3   Unit 4   Unit 5

| Weeks 1-6 | Weeks 7-12 | Weeks 13-18 | Weeks 19-24 | Weeks 25-30 | Weeks 31-36 |

Outside assessments, such as *TPRI, DRA,* and *DIBELS,* may recommend regrouping at other times during the year.

STEP 4 Summative Assessment

Use these tools after lesson teaching to **assess students.**

- **Unit Benchmark Tests** Use to measure a student's mastery of each unit's skills.

- **End-of-Year Benchmark Test** Use to measure a student's mastery of program skills covered in all six units.

Unit and End-of-Year Benchmark Tests

UNIT 3

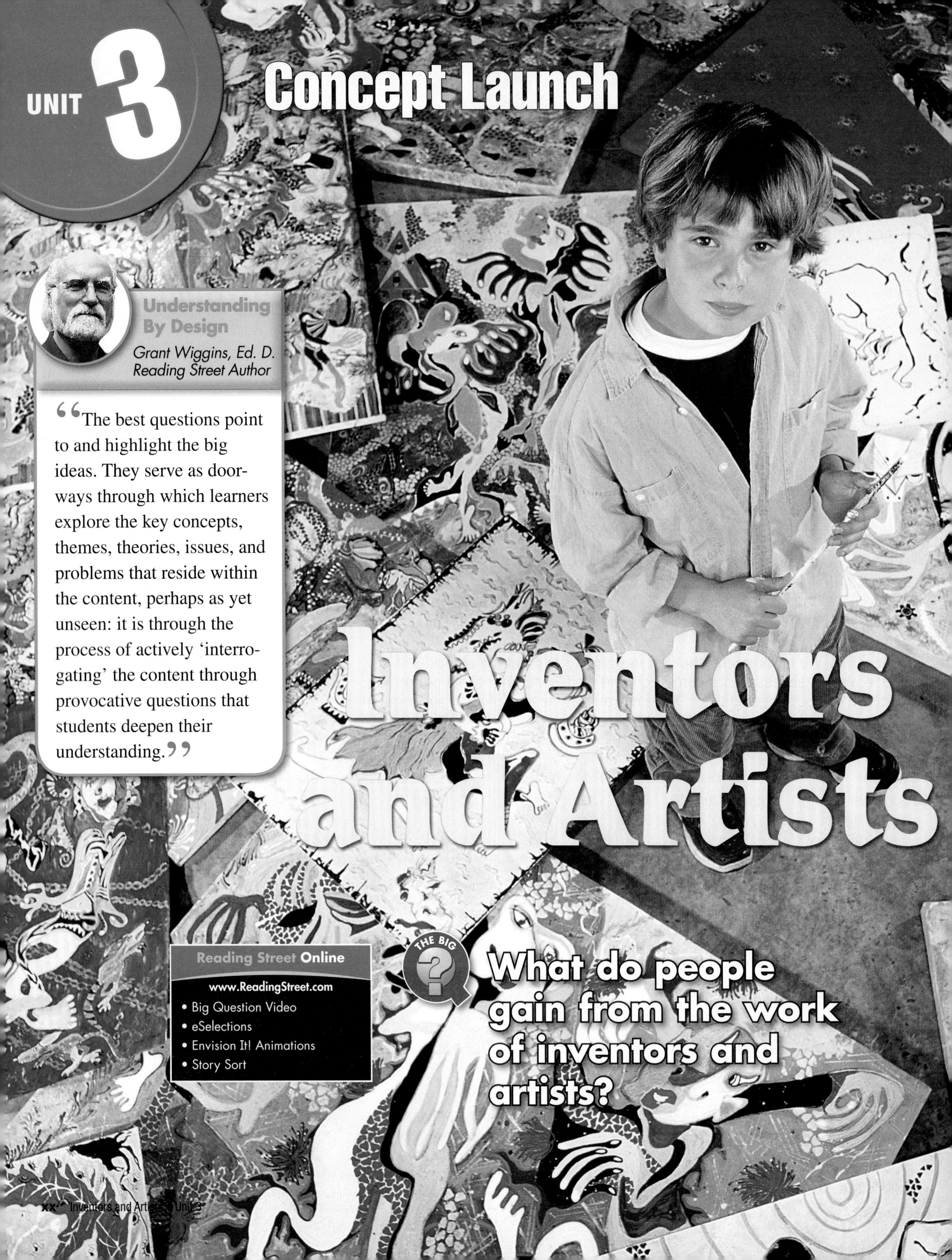

Concept Launch

Understanding By Design

Grant Wiggins, Ed. D.
Reading Street Author

"The best questions point to and highlight the big ideas. They serve as doorways through which learners explore the key concepts, themes, theories, issues, and problems that reside within the content, perhaps as yet unseen: it is through the process of actively 'interrogating' the content through provocative questions that students deepen their understanding."

Inventors and Artists

THE BIG ?

What do people gain from the work of inventors and artists?

Reading Street Online

www.ReadingStreet.com

- Big Question Video
- eSelections
- Envision It! Animations
- Story Sort

 Let's **Think** About Reading!

 connect to **SCIENCE**

The Fabulous Perpetual Motion Machine DRAMA

How do inventors inspire our imaginations?

Paired Selection
The Toy Space Shuttle Is Here! PERSUASIVE TEXT

connect to **SOCIAL STUDIES**

Leonardo's Horse BIOGRAPHY

How do artists inspire future generations?

Paired Selection
A Job for Michelangelo HISTORICAL FICTION

 connect to **SCIENCE**

The Dinosaurs of Waterhouse Hawkins BIOGRAPHY

How can paleontologists help us understand the past?

Paired Selection
A Model Scientist EXPOSITORY TEXT

connect to **SOCIAL STUDIES**

Mahalia Jackson EXPOSITORY TEXT

How does an artist use music to inspire others?

Paired Selection
Perfect Harmony POETRY

connect to **SCIENCE**

Special Effects in Film and Television EXPOSITORY TEXT

How do artists create special effects to entertain us?

Paired Selection
Searching for Animation SEARCH ENGINES

Theme Launch **xxi**

Key

- **SI** Strategic Intervention
- **OL** On-Level
- **A** Advanced
- **ELL** ELL

SI OL A

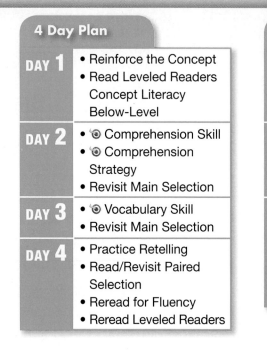

5 Day Plan

DAY 1
- Reinforce the Concept
- Read Leveled Readers Concept Literacy Below-Level

DAY 2
- Comprehension Skill
- Comprehension Strategy
- Revisit Main Selection

DAY 3
- Vocabulary Skill
- Revisit Main Selection

DAY 4
- Practice Retelling
- Read/Revisit Paired Selection

DAY 5
- Reread for Fluency
- Reread Leveled Readers

4 Day Plan

DAY 1
- Reinforce the Concept
- Read Leveled Readers Concept Literacy Below-Level

DAY 2
- Comprehension Skill
- Comprehension Strategy
- Revisit Main Selection

DAY 3
- Vocabulary Skill
- Revisit Main Selection

DAY 4
- Practice Retelling
- Read/Revisit Paired Selection
- Reread for Fluency
- Reread Leveled Readers

3 Day Plan

DAY 1
- Reinforce the Concept
- Read Leveled Readers Concept Literacy Below-Level

DAY 2
- Comprehension Skill
- Comprehension Strategy
- Revisit Main Selection

DAY 3
- Practice Retelling
- Read/Revisit Paired Selection
- Reread for Fluency
- Reread Leveled Readers

ELL

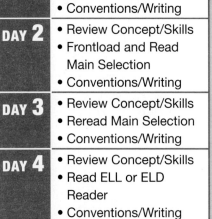
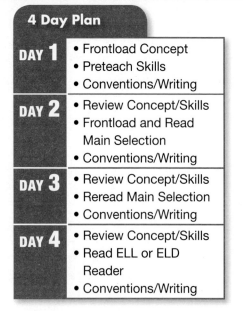
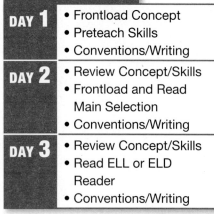

5 Day Plan

DAY 1
- Frontload Concept
- Preteach Skills
- Conventions/Writing

DAY 2
- Review Concept/Skills
- Frontload and Read Main Selection
- Conventions/Writing

DAY 3
- Review Concept/Skills
- Reread Main Selection
- Conventions/Writing

DAY 4
- Review Concept/Skills
- Read ELL or ELD Reader
- Conventions/Writing

DAY 5
- Review Concept/Skills
- Reread ELL or ELD Reader
- Conventions/Writing

4 Day Plan

DAY 1
- Frontload Concept
- Preteach Skills
- Conventions/Writing

DAY 2
- Review Concept/Skills
- Frontload and Read Main Selection
- Conventions/Writing

DAY 3
- Review Concept/Skills
- Reread Main Selection
- Conventions/Writing

DAY 4
- Review Concept/Skills
- Read ELL or ELD Reader
- Conventions/Writing

3 Day Plan

DAY 1
- Frontload Concept
- Preteach Skills
- Conventions/Writing

DAY 2
- Review Concept/Skills
- Frontload and Read Main Selection
- Conventions/Writing

DAY 3
- Review Concept/Skills
- Read ELL or ELD Reader
- Conventions/Writing

Common Core Standards
Weekly Planning Guide

Selection: The Fabulous Perpetual Motion Machine
Genre: Drama

Alignment of the Common Core Standards with This Week's Skills and Strategies

This Week's Common Core Standards for English Language Arts	Instructional Summary
Reading Standards for Literature/Informational Text	
Literature 1. Quote accurately from a text when explaining what the text says explicitly and when drawing inferences from the text.	This week's comprehension lesson focuses on how the events of a story happen in a certain order called a **sequence.** Students practice the strategy of **summarizing** in order to identify the most important parts of a story and to help them understand and remember what they read.
Literature 2. Determine a theme of a story, drama, or poem from details in the text, including how characters in a story or drama respond to challenges or how the speaker in a poem reflects upon a topic; summarize the text.	
Informational Text 8. Explain how an author uses reasons and evidence to support particular points in a text, identifying which reasons and evidence support which point(s).	
Foundational Skills Standards	
Foundational Skills 4. Read with sufficient accuracy and fluency to support comprehension.	This week's word analysis instruction helps students recognize that words have various **shades of meaning** that can affect comprehension. This week's fluency work helps students use appropriate voice tone and **expression.**
Foundational Skills 4.b. Read on-level prose and poetry orally with accuracy, appropriate rate, and expression on successive readings.	
Writing Standards	
Writing 3.a. Orient the reader by establishing a situation and introducing a narrator and/or characters; organize an event sequence that unfolds naturally.	Students write a **short play** about something they could invent patterned after the young inventors who created a special machine in *The Fabulous Perpetual Motion Machine.* They use the writing process to plan, draft, revise, edit, and publish their written work. The play includes a plot, setting, stage directions, and theme as well as **dialogue** for the characters. This week's Research and Inquiry instruction has students use their research as they write an **advertisement** about inventions.
Writing 3.b. Use narrative techniques, such as dialogue, description, and pacing, to develop experiences and events or show the responses of characters to situations.	
Writing 3.c. Use a variety of transitional words, phrases, and clauses to manage the sequence of events.	
Writing 8. Recall relevant information from experiences or gather relevant information from print and digital sources; summarize or paraphrase information in notes and finished work, and provide a list of sources.	
Speaking and Listening Standards	
Speaking/Listening 1.c. Pose and respond to specific questions by making comments that contribute to the discussion and elaborate on the remarks of others.	Students create a **play review,** a short piece that gives opinions about the play and makes recommendations. In the Research and Inquiry section, students display their **advertisement** and tell people why their invention is important.
Speaking/Listening 4. Report on a topic or text or present an opinion, sequencing ideas logically and using appropriate facts and relevant, descriptive details to support main ideas or themes; speak clearly at an understandable pace.	
Language Standards	
Language 1. Demonstrate command of the conventions of standard English grammar and usage when writing or speaking.	In the Conventions section, students identify and use **verbs** in the **present, past, and future tense forms.**
Language 1.c. Use verb tense to convey various times, sequences, states, and conditions.	
Language 1.d. Recognize and correct inappropriate shifts in verb tense.	

Additional Support for a Common Core Standard This Week

Use the following instruction to supplement the teaching of one of this week's Common Core Standards.

Common Core Standard: Informational Text 8.
Display Student Edition pages 348 and 351 to explore the features of persuasive text. Point out to students that the advertisement is an example of persuasive text in which the writer is sharing his or her opinion about the toy space shuttle.

- Have students retell the content of the advertisement. Ask them to tell if it recommends that you buy a toy space shuttle.
- Ask students to write an advertisement for a toy. Ask them to work in groups to present their advertisements and have the groups decide whether they would want the toy, based on the advertisement.

ISBN-13: 978-0-328-64415-5 ISBN-10: 0-328-64415-3

Grade 5 • Unit 3 • Week 1

The Fabulous Perpetual Motion Machine

Unit 3

THE BIG QUESTION
What do people gain from the work of inventors and artists?

Common Core Standards and Concept Development

- Introduce and explore this unit's weekly concepts through rich, structured conversations
- Develop complex content knowledge and vocabulary
- Expand on a single concept with engaging literature and nonfiction
- Build better readers in all content areas
- Align instruction to **Common Core Anchor Standards**

You Are Here: Week 1

connect to SCIENCE

The Fabulous Perpetual Motion Machine

Question of the Week
How do inventors inspire our imaginations?

As students answer this unit's Big Question and this week's Question of the Week, they will address:

Reading 1. Read closely to determine what the text says explicitly and to make logical inferences from it; cite specific textual evidence when writing or speaking to support conclusions drawn from the text. **(Also Reading 2.)**

Concept Talk Guide students as they discuss questions such as:
- What are some important inventions we use? Why are they important?
- What books, movies, or TV shows do you know that feature inventors and inventions?

As students answer this week's Concept Talk questions, they will address:

Speaking/Listening 1. Prepare for and participate effectively in a range of conversations and collaborations with diverse partners, building on others' ideas and expressing their own clearly and persuasively. **(Also Speaking/Listening 4.)**

Writing In *The Fabulous Perpetual Motion Machine*, young inventors create a special machine. Think about something that could be invented. Now write a short play based on your idea.

As students write about this week's prompt, they will address:

Writing 3. Write narratives to develop real or imagined experiences or events using effective technique, well-chosen details, and well-structured event sequences.

Listening and Speaking On page 353, students learn that they should listen closely to determine the main and supporting ideas in a speaker's message. By doing so, they address:

Speaking/Listening 4. Present information, findings, and supporting evidence such that listeners can follow the line of reasoning and the organization, development, and style are appropriate to task, purpose, and audience. **(Also Speaking/Listening 1.)**

Week 2

connect to SOCIAL STUDIES

Leonardo's Horse

Question of the Week
How do artists inspire future generations?

Concept Talk Guide students as they discuss questions such as:
- What might inspire an artist to create?
- How can an artist's work inspire other people?

Writing Think about modern inventions. Which recent invention changed people's lives the most? Write a persuasive speech that answers this question.

Week 3

connect to SCIENCE

The Dinosaurs of Waterhouse Hawkins

Question of the Week
How can paleontologists help us understand the past?

Concept Talk Guide students as they discuss questions such as:
- What selections or books have you read about dinosaurs?
- What do you know about paleontologists and their work?

Writing *The Dinosaurs of Waterhouse Hawkins* tells about the introduction of dinosaur models to the world. Prepare an advertisement for one of the events, enticing people to come.

Week 4

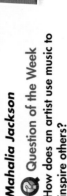

connect to SOCIAL STUDIES

Mahalia Jackson

Question of the Week
How does an artist use music to inspire others?

Concept Talk Guide students as they discuss questions such as:
- What did you discuss about music as an inspiration?
- What kind of music do you like most?

Writing *Mahalia Jackson* describes the voice of a talented singer. Think about music or another unique sound. Now write a description of that sound, using vivid sensory words.

Week 5

connect to SCIENCE

Special Effects in Film and Television

Question of the Week
How do artists create special effects to entertain us?

Concept Talk Guide students as they discuss questions such as:
- What examples of special effects did you discuss?
- Where have you seen special effects?

Writing Think about which form of entertainment you prefer: watching a movie or watching a television program. Compare and contrast the two, using specific details to make your point.

This Week's ELL Overview

ELL Handbook

- Maximize Literacy and Cognitive Engagement
- Research Into Practice
- Full Weekly Support for Every Selection

The Fabulous Perpetual Motion Machine

- Multi-Lingual Summaries in Five Languages
- Selection-Specific Vocabulary Word Cards
- Frontloading/Reteaching for Comprehension Skill Lessons
- ELD and ELL Reader Study Guides

- Transfer Activities
- Professional Development

Daily Leveled ELL Notes

ELL notes appear throughout this week's instruction and ELL Support is on the DI pages of your Teacher's Edition. The following is a sample of an ELL note from this week.

English Language Learners

Beginning Have student pairs read the details from their Story Sequence charts to each other.

Intermediate Partners should provide feedback about whether additional details are needed, and writers should incorporate suggestions into their charts.

Advanced Have students analyze their partner's solution to the problem addressed in the play and determine whether it's a good one. Monitor feedback that students provide to each other.

Advanced High Have students write a paragraph explaining the solution to the problem addressed in the play and suggesting a different solution.

ELL by Strand

The ELL lessons on this week's Support for English Language Learners pages are organized by strand. They offer additional scaffolding for the core curriculum. Leveled support notes on these pages address the different proficiency levels in your class. See pages DI•16–DI•25.

ELL Guy
Dr. Jim Cummins

The Three Pillars of ELL Instruction

ELL Strands	Activate Prior Knowledge	Access Content	Extend Language
Vocabulary pp. DI•17–DI•18	Preteach	Reteach	Leveled Writing Activities
Reading Comprehension p. DI•22	Frontloading	Sheltered Reading	After Reading
Phonics, Spelling, and Word Analysis p. DI•20	Preteach	Teach/Model	Leveled Practice Activities
Listening Comprehension p. DI•19	Prepare for the Read Aloud	First Listening	Second Listening
Conventions and Writing pp. DI•24–DI•25	Preteach	Reteach	Leveled Writing Activities
Concept Development p. DI•16	Activate Prior Knowledge	Discuss Concept	Daily Concept and Vocabulary Development

This Week's Practice Stations Overview

Six Weekly Practice Stations with Leveled Activities can be found at the beginning of each week of instruction. For this week's Practice Stations, see pp. 324h–324i.

Small Group Teacher-led

Classroom Management Handbook for Differentiated Instruction Practice Stations

Practice Stations

Daily Leveled Center Activities
- ○ Below
- △ On-Level
- ▢ Advanced
- **ELL**

Practice Stations Flip Charts

	Word Wise	Word Work	Words to Know	Let's Write	Read for Meaning	Get Fluent
Objectives	• Spell words ending with the syllables -*er*, -*ar*, -*or*.	• Identify and write words ending with syllables -*er*, -*ar*, -*or*.	• Identify the meaning of words with endings -*s*, -*ed*, -*ing*.	• Write a narrative set in the past.	• Understand the author's purpose for writing.	• Read aloud at an appropriate rate.
Materials	• *Word Wise* Flip Chart Activity 11 • Teacher-made word cards • Letter Tiles • paper • pencils	• *Word Work* Flip Chart Activity 11 • Teacher-made word cards • paper • pencils	• *Words to Know* Flip Chart Activity 11 • Teacher-made word cards • paper • pencils	• *Let's Write* Flip Chart Activity 11 • paper • pens or pencils	• *Read for Meaning* Flip Chart Activity 11 • Leveled Readers • paper • pencils	• *Get Fluent* Flip Chart Activity 11 • Leveled Readers

This Week on Reading Street!

Question of the Week
How do inventors inspire our imaginations?

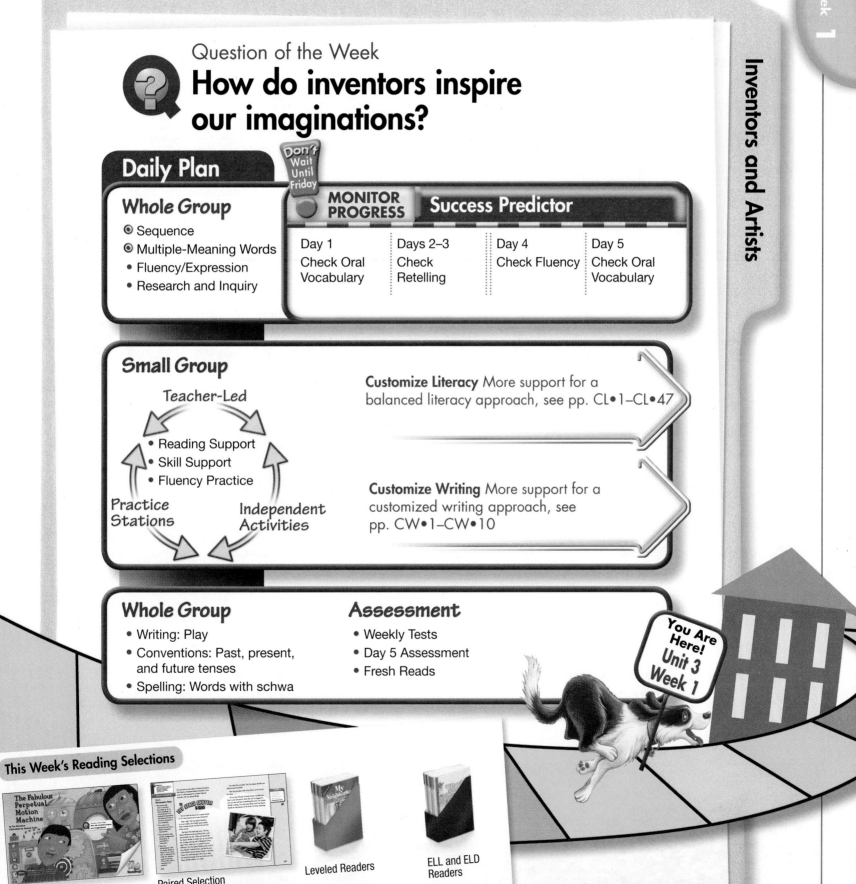

Daily Plan

Don't Wait Until Friday

Whole Group
◎ Sequence
◎ Multiple-Meaning Words
• Fluency/Expression
• Research and Inquiry

MONITOR PROGRESS | **Success Predictor**

Day 1	Days 2–3	Day 4	Day 5
Check Oral Vocabulary	Check Retelling	Check Fluency	Check Oral Vocabulary

Small Group

Teacher-Led

• Reading Support
• Skill Support
• Fluency Practice

Practice Stations   Independent Activities

Customize Literacy More support for a balanced literacy approach, see pp. CL•1–CL•47

Customize Writing More support for a customized writing approach, see pp. CW•1–CW•10

Whole Group
• Writing: Play
• Conventions: Past, present, and future tenses
• Spelling: Words with schwa

Assessment
• Weekly Tests
• Day 5 Assessment
• Fresh Reads

You Are Here!
Unit 3
Week 1

This Week's Reading Selections

The Fabulous Perpetual Motion Machine

Leveled Readers

ELL and ELD Readers

Main Selection
Genre: **Drama**

Paired Selection
Genre: **Persuasive Text**

Resources on Reading Street!

	Build Concepts	Comprehension
Whole Group	Let's Talk About pp. 324–325	Envision It! Skills/ Strategies Comprehension Skills Lesson pp. 326–327
Go Digital	• Concept Talk Video	• Envision It! Animations • eSelections
Small Group and Independent Practice	The Fabulous Perpetual Motion Machine pp. 330–331 ELL and ELD Readers Leveled Readers	The Fabulous Perpetual Motion Machine pp. 330–331 ELL and ELD Readers Leveled Readers Envision It! Skills/ Strategies Reader's and Writer's Notebook Practice Station Flip Chart
Go Digital	• eReaders • eSelections	• Envision It! Animations • eSelections • eReaders
Customize Literacy	• Leveled Readers	• Envision It! Skills and Strategies Handbook • Leveled Readers
Go Digital	• Concept Talk Video • Big Question Video • eReaders	• Envision It! Animations • eReaders

a b

How do inventors inspire our imaginations?

Vocabulary

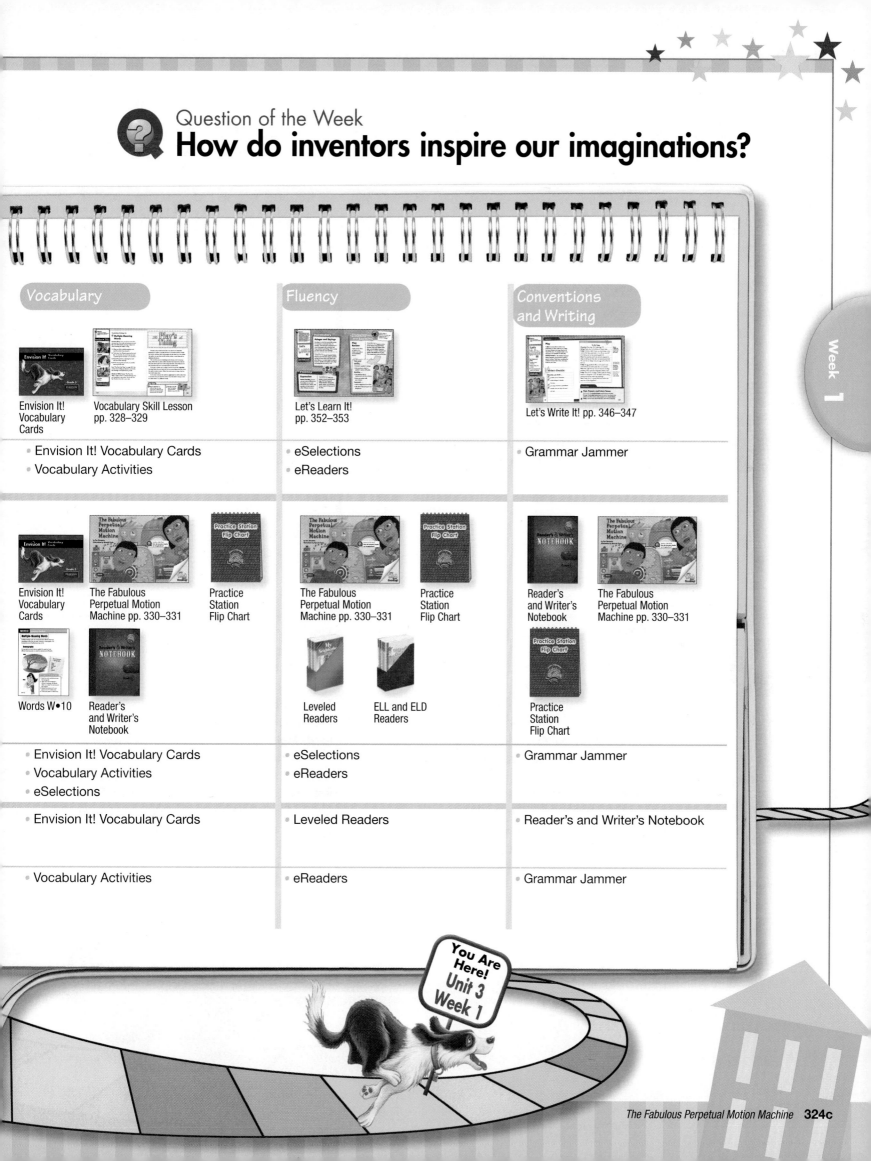

Envision It! Vocabulary Cards

Vocabulary Skill Lesson pp. 328–329

- Envision It! Vocabulary Cards
- Vocabulary Activities

Envision It! Vocabulary Cards

The Fabulous Perpetual Motion Machine pp. 330–331

Practice Station Flip Chart

Words W•10

Reader's and Writer's Notebook

- Envision It! Vocabulary Cards
- Vocabulary Activities
- eSelections

- Envision It! Vocabulary Cards

- Vocabulary Activities

Fluency

Let's Learn It! pp. 352–353

- eSelections
- eReaders

The Fabulous Perpetual Motion Machine pp. 330–331

Practice Station Flip Chart

Leveled Readers

ELL and ELD Readers

- eSelections
- eReaders

- Leveled Readers

- eReaders

Conventions and Writing

Let's Write It! pp. 346–347

- Grammar Jammer

Reader's and Writer's Notebook

The Fabulous Perpetual Motion Machine pp. 330–331

Practice Station Flip Chart

- Grammar Jammer

- Reader's and Writer's Notebook

- Grammar Jammer

You Are Here!
Unit 3
Week 1

Week 1

My 5-Day Planner for Reading Street!

Don't
Wait
Until
Friday

MONITOR PROGRESS

	Check Oral Vocabulary **Day 1** pages 324j–327f	Check Retelling **Day 2** pages 328a–337e

Get Ready to Read	**Concept Talk,** 324j
	Oral Vocabulary, 325a
	  theory, experiment, suggested
	Listening Comprehension, Read Aloud, 325b
		Concept Talk, 328a
		Oral Vocabulary, 328b
		  device, vehicle, enterprise
		Word Analysis, 328c
		  Shades of Meaning
		Literary Terms, 328d
		  Foreshadowing
		Story Structure, 328d
		  Rising Action

Read and Comprehend	**Comprehension Skill,**
	  ◉ Sequence, 325c
	Comprehension Strategy,
	  ◉ Summarize, 325c
	READ Comprehension, 326–327
	Model Fluency, Expression, 326–327
	Introduce Lesson Vocabulary, 327a
	  applauds, browsing, fabulous, inspecting, project
		Vocabulary Skill, ◉ Multiple-Meaning Words, 328e
		Vocabulary Strategy, Context Clues, 328e
		Lesson Vocabulary, 328–329
		  applauds, browsing, fabulous, inspecting, project
		READ Vocabulary, 328–329
		Model Fluency, Expression, 328–329
		READ Main Selection, *The Fabulous Perpetual Motion Machine,* 330–337a

Language Arts	**Research and Inquiry,** Identify Questions, 327b **Spelling,** Words with schwa, 327c **Conventions,** Past, present, and future tenses, 327d **Handwriting,** Cursive Letter *e* and *E,* 327d **Writing,** Play, 327e–327f	**Research and Inquiry,** Navigate/Search, 337b **Conventions,** Past, present, and future tenses, 337c **Spelling,** Words with schwa, 337c **Writing,** Play, Organization, 337d

You Are Here!
Unit 3
Week 1

How do inventors inspire our imaginations?

Check Retelling	**Check Fluency**	**Check Oral Vocabulary**
Day 3 pages 338a–347c	**Day 4** pages 348a–353e	**Day 5** pages 353f–353q

Concept Talk, 338a
Oral Vocabulary, 338b
  improvement, design
Comprehension Check, 338c
Check Retelling, 338d
	Concept Talk, 348a
	Oral Vocabulary, 348b
	  entrepreneur, innovation
	Genre,
	  Persuasive Text, 348c
		Concept Wrap Up, 353f
		Check Oral Vocabulary, 353g
		  theory, experiment, suggested,
		  device, vehicle, enterprise,
		  improvement, design, entrepreneur,
		  innovation
		Amazing Ideas, 353g
		  Review ⊙ Sequence, 353h
		  Review ⊙ Multiple-Meaning Words, 353h
		  Review Word Analysis, 353i
		  Review Literary Terms, 353i

READ Main Selection, *The Fabulous Perpetual Motion Machine,* 338–343a
Retelling, 344–345
Think Critically, 345a
Model Fluency, Expression, 345b
Research and Study Skills,
  Advertisement, 345c
	READ Paired Selection, "The Toy Space Shuttle Is Here!" 348–351a
	Let's Learn It! 352–353a
	  Fluency: Expression
	  Vocabulary: Adages and Sayings
	  Listening and Speaking: Play Review
		Fluency Assessment, WCPM, 353j–353k
		Comprehension Assessment,
		  ⊙ Sequence, 353l–353m

Research and Inquiry, Analyze, 345d **Conventions,** Past, present, and future tenses, 345e **Spelling,** Words with schwa, 345e **Let's Write It!** Play, 346–347a **Writing,** Play, Word Choice, 347a–347c	**Research and Inquiry,** Synthesize, 353b **Conventions,** Past, present, and future tenses, 353c **Spelling,** Words with schwa, 353c **Writing,** Play, Revising, 353d–353e	**Research and Inquiry,** Communicate, 353n **Conventions,** Past, present, and future tenses, 353o **Spelling Test,** Words with schwa, 353o **Writing,** Play, Past, present, and future tenses, 353p **Quick Write for Fluency,** 353q

Week 1

Grouping Options for Differentiated Instruction
Turn the page for the small group time lesson plan.

Planning Small Group Time on Reading Street!

SMALL GROUP TIME RESOURCES

Look for this Small Group Time box each day to help meet the individual needs of all your students. Differentiated Instruction lessons appear on the DI pages at the end of the week.

DAY 1

Teacher Led

SI Strategic Intervention

Teacher Led
• Reinforce the Concept
• **Read** *Concept Literacy* or *Below Level Reader*

OL On-Level

Teacher Led
• Expand the Concept
• **Read** *On-Level Reader*

A Advanced

Teacher Led
• Extend the Concept
• **Read** *Advanced Reader*

ELL Place English language learners in the groups that correspond to their reading abilities in English.

Practice Stations
• Read for Meaning
• Get Fluent
• Word Work

Independent Activities
• Concept Talk Video
• Reader's and Writer's Notebook
• Research and Inquiry

ELL

Scientific Methods in Action
by D. Michael Kim
Illustrated by Bruce Day

ELL Reader
Advanced
Advanced High

Scientific Methods in Action
by D. Michael Kim
Illustrated by Bruce Day

ELD Reader
Beginning
Intermediate

ELL Poster

You Are Here!
Unit 3
Week 1

Day 1

SI Strategic Intervention	**Reinforce the Concept,** DI•1–DI•2 **Read Concept Literacy Reader** or **Below-Level Reader**	
OL On-Level	**Expand the Concept,** DI•7 **Read On-Level Reader**	
A Advanced	**Extend the Concept,** DI•12 **Read Advanced Reader**	
ELL English Language Learners	DI•16–DI•25 **Frontload Concept** **Preteach Skills** **Writing**	

Reading Street Response to Intervention Kit

Reading Street Practice Station Kit

SI Strategic Intervention

OL On-Level

A Advanced

Below-Level Reader

Concept Literacy Reader

On-Level Reader

Advanced Reader

The Fabulous Perpetual Motion Machine pp. 330–331

The Toy Space Shuttle is Here! pp. 348–349

Small Group Weekly Plan

Day 2	Day 3	Day 4	Day 5
Reinforce Comprehension, DI•3 **Revisit Main Selection**	Reinforce Vocabulary, DI•4 **Read/Revisit Main Selection**	Reinforce Comprehension, Practice Retelling DI•5 Genre Focus **Read/Revisit Paired Selection**	Practice Fluency, DI•6 **Reread Concept Literacy Reader** or **Below-Level Reader**
Expand Comprehension, DI•8 **Revisit Main Selection**	Expand Vocabulary, DI•9 **Read/Revisit Main Selection**	Expand Comprehension, Practice Retelling DI•10 Genre Focus **Read/Revisit Paired Selection**	Practice Fluency, DI•11 **Reread On-Level Reader**
Extend Comprehension, DI•13 **Revisit Main Selection**	Extend Vocabulary, DI•14 **Read/Revisit Main Selection**	Extend Comprehension, Genre Focus DI•15 **Read/Revisit Paired Selection**	Practice Fluency, DI•15 **Reread Advanced Reader**
DI•16–DI•25 **Review Concept/Skills** **Frontload Main Selection** **Practice**	DI•16–DI•25 **Review Concept/Skills** **Reread Main Selection** **Practice**	DI•16–DI•25 **Review Concept** **Read ELL/ELD Readers** **Practice**	DI•16–DI•25 **Review Concept/Skills** **Reread ELL/ELD Reader** **Writing**

Week 1

Practice Stations for Everyone on Reading Street!

Word Wise
Words ending with the syllables *-er, -ar, -or*

Objectives
• Spell words ending with the syllables *-er, -ar, -or*.

Materials
• *Word Wise* Flip Chart Activity 11
• Teacher-made word cards
• Letter Tiles • paper • pencils

Differentiated Activities

⬤ Find two word cards for each of the following final syllables: *-er, -ar, -or*. Use the letter tiles to spell the words. Write sentences using each of the words.

▲ Choose ten word cards, and write your words in a list. Underline the final syllable in each word. Write sentences using six of your words.

◼ Choose ten word cards, and write your words in a list. Underline the final syllable in each word. Write sentences using the words. Add other words you know with these endings to your list.

Technology
• Online Dictionary

Word Work
Words ending with the syllables *-er, -ar, -or*

Objectives
• Identify and write words ending with syllables *-er, -ar, -or*.

Materials
• *Word Work* Flip Chart Activity 11
• Teacher-made word cards
• paper • pencils

Differentiated Activities

⬤ Find two word cards for each of the following final syllables: *-er, -ar, -or*. Write the words in a list. Say each word quietly to yourself. Add other words ending with these syllables to your list.

▲ Choose ten word cards that end with the syllable *-er, -ar, or -or*. Write the words in a list. Say each word quietly to yourself. Add other words ending with these syllables to your list.

◼ Make a three-column chart using final syllables *-er, -ar, -or* as headings. Use the word cards to fill in the chart. Quietly read the words aloud. Add other words with these final syllables to the chart.

Technology
• Modeled Pronunciation Audio CD

Words to Know
Words with endings *-s, -ed, -ing*

Objectives
• Identify the meaning of words with endings *-s, -ed, -ing*.

Materials
• *Words to Know* Flip Chart Activity 11
• Teacher-made word cards
• paper • pencils

Differentiated Activities

⬤ Choose three word cards. List the base words on paper. Next to each, write the *-s, -ed,* and *-ing* forms of the word. Then write one sentence for each base word, using one of the words you formed.

▲ Choose five word cards. Write the base words on paper. Next to each, write the *-s, -ed,* and *-ing* forms of the word. Then write one sentence for each base word, using one of the words you formed.

◼ Choose seven word cards. Next to each one, write the *-s, -ed,* and *-ing* forms of the word. Then use a variety of the words to write a short, fictional paragraph.

Technology
• Online Dictionary

You Are Here!
Unit 3
Week 1

Key
● Below-Level Activities
▲ On-Level Activities
■ Advanced Activities

Practice Station
Flip Chart

Use this week's materials from the Reading Street Leveled Practice Stations Kit to organize this week's stations.

Let's Write!
Narrative fiction set in the past

Objectives
• Write a narrative set in the past.

Materials
• *Let's Write!* Flip Chart Activity 11
• paper • pens or pencils

Differentiated Activities

● Write a story of historical fiction set 100 years ago. What would life have been like? Use imagery to describe the setting of your story. Include sensory details that appeal to the five senses.

▲ Write a story of historical fiction that takes place 100 years ago. Use imagery to describe the setting of your story, and include sensory details.

■ Write a story of historical fiction that imagines an event that happened 100 years ago. Use imagery to describe the story's setting. Include sensory details in your story.

Technology
• Online Graphic Organizers

Read for Meaning
Author's purpose

Objectives
• Understand the author's purpose for writing.

Materials
• *Read for Meaning* Flip Chart Activity 11
• Leveled Readers
• paper • pencils

Differentiated Activities

● Choose a book from those your teacher provided. As you read, think about the author's purpose for writing. Write one sentence that tells what the author's purpose is. Write a sentence with one detail from the story to support your thinking.

▲ Choose a book from those your teacher provided. As you read, think about the author's purpose. Write a short paragraph stating the author's purpose. Include at least two details from the story from the selection to support your reasoning.

■ Choose a book from those your teacher provided. As you read, think about the author's purpose for writing. Write a paragraph that explains the author's purpose, and include three details from the selection to support your reasoning.

Technology
• Leveled Reader Database

Get Fluent
Practice fluent reading.

Objectives
• Read aloud at an appropriate rate.

Materials
• *Get Fluent* Flip Chart Activity 11
• Leveled Readers

Differentiated Activities

● Work with a partner. Choose a Concept Literacy Reader or Below-Level Reader. Take turns reading a page from the book. Use the reader to practice appropriate rate. Provide feedback as needed.

▲ Work with a partner. Choose an On-Level Reader. Take turns reading a page from the book. Use the reader to practice appropriate rate. Provide feedback as needed.

■ Work with a partner. Choose an Advanced Reader. Take turns reading a page from the book. Use the reader to practice appropriate rate. Provide feedback as needed.

Technology
• Leveled Reader Database
• Reading Street Readers CD-ROM.

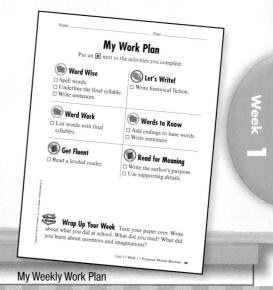

My Weekly Work Plan

week 1

Objectives
- Introduce the weekly concept.
- Develop oral vocabulary.

Today at a Glance

Oral Vocabulary
theory, experiment, suggested

Comprehension
- ◉ Sequence
- ◉ Summarize

Reading
"Kid Inventor"

Fluency
Expression

Lesson Vocabulary
Tested vocabulary

Research and Inquiry
Identify questions

Spelling
Words with schwa

Conventions
Past, present, and future tenses

Handwriting
Cursive *e* and *E*

Writing
Drama: Play

Concept Talk

Question of the Week

How do inventors inspire our imaginations?

Introduce the concept

To explore the unit concept of Inventors and Artists, this week students will read, write, and talk about how inventors stretch our ideas with their work. Write the Question of the Week on the board.

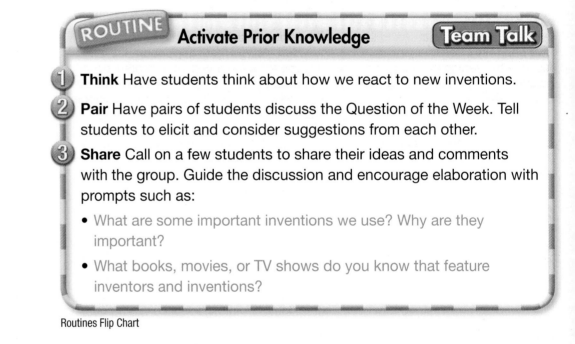

ROUTINE **Activate Prior Knowledge** **Team Talk**

1. **Think** Have students think about how we react to new inventions.

2. **Pair** Have pairs of students discuss the Question of the Week. Tell students to elicit and consider suggestions from each other.

3. **Share** Call on a few students to share their ideas and comments with the group. Guide the discussion and encourage elaboration with prompts such as:
   - What are some important inventions we use? Why are they important?
   - What books, movies, or TV shows do you know that feature inventors and inventions?

Routines Flip Chart

Anchored Talk

Develop oral vocabulary

Have students turn to pp. 324–325 in their Student Editions. Look at each of the photos. Then, use the prompts to guide discussion and create the *How inventors inspire our imaginations* concept map.

- What do you think people thought and felt when they saw the earliest vehicles? (They were probably amazed and excited. They were probably happy that it would make traveling so much easier.) Cars definitely make it easier to get around. Let's add *Make life easier* to our map.

- What are the students doing in the photo? (They are doing a science *experiment*.) Inventors usually have to try different approaches before they succeed. Let's add *Experiment* to our map.

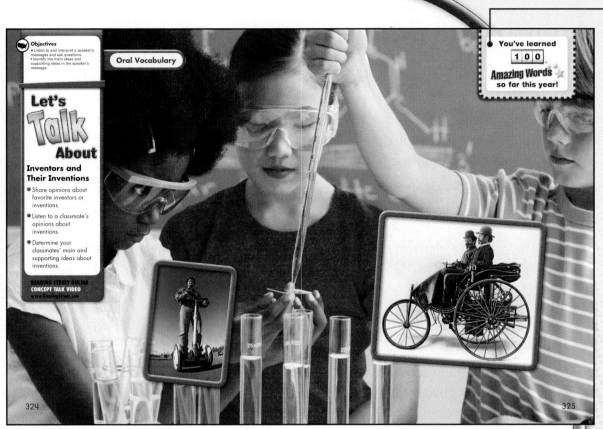

Objectives
- Listen to and interpret a speaker's messages and ask questions.
- Identify the main ideas and supporting ideas in the speaker's message.

Oral Vocabulary

Let's Talk About

Inventors and Their Inventions
- Share opinions about favorite inventors or inventions.
- Listen to a classmate's opinions about inventions.
- Determine your classmates' main and supporting ideas about inventions.

READING STREET ONLINE
CONCEPT TALK VIDEO
www.ReadingStreet.com

324

325

You've learned
1 0 0
Amazing Words ★
so far this year!

Student Edition pp. 324–325

Amazing Words

You've learned **1 0 0** words so far.

You'll learn **0 1 0** words this week!

theory	enterprise
experiment	improvement
suggested	design
device	entrepreneur
vehicle	innovation

 **Writing on Demand**

Writing Fluency
Ask students to respond to the photos on pp. 324–325 by writing as well as they can and as much as they can about how inventors inspire our imaginations.

- How does that two-wheeled *vehicle* compare with a car? (It might be better for going short distances.)
- Ask: How do inventors inspire our imaginations?

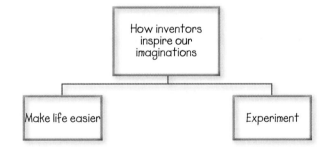

How inventors inspire our imaginations

Make life easier

Experiment

Connect to reading

Tell students that they will be reading about inventors and inventions. Encourage students to add concept-related words to the week's concept map.

ELL **Preteach Concepts** Use the Day 1 instruction on ELL Poster 11 to assess and build background knowledge, develop concepts, and build oral vocabulary.

 **ELL**

English Language Learners
ELL support Additional ELL support and modified instruction is provided in the *ELL Handbook* and in the ELL Support lessons on pp. DI•16–DI•25.

Listening comprehension
English learners will benefit from additional visual support to understand the key terms in the concept map. Use the pictures on pp. 324–325 to scaffold understanding.

Frontload for Read Aloud Use the modified Read Aloud on p. DI•19 in the ELL Support lessons to prepare students to listen to "What's the Big Idea, Ben Franklin?" (p. 325b).

ELL Poster 11

The Fabulous Perpetual Motion Machine **324–325**

Objectives
- Develop listening comprehension.
- Develop oral vocabulary.

Check Oral Vocabulary
SUCCESS PREDICTOR

Oral Vocabulary
Amazing Words

Introduce Amazing Words

"What's the Big Idea, Ben Franklin?" on p. 325b is about a famous American inventor. Tell students to listen for this week's Amazing Words—*theory, experiment,* and *suggested*—as you read.

Model fluency

As you read "What's the Big Idea, Ben Franklin?" model appropriate expression by adjusting your voice to demonstrate a lively, fluent reader.

Teach Amazing Words

Amazing Words Oral Vocabulary Routine

> theory
> experiment
> suggested

① **Introduce** Write the word *experiment* on the board. Have students say the word aloud with you. In "What's the Big Idea, Ben Franklin?" we learn that Franklin did an *experiment* with a pot of molasses and an ant. Does the author include any context clues that help me determine the meaning of this word? Supply a student-friendly definition.

② **Demonstrate** Have students answer questions to demonstrate understanding. What did Franklin learn from his ant *experiment*? Can you think of another *experiment* to find out about ants?

③ **Apply** Ask students to give examples of *experiments* they have done.

See p. OV•1 to teach *theory*.

Routines Flip Chart

Apply Amazing Words

To build oral language, lead the class in a discussion about the meanings of the Amazing Words.

Don't Wait Until Friday

MONITOR PROGRESS **Check Oral Vocabulary**

During discussion, listen for students' use of the Amazing Words.

If... students are unable to use the Amazing Words to discuss the concept,

Then... use Oral Vocabulary Routine in the Routines Flip Chart to demonstrate words in different contexts.

Day 1	Days 2–3	Day 4	Day 5
Check Oral Vocabulary	Check Retelling	Check Fluency	Check Oral Vocabulary

Success Predictor

What's the Big Idea, Ben Franklin?

by Jean Fritz

Benjamin Franklin was a famous American author, diplomat, inventor, and philosopher who lived from 1706 to 1790.

No matter how busy he was, Benjamin found time to try out new ideas. Sometimes he had ideas on why things happen the way they do. He wrote about comets. He formed a theory about hurricanes; they moved, he said, from the southwest to the northeast, contrary to the way winds usually move. Once he made an experiment with a pot of molasses and an ant. He hung the pot on a string and watched for the ant to crawl down. Soon there was a swarm of ants crawling up the string, so Benjamin concluded that ants have a way of telling each other news.

Sometimes Benjamin's ideas were for the improvement of Philadelphia. He formed the first circulating library in America. He helped organize Philadelphia's fire department. He suggested ways to light the streets, deepen the rivers, dispose of garbage, and keep people from slipping on ice in winter.

Sometimes his ideas turned into inventions. At the head of his bed he hung a cord that was connected to an iron bolt on his door. When he wanted to lock his door at night, he didn't have to get out of bed. He just pulled the cord, rolled over, and shut his eyes.

He invented a stepladder stool with a seat that turned up. And a rocking chair with a fan over it. When he rocked, the fan would turn and keep the flies off his head. He fixed up a pole with movable fingers to use when he wanted to take books down from high shelves. He cut a hole in his kitchen wall and put in a windmill to turn his meat roaster. And he invented an iron stove with a pipe leading outside. The stove produced more heat than an ordinary fireplace, cost less to operate, was less smoky, and became very popular.

In 1732, when he was 26 years old, Benjamin Franklin had one of his best ideas. He decided to publish an almanac. Every family bought an almanac each year. People read it to find out the holidays, the weather forecasts, the schedule of tides, the time the sun came up and went down, when the moon would be full, when to plant what. It was just the kind of book that Benjamin loved—full of odd pieces of information and bits of advice on this and that. It was, in addition to being a calendar, a grand how-to book and

(continued on p. 353s)

Oral Vocabulary

Success Predictor

Objectives
○ Identify sequence to aid comprehension.
○ Use the summarizing strategy to aid comprehension.
● Read grade-level text with expression.

Skills Trace
◎ **Sequence**

Introduce/Teach U2W2D1; U3W1D1; U6W5D1

Practice U2W2D2; U2W2D3; U3W1D2; U3W1D3; U6W5D2; U6W5D3

Reteach/Review U1W1D2; U1W1D3; U2W2D5; U2W3D3; U3W1D5; U6W2D2; U6W5D5

Assess/Test Weekly Tests U2W2; U3W1; U6W5

Benchmark Tests U2; U6

KEY:
U=Unit   W=Week   D=Day

Skill ↔ Strategy
◎ Sequence
◎ Summarize

Student Edition p. EI•13

Introduce sequence

Envision It!

A sequence of events is the order in which things happen. How can readers tell the order in which events happen? (by looking for specific dates and times or clue words, such as *first, next, before, after, while, at the same time,* and so on) Why is it important to know the order of events? (Possible response: because one event might cause another or lead to another) Have students turn to p. EI•13 in the Student Edition to review sequence of events. Then read "Kid Inventor" with students.

Model the skill

Think Aloud Today we're going to read about a product invented by a kid. Have students follow along as you read the first two paragraphs of "Kid Inventor." In the second paragraph, I see these sequence clues: *1905, first, overnight, then,* and *next morning.* The events took place in 1905 and happened like this: 1. The boy made a drink and left it outside. 2. Temperatures fell. 3. The drink froze. 4. The boy tasted it and liked it.

Guide practice

Have students finish reading "Kid Inventor" on their own. After they read, have them use a graphic organizer like the one on p. 326 and identify the sequence of events from the passage.

Strategy check

Summarize Remind students that if they have difficulty understanding the sequence of events in "Kid Inventor," they can use the summarize strategy. Model the strategy.

Model the strategy

Envision It!

Think Aloud When I first read the selection, I noticed a lot of facts, but I didn't get a clear idea of how they fit together. I'll summarize and paraphrase, using my own words to tell just the main ideas in a way that maintains meaning and logical order. I'll use clue words to reinforce the sequence of events. When Frank was a child, he left a drink outside and it froze. He thought the frozen drink was tasty. When he grew up, he patented the idea and later sold it to a company, which then began producing the treats. Have students review the summarize strategy on p. EI•23 of the Student Edition.

Student Edition p. EI•23

On their own

Use p. 178 in the *Reader's and Writer's Notebook* for additional practice with sequence.

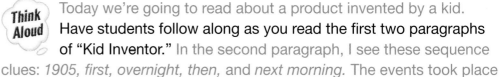

Reader's and Writer's Notebook p. 178

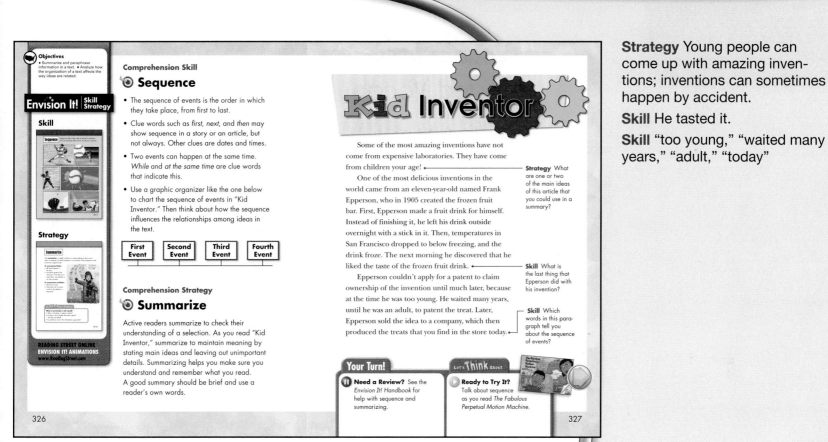

Student Edition pp. 326–327

Model Fluency
Expression

Model fluent reading

Have students listen as you read the first paragraph of "Kid Inventor" with expression. Explain that you will adjust the tone and level of your voice to stress important words and phrases.

ROUTINE Choral Reading

1. **Select a passage** Read paragraph 1 of "Kid Inventors" aloud.

2. **Model** Have students listen as you read with appropriate expression.

3. **Guide practice** Have students read along with you.

4. **On their own** For optimal fluency, have the class read aloud three or four times with expression. Encourage students to adjust the tone of level of their voices.

Routines Flip Chart

ELL

English Language Learners

Sequence of Events Draw a time line on the board. Have volunteers identify things that have happened at your school this year. For each event, ask *Where should I place this event on my time line?* When you have included several events on the time line, have students tell about the events, using clue words, such as *In September, we returned to school. The first field trip we had was…* and so on.

Objectives
- Activate prior knowledge of words.
- Identify questions for research.

Vocabulary
Tested Vocabulary

Lesson vocabulary

Have students complete sentences by filling in the blanks with lesson vocabulary.

Activate prior knowledge

Display the lesson vocabulary and discuss what students already know about these words. Then write incomplete sentences on the board, such as those below. Have students identify the word that completes each sentence and makes sense in context. Students may need to check the meanings of the words in the glossary.

- Everyone _____ when the magician finishes his amazing act. (applauds)
- I use my magnifying glass when I'm _____ the new mold growth. (inspecting)
- The red feathers on her hat looked _____ with a dark brown background. (fabulous)
- Jane worked hard to make her _____ a success. (project)
- Dylan spends hours _____ in stores but rarely buys anything. (browsing)

Related words

Ask students to clap their hands in approval. Ask how *applause* and *applauds* are related in meaning.

Preteach Academic Vocabulary

E L L **Academic Vocabulary** Write the following words on the board:

persuasive text	tone of voice
product review	verb tenses
rising action	schwa

Have students share what they know about this week's academic vocabulary. Use the students' responses to assess their prior knowledge. Preteach the Academic Vocabulary by providing a student-friendly description, explanation, or example that clarifies the meaning of each term. Then ask students to restate the meaning of the Academic Vocabulary term in their own words.

Research and Inquiry
Identify Questions

Teach

Discuss the Question of the Week: *How do inventors inspire our imaginations?* Tell students they will research how an inventor or an invention inspired others. They will create an advertisement for the invention and present it to the class on Day 5.

Model

Think Aloud

I'll start by talking with others about how one inventor's work inspires another's. I know that the invention of the airplane started a whole new way of traveling. Some research questions could be *When did the first successful airplane flight take place? How did news spread about the first airplane? How did the invention of the airplane help inspire the invention of other flying machines?*

Guide practice

Have students consult with others as they decide upon a topic. They should formulate an open-ended question about their topic.

On their own

Tell students that tomorrow they will conduct research using their questions. Help them outline their research plans. They should find historic advertisements and information about inventions in nonfiction books, reference books, and online.

INTERNET GUY
Don Leu

21st Century Skills

Weekly Inquiry Project

Day 1 Identify Questions

Day 2 Navigate/Search

Day 3 Analyze

Day 4 Synthesize

Day 5 Communicate

Small Group Time

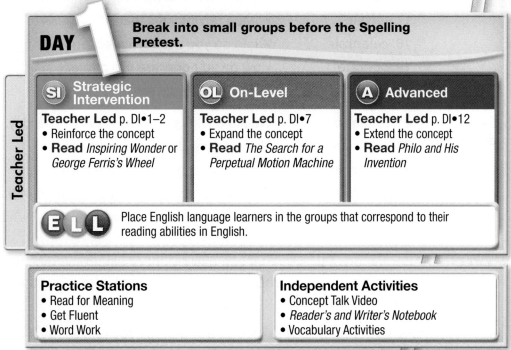

DAY 1

Break into small groups before the Spelling Pretest.

Teacher Led

SI Strategic Intervention
Teacher Led p. DI•1–2
• Reinforce the concept
• **Read** *Inspiring Wonder* or *George Ferris's Wheel*

OL On-Level
Teacher Led p. DI•7
• Expand the concept
• **Read** *The Search for a Perpetual Motion Machine*

A Advanced
Teacher Led p. DI•12
• Extend the concept
• **Read** *Philo and His Invention*

ELL Place English language learners in the groups that correspond to their reading abilities in English.

Practice Stations
• Read for Meaning
• Get Fluent
• Word Work

Independent Activities
• Concept Talk Video
• *Reader's and Writer's Notebook*
• Vocabulary Activities

English Language Learners
Multilingual vocabulary
Students can apply knowledge of their home languages to acquire new English vocabulary by using Multilingual Vocabulary Lists (*ELL Handbook*, pp. 431–444.)

Objectives
- Spell words with the schwa sound.
- Use and understand past, present, and future verb tenses.
- Write cursive lowercase *e* and capital letter *E* in words.

Spelling Pretest
Words with Schwa

Introduce Tell students to think of words with the schwa sound. This week we will learn rules and patterns to help us spell words with the schwa sound.

Pretest Use these sentences to administer the spelling pretest. Say each word, read the sentence, and repeat the word.

1. jewel	The **jewel** fell out of the ring.
2. kingdom	The king ruled the **kingdom**.
3. gasoline	We need an alternative to **gasoline**.
4. factory	What do they make at the **factory?**
5. garage	The truck will not fit in the **garage**.
6. tropical	**Tropical** fish are colorful.
7. pajamas	My **pajamas** are under the pillow.
8. estimate	Will you give us an **estimate** of the cost?
9. tomorrow	The book report is due **tomorrow.**
10. humidity	Before the storm, the air was full of **humidity.**
11. Chicago	**Chicago** has many sports teams.
12. bulletin	Look at the display on the **bulletin** board.
13. carnival	We rode the rides at the **carnival.**
14. illustrate	Draw a picture to **illustrate** your story.
15. elegant	The hotel is **elegant** and formal.
16. census	The **census** is taken every ten years.
17. terrific	What a **terrific** idea that is!
18. celebrate	When do you want to **celebrate** your birthday?
19. operate	How do you **operate** this printer?
20. celery	I like **celery** in my salad.

Challenge words

21. rehearsal	We are having play **rehearsal** on Tuesday.
22. salamander	The **salamander** looks like a lizard.
23. prominent	The museum features **prominent** artists.
24. significant	The results of the experiment were **significant.**
25. parakeet	My favorite bird is the **parakeet.**

Self-correct After the pretest, students can use a print or electronic dictionary to check their work. Have students self-correct their pretests by writing misspelled words.

Let's Practice It!
TR DVD•123

On their own Use *Let's Practice It!* p. 123 on the *Teacher Resources DVD-ROM* for additional practice.

Conventions
Past, Present, and Future Tenses

Teach
Display Grammar Transparency 11, and read aloud the explanation and examples in the box. Point out the present tense verbs *covers* and *wait,* the past tense verb *constructed,* and the future tense verb phrase *will move.*

Model
Model identifying the correct verb tense for items 1 and 2. Apply the rules for identifying verb tenses to show how you determined the correct tense.

Guide practice
Guide students to complete items 3–7. Record the correct responses on the transparency.

Daily Fix-It
Use Daily Fix-It numbers 1 and 2 in the right margin.

Connect to oral language
Have students read items 8 to 10 on the transparency and write the correct present, past, and future tense of each verb.

Grammar Transparency 11, TR DVD

Handwriting
Cursive Letter *e* and *E*

Model letter formation
Display the capital cursive letter *E* and the lower-case letter *e.* Follow the stroke instruction pictured to model letter formation.

Model letter size
Explain that writing legibly means letters are the correct size, form, and slant. Capital letters should be larger than lower-case letters. For example, the capital *E* touches the top line, while the lower-case *e* touches the middle line. Model writing this sentence smoothly: *Everyone enjoys eggs and ham.* Make sure the letters aren't too light, dark, or jagged.

Guide practice
Have students write this sentence: *Everyone was excited about the evening's entertainment.* Circulate around the room, guiding students.

Academic Vocabulary

Verb tenses are verb forms that show when something happens.

Schwa is a vowel sound in an unstressed syllable.

Daily Fix-It

1. Once I write a story about a king? (wrote; king.)
2. *King wrong* was a funny ferry tale. (*Wrong*; fairy)

English Language Learners

Past, Present, and Future Tenses On the board, write two or three examples each of words with past, present, and future tenses. Identify how to tell the tense for each word. Then have pairs create their own lists, writing two or three examples of each verb tense. Ask for volunteers to add these words to the board.

Handwriting: Verbs
Have students write present-tense verbs containing the letter *e,* such as *exercise, excite, engage,* and *endure.* Students should write each word beginning with a capital *E,* and then again with a lower-case *e.*

Objectives
- Understand and identify the features of a short play.

Writing—Play
Introduce

MINI-LESSON

5 Day Planner
Guide to Mini-Lessons

DAY 1	Read Like a Writer
DAY 2	Developing a Story Sequence
DAY 3	Writing Effective Dialogue
DAY 4	Revising Strategy: Clarifying
DAY 5	Proofread for Correct Tenses

MINI-LESSON

Read Like a Writer

Introduce This week you will write a short play. A short play is a story that is acted out on stage.

Prompt In *The Fabulous Perpetual Motion Machine,* young inventors create a special machine. Think about something that could be invented. Now write a short play based on your ideas.

Trait   Word Choice

Mode   Narrative

INTERAC with TEXT

Reader's and Writer's Notebook p. 179

Examine Model Let's read an example of a short play that is about an invention. Have students read "Summer Dreams" on p. 179 of their *Reader's and Writer's Notebook.*

Key Features Short plays include a list of **characters** and a **setting** and **time** that tell where and when the play is taking place. Find the characters, setting, and time in the play and circle them. Have students interact by circling the characters, setting, and time. Discuss how this information helps the reader picture the scene.

Short plays also include **stage directions** that give information about characters' actions and behavior. These directions are contained in parentheses. Have students underline all the stage directions in the play.

The **dialogue** in a short play shows the distinct way that characters speak. Have students draw a box around an example of dialogue from each character. Ask them to think about what each example of dialogue tells them about the characters.

Review
key features

Review the key features of a short play with students. You may want to post the key features in the classroom for students to refer to as they work on their compositions.

Key Features of a Short Play

- includes a list of characters
- describes the setting, time, or place
- characters often speak or act distinctly

ROUTINE   Quick Write for Fluency   Team Talk

1. **Talk** Have paired groups of students discuss the features of a short play.

2. **Write** Students should write a few sentences defining a short play.

3. **Share** Partners should read each other's writing.

Routines Flip Chart

Wrap Up Your Day

Write Guy
Jeff Anderson

Let Me Check My List

Encourage students to keep lists of words they come across that are exciting or interesting to them. They can use their lists to increase their vocabulary and incorporate them in their own writing. This is a great way to improve vocabulary and word choice.

✔ **Build Concepts** Have students discuss how inventors inspire our imaginations.

✔ **Oral Vocabulary** Have students use the Amazing Words they learned in context sentences.

✔ **Homework** Send home this week's Family Times newsletter on *Let's Practice It!* pp. 124–125 on the *Teacher Resources DVD-ROM.*

Let's Practice It!
TR DVD•124–125

English Language Learners
Have students exchange their marked-up copies of the writing models with each other. Ask them to review each other's papers to ensure that the characters, setting, time, and stage directions have been appropriately marked. Students should then provide feedback to each other.

Preview DAY 2

Tell students that tomorrow they will read a play about twins who come up with a new invention.

Objectives
- Expand the weekly concept.
- Develop oral vocabulary.

Today at a Glance

Oral Vocabulary
device, vehicle, enterprise

Word Analysis
Shades of Meaning

Literary Terms
Foreshadowing

Story Structure
Rising action

⊙ Lesson Vocabulary
Multiple-meaning words

Reading
"The Play's the Thing"

The Fabulous Perpetual Motion Machine

Fluency
Expression (tone of voice)

Research and Inquiry
Navigate/Search

Spelling
Words with schwa

Conventions
Past, present, and future tenses

Writing
Drama: Short Play

Concept Talk

Question of the Week

How do inventors inspire our imaginations?

Expand the concept

Remind students of the Question of the Week. Tell students that today they will begin reading *The Fabulous Perpetual Motion Machine.* As they read, encourage students to think about how inventors get ideas for new inventions.

Anchored Talk

Develop oral vocabulary

Use the photos on pp. 324–325 and the Read Aloud "What's the Big Idea, Ben Franklin?" to talk about the Amazing Words: *theory, experiment,* and *suggested.* Add the words to the concept map to develop students' knowledge of the topic. Break the class into groups. Have students discuss the following questions, considering suggestions from other group members.

- Have you ever *suggested* ways a product could be made better?
- What are some ways to prove a *theory*?
- Discuss a time when you tried an *experiment* to find out if you were right about something.

Oral Vocabulary
Amazing Words

Amazing Words

theory | enterprise
experiment | improvement
suggested | design
device | entrepreneur
vehicle | innovation

Teach Amazing Words

Amazing Words Oral Vocabulary Routine

1 Introduce Write the Amazing Word *device* on the board. Have students say it aloud with you. Relate *device* to the photographs on pp. 324–325 and "What's the Big Idea, Ben Franklin?" Ben Franklin invented a special stove, a pole to grip books, and many other *devices.* How can the context of those inventions help us understand what a *device* is? Have students determine the definition of the word. (A *device* is an invention made to do a certain job.)

2 Demonstrate Have students answer questions to demonstrate understanding. What are some *devices* you use? If you could invent a new *device,* what would it be?

3 Apply Have students apply their understanding. Can you think of a synonym for *device*?

See p. OV•1 to teach *vehicle* and *enterprise.*

Routines Flip Chart

Apply Amazing Words

Have students establish a purpose for reading before they read "The Play's the Thing" on p. 329. Have them consider how the Amazing Word *enterprise* applies to the process of putting on a play.

Connect to reading

Explain that today students will read about some students working on an amazing invention. As they read, they should think about how the Question of the Week and the Amazing Words *device, vehicle,* and *enterprise* apply to the characters in the play.

ELL Reinforce Vocabulary Use the Day 2 instruction on ELL Poster 11 to teach the selection vocabulary and discuss the lesson concept.

ELL Poster 11

Objectives

- Use the context to clarify shades of meaning.
- Identify how story incidents foreshadow future story events.
- Use story structure to enhance comprehension.

Word Analysis
Shades of Meaning

Teach shades of meaning
Remind students that sometimes two words have similar meanings, and that the differences between the meanings are called shades of meaning. Display the following sentence: *Mel's invention was a _____ idea.* List the following words: *modern, new, cutting-edge, fresh, newfangled.* Ask students to tell which word makes Mel's invention sound most appealing and which makes it sound least appealing.

Model

Think Aloud I notice that the words are all synonyms for *new,* but they don't mean quite the same thing. *Modern* doesn't necessarily mean *up-to-the-minute,* and *new* doesn't sound very exciting. *Fresh* suggests something that hasn't been done before. *Newfangled* sounds like the way my grandpa described technology he couldn't understand, so I don't feel too positive about that one. *Cutting-edge* sounds new and exciting—perhaps a little dangerous? I think *fresh* appeals to me most.

Guide practice
Have students determine the shades of meaning of the words *inspecting, watching, observing,* and *looking at.*

On their own
Have students check an electronic dictionary to see how the definitions of the words compare. Follow the strategy for Meaningful Word Parts to teach the word *inspecting.*

ROUTINE **Strategy for Meaningful Word Parts**

1. **Introduce word parts** Circle each word part in the word *inspecting.* I will circle *in, spect,* and *ing.*

2. **Connect to meaning** Define each word part. *In* means "into" or "within." *Spect* means "look at." I know that word part from *spectacles* and *spectacular.* The ending, *-ing,* means something is happening now. It signals a present-tense verb.

3. **Read the word** Blend the meaningful word parts together to read *inspecting.* Then blend the meanings to find the meaning of *inspecting. Inspecting* means "looking into something or looking very closely at it." Continue the Routine with the words *project* and *browsing.*

Routines Flip Chart

Literary Terms
Foreshadowing

Teach foreshadowing

Tell students that the word *foreshadowing* refers to hints authors give about what will happen later in a story. Used in narrative genres, foreshadowing builds curiosity or suspense.

Model foreshadowing

 **Think Aloud** Let's look back at *A Summer's Trade* on page 271. I read that Tony's uncle is home early. How does that foreshadow, or hint at, what will happen later? (It's a clue that something is wrong—his uncle is injured and can't work.)

Guide practice

Discuss the example of foreshadowing in title of *The Fabulous Perpetual Motion Machine*. (Perpetual motion is impossible.) Point out that authors do not usually include details without a reason. If readers wonder why a detail is given, it might be a clue to something that will be important later.

On their own

Have students look for and describe examples of foreshadowing in other selections in their Student Edition.

Story Structure
Rising Action

Teach rising action

Tell students that the term *rising action* describes how one conflict or action builds on another, increasing the stakes as a character seeks to achieve a goal or solve a problem.

Model

Think Aloud In *A Summer's Trade,* Tony is saving money to buy a saddle. I can tell Tony feels bad that his grandmother pawned her bracelet, but when his mother tells him to mind his own business, he does. When he finds his grandmother is sick, though, he gets really worried. This chain of events is an example of rising action. It forces him to make a decision—and help his grandmother with the money he was saving for his saddle.

Guide practice

Have students look for another example of rising action in *A Summer's Trade*. Ask them to explain how each example helps advance the story.

On their own

Have students look for and describe examples of foreshadowing as they read *The Fabulous Perpetual Motion Machine*.

Academic Vocabulary

Rising action tells how scenes or story events build on one another, increasing the drama and excitement to higher and higher levels.

Objectives
- Use context clues to identify meaning of multiple-meaning words.
- Read grade level text with expression.

Vocabulary Strategy for
Multiple-Meaning Words

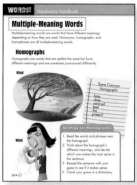

Student Edition p. W•10

Teach multiple-meaning words

Envision It!

Tell students that when they encounter words with multiple meanings, they should look for context clues. Explain how using the strategy of context clues can help readers choose the correct meaning for the word in a sentence. Refer students to *Words!* on p. W•10 in the Student Edition for additional practice.

Model the strategy

Think Aloud

Write on the board: *We will be growing plants for a class project.* and *I will project these images onto that movie screen.* I see one word that appears in both sentences. Circle the word *project* in both. I know this word can mean different things, such as *undertaking* or *activity* and *to show in a large size.* I'll look for context clues to help me decide which meaning belongs in each sentence. In the first sentence, I see *growing plants* and *class.* In the second, I see *images* and *movie screen.* I will choose a meaning based on these context clues. When I try to replace the word with the meanings I chose, I get *We will be growing plants for a class activity* and *I will show these images in a large size on that movie screen.* I think those are the right meanings.

Guide practice

Write this sentence on the board: *Our principal applauds our effort to beautify the school.* Have students look in a dictionary for definitions of *applaud.* Then tell students to choose the correct meaning and explain why they chose the meaning they did. For additional support, use *Envision It! Pictured Vocabulary Cards* or *Tested Vocabulary Cards.*

On their own

Have students reread "The Play's the Thing" and use context clues to help them clarify the meanings of the lesson vocabulary. Have students share their choices and explain their reasoning. For additional practice use *Reader's and Writer's Notebook,* p.180.

Reader's and Writer's Notebook p. 180

Go Digital! | **Vocabulary Activities**

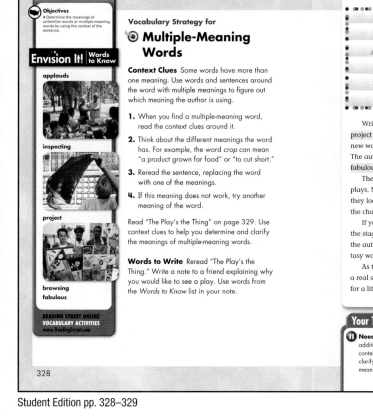

Student Edition pp. 328–329

Objectives
• Determine the meanings of unfamiliar words or multiple-meaning words by using the context of the sentence.

Envision It! | Words to Know

applauds

inspecting

project

browsing
fabulous

**READING STREET ONLINE
VOCABULARY ACTIVITIES**
www.ReadingStreet.com

328

Vocabulary Strategy for
Multiple-Meaning Words

Context Clues Some words have more than one meaning. Use words and sentences around the word with multiple meanings to figure out which meaning the author is using.

1. When you find a multiple-meaning word, read the context clues around it.

2. Think about the different meanings the word has. For example, the word *crop* can mean "a product grown for food" or "to cut short."

3. Reread the sentence, replacing the word with one of the meanings.

4. If this meaning does not work, try another meaning of the word.

Read "The Play's the Thing" on page 329. Use context clues to help you determine and clarify the meanings of multiple-meaning words.

Words to Write Reread "The Play's the Thing." Write a note to a friend explaining why you would like to see a play. Use words from the *Words to Know* list in your note.

The **Play's** *the* **Thing**

Writing a play is hard work. But it can also be an enjoyable project for an author—and the audience. An author creates a whole new world, and then fills it with people who do what he or she wishes. The author can use them to tell realistic stories, or send them off on fabulous adventures.

The next time you are browsing in the library, look for famous plays. Notice the way that authors describe their characters. How do they look and sound? Look at the stage directions. They tell you how the characters will move and what will be around them.

If you get a chance, go to a play. It can be lots of fun. Inspecting the stage before the play starts will tell you something about the mood the author wants to create. When the actors come on stage, this fantasy world comes alive.

As the play ends and the audience applauds, the author often feels a real sense of joy. So does the crowd. They were able to escape—even for a little while—to a different world.

Your Turn!

ⓘ **Need a Review?** For additional help with using context clues to determine and clarify the meaning of multiple-meaning words, see *Words!*

▶ **Ready to Try It?** Read *The Fabulous Perpetual Motion Machine* on pp. 330–343.

329

Reread for Fluency
Expression

Model fluent reading

Read the first paragraph of "The Play's the Thing" aloud, paying attention to your expression. Tell students you are changing your tone of voice as you read to add interest and convey meaning.

ROUTINE **Choral Reading** **Team Talk**

① **Select a passage** Read paragraph 2 of "The Play's the Thing" aloud.

② **Model** Have students listen as you read with appropriate expression.

③ **Guide practice** Have students read along with you.

④ **Corrective feedback** For optimal fluency, students should reread three or four times with expression. Provide corrective feedback.

Routines Flip Chart

Lesson Vocabulary

applauds shows approval by clapping hands, shouting, etc.

browsing looking here and there

fabulous wonderful; exciting

inspecting looking over carefully; examining

project a special assignment planned and carried out by a student or group of students

Differentiated Instruction

SI Strategic Intervention

Multiple-meaning words
To reinforce the concept of multiple-meaning words, ask volunteers to identify different meanings of the word *run*. Then assign a common multiple-meaning word, such as *stand, part,* and *right,* to small groups of students. Ask them to identify as many meanings for their word as they can.

Academic Vocabulary

tone of voice the quality, pitch, strength, etc., of a person's voice.

ELL

English Language Learners
Build Academic Vocabulary
Use the lesson vocabulary pictured on p. 328 to teach the meanings of *device, vehicle,* and *enterprise.* Call on pairs to write the words on sticky notes and use them to label images of the words on the ELL Poster.

Objectives
- Understand the elements and structure of drama.
- Use illustrations and the structure of drama to preview and predict.
- Set a purpose for reading.

The Fabulous Perpetual Motion Machine

by Don Abramson
illustrations by Gerardo Suzán

Question of the Week
How do inventors inspire our imaginations?

Genre **A drama** is a story written to be acted out for an audience. As you read, imagine the actors speaking the lines and acting out the action.

330

Let's **Think About Reading!**

Student Edition pp. 330–331

Build Background

Discuss inventors

Team Talk Have students turn to a partner and discuss the Question of the Week and these questions about inventors.

- Where do inventors get their ideas?
- What makes a good invention?
- What do you think inventors do if their first plan fails?

Connect to selection

Have students discuss their answers with the class. Possible responses: Inventors see a need and try to figure out a way to satisfy that need. A good invention is often something that solves a problem or makes something easier to do. Inventors might run into many problems before they create a successful invention; they might change the design or approach the problem in a new way if their first plan fails. For additional opportunities to build background, use the Background Building Audio.

Prereading Strategies

Genre
Explain that a **drama**, or play, is a story written to be acted out for an audience. A drama consists mainly of dialogue and stage directions, which tell the actors where to move on stage. A written drama usually lists a cast of characters and describes the setting. Plays are divided into numbered acts and scenes.

Preview and predict
Have students preview the title and illustrations and note the format, the list of characters, and the description of the setting. Point out the numbered scenes and the characters' names in bold. Then have students predict what the play will be about.

Set purpose
Prior to reading, have students set their own purposes for reading this selection. To help students set a purpose, ask them to think about what it would be like to create a very special invention.

Strategy Response Log

INTERACT with TEXT

Have students use p. 17 in the *Reader's and Writer's Notebook* to identify the characteristics of drama.

Small Group Time

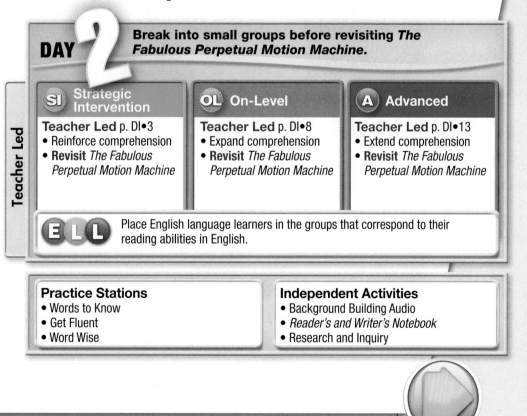

DAY 2

Break into small groups before revisiting *The Fabulous Perpetual Motion Machine.*

Teacher Led

SI Strategic Intervention
Teacher Led p. DI•3
• Reinforce comprehension
• **Revisit** *The Fabulous Perpetual Motion Machine*

OL On-Level
Teacher Led p. DI•8
• Expand comprehension
• **Revisit** *The Fabulous Perpetual Motion Machine*

A Advanced
Teacher Led p. DI•13
• Extend comprehension
• **Revisit** *The Fabulous Perpetual Motion Machine*

ELL Place English language learners in the groups that correspond to their reading abilities in English.

Practice Stations
• Words to Know
• Get Fluent
• Word Wise

Independent Activities
• Background Building Audio
• *Reader's and Writer's Notebook*
• Research and Inquiry

Differentiated Instruction

A Advanced
Have students think of a need that could be filled by a new invention. Then ask them to write a paragraph telling about what the new invention would have to do to meet that need.

Double Day Read Multidraft Reading

For **Whole Group** instruction, choose one of the reading options below. For each reading, have students set the purpose indicated.

Option 1
Day 2 Read the selection. Use Guide Comprehension to monitor and clarify understanding.
Day 3 Reread the selection. Use Extend Thinking to develop higher-order thinking skills.

Option 2
Day 2 Read the first half of the selection, using both Guide Comprehension and Extend Thinking instruction.
Day 3 Read the second half of the selection, using both Guide Comprehension and Extend Thinking instruction.

ELL

English Language Learners
Build Background To build background, review the selection summary in English (9) *ELL Handbook* p. 191. Use the Retelling Cards to provide visual support for the summary.

Objectives

◎ Use context clues to determine the meaning of multiple-meaning words.

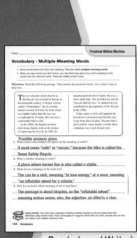

Reader's and Writer's Notebook p. 184.

OPTION 1 Guide Comprehension Skills and Strategies

Teach Multiple-Meaning Words

Multiple-Meaning Words Write these sentences on the board: *Effie found it hard to be patient as she waited to see the project. If the project is a medical one, maybe it will cure a doctor's patient someday.* Have students determine the correct meaning of *patient* in each sentence.

Corrective Feedback

If... students are unable to figure out the meanings of *patient,*

then... model using context clues to determine the correct meanings.

Model the Skill

Think Aloud How can I figure out the meaning of the word *patient* in the first sentence? I see the context clues "found it hard" and "as she waited."

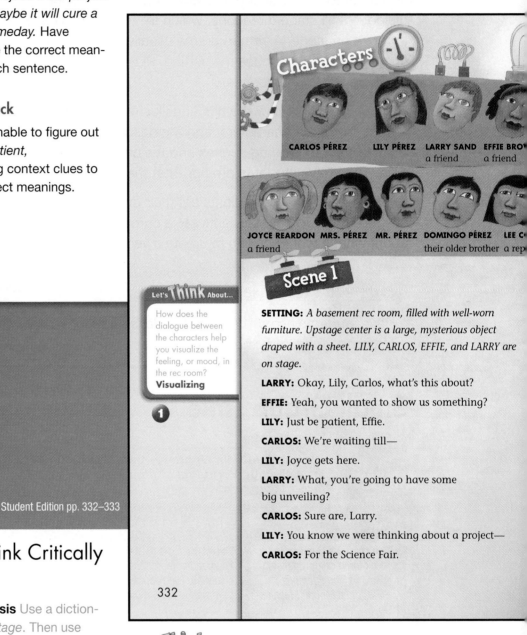

Student Edition pp. 332–333

OPTION 2 Extend Thinking Think Critically

Higher-Order Thinking Skills

Multiple-Meaning Words • Synthesis Use a dictionary to find two meanings for the word *stage*. Then use context clues to clarify the meaning of *stage* at the top of page 332. Possible response: The word *stage* can mean "a raised platform in a theater" or "a step in a process." Here the word *stage* appears in the context of the setting for a play, so I can clarify that *stage* means "a raised platform in a theater."

Let's Think About...

❶ The characters are talking quietly. It helps me visualize a roomful of impatient people.

❷ She likes original ideas. She's not very patient.

❸ Lilly and Carlos have something to show their friends. It involves the upcoming Science Fair. They think their project will win first prize and blow everyone away.

The clues help me to determine that here, *patient* means "able to wait calmly." Which context clues do you see in the second sentence? (medical, cure, doctor) What does *patient* mean there? (someone treated by a doctor)

EFFIE: We were all trying to come up with something that hadn't been done to death.

LARRY: That wasn't so easy. I'm doing a dinosaur diorama.

EFFIE: Done to death.

LARRY: I said it wasn't easy.

EFFIE: Carlos, Lily, you're driving us crazy here.

LARRY: Yeah, give us a little hint!

CARLOS: All right. Prepare to be blown away.

LILY: This year, first prize at the Science Fair—

CARLOS: Will be awarded to—

LILY: The fabulous Pérez Twins! Take a bow, Carlos. *(She applauds as he bows.)*

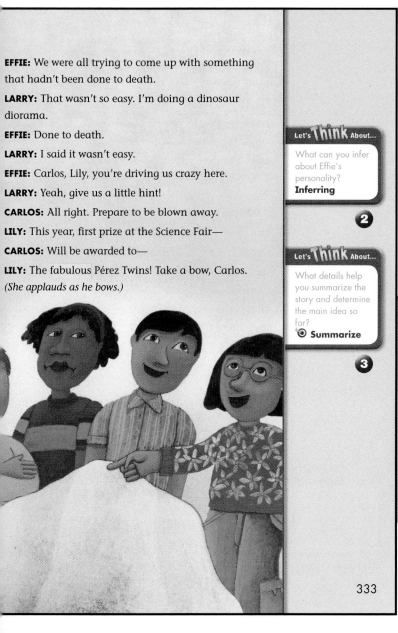

On Their Own

Have students look for other examples of multiple-meaning words on p. 332. *(stage, sheet)* Have them copy the sentences and underline clue words that point to the meaning of the multiple-meaning words. For additional practice, use the *Reader's and Writer's Notebook* p. 184.

Let's **Think** About...

What can you infer about Effie's personality?
Inferring

②

Let's **Think** About...

What details help you summarize the story and determine the main idea so far?
◉ **Summarize**

③

333

Genre • Evaluation In this play, we do not hear from a narrator—only the characters themselves. How would adding a narrator change what you know about the characters? Possible response: A narrator could tell more about what the characters are thinking and feeling. A narrator might also tell what is under the sheet.

Foreshadowing • Evaluation Reread the stage directions on page 332. How does the author use the setting to foreshadow what may happen later in the play? Possible response: By showing the "large, mysterious object draped with a sheet," the author foreshadows that the sheet will be lifted and the object will be revealed.

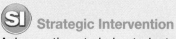

Objectives

◎ Summarize to enhance comprehension.

OPTION 1 Skills and Strategies, continued

Teach Summarize

◉ **Summarize** Have students read p. 334. Ask students to summarize what they know about how the twins found their idea for the science fair project. (Carlos searched for ideas on the Internet and found information about an invention that many people have tried before but failed.)

Corrective Feedback

If... students are unable to summarize what they know about the project, **then...** model how to summarize information.

Student Edition pp. 334–335

OPTION 2 Think Critically, continued

Higher-Order Thinking Skills

◉ **Summarize • Analysis** Summarize the strategies the twins use to build suspense around their project. Be sure to maintain the order of the events as you tell your summary. Possible response: The twins cover the project with a sheet, tell everyone that it is sure to win first prize, give hints about it without telling what it is, and wait until everyone comes over before they unveil it.

Model the Strategy

Think Aloud When I summarize, I paraphrase, or use my own words, to tell the main points while maintaining the meaning of the text. What does Lily say about how Carlos found the idea for the project? (She says he was browsing the Internet.)

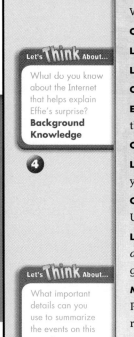

CARLOS: And Lily. Yea-a-a! *(He applauds as she bows; then turns to EFFIE and LARRY.)* You're not getting into t spirit, you two.

LARRY: We haven't seen anything yet.

EFFIE: And you're really going to have to be fabulous win first prize at that Science Fair.

LARRY: It's usually somebody from Higgins School. They've got that hot-shot science teacher.

LILY: Well, not this year. This year the Mary Dimity Witherspoon Elementary School—

CARLOS: Will go down in history!

LARRY: Enough, already! What is this project?

LILY: Well, Carlos was browsing the Internet—

CARLOS: Looking for failed inventions.

EFFIE: Hey, you can't take your science project off the Internet!

CARLOS: We found the idea, not the plan.

LILY: People have been playing around with this for years—

CARLOS: For centuries! But until now, nobody's done Until us, the fabulous—

LILY: Pérez Twins! Yea-a-a! *(CARLOS and LILY both chee applaud, and bow. She turns to LARRY and EFFIE.)* C'mo guys!

MRS. PÉREZ *(entering):* And just what is it the fabulou Pérez Twins have achieved to warrant a spontaneou round of applause?

CARLOS: Hi, Mom. We were just telling Effie and Lar

MRS. PÉREZ: Well, tell Joyce too. She just got here.

Let's Think About...

What do you know about the Internet that helps explain Effie's surprise? **Background Knowledge** ❹

Let's Think About...

What important details can you use to summarize the events on this page? ◉ **Summarize** ❺

334

Let's Think About...

❹ The Internet probably has plans from other successful projects that were already done.

❺ Students from Higgins School usually win first prize at the Science Fair because of their teacher. Lily and Carlos found the idea for their project on the Internet.

❻ Mrs. Pérez likes to know what her children are up to. She's excited to learn about their secret project.

What does Carlos say he was looking for? **(failed inventions)** What did he find? **(an idea that people have been playing around with for centuries)** So I could summarize by saying they found information on the Internet about an invention that has been tried before without success.

On Their Own

Have students read pp. 334–335 and summarize Carlos and Lily's goals for the Science Fair by paraphrasing the main points in order.

OYCE *(entering)*: Hi, guys. *(Everyone adlibs greetings.)* What's up? Is this your Science Fair idea?

LY: Yes, and I tell you—

RS. PÉREZ: Aha! So that's what you've been banging round down here about.

ARLOS: We're going to win the—

ARRY: We've heard this already!

RS. PÉREZ: If you're finally going to disclose this big cret, do you mind if your mother sits in? *(to the others)* hey've been driving the whole family crazy.

LY: Sure, Mom.

ARLOS: Sit over here.

OYCE *(inspecting the draped thing)*: Is this it?

LY: Yes! But first let us tell you—

OYCE has tugged at a corner of the sheet, hich falls away, revealing a contraption th dials, levers, pulleys, etc.)

Let's Think About...

What do Mrs. Perez's comments tell about the kind of person she is? **Inferring**

6

335

Author's Purpose • Evaluation Read the stage directions that appear in parentheses on page 334. Why do you think the author has the twins bow, cheer, and applaud so much? Possible response: It would be entertaining when performed by actors on stage; it shows how they feel about themselves and their project even though there is no narrator to tell us directly.

Character and Plot • Synthesis At the bottom of page 335, Joyce pulls the sheet off the science project. How do you think that event will help move the story forward? Possible response: The twins have been stalling. Now that everyone sees the machine, they will have to tell about it.

English Language Learners
Vocabulary: Exaggeration Focus students' attention on Carlos's statement on p. 334 that his school "will go down in history." *Will go down in history* is an example of exaggeration. When we exaggerate, we make something seem greater than it actually is. I could say that a big shopping trip will go down in history to make it seem bigger than it actually is. Ask students to think of events they might describe in this way.

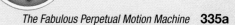

Objectives

◎ Identify sequence.

OPTION 1 Skills and Strategies, continued

Teach Sequence

🔘 **Sequence** Have students read p. 336. Then have them determine which of the following events happens first: the guests applaud or the twins try the machine for the very first time. (The twins turn on the machine first. It comes to life and impresses the guests, who then applaud.)

Corrective Feedback

If... students have difficulty following the sequence,
then... model how to follow the sequence.

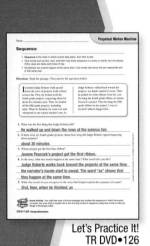

Let's Practice It!
TR DVD•126

OPTION 2 Think Critically, continued

Higher-Order Thinking Skills

🔘 **Sequence • Evaluation** Lily and Carlos invited friends to see the machine before testing it themselves. Do you think that was a good plan? Why or why not? **Possible response: No, because they don't know whether it works and they might be embarrassed in front of their friends if it doesn't work.**

Model the Skill

Think Aloud To follow the sequence, I look for the order in which events happen in the play. In the stage directions I see that Lily flips a switch on the machine. What happens next?

Student Edition pp. 336–337

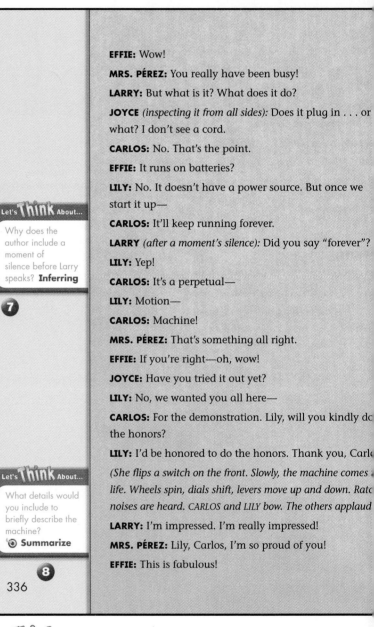

EFFIE: Wow!

MRS. PÉREZ: You really have been busy!

LARRY: But what is it? What does it do?

JOYCE *(inspecting it from all sides):* Does it plug in . . . or what? I don't see a cord.

CARLOS: No. That's the point.

EFFIE: It runs on batteries?

LILY: No. It doesn't have a power source. But once we start it up—

CARLOS: It'll keep running forever.

LARRY *(after a moment's silence):* Did you say "forever"?

LILY: Yep!

CARLOS: It's a perpetual—

LILY: Motion—

CARLOS: Machine!

MRS. PÉREZ: That's something all right.

EFFIE: If you're right—oh, wow!

JOYCE: Have you tried it out yet?

LILY: No, we wanted you all here—

CARLOS: For the demonstration. Lily, will you kindly do the honors?

LILY: I'd be honored to do the honors. Thank you, Carl[os]

(She flips a switch on the front. Slowly, the machine comes [to] life. Wheels spin, dials shift, levers move up and down. Ratc[het] noises are heard. CARLOS and LILY bow. The others applaud[.]

LARRY: I'm impressed. I'm really impressed!

MRS. PÉREZ: Lily, Carlos, I'm so proud of you!

EFFIE: This is fabulous!

336

Let's Think About...
Why does the author include a moment of silence before Larry speaks? **Inferring**
7

Let's Think About...
What details would you include to briefly describe the machine?
🔘 **Summarize**
8

Let's Think About...

7 The author is telling the reader that Larry is shocked.

8 It's a machine that doesn't require a plug, batteries, or any other power source. It runs on perpetual motion. It has wheels, dials, and levers.

9 I can look back in the story to find details about them.

Check Predictions Have students look back at the predictions they made earlier and discuss whether they were accurate. Then have students preview the rest of the selection and either adjust their predictions accordingly or make new predictions.

(The machine comes to life, and the guests applaud.) How does the first incident give rise to the next? (Lily must turn on the machine before the guests can be impressed enough to applaud.)

Let's **Think** About...

What can you do to help remember all the characters?
Monitor and Clarify

9

337

On Their Own

Have students find other examples of sequence on p. 336. For additional practice, see *Let's Practice It!* p. 126 on the *Teacher Resources DVD-ROM.*

Compare and Contrast • Analysis What do the twins' friends say about the machine on page 336? Compare and contrast the way they felt about the project before it was turned on with how they felt after. Possible response: Before, they were curious but skeptical about the project; afterward, they were amazed and thought it was "fabulous."

Background Knowledge • Evaluation • Text to World Think about what you know about how machines work. Do you think the twins have actually built a perpetual motion machine? Explain. Possible response: Probably not; machines need energy to work, and it seems unlikely that the twins could do something that people have been trying unsuccessfully to do for centuries.

Differentiated Instruction

SI **Strategic Intervention**

Sequence of events Explain that the events in this play, as in most stories and plays, are told in the order in which they happen. However, sometimes characters tell about something that happened earlier. Have students reread p. 336 and find places where the characters talk about something that has happened in the past. (Mrs. Pérez says the twins have been busy. The twins tell about making the decision not to test the machine before showing it to their friends.)

A **Advanced**

Genre: Drama Have students act out the dialogue. Encourage students to imagine that they are the actual characters and put appropriate expression in their voices to help the audience understand the characters.

ELL

English Language Learners
Monitor comprehension Write the question words *Who, What, When, Where, Why,* and *How* on the board. Have students ask questions about aspects of the play using the question words. Allow classmates to answer each other's questions.

If you want to teach this selection in two sessions, stop here.

Objectives
- Find pertinent information from online sources.
- Practice correctly spelling words with schwa.
- Recognize and correctly use past, present, and future tenses.

Research and Inquiry
Navigate/Search

Teach

Have students follow their research plans to collect information on the Internet using their inquiry questions and keywords. Tell them to skim and scan each site for information that helps answer their inquiry question. Remind them to use print resources as well. Students who are researching individual inventors could look for entries in encyclopedias or biographies in the library.

Model

Think Aloud When searching for information about how the airplane helped inspire future flying machines, I know I should make my research as specific as possible. A keyword like *inventions* is too broad. I can streamline my search by using keywords such as *flight inventions* or *early flying machines* to find Web sites that will answer my questions. I can also use keywords such as *aviation* and *history*.

Guide practice

Have students review the print and online resources they've identified. Have them evaluate the relevance, validity, and reliability of each source. Point out that commercial Web sites and advertisements often contain persuasive text. Since they are looking for advertisements, students will run into text that is persuasive and commercial. Give an example to show them how to recognize it.

On their own

As they research, students should look for quotes about their inventions. Stress the importance of recording the sources of the quotations they will use in the ads.

Conventions
Past, Present, and Future Tenses

Teach

Write on the board: *The prize was good* and *She wants to win.* Point out that *was* is in the past tense and *wants* is in the present tense.

Guide Practice

Explain to students that verb tenses should be logical and consistent in a piece of writing. Write on the board:

> *Incorrect:* **The people cheered for the king as he passes by.**
> *Correct:* **The people cheered for the king as he passed by.**

In the correct version of this sentence, both *cheered* and *passed* are written in the past tense.

Daily Fix-It

Use Daily Fix-It numbers 3 and 4 in the right margin.

Connect to oral language

Have students look for past, present, and future tense verbs in *The Fabulous Perpetual Motion Machine.*

On their own

For additional practice, use the *Reader's and Writer's Notebook,* p. 181.

Reader's and Writer's Notebook, p. 181.

Spelling
Words with Schwa

Teach

Remind students of the pattern that vowels in unaccented syllables often have the schwa sound, and the rule that the schwa in an unaccented syllable gives no clue to its spelling.

Guide practice

Write *kingdom* and say it slowly, exaggerating the accented syllable. Underline the unaccented syllable *dom* and say the vowel sound /ə/.

On their own

For additional practice, use the *Reader's and Writer's Notebook,* p. 182.

Reader's and Writer's Notebook, p. 182

Daily Fix-It

3. In this kingdum, the king surved everyone. *(kingdom, served))*

4. He payed taxes to his loyel subjects. *(paid, loyal)*

ELL

English Language Learners

Conventions To provide students with practice on past, present, and future tenses, use the modified grammar lessons in the *ELL Handbook* and the Grammar Jammer! online at: www.ReadingStreet.com.

Practice Pronunciation: Words with Schwa Have students choose five words from their spelling pretests. Students should copy the words, look them up in a dictionary, and circle the vowels that are represented by the schwa symbol in the pronunciation key. They should then pronounce each word out loud, paying attention to the schwa sound as they say it.

Objectives
- Choose a topic for writing.
- Develop a story sequence.

Writing—Play
Writing Trait: Organization

Introduce the prompt

Review the key features of a play. Remind students that they should think about these features as they plan their writing. Then explain that they will begin writing a short play today. Read aloud the writing prompt.

> **Writing Prompt**
>
> In *The Fabulous Perpetual Motion Machine,* young inventors create a special machine. Think about something that could be invented. Now write a short play based on your ideas.

Select a topic

Think Aloud To help choose a topic, let's make a list of useful inventions that could solve problems or make life easier. I will write *a machine that saves time on homework* on my list. Can you think of any other useful inventions? (Possible response: a machine that transports you anywhere in an instant) Add a *machine that transports you anywhere in an instant* to the list. Can you think of one more useful invention? (Possible response: a machine that turns trash into energy) Continue filling in the chart with *a machine that turns trash into energy.*

I am very interested in recycling, so I will write a play about a machine that changes household garbage into an energy source because that is the subject that is most interesting to me.

Gather information

Remind students that they can do research to help them find more information about inventions. Remember to keep this chart as the students will refer back to it tomorrow as they draft.

Useful Inventions

a machine that saves time on homework

a machine that transports you anywhere in an instant

a machine that changes trash into energy

Corrective feedback

Circulate around the room and conference briefly with students having problems making a choice. Mention the following ideas as possible topics for inventions: a type of transportation, a type of appliance, a special robot.

Differentiated Instruction

A **Advanced**

Problem Finding Have partners find possible problems with each other's inventions and make suggestions for how to correct these difficulties.

Reader's and Writer's Notebook p. 183

MINI-LESSON

Developing a Story Sequence

▉ Now that I have selected a topic, I will brainstorm ideas for a play. I will use a story chart to help develop and organize my ideas. **Display a story sequence chart.** I begin my story chart by writing the names of the characters in my play. My characters will be two friends, named Dana and Roberto, who are working on the invention together. The setting will be Dana's parents' garage. The first event I will list has to do with Dana and Roberto discussing what to do with all the garbage.

Continue modeling how to complete a story chart to organize ideas. Then, allow students time to fill in a story sequence chart to develop and organize the ideas for their own plays.

ROUTINE Quick Write for Fluency   Team Talk

1 **Talk** Have pairs discuss the inventions they've chosen.

2 **Write** Each student should write about his or her invention.

3 **Share** Have partners exchange their writings with each other. Each should ask the other one a question about the invention.

Routines Flip Chart

Teacher Tip

Do a periodic check of students' Quick Writes to make sure they are on task and communicating effectively with their partners.

Wrap Up Your Day

✔ **Build Concepts** What did you learn about where inventors get their ideas?

✔ **Sequence** How did following the sequence help you understand how the twins impressed their guests with their invention?

✔ **Summarize** How did summarizing the text help you understand how the twins came up with their idea for the science fair project?

Preview DAY 3

Tell students that tomorrow they will find out what happened with the twins' invention.

Objectives
• Expand the weekly concept.
• Develop oral vocabulary.

Today at a Glance

Oral Vocabulary
improvement, design

Comprehension Check/Retelling
Discuss questions

Reading
The Fabulous Perpetual Motion Machine

Think Critically
Retelling

Fluency
Expression

Research and Study Skills
Advertisement

Research and Inquiry
Analyze

Spelling
Words with schwa

Conventions
Past, present, and future tenses

Writing
Drama: Play

Concept Talk

Question of the Week

How do inventors inspire our imaginations?

Expand the concept

Remind students of the weekly concept question. Discuss how the question relates to Carlos and Lily's science fair project. Tell students that today they will read about the twins' plans for the machine. Encourage students to think about how the *device* might lead to an important *enterprise* for the twins.

Anchored Talk

Develop oral vocabulary

Have students scan illustrations to review pp. 330–337 of *The Fabulous Perpetual Motion Machine.* Then discuss the Amazing Words *device, vehicle,* and *enterprise* and add these words to the concept map. Use the following questions to guide discussion and broaden students' understanding of the concept.

• Think about how the twins plan to use their *device.* Think of some ways that *devices* are used to help people in society.

• What do people need to do to make sure a new *enterprise* succeeds?

Oral Vocabulary
Amazing Words

Amazing Words

theory	enterprise
experiment	improvement
suggested	design
device	entrepreneur
vehicle	innovation

Teach Amazing Words

Amazing Words Oral Vocabulary Routine

1 Introduce Write the word *improvement* on the board. Have students say it with you. In "What's the Big Idea, Ben Franklin?" we learned that Ben had ideas for the *improvement* of Philadelphia, such as forming a circulating library. Have students use context clues to determine a definition of *improvement*. (*Improvement* is the act of improving, or making something better.)

2 Demonstrate Have students answer questions to demonstrate understanding. Why would having a city fire department be an *improvement*? (Having a group of people trained and ready to fight fires would help save lives and property.)

3 Apply Have students apply their understanding. Name an *improvement* you would like to make in your classroom.

See p. OV•1 to teach *design.*

Routines Flip Chart

Apply Amazing Words

As students read pp. 338–343 of *The Fabulous Perpetual Motion Machine,* have them consider how the Amazing Words *improvement* and *design* apply to Carlos and Lily's project.

Connect to reading

Explain that today students will read about how the twins' project works. As they read, students should think about how this week's concept question and the Amazing Words *improvement* and *design* apply to Carlos and Lily's work.

ELL Expand Vocabulary Use the Day 3 instruction on ELL Poster 11 to help students expand vocabulary.

ELL Poster 11

Objectives

◎ Identify sequence to aid comprehension.

◎ Use the summarizing strategy to aid comprehension.

◎ Use context clues to clarify the meanings of multiple-meaning words.

Comprehension Check

Have students discuss each question with a partner. Ask several pairs to share their responses.

☑ **Genre • Analysis**

In *The Fabulous Perpetual Motion Machine,* Lily and Carlos often finished each other's sentences. Why do you think the author had them talk this way? **Possible response: To show that they are so close to each other that they think the same thoughts. It would be funny to see them talk that way on stage.**

☑ **Sequence • Analysis**

The author doesn't show every event, such as Lily and Carlos choosing an idea. How do we learn about that? **Possible response: The twins tell their guests about things that happened before the action of the play begins.**

☑ **Summarize • Analysis**

Come up with a one-sentence summary to answer these questions: What is the twins' goal? Why do their friends think it's a difficult one? **Possible response: They want to win first prize at the Science Fair, but the top prize usually goes to a student from a different school with a hot-shot science teacher.**

☑ **Multiple-Meaning Words • Analysis**

In *The Fabulous Perpetual Motion Machine,* Lily tells Carlos to "take a bow." Write the phrase on the board. Think of as many meanings as you can for *bow.* Then describe how this command could mean something different in a different context. **Possible response: A person wrapping packages could "take a bow." An archery teacher might also "take a bow."**

☑ **Connect text to self**

If you had what you thought was an earth-shaking idea, would you present it to your friends in the way Lily and Carlos do? Would you do it differently? Explain your answer. **Possible responses: I would not keep telling everyone how great my idea was because it might not work; I would test it myself before I showed it to anyone else.**

Strategy Response Log

Have students revisit p. 17 in the *Reader's and Writer's Notebook* to add additional information about drama.

Check Retelling

Have students retell yesterday's reading of *The Fabulous Perpetual Motion Machine.* Encourage students to paraphrase the selection in their retellings.

Corrective feedback

If... students leave out important details,
then... have students look back through the illustrations in the selection.

Small Group Time

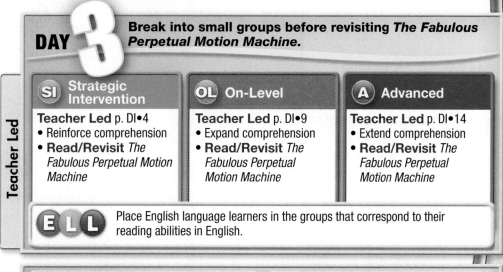

DAY 3 **Break into small groups before revisiting *The Fabulous Perpetual Motion Machine.***

Teacher Led

SI Strategic Intervention
Teacher Led p. DI•4
• Reinforce comprehension
• **Read/Revisit** *The Fabulous Perpetual Motion Machine*

OL On-Level
Teacher Led p. DI•9
• Expand comprehension
• **Read/Revisit** *The Fabulous Perpetual Motion Machine*

A Advanced
Teacher Led p. DI•14
• Extend comprehension
• **Read/Revisit** *The Fabulous Perpetual Motion Machine*

ELL Place English language learners in the groups that correspond to their reading abilities in English.

Practice Stations
• Let's Write
• Get Fluent
• Word Work

Independent Activities
• AudioText: *Perpetual Motion Machine*
• *Reader's and Writer's Notebook*
• Research and Inquiry

English Language Learners
Check retelling To support retelling, review the multilingual summary for *The Fabulous Perpetual Motion Machine* with the appropriate Retelling Cards to scaffold understanding.

Objectives
◎ Identify sequence to improve comprehension.

OPTION 1 Skills and Strategies, continued

Teach Sequence

Sequence Remind students that authors put events in a certain order for a purpose. Each event gives rise to the next, and some events may foreshadow future events. Ask students to identify at what point in the drama's plot Domingo enters. (He comes in after everyone has seen and been amazed by the machine.)

Corrective Feedback

If... students have trouble identifying a sequence of events,
then... model how to put events in context.

Multidraft Reading

If you chose...

Option 1 Return to Extend Thinking instruction starting on p. 332–333.
Option 2 Read pp. 338–343. Use the Guide Comprehension and Extend Thinking instruction.

Student Edition pp. 338–339

OPTION 2 Think Critically, continued

Higher-Order Thinking Skills

Sequence • Analysis Read the stage directions at the top of page 338. What has happened since we last saw the characters? They have spent three hours watching the machine. How does knowing this help you understand how the characters are feeling? Possible response: It shows that the characters are now bored, in contrast to the enthusiasm they showed earlier in the play.

Model the Skill

Think Aloud I know that plays, like stories, usually tell events in time order. On page 338, I read that the guests have been watching the machine for a long time.

Scene 2

Let's Think About...
How does the author use descriptions to set the scene?
Story Structure

10

About three hours later. LILY, CARLOS, EFFIE, LARRY, and JOYCE sit watching the machine, which is still running merrily along. They each have an almost-finished glass of lemonade.

LARRY: Well, it's better than watching paint dry. At least you've got some things that go round and round.

EFFIE: And some things that go up and down.

LARRY: But why are we sitting here watching things go round and round and up and down?

LILY: We have to make sure it's perpetual. That it keeps going.

JOYCE: But what does it do?

CARLOS: You've got to think big, Joyce.

LILY: We can attach stuff to it.

CARLOS: Run other machines, lots of them.

LILY: Just think—free power for everybody!

CARLOS: We're going to be rich!

EFFIE: How are you going to get rich if it's free power?

LILY: Somebody has to build the machines.

LARRY: But how does it work?

CARLOS: Oh, we can't disclose its secrets—

LILY: Until we apply for our patents.

EFFIE: Hmm. How long is it now?

LARRY: Must be nearly three hours. *(He looks at his watch and then shakes it.)* That's funny. My watch must be running slow.

Let's Think About...
What details help you to summarize how the characters feel about the machine?
Summarize

338 **11**

Let's Think About...

10 The author tells where the characters are and what they are doing.

11 Carlos and Lily think they're going to be rich, but Effie is wondering how they can charge for free power. Larry is wondering how it works.

12 The author uses dialogue to show how some characters are skeptical of this perpetual motion machine.

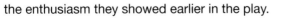

They wonder how it works. Then Domingo enters. So, I know that he arrives *after* everyone else has already seen the machine. What does he say about the machine? (He says it can't possibly work.)

On Their Own

Ask students how Domingo's statement may fore-shadow future events.

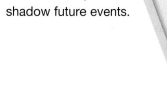

EFFIE *(finishing her lemonade):* I should be getting home.

JOYCE: Yeah, I should go too. Thanks for the lemonade.

DOMINGO *(entering):* So, what's going on down here? Mom said you've got a special science project.

LILY: Domingo, come look!

DOMINGO: Yow! What on Earth is that?

CARLOS: It's a perpetual motion machine.

LILY: That means it runs forever.

DOMINGO: I know what that means. Well, I'll be darned. Wait a minute, where's the power?

LILY: There isn't any. That's what we're telling you.

CARLOS: It just keeps running and running.

DOMINGO: It's impossible. Perpetual motion. Can't work.

CARLOS: But look at it!

DOMINGO: Okay, look, I know there's something wrong with this. I don't know what, but I'm going to find out!

Let's Think About...
How does the author use dialogue to set up the problem?
Story Structure

12

339

Foreshadowing • Analysis At the bottom of page 338, Larry says his watch is running slow. Why do you think the author would include an ordinary experience like this in the play? Possible response: The twins have invented a machine that is supposed to run forever, and it's already been running for three hours. I think the machine will have something to do with Larry's watch slowing down.

Make Inferences • Synthesis Based on what you know about how businesses work in the real world, why do you think the twins won't tell how the machine works just yet? Possible response: They're afraid someone will steal their idea and the rewards from it. They want to protect themselves by getting a patent first.

English Language Learners
Monitor comprehension Have students read the first two lines of Larry's dialogue on p. 338. Ask: Do you think it would be interesting to watch paint dry? (no) When we say that something is like watching paint dry, we mean it's very slow and boring. Larry says watching the machine is better than that, but that's not saying too much. How would the meaning change if he said it was better than watching a circus? (A circus is exciting, so the machine must be *really* exciting.)

Objectives

◎ Summarize and paraphrase text to enhance comprehension.

OPTION 1 Skills and Strategies, continued

Teach Summarizing

👁 **Summarize** Ask students to summarize what happens on pp. 340–341. Remind students to summarize by paraphrasing only the most important events in ways that maintain meaning and logical order. (Possible response: As Domingo sets out to prove the machine won't work, his father brings a reporter to interview the twins about their invention. The machine is still running, but other things—watches, the oven, the camera flash—have suddenly stopped working.)

Corrective Feedback

If... students are unable to summarize the section,
then... model how to tell only the important points.

Model the Strategy

Think Aloud When I summarize a story, I tell the most important events. I paraphrase, or use my own words, but I maintain the meaning and order of the text. Why does Domingo leave?

(He leaves.)

EFFIE: Well, see you, Lily, Carlos. Good work! I think you're right about that first prize.

MR. PÉREZ *(offstage):* It's just down here, Lee. Watch your step. *(He enters, followed by LEE, who carries a camera.)* What's this about first prize?

CARLOS: At the Science Fair, Dad.

MR. PÉREZ: If this thing really works, they'll have to make up a special prize just for you! Lee, you remember my kids.

LEE: I sure do. Hi, Lily, Carlos.

LILY: Hello, Mrs. Comer. Um—these are our friends.

MR. PÉREZ: When your mother called me at work about this, I thought, hey, what luck we've got a friend who's a newspaper reporter. This is some real

Let's Think About...
What can you do to help understand the scene so far? **Monitor and Clarify**

13

340

Student Edition pp. 340–341

OPTION 2 Think Critically, continued

Higher-Order Thinking Skills

👁 **Summarize • Analysis** Reread the dialogue on pages 340–341. Summarize how the different characters feel about the twins' invention. Be sure to paraphrase only the most important points in your summary. Possible response: Domingo is sure it doesn't work. Effie and Larry are impressed. Mr. and Mrs. Pérez are proud and excited. Lee thinks she has a good story to report.

Let's Think About...

13 I can reread to look for details to help me summarize the scene.

14 Mr. Pérez is excited about the machine. He brought a newspaper reporter to look at it.

15 I think the perpetual motion machine is somehow causing everything else to stop working.

(to prove the machine can't work) Who does the twins' father bring? (He brings a reporter.) What is happening to other gadgets? (They've stopped working.)

On Their Own

Have students reread p. 341 and summarize what Lee Comer plans to do.

Connect to Science

Perpetual motion Domingo is correct—perpetual motion is impossible. Perpetual motion is impossible because of friction. Think about a pendulum. The friction between the rod and the pendulum causes the pendulum to slow down and eventually stop. It requires energy to overcome friction. Until scientists develop a perfect lubricant, or find some other way to eliminate friction completely, perpetual motion will remain nothing more than a dream.

news. *(He approaches the machine.)* This it? Come see this, Lee. *(LEE joins him. They inspect the machine from all sides.)* Perpetual motion. The dream of ages. How long has it been running, kids?

CARLOS: About three hours.

LARRY: We lost track. My watch stopped.

JOYCE *(looking):* Funny, mine too.

MRS. PÉREZ *(entering with a tray with a pitcher and glasses):* Are you going to make my children famous, Lee?

LEE: I'd say they did that themselves. All I can do is report it.

MRS. PÉREZ: Funniest thing. I've had some chicken in the oven for the last hour, but it's not cooking at all. Here, I brought you some lemonade. *(She sets down the tray.)*

LEE: Thanks.

MR. PÉREZ: Well, what do you think, Lee?

LEE: I'll take some pictures first and then do an interview. We'll get one with Lily and Carlos beside the machine—tinkering—and maybe another one with their friends looking on in admiration. *(EFFIE, LARRY, and JOYCE perk up and start fixing their hair and clothes.)*

MR. PÉREZ: Sounds good. Where do you want the kids now?

LEE: One on either side, I think. Where's Domingo? Did he have anything to do with this?

LILY: He did not. He said it wouldn't work.

CARLOS: But it's been going for three hours.

LEE: Hold it! *(She presses the shutter, but there's no flash.)* That's funny.

DOMINGO *(entering, waving an encyclopedia):* I knew it,

Let's **Think** About...

How would you describe Mr. Perez's opinion of the machine?
🔵 **Summarize**

14

Let's **Think** About...

Why do you think so many different things have stopped working?
Questioning

15

341

Fact and Opinion • Evaluation Reread Lee Comer's lines of dialogue on page 341. What can you infer about the way she would write her article? Do you think an article she would write about the invention would include only facts or both facts and opinions? Use evidence from the text to support your answer. **Possible responses:** She would probably include only facts because she is a reporter and says all she can do "is report" what the kids did. She would probably include both facts and opinions because she wants to photograph the friends "looking on with admiration."

Draw Conclusions • Evaluation The machine has been running for three hours. Do you think that is long enough to know it will run forever? Why or why not? **Possible response:** No. Three hours might seem like a long time to the people watching, but it's really a very short amount of time.

English Language Learners
Extend vocabulary Point out the word *tinkering* on p. 341. Explain that *to tinker* means "to adjust or fix." Ask students to describe something they might tinker with.

Objectives

⦿ Identify cause-and-effect relationships to improve comprehension.

OPTION 1 Skills and Strategies, continued

Teach Cause and Effect

Review **Cause and Effect** Have students explain what caused the lights to flicker on p. 343. (The perpetual motion machine was borrowing power from the lights, so the lights had less power to draw on.)

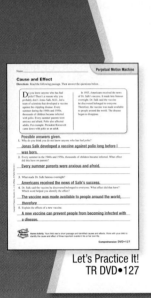

Let's Practice It!
TR DVD•127

Corrective Feedback

If... students are unable to explain the cause,

then... model how to identify cause-and-effect relationships.

Model the Skill

Think Aloud In the stage directions on page 342, I read that the lights flicker. The lights flickering is the effect—the thing that happens. The cause is what *makes* that thing happen.

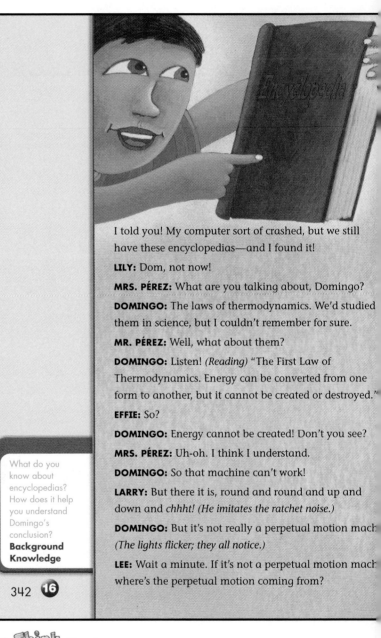

I told you! My computer sort of crashed, but we still have these encyclopedias—and I found it!

LILY: Dom, not now!

MRS. PÉREZ: What are you talking about, Domingo?

DOMINGO: The laws of thermodynamics. We'd studied them in science, but I couldn't remember for sure.

MR. PÉREZ: Well, what about them?

DOMINGO: Listen! *(Reading)* "The First Law of Thermodynamics. Energy can be converted from one form to another, but it cannot be created or destroyed."

EFFIE: So?

DOMINGO: Energy cannot be created! Don't you see?

MRS. PÉREZ: Uh-oh. I think I understand.

DOMINGO: So that machine can't work!

LARRY: But there it is, round and round and up and down and *chhht!* (He imitates the ratchet noise.)

DOMINGO: But it's not really a perpetual motion mach (The lights flicker; they all notice.)

LEE: Wait a minute. If it's not a perpetual motion mach where's the perpetual motion coming from?

What do you know about encyclopedias? How does it help you understand Domingo's conclusion? **Background Knowledge**

342 **16**

Student Edition pp. 342–343

OPTION 2 Think Critically, continued

Higher-Order Thinking Skills

Review **Cause and Effect • Evaluation** If the twins' invention actually worked the way they said it would, what effects do you think it would have on people? **Possible response:** People would have as much power as they needed and with less pollution, they would be healthier.

⦿ **Sequence • Analysis** If the play continued, what do you think Carlos would say next? Why? **Possible response:** Carlos would invent new projects because he is bright and creative.

Let's Think About...

16 Encyclopedias have information about different topics. Domingo understood how the perpetual motion machine was working after he looked up thermodynamics.

17 It gets energy from computers, lights, ovens, and watches.

18 I think it's a clever way for the author to end a story about electricity, instead of saying *the end.*

I read the dialogue that comes before and after. Where does the perpetual motion machine get its power? (It borrows it from other energy sources.) So the lights flicker because the perpetual motion machine is stealing power from them.

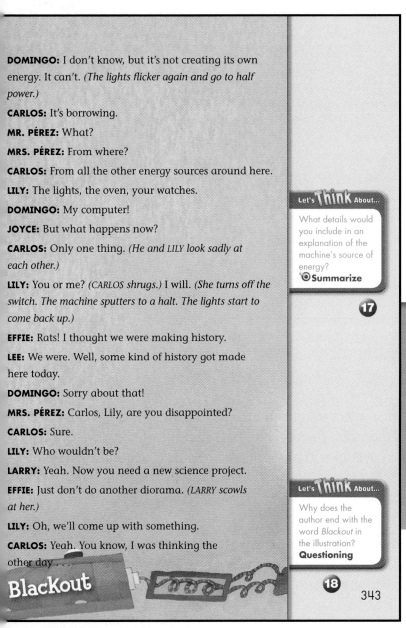

DOMINGO: I don't know, but it's not creating its own energy. It can't. *(The lights flicker again and go to half power.)*

CARLOS: It's borrowing.

MR. PÉREZ: What?

MRS. PÉREZ: From where?

CARLOS: From all the other energy sources around here.

LILY: The lights, the oven, your watches.

DOMINGO: My computer!

JOYCE: But what happens now?

CARLOS: Only one thing. *(He and LILY look sadly at each other.)*

LILY: You or me? *(CARLOS shrugs.)* I will. *(She turns off the switch. The machine sputters to a halt. The lights start to come back up.)*

EFFIE: Rats! I thought we were making history.

LEE: We were. Well, some kind of history got made here today.

DOMINGO: Sorry about that!

MRS. PÉREZ: Carlos, Lily, are you disappointed?

CARLOS: Sure.

LILY: Who wouldn't be?

LARRY: Yeah. Now you need a new science project.

EFFIE: Just don't do another diorama. *(LARRY scowls at her.)*

LILY: Oh, we'll come up with something.

CARLOS: Yeah. You know, I was thinking the other day . . .

Let's **Think** About...

What details would you include in an explanation of the machine's source of energy?
Summarize

⑰

Let's **Think** About...

Why does the author end with the word *Blackout* in the illustration?
Questioning

⑱

343

On Their Own

Have students reread Domingo's first lines of dialogue at the top of p. 342. Ask them to identify a cause-and-effect relationship in how Domingo did his research. (His computer crashed, so he used a print encyclopedia to find the answer.) For additional practice, use *Let's Practice It!* p. 127 on the *Teacher Resources DVD-ROM.*

Comprehension Check

Spiral Review

Literary Elements: Setting • Analysis Why do you think the author chose an indoor setting for this play? The play needed to be set in a place where electrical appliances such as lights and ovens could stop functioning.

Literary Elements: Character • Analysis What is the function of Domingo's character? How does he resolve a conflict within the play?

Domingo's function is to prove through research that the twins' invention cannot work. This resolves the conflict that arose earlier, when they disagreed about whether the machine could work.

Check Predictions Have students return to the predictions they made earlier and confirm whether they were accurate.

Differentiated Instruction

SI Strategic Intervention

Cause and effect Have students work in pairs to fill in cause-and-effect charts. Give them the following effects and have them supply the causes: *The oven isn't working right. The twins are disappointed.*

A Advanced

Generating ideas Have students generate a list of amazing science projects Lily and Carlos might want to tackle next.

ELL

English Language Learners

Determine meaning Point out the word *thermodynamics*. Tell students that the prefix *thermo-* means "having to do with heat," and one meaning of *dynamic* is "relating to objects in motion." Have students suggest a definition for *thermodynamics.* (The branch of science that studies the relationship between motion and forms of energy such as heat.)

Objectives
◎ Identify sequence to enhance comprehension.
◎ Summarize important ideas to aid comprehension.

Check Retelling
SUCCESS PREDICTOR

Objectives
• Provide evidence from text to support understanding. • Read independently for a sustained period of time and paraphrase the reading, including the order in which events occur.

Envision It! Retell

READING STREET ONLINE
STORY SORT
www.ReadingStreet.com

344

Think Critically

1. Think about how Lily and Carlos created their invention together. Then think about a time when you and a partner worked together to create something. How does the way you worked compare to the way Lily and Carlos worked? **Text to Self**

2. The author presents Lily and Carlos as a sister and brother who are close. How does he do this? **Think Like an Author**

3. Reread Scene 2. In your own words, describe the sequence of events that occurs when the Perez twins demonstrate the perpetual motion machine to their friends and family. Be sure to use sequence words, such as *first, then,* and *next.* **Sequence**

4. Summarize the events that occur when Carlos and Lily reveal the perpetual motion machine in Scene 1. **Summarize**

5. **Look Back and Write** Look through the play. What goals do Lily and Carlos have for inventing their machine other than winning the prize at the science fair? Are these the goals you would have if you invented such a machine? Provide evidence to support your answer.

TEST PRACTICE Extended Response

Meet the Author

Don Abramson

Don Abramson became involved in theater as a high school freshman. Since then, he has directed and acted in plays and designed and built theatrical sets. Several of his plays have been published in textbooks. One of his works (a collection of poetry) was staged in Phoenix, Chicago, New York, and London. Mr. Abramson has also written books and lyrics for musical theater. His children's musical *The Well of the Guelphs* was produced in Iowa and Nebraska.

Recently, he had fun doing research on Cinderella. Do you know there are hundreds of Cinderella stories from countries all around the world? He read dozens of these stories and then chose four—from China, India, the Philippines, and America—to combine into one musical entitled *Who Is Cinderella?*

Use the Reader's and Writer's Notebook to record your independent reading.

345

Student Edition pp. 344–345

Retelling

Envision It! Have students work in pairs to retell the selection, using the Envision It! Retelling Cards as prompts. Remind students that they should accurately summarize the main events and paraphrase important ideas using key vocabulary. Monitor students' retellings to be sure they maintain the meaning and logical order of the text.

Scoring rubric

> **Top-Score Response** A top-score response makes connections beyond the text, describes the main events and important ideas using accurate information, and draws conclusions from the text.

Plan to Assess Retelling

☑ **This week assess Strategic Intervention students.**

☐ **Week 2** Assess Advanced students.

☐ **Week 3** Assess Strategic Intervention students.

☐ **Week 4** Assess On-Level students.

☐ **Week 5** Assess any students you have not yet checked during this unit.

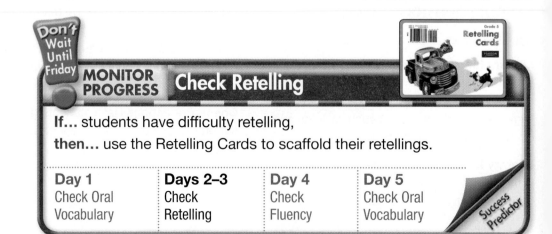

Don't Wait Until Friday

Grade 5
Retelling Cards

MONITOR PROGRESS Check Retelling

If... students have difficulty retelling,

then... use the Retelling Cards to scaffold their retellings.

Day 1	Days 2–3	Day 4	Day 5
Check Oral Vocabulary	Check Retelling	Check Fluency	Check Oral Vocabulary

Success Predictor

Think Critically

Text to self

1. Possible response: I worked with a friend on a science fair project, but we argued a lot. Both of us thought the other one wasn't working hard enough. Still, working together made our project better.

Think like an author

2. Possible response: He has them finish each other's sentences. Also, he shows them working very well together as team. Neither one tries to take all the credit.

 **Sequence**

3. Possible response: First, the twins explain how it will be used. Then Larry notices his watch is not working right. Then Domingo tells everyone the machine can't work and sets out to prove it. After that, Mr. Pérez brings a reporter to write a story about it. Then they figure out that the machine is just borrowing power from other devices. Finally, they shut off the machine.

Summarize

4. Possible response: Lily and Carlos gather their friends for a grand unveiling of their science fair project. They try to build suspense by telling everyone how great it is—without giving them any details. Finally, Joyce pulls the cover off the project and reveals a machine with dials, levers, and pulleys.

5. **Look Back and Write** To build writing fluency, assign a 10–15 minute time limit.

Suggest that students use a prewriting strategy, such as brainstorming or using a graphic organizer, to organize their ideas. Remind them to establish a topic sentence and support it with facts, details, or explanations. As students finish, encourage them to reread their responses, revise for organization and support, and proofread for errors in grammar and conventions.

Scoring rubric

> **Top-Score Response** A top-score response uses details to tell about Lilly's and Carlos's goals for their invention other than winning the science fair.
>
> **A top-score response should include:**
>
> - Lily and Carlos want to offer free power to everybody.
>
> - They want to get rich from producing the machines that create the power.
>
> - Response should explain what the student's goals would be and compare and/or contrast those goals with the goals of Lily and Carlos.

Differentiated Instruction

SI **Strategic Intervention**

Have students work in pairs to identify the twins' goals in inventing the machine and discuss what their own goals would be. Ask: What could you do with a machine like this?

Meet the Author

Have students read about author Don Abramson on page 345. Ask them if they think *Who Is Cinderella?* would be funny, serious, or both.

Independent Reading

After students read independently for a sustained period of time, have them enter their independent reading information into their Reading Logs. Then have them paraphrase a portion of the text. Remind students that when we paraphrase, we express the meaning of a passage using other words and maintaining logical order.

ELL

English Language Learners
Retelling Use the Retelling Cards to discuss the selection with students. Place the cards in any order and read aloud a passage that relates to one of the cards. Ask a volunteer to choose the corresponding card and to explain why he or she chose that card.

Retelling

Success Predictor

Objectives
- Read grade-level text with expression.
- Reread for fluency.
- Identify propaganda techniques in advertisements.

Model Fluency
Expression

Model fluent reading

Have students turn to p. 338 of *The Fabulous Perpetual Motion Machine*. Have students follow along as you read this page. Tell them to listen to the expression of your voice as you read the lines of different characters. Read the character names in a calm, plain voice, but adjust your tone and delivery to emphasize the personality and emotional state of each character.

Guide practice

Have the students follow along as you read the page again. Then have them reread the page as a group without you until they read with expression and with no mistakes. Ask questions to be sure students comprehend the text. Continue in the same way on p. 339.

Corrective feedback

If... students are having difficulty reading with expression,
then... prompt:

- Which word is a problem? Let's read it together.
- Read the sentence again to be sure you understand it.
- Tell me the sentence. Now read it as if you are speaking to me.

ROUTINE Choral Reading

1) **Select a passage** For *The Fabulous Perpetual Motion Machine,* use p. 339.

2) **Model** Read aloud p. 339. Have students notice how you change your expression and tone of voice to fit the character and the mood.

3) **Guide practice** Have students practice by reading along with you. If you like, you may read the character names yourself.

4) **On their own** Have the class read the passage without you. You may read the character names if you prefer. For optimal fluency, students should reread three or four times. Provide corrective feedback as needed, paying special attention to expression.

Routines Flip Chart

Research and Study Skills
Advertisement

Teach

Ask students to tell about the purpose of an advertisement. (to persuade people to do something—usually to buy a certain product) Display some advertisements and use them to discuss these propaganda techniques:

- The purpose of an **advertisement** is to sell a product or service. Advertisers use many propaganda techniques to sell products.

- **Loaded words** affect the consumer by creating certain emotions or making value judgments.

- A **slogan** can have catchy words that appeal to people's emotions rather than logic. It is easily remembered.

- A **generality** is a vague statement. It doesn't give specific details or facts and opinions that are well supported.

- A **bandwagon statement** claims that a lot of people are buying the product. Bandwagon means "everyone else is doing it."

- A **testimonial** is an endorsement of a product from a celebrity or well-known person.

Provide groups with different types of advertisements and have them use the text features to gain an overview of the contents and locate information. Encourage students to look for exaggerated and misleading statements in the text. Then have each group present its advertisement to the class, identifying which (if any) propaganda techniques they found.

Guide practice

Discuss these questions:

Were any of the advertisements completely factual? (Some advertisements may depend more on facts than others, but most or all will also contain opinions, including propaganda techniques.)

Why should you be on the lookout for propaganda techniques? (to keep from making bad judgments based on bad information)

After students discuss their advertisements, ask them to consider the difference in techniques used by different types of advertisements (TV commercials, print ads, radio ads).

On their own

Have students complete pp. 185–186 of the *Reader's and Writer's Notebook.*

Reader's and Writer's Notebook pp. 185–186

Academic Vocabulary

Persuasive text Persuasive text is text that is written for the purpose of convincing readers to do something, such as buy a product, or to think in a certain way.

Tone of voice Tone of voice describes the sound quality and the emotions that show in a reader's voice. By changing the tone of voice, a reader can show surprise, anger, worry, old age, and so on, to add depth to the text being read.

ELL

English Language Learners
Expand vocabulary To help students understand and identify slogans, give them some examples, such as: *ExtraMint— the best your breath can be!* or *Pencil Perfect—the pencil of the future.*

Research and Inquiry
Analyze

Teach

Tell students that today they will analyze their findings. They may need to refine their inquiry question to be more specific.

Model

Think Aloud Originally I was looking for information about how the airplane inspired the invention of future flying machines. To refine my research question, I asked myself, *What have I found so far?* I found a lot of information about how flying machines have changed over time, and how different designs evolved from the work of inventors who came before. I think I will change my inquiry question so that I can use the information I am finding. Now, my inquiry question is *How has flight changed since the invention of the airplane?* The new question still explores how the invention of the airplane inspired future inventors, but it looks more closely at the inventions that were produced to improve flight. I can use these ideas in my advertisement for airplanes.

Guide practice

Have students analyze their findings and ask themselves what they have found. They may need to refocus their inquiry question to better fit the information they have found. Some students may need to look for different ways to find information they seek. Point out that at any time they can formulate new open-ended questions to address the topic.

On their own

Have students evaluate the advertisements they have found about inventions for exaggerated, contradictory, or misleading statements. Suggest they look for evidence of propaganda techniques, such as slogans or loaded words. Point out that they may use some of these techniques as they write their advertisements for Day 5.

Conventions
Past, Present, and Future Tenses

Review Remind students that this week they learned about past, present, and future verb tenses.

- The past tense shows action that has already happened. The present tense shows action that happens now. The future tense shows action that will happen.

- Also explain the perfect tenses, which show action that began and was completed in the past (past perfect: *had finished*), began in the past and was completed in the present (present perfect: *has given*), or began in the past or present and will be completed in the future (future perfect: *will have written*).

Daily Fix-It Use Daily Fix-It numbers 5 and 6 in the right margin.

Connect to oral language Have students say the past and future tenses for the following underlined present tense verbs.

> **She <u>saves</u> money. They <u>skate</u> on the ice. Mom <u>walks</u> to work.**

On their own For additional practice, use *Let's Practice It!* p. 128 on the *Teacher Resources DVD-ROM*.

Let's Practice It!
TR DVD•128

Spelling
Words with Schwa

Frequently misspelled words *Christmas, beautiful,* and *probably* are words that students often misspell. I'm going to read a sentence. Choose the right word to complete the sentence and then write it correctly.

> 1. You will _____ be cold if you don't wear a jacket. (probably)
>
> 2. Does your family celebrate _____ ? (Christmas)
>
> 3. The stars make the sky look bright and _____. (beautiful)

Reader's and Writer's Notebook p. 187

On their own For additional practice, use the *Reader's and Writer's Notebook* p. 187.

Differentiated Instruction

SI Strategic Intervention

Practice identifying verb tense Have students work in pairs to practice verb tense identification. Students should write a few simple sentences and then have their partners identify the verb tenses being used.

Daily Fix-It

5. Everyone will celebrat the queens' birthday.
   (celebrate; queen's)

6. A carnivle of actors performed tomorrow.
   (carnival; will perform)

Objectives

- Write a first draft of a short play.
- Use past, present, and future verb tenses correctly.

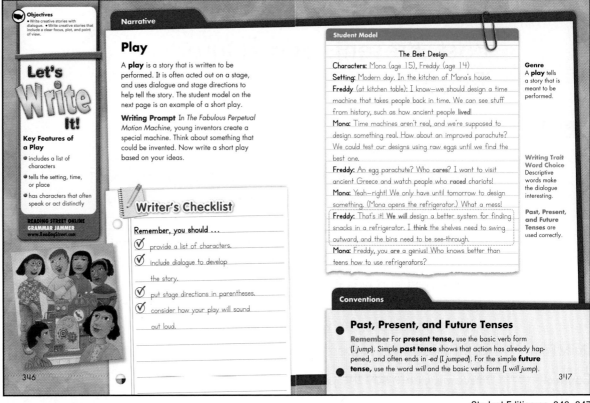

Student Edition pp. 346–347

Let's Write It!
Play

Teach

Use pp. 346–347 in the Student Edition. Direct students to read the key features of a short play, which appear on p. 346. Remind students that they can refer to the information in the Writer's Checklist as they write their own short play.

Read the student model on p. 347. Point out the list of characters, setting, and time in the model along with examples of dialogue and stage directions.

Connect to conventions

Remind students that verb tenses should be logical and consistent in a piece of writing. Point out the correct use of verb tenses in the model. Direct students' attention to the verb *will design* in Freddy's last piece of dialogue. Explain that here the verb tense changes to the future tense in order to indicate an action that has not yet occurred.

Writing—Play
Writing Trait: Word Choice

Display rubric

Display Scoring Rubric 11 from the *Teacher Resources DVD-ROM* and go over the criteria for each trait under each score. Then, using the model in the Student Edition, choose students to explain why the model should score a 4 for one of the traits. If a student offers that the model should score below 4 for a particular trait, the student should offer support for that response. Remind students that this is the rubric that will be used to evaluate the short play they write.

Scoring Rubric: Play

	4	3	2	1
Focus/Ideas	Excellent, focused play; setting and stage directions are clear and well-described	Focused play; setting and stage directions are clear	Play lacks focus; setting and stage directions are vague	Unfocused play; setting and stage directions are not included
Organization	Strong beginning, middle, end; clear sequence of events	Coherent beginning, middle, end; sequence understandable	Little connection from beginning to end; sequence of events not clear	No connection between beginning, middle, end; incorrect or no sequence of events
Voice	Involved throughout; engages readers	Involved most of the time	Not fully engaged	Writer not engaged
Word Choice	Strong word choice; dialogue is clear and sounds like natural speech	Word choice and some natural sounding dialogue make ideas clear	Lack of interesting word choice; dialogue occasionally sounds natural	Poor word choice and vague language; no natural sounding dialogue
Sentences	Sentences in dialogue reflect natural speech patterns	Most sentences in dialogue reflect natural speech patterns	Many sentences in dialogue do not reflect natural speech patterns	Sentences in dialogue do not reflect natural speech patterns
Conventions	Excellent control and accuracy; confident and consistent use of verb tenses	Good control; verb tenses used correctly but not consistently	Errors that may prevent understanding; shows lack of understanding of correct verb tenses	Frequent errors that interfere with meaning; conveys no understanding of verb tenses

Story Sequence Chart

Have students take out the story sequence charts they worked on yesterday. Allow students extra time to complete their charts if they are not yet finished.

Write

You will be using your story sequence chart as you write the draft of your play. As you draft, don't worry about getting the wording exactly right. You will have time tomorrow to revise it. Focus on building on your ideas and creating a focused piece of writing.

Differentiated Instruction

A Advanced

Elaborating As students review their story sequence charts, have them elaborate on any information that will enhance their plays, such as additional details about setting, characters, or stage directions.

English Language Learners
Leveled Support: Story Sequence chart
Beginning Have student pairs read the details from their Story Sequence charts to each other.

Intermediate Partners should provide feedback about whether additional details are needed, and writers should incorporate suggestions into their charts.

Advanced/Advanced High Have students analyze their partner's solution to the problem addressed in the play and determine whether it's a good one. Monitor feedback that students provide to each other.

Objectives
- Write a first draft of a short play.
- Use effective word choice and dialogue.

Writing, continued
Writing Trait: Word Choice

MINI-LESSON

Writing Effective Dialogue

■ **Introduce** Explain to students that dialogue is the words characters say to each other. In order for dialogue to be believable, it should sound natural and fit the characters. Display the Drafting Tips for students. Remind them that the focus of drafting is to get their ideas down in an organized way.

How Howie Helps

CHARACTERS
MOM, Howie's mother
DAD, Howie's father
HOWIE, an 11-year-old boy
SETTING: The kitchen of Howie's home
AT RISE: *MOM and DAD enter the kitchen carrying golf bags.*
MOM: I won. You lose, so you have to make dinner. I'll just sit here and drink a tall, cool glass of iced tea.
DAD: *(throwing golf bag on floor)* You won. I still think something's not right. Your score was better than a professional golfer's.
MOM: I told you I've been practicing. Don't be a sore loser. Now let's see, what do I want for dinner? Maybe I should ask what Howie wants. *(Calling)* Howie, Dad's making dinner tonight. What would you like him to cook?
(HOWIE enters kitchen.)
HOWIE: So, Mom, you won? Congratulations. *(HOWIE winks at MOM who winks back.)* How did you do, Dad?
DAD: Never mind. What do you want for dinner?
HOWIE: I'd liked Mom's special grilled fish. I know it's hard to make, but I've got an invention that'll make it easier for you to cook. . . .
DAD: No thanks! You and your crazy inventions, they either blowed up or never work. I'll just go to the market and shop for dinner. *(HOWIE and MOM giggle.)* What's so funny? I think there's something fishie going on. And I don't mean dinner. *(Exits.)*
MOM: It worked! The special golf clubs you invented worked!
HOWIE: Dad looked upset. Maybe we should tell him?
MOM *(laughing):* Not until after he's finished making dinner!

Unit 3: The Fabulous Perpetual Motion Machine   Writing: Model **11A**

Writing Transparency 11A, TR DVD

Drafting Tips

✔ To get started, review your Story Sequence Chart.

✔ Think about how your characters should sound. Then write dialogue that is appropriate for them.

✔ Don't worry about grammar and mechanics when drafting. You'll focus on these during the proofreading stage.

Think Aloud I'm going to write the first draft of my short play. As I draft, I should be careful to use dialogue that is realistic for my characters. I won't worry about proofreading or revising for now. That will come later. I will use my Story Sequence Chart to make sure I include all the information and keep the writing organized.

Display Writing Transparency 11A for the week and explain the process of drafting using the Writing Transparency. Have students use the drafting tips to guide them in writing their plays. Remind them to use realistic dialogue for the characters in their plays.

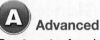

ROUTINE **Quick Write for Fluency** **Team Talk**

1. **Talk** Pairs should talk about the inventions they are discussing in their plays.

2. **Write** Students should write two sentences from their draft that describes their inventions, using appropriate verb tenses.

3. **Share** Partners should check each other's sentences for correct use of verb tenses.

Routines Flip Chart

Differentiated Instruction

A **Advanced**

Restructuring Have pairs read each other's first drafts. Students should provide feedback on the play's organization, making suggestions if the order of events seems unclear.

Wrap Up Your Day

✔ **Build Concepts** Have students discuss the lesson the twins learned about inventing.

✔ **Sequence** How did following the sequence help you understand what happened between Scenes 1 and 2?

✔ **Summarize** How did the summarizing strategy help you understand how the different characters feel about the twins' invention?

Preview 4 DAY

Tell students that tomorrow they will read an advertisement for another fictional invention.

Objectives
• Expand the weekly concept.
• Develop oral vocabulary.

Today at a Glance

Oral Vocabulary
entrepreneur, innovation

Genre
Persuasive text

Reading
"The Toy Space Shuttle Is Here!"

Let's Learn It!
Fluency: Expression
Vocabulary: Adages and sayings
Listening/Speaking: Play review

Research and Inquiry
Synthesize

Spelling
Words with schwa

Conventions
Past, present, and future tenses

Writing
Drama: Short Play

Concept Talk

 Question of the Week

How do inventors inspire our imaginations?

Expand the concept

Remind students that this week they have read about inventors who worked to make improvements in our lives. Tell students that today they will read about a toy with an unusual new design—a tiny space shuttle that can actually orbit the Earth.

Anchored Talk

Develop oral vocabulary

Use text features—illustrations, dialogue, stage directions—to review pp. 338–343 of *The Fabulous Perpetual Motion Machine*. Discuss the Amazing Words *improvement* and *design*. Add these and other concept-related words to the concept map. Use the following questions to develop students' understanding of the concept.

• Think about the *improvement* Carlos and Lily thought they made with the perpetual motion machine. What role does *improvement* play in ideas for new inventions?

• There was a problem with Carlos and Lily's *design*—the machine borrowed energy rather than creating it. Is it possible to have a good idea but a bad *design*? If so, what do you think would happen to the invention?

Strategy Response Log

Have students review the characteristics of drama on p. 17 of the *Reader's and Writer's Notebook*. Then have them compare *The Fabulous Perpetual Motion Machine* to another example of drama that they have read or know about.

Oral Vocabulary
Amazing Words

Amazing Words

theory	enterprise
experiment	improvement
suggested	design
device	entrepreneur
vehicle	innovation

Teach Amazing Words

Amazing Words — Oral Vocabulary Routine

1 Introduce Write the word *innovation* on the board. Have students say it aloud with you. Use context clues in this sentence to help you come up with a definition for the word *innovation*: Creating a new machine instead of a typical diorama was a real *innovation*. (The words *creating* and *new* help me understand that the word means "new idea or new way of doing something.")

2 Demonstrate Have students answer questions to demonstrate understanding. In what way was the twins' machine meant to be an energy *innovation*? (If it worked it would create its own energy. No machine has created its own energy before.)

3 Apply Have students apply their understanding. What would some antonyms be for the word *innovation*?

See p. OV•1 to teach *entrepreneur*.

Routines Flip Chart

Apply Amazing Words

As students read "The Toy Space Shuttle Is Here!" on pp. 346–349, have them think about why *innovations* are important in society and how *entrepreneurs* use them to become successful.

Connect to reading

As students read today's selection about the Toy Space Shuttle, have them think about how this week's concept question and the Amazing Words *innovation* and *entrepreneur* apply to the Toy Space Shuttle and its inventor.

ELL Produce Oral Language
Use the Day 4 instruction on ELL Poster 11 to extend and enrich language.

ELL Poster 11

Let's Think About Genre

Persuasive Text: Product Review

Introduce the genre

Explain to students that what we read is structured differently depending on the author's reasons for writing and what kind of information he or she wishes to convey. Different types of texts are called genres. Tell them that persuasive text is one type of genre.

Discuss the genre

Discuss with students the techniques advertisers use to persuade people to buy a product. Ask: What is the purpose of an advertisement? (Possible response: to get people to buy a product) Can you believe everything an advertiser tells you? (no) Why not? (Possible response: Advertisers try to make their products sound as good as possible, so they won't mention any drawbacks or flaws.) Explain that the authors of product reviews always have a definite viewpoint—one that favors their product—and position—to convince the reader to buy it. Therefore, readers should not count on product reviews for unbiased information. Readers should learn how to recognize exaggerated, contradictory, or misleading statements. Ask volunteers for examples of these types of statements.

On the board, draw a T-chart like the one below, labeled *Good information* and *Faulty information.* Ask the following questions:

- Suppose you read an advertisement for a new camera. What kind of information would you pay attention to? Possible responses: factual information about the product, what it costs, who is selling it

- What kind of information would you ignore? Possible responses: descriptions of how it will make me feel, things that sound too good to be true

Good information	Faulty information
Amount of memory	How popular it is
Cost	
Size	

Guide practice

Provide advertisements for students. Then, have students work in pairs to identify words or phrases they could add to either side of the T-chart using the advertisements as examples.

Connect to reading

Tell students that they will now read an advertisement for a fictional new toy. Have the class think about techniques the advertiser uses to make readers want to buy the toy.

Small Group Time

Academic Vocabulary

Persuasive text Persuasive text is text that is written for the purpose convincing readers to do something, such as buy a product, or to think in a certain way.

DAY 4

Break into small groups before reading or revisiting "The Toy Space Shuttle is Here!"

Teacher Led

SI Strategic Intervention

Teacher Led p. DI•5
• Practice retelling
• Genre focus
• **Read/Revisit** "The Toy Space Shuttle is Here!"

OL On-Level

Teacher Led p. DI•10
• Practice retelling
• Genre focus
• **Read/Revisit** "The Toy Space Shuttle is Here!"

A Advanced

Teacher Led p. DI•15
• Genre focus
• **Read/Revisit** "The Toy Space Shuttle is Here!"

ELL Place English Language learners in the groups that correspond to their reading abilities in English.

Practice Stations
• Read for Meaning
• Get Fluent
• Words to Know

Independent Activities
• AudioText: "The Toy Space Shuttle is Here!"
• *Reader's and Writer's Notebook*
• Research and Inquiry

Objectives

- Understand persuasive text.
- Identify exaggerated statements in text.

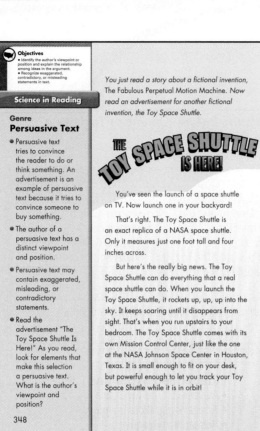

Student Edition pp. 348–349

Guide Comprehension
Skills and Strategies

Teach the genre

Persuasive Text: Product Review Have students read p. 348. Then ask: What is the purpose of this advertisement? Which parts might be true? Which are probably exaggerated or misleading statements?

Corrective feedback

If... students have difficulty identifying exaggerating and/or misleading statements,

then... use the model to guide students in identifying these statements.

Model the skill

Think Aloud I read that the Toy Space Shuttle is a foot tall and four inches across. That is probably true—I could easily measure it. It could also be a close replica of a real shuttle, but could it really do *everything* a real space shuttle can do? I don't believe it could go into orbit, but even if it could, it is too small to do everything a real space shuttle can do. When I see extreme words, such as *every, all, best, always, never,* and *only,* I think a writer might be exaggerating and providing misleading information.

On their own

Have students identify the viewpoint of the author of this ad. Then have students work in pairs to write exaggerated and misleading claims for a product of their choosing.

Extend Thinking
Think Critically

Higher-order thinking skills

Writer's Craft • Evaluation On page 349, the writer includes the question *How do you play with a toy that is so far away? Why do you think the writer does this? Is it effective? Why or why not?* Possible response: I think the writer does this to make you think the same question in your mind. Yes, I think it's effective because it brings you into a dialogue with the writer.

Drawing Conclusions • Synthesis How does the picture of the children add to ideas presented in the text? How is this different from the pictures of the characters in *The Fabulous Perpetual Motion Machine?* Possible response: The picture in "The Toy Space Shuttle Is Here!" shows happy, excited kids, suggesting that I would also be happy and excited if I got the toy. The pictures in *The Fabulous Perpetual Motion Machine* are meant to help me visualize who the characters are and what is happening in the play.

Comparison • Analysis Why does the advertisement mention Houston, Texas? Possible response: The ad is trying to sound factual when it compares the Toy Space Shuttle Mission Control Center to the real shuttle's mission control center, which is in Houston.

Let's Think About...

1 Yes, there are many exaggerations included in this example: *The Toy Space Shuttle comes with its own Mission Control Center, just like the one at the NASA Johnson Space Center in Houston, Texas.*

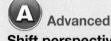

Objectives
- Identify contradictory and misleading statements in text.
- Summarize ideas across texts.
- Make logical connections between texts of different genres.

Ever wondered what Iceland looks like? Direct your Toy Space Shuttle to fly above it. Punch in the code to tell your Toy Space Shuttle to take some pictures of Iceland. Then download the photos to your computer. Whatever fun you've ever had in your life, there is no way it compares to this!

It's even better if your friend also has a Toy Space Shuttle. Then, you can view each other's shuttle missions. You can even arrange for your Toy Space Shuttles to meet up in orbit! How cool is that?

When you're ready to have your Toy Space Shuttle come back, simply key in the code for HOME. This tells the Toy Space Shuttle to head on home. You can monitor your shuttle's progress from your Mission Control Center. You can even program the Toy Space Shuttle to fly into your bedroom window. Just be sure to leave your window open!

Here's what one happy customer had to say about the Toy Space Shuttle:

"Ever since I got the Toy Space Shuttle, I have been smiling twenty-four hours a day. I rush home from school in order to check in at Mission Control. Will my shuttle be flying near Asia today? or Australia? I can't wait to find out. Because of the Toy Space Shuttle, I have become really interested in space travel. I think I may want to become an astronaut. And I owe it all to this remarkable invention."

Parents will love the Toy Space Shuttle too. One parent who bought it said, "We used to get

our children all these fancy toys, which they would misplace or lose. But with the Toy Space Shuttle, we know exactly where that toy is. All we have to do is look at the Mission Control Center."

There is something wonderful about having a toy that can go into orbit. Every time your Toy Space Shuttle comes home, you can give it a hug. It's pretty amazing to have a toy that has flown so high!

In short, if you want to have fun, if you want to learn about space, if you want to be happy, you should run out and buy the Toy Space Shuttle. It is more exciting than any video game. It is more educational than any book about space travel. It is the invention of the century.

So get your Toy Space Shuttle now before they're all gone! For a special price of just $10,000, you will agree that this fabulous and amazing toy is well worth the money.

Let's Think About...

Why does the Toy Space Shuttle make the customer happy?
Persuasive Text

②

Let's Think About...

How does the author use comparison in this argument?
Persuasive Text

③

350

JUST $10,000!

Let's Think About...

What is misleading or contradictory about the paragraphs on this page?
Persuasive Text

④

Let's Think About...

Reading Across Texts Look back at *The Fabulous Perpetual Motion Machine* and "The Toy Space Shuttle Is Here!" Why do you think inventions are so useful to people? List your reasons.

Writing Across Texts Create your own invention and write about it. Why would your invention be useful to people?

351

Student Edition pp. 350–351

Guide Comprehension
Skills and Strategies

Teach the genre

Persuasive Text: Product Review Explain that advertisements often contain misleading or contradictory statements. Have students read pp. 350–351. Then ask: Which parts of the last paragraph on p. 351 are misleading or contradictory?

Corrective feedback

If... students are unable to identify misleading or contradictory statements,
then... model how to evaluate statements in persuasive text.

Model the skill

Think Aloud I read that the Toy Space Shuttle sells for a special price of just $10,000. *Just $10,000* is contradictory because it suggests that this is a low price and a good bargain. The text also tells me to *hurry and buy one before they're all gone.* That's misleading since it makes me think that if I don't act now, they will run out. When these toys cost $10,000, I doubt they will run out very soon.

On their own

Have students look through other advertisements to locate examples of misleading and contradictory statements.

Extend Thinking
Think Critically

Higher-order thinking skills

Draw Conclusions • Analysis *If you want to be happy, you should run out and buy the Toy Space Shuttle.* What does the author want you to infer will happen if you *don't* buy the toy? Possible response: You will not be happy.

Draw Conclusions • Analysis *It's even better if your friend also has a Toy Space Shuttle.* What inference can you make about the author's viewpoint that is supported by this piece of textual evidence? Possible response: The author thinks this toy is great and wants you to convince your friend to buy one.

2 It gives him or her a chance to see all different parts of the world from the air; it makes him or her curious about the world and space travel.

3 The author compares the Toy Space Shuttle to fancy toys that get misplaced or lost, but points out that the Toy Space Shuttle is different because its Mission Control Center can tell parents exactly where it is.

4 Just because a toy can do wonderful or amazing things doesn't mean you would want to hug it.

Reading Across Texts

Have students summarize or paraphrase what they read about the inventions in *The Fabulous Perpetual Motion Machine* and "The Toy Space Shuttle Is Here!" in a way that maintains the meaning and order of the texts, and also makes thematic connections between the selections.

Writing Across Texts

Have students compose a list of selling points they might use to help them create an advertisement for their invention.

Objectives

- Read with fluency and comprehension.
- Identify and explain adages and sayings.
- Prepare a play review.

Check Fluency: WCPM
SUCCESS PREDICTOR

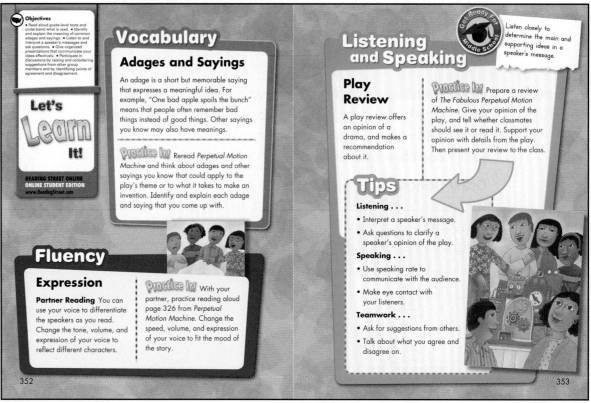

Student Edition pp. 352–353

Fluency
Expression

Guide practice

Use the Student Edition activity as an assessment tool. Make sure the reading passage is at least 200 words in length. As students read aloud with partners, make sure their expression is appropriate and enhances the meaning of what they are reading.

Don't Wait Until Friday

MONITOR PROGRESS Check Fluency: WCPM

As students reread, monitor their progress toward their individual fluency goals.
Current Goal: 115–122 words correct per minute
End-of-Year Goal: 140 words correct per minute

If... students cannot read fluently at a rate of 115–122 WCPM,

then... make sure students practice with text at their independent levels.

Day 1	Days 2–3	Day 4	Day 5
Check Oral Vocabulary	Check Summarizing	Check Fluency	Check Oral Vocabulary

Success Predictor

Vocabulary
Adages and Sayings

Teach adages and sayings

Write this sentence on the board. *There's nothing new under the sun.* Explain that this expression is an adage that expresses the idea that no matter how new something seems, it has been done before in some way.

Guide practice

Have students use the context of *The Fabulous Perpetual Motion Machine* to clarify the meaning of the adage.

On their own

Have students work in small groups to brainstorm a list of adages and other sayings. If they have trouble coming up with adages and sayings, encourage them to use print or online resources to locate adages and sayings. Be sure they understand the meaning of the adages and sayings they choose and can explain how the expressions relate to the selection.

Listening and Speaking
Play Review

Teach

Tell students that play reviews offer opinions, but that reviewers must explain why they think and feel as they do, supporting their opinions with details about the performance or script. Remind students that to communicate effectively, they should make eye contact with their audience and speak at an appropriate rate and volume. Remind listeners to listen for main ideas and supporting details. Point out that they should pay attention to the reviewer's verbal as well as nonverbal cues to help them interpret the speaker's message and understand his or her perspective.

Guide practice

To be sure students are listening attentively and understanding each reviewer's ideas, explain to students that after each review you will take a poll by show of hands to determine whether the review was mostly favorable or mostly unfavorable.

On their own

Have students present their review to the class. Afterwards, ask volunteers to tell whether or not they would see the play, based on the reviews they heard. Ask them to identify the main ideas and supporting ideas that helped them decide.

Play Review

Explain to students that they should choose and follow an appropriate organizational pattern to present their ideas. For example, they may wish to group all comments about plot together, followed by all comments about character, and so on. Alternatively, they may wish to organize their comments chronologically, moving through the play in sequential order.

English Language Learners
Practice pronunciation Assist students as they prepare for their play reviews. Model correct pronunciation of words they have difficulty with. Have them repeat the words after you.

Success Predictor

Fluency

Objectives
- Synthesize data by composing an advertisement for a product.
- Distinguish and correctly use verb tenses.
- Practice correctly spelling words with the schwa sound.

Research and Inquiry
Synthesize

Teach

Have students synthesize their research findings. Review how to choose relevant information from a number of sources and organize it logically. Remind students that the point of their advertisement is to persuade people to buy a product, so they should concentrate on presenting positive information and convincing arguments, as well as testimonials and other quotations. Point out that they may wish to include arguments against the product if they can counterbalance them with better, positive arguments.

Guide practice

Have students use a word processing program to create their advertisements, and suggest they include photos, diagrams, or other visuals. They also may want to use colorful or special fonts to catch the consumer's attention. They can then mount their advertisements on a poster board to prepare for their presentations on Day 5.

On their own

Have students try out their presentations on a partner. Partners should offer constructive suggestions for improving the advertisements, paying special attention to quotations and visuals. They may suggest persuasive techniques.

 Go Digital!

Grammar Jammer

Conventions
Past, Present, and Future Tenses

Test practice

Remind students that grammar skills such as past, present, and future verb tenses are often assessed on important tests.

- Past tense shows action that has already happened.
- Present tense shows action that happens now.
- Future tense shows action that will happen.

Daily Fix-It

Use Daily Fix-It numbers 7 and 8 in the right margin.

On their own

For additional practice, use the *Reader's and Writer's Notebook* p. 188.

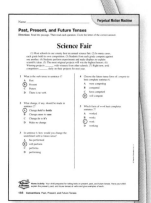

Reader's and Writer's
Notebook p. 188

Spelling
Words with Schwa

Practice spelling strategy

Have partners play a word scramble. Each student scrambles ten different list words. Then students should exchange scrambled words with their partners and have the partner unscramble the words, keeping in mind the rules and patterns regarding words with schwa. Play continues until each partner has unscrambled the other partner's words. Students can use print or electronic dictionaries to check their work.

Let's Practice It!
TR DVD•129

On their own

For additional practice, use *Let's Practice It!* p. 129 on the *Teacher Resources DVD-ROM.*

Daily Fix-It

7. What book is you reading *(are; reading?)*

8. *Alice In Wonderland* is about a girls wild dream. *(in; girl's)*

Differentiated Instruction

A Advanced

Compare verb tenses Give students a list of ten verbs of varying tenses (past, present, and future). Have them write down the tense of each verb. Then have them circle the verbs' beginnings and endings that indicate the tense of the verb (*-ed* for past tense, *will* for future tense, etc.) to see how they differ.

Writing—Play
Revising Strategy

MINI-LESSON

Revising Strategy: Clarifying

▨ Yesterday we wrote short plays about inventions. Today we will revise our drafts. The goal is to make your writing more coherent or clear, more interesting, and more informative.

Writing Transparency 11B,
TR DVD

▨ Display Writing Transparency 11B. Remind students that revising does not include corrections of grammar and mechanics. Then introduce the revising strategy Clarifying.

▨ When we revise, we ask ourselves *Does my word choice make the dialogue sound natural? Does my dialogue show my characters' thoughts, feelings, and motivations?* The revising strategy Clarifying is the process by which we replace words in our dialogue that sound awkward with words that sound like natural speech. I can clarify Mom's words to Dad. To make Mom sound more natural and reveal her feelings about winning, I'll change "I won," to "Ha! I can't believe I beat you!"

Tell students that as they revise, they should look for places where they could make the dialogue sound more natural.

Revising Tips

✔ Choose words that make your dialogue sound like natural speech.

✔ Use words that reveal your characters' thoughts, feelings, and motivations.

✔ Add or subtract details to clarify meaning where necessary.

Peer conferencing

Peer Revision Have pairs exchange papers for peer revision. Students should write three questions about their partners' writing. These questions should focus on making the dialogue more realistic. Refer to *First Stop* for more information about peer conferencing.

Have students revise their compositions using the questions their partners wrote during Peer Revision as well as the key features of short plays to guide them. Be sure that students are using the revising strategy Clarifying.

Corrective feedback

Circulate around the room to monitor students and have conferences with students as they revise. Remind students correcting errors that they will have time to proofread tomorrow. They should be focusing on content and word choice today.

ROUTINE   **Quick Write for Fluency**   **Team Talk**

1. **Talk** Pairs discuss what they read about in *The Fabulous Perpetual Motion Machine.*

2. **Write** Have students write one paragraph about their discussions.

3. **Share** Pairs should check each other's writing, making sure it includes believable dialogue.

Routines Flip Chart

Wrap Up Your Day

✔ **Build Concepts** What did you learn about the Toy Space Shuttle?

✔ **Oral Vocabulary** Monitor students' use of oral vocabulary as they respond to the question: How would you describe the *design* of the Toy Space Shuttle?

✔ **Persuasive Techniques** Which persuasive techniques did you find most persuasive in "The Toy Space Shuttle Is Here!"?

Write Guy
Jeff Anderson

Teaching Trait-by-Trait: Focus

In a writing conference, choose one aspect of a student's draft, not many things. Maybe there is one skill at this student's growing edge of knowledge that I can help him or her improve. I'd hate to see that lost in a swarm of my other comments.

English Language Learners
Leveled Support: Language Production To create more realistic dialogue in writing:

Beginning Review contractions, such as *it's, we're,* and *they're.*

Intermediate Review interjections, such as *oh* and *my.*

Advanced/Advanced High Introduce the idea of informal versus formal language with students. Explain that the elements of informal writing help create more realistic dialogue.

Preview DAY 5

Remind students to think about how inventors inspire our imaginations.

Objectives
- Review the weekly concept.
- Review oral vocabulary.

Today at a Glance

Oral Vocabulary

Comprehension
◉ Sequence

Lesson Vocabulary
◉ Multiple-meaning words

Word Analysis
Shades of meaning

Literary Terms
Foreshadowing

Assessment
Fluency
Comprehension

Research and Inquiry
Communicate

Spelling
Words with schwa

Conventions
Past, present, and future tenses

Writing
Drama: Short Play

Check Oral Vocabulary
SUCCESS PREDICTOR

Concept Wrap Up

Question of the Week
How do inventors inspire our imaginations?

Review the concept

Have students look back at the reading selections to find examples that best demonstrate how inventors inspire our imaginations.

Review Amazing Words

Display and review this week's concept map. Remind students that this week they have learned ten Amazing Words related to inventors and inventions. Have students use the Amazing Words and the concept map to answer the question *How do inventors inspire our imaginations?*

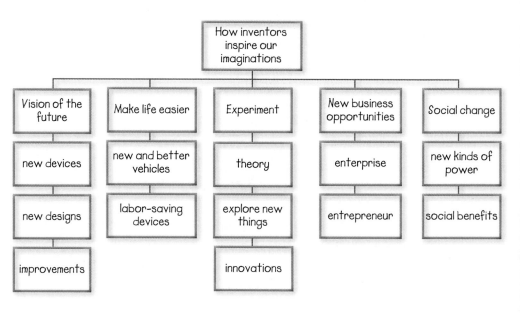

How inventors inspire our imaginations				
Vision of the future	Make life easier	Experiment	New business opportunities	Social change
new devices	new and better vehicles	theory	enterprise	new kinds of power
new designs	labor-saving devices	explore new things	entrepreneur	social benefits
improvements		innovations		

ELL Check Concepts and Language Use the Day 5 instruction on ELL Poster 11 to monitor students' understanding of the lesson concept.

ELL Poster 11

Amazing Ideas

Connect to the Big Question

Have pairs of students discuss how the Question of the Week connects to the Big Question: *What do people gain from the work of inventors and artists?* Tell students to use the concept map and what they have learned from this week's Anchored Talks and reading selections to form an Amazing Idea—a realization or "big idea" about Inventors and Artists. Remind students to elicit and consider each other's suggestions. Then ask each pair to share their Amazing Idea with the class.

Amazing Ideas might include these key concepts:

- Inventors have to be willing to experiment with their designs, because they might not work the first time.

- Inventors can get ideas for inventions by thinking about what new devices could make people's lives easier or more enjoyable.

- Inventors must think about whether their inventions cause problems as well as solutions.

Write about it

Have students write a few sentences about their Amazing Idea, beginning with "This week I learned …"

It's Friday

MONITOR PROGRESS | **Check Oral Vocabulary**

Have individuals use this week's Amazing Words to describe the work of inventors. Monitor students' abilities to use the Amazing Words and note which words you need to reteach.

If… students have difficulty using the Amazing Words,

then… reteach using the Oral Vocabulary Routine, pp. 325a, 328b, 338b, 348b, OV•1.

Day 1	**Days 2–3**	**Day 4**	**Day 5**
Check Oral Vocabulary	Check Retelling	Check Fluency	Check Oral Vocabulary

Success Predictor

Amazing Words

theory	enterprise
experiment	improvement
suggested	design
device	entrepreneur
vehicle	innovation

English Language Learners
Concept map Work with students to add new words to the concept map.

 Oral Vocabulary **Success Predictor**

Objectives
◎ Review sequence.
◎ Review multiple-meaning words.
• Review shades of meaning.
• Review foreshadowing.

Comprehension Review
⦿ Sequence

Teach Sequence

Review the definition of sequence on p. 326. Remind students that the sequence is the order in which events happen, from first to last. Clue words such as *first, next, then,* and *while,* as well as dates and times, can help readers understand the time order of story or article events. For additional support, have students review p. EI•13 on sequence.

Student Edition p. EI•13

Guide practice

Have student pairs find an example of a sequence in *The Fabulous Perpetual Motion Machine.* Then have the pairs tell what evidence they used to determine the sequence.

On their own

For additional practice with sequence, use *Let's Practice It!* p. 130 on the *Teacher Resources DVD-ROM.*

Let's Practice It!
TR DVD•130

Vocabulary Review
⦿ Multiple-Meaning Words

Teach multiple-meaning words

Remind students to use context clues to help them choose the correct meaning for multiple-meaning words.

Guide practice

Review with students how to determine and clarify the correct meaning of *project* by using context clues.

On their own

Have students look up the lesson vocabulary words in a dictionary to find additional meanings. Then have them write sentences for each word, including context clues to help readers choose the correct meaning for each instance. Then have students trade sentences with a partner and identify which meaning of each word fits in the context of the sentence.

Word Analysis Review
Shades of Meaning

Teach shades of meaning

Review with students that shades of meaning refers to the differences in meaning between two words. Discuss shades of meaning for *device* and *gadget*.

Guide practice

Display the following words: *extraordinary* and *incredible*. Use the Strategy for Meaningful Word Parts to teach the word *extraordinary*.

On their own

Have students work in pairs to identify word parts and define *incredible*.

ROUTINE Strategy for Meaningful Word Parts

1 Introduce word parts Have students circle each smaller word in *extraordinary*.

2 Connect to meaning Define each smaller word. *Extra* means "more or better than." *Ordinary* means "plain, common, usual."

3 Blend Blend the meaningful word parts together to read *extraordinary*. Then use the meanings of the smaller words to determine the meaning of the new word. Something that is *extraordinary* is "beyond the commonplace."

Routines Flip Chart

Literary Terms Review
Foreshadowing

Teach foreshadowing

Have students reread the first half of *The Fabulous Perpetual Motion Machine.* Remind students that foreshadowing refers to hints about what will happen in a story.

Guide practice

Find an example of foreshadowing, such as "until now, nobody's done it" on p. 334. Discuss why the author included this phrase. Have students find and discuss other examples of foreshadowing in the selection.

On their own

Have students make a T-chart with the headings *hint* and *what it foreshadows.* Ask them to find examples of foreshadowing and explain what future event each foreshadows.

English Language Learners
Sequence of events If students have trouble ordering events, explain that clue words about time, such as *first, then, finally, since,* and *after* can help them determine the sequence of events. Have them work in pairs to identify more time-related words that can serve as clues.

Objectives
- Read grade-level text with fluency.

Plan to Assess Fluency

☑ **This week assess Advanced students.**

☐ **Week 2** Assess Strategic Intervention students.

☐ **Week 3** Assess On-Level students.

☐ **Week 4** Assess Strategic Intervention students.

☐ **Week 5** Assess any students you have not yet checked during this unit.

Set individual goals for students to enable them to reach the year-end goal.

- Current Goal: 115–122 WCPM

- Year-End Goal: 140 WCPM

Assessment

Check words correct per minute

Fluency Make two copies of the fluency passage on page 353k. As the student reads the text aloud, mark mistakes on your copy. Also mark where the student is at the end of one minute. To check the student's comprehension of the passage, have him or her retell what was read. To figure words correct per minute (WCPM), subtract the number of mistakes from the total number of words read in one minute.

Corrective feedback

If... students cannot read fluently at a rate of 115–122 WCPM,
then... make sure they practice with text at their independent reading levels. Provide additional fluency practice by pairing nonfluent readers with fluent readers.

If... students already read at 140 WCPM,
then... have them read a book of their choice independently.

Small Group Time

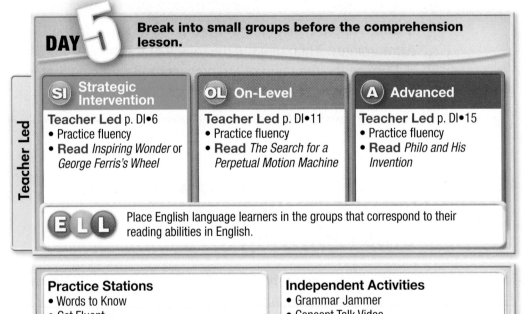

DAY 5 Break into small groups before the comprehension lesson.

Teacher Led

SI Strategic Intervention
Teacher Led p. DI•6
- Practice fluency
- **Read** *Inspiring Wonder* or *George Ferris's Wheel*

OL On-Level
Teacher Led p. DI•11
- Practice fluency
- **Read** *The Search for a Perpetual Motion Machine*

A Advanced
Teacher Led p. DI•15
- Practice fluency
- **Read** *Philo and His Invention*

ELL Place English language learners in the groups that correspond to their reading abilities in English.

Practice Stations
- Words to Know
- Get Fluent
- Read for Meaning

Independent Activities
- Grammar Jammer
- Concept Talk Video
- Vocabulary Activities

Bette Nesmith Graham

Bette Nesmith Graham dreamed of being an artist. But she was a single   13
mother. She had a young son to feed. So she took a job as a secretary.   29

This was the 1950s. There were no computers. Letters and documents   40
were written on typewriters. What was that like? Imagine you are sitting at   53
your keyboard. When you hit the keys, the words are printed on paper. There   67
is no computer in-between. What if you made a mistake? You had to   80
start over.   82

Bette knew there was a better way. Artists painted over their mistakes.   94
Maybe she could paint over typing mistakes. She mixed up a batch of paint   108
the same color as the paper at work. When she made a typing mistake, she   123
painted over it. The other secretaries wanted some too. Bette brought the   135
paint to work in small bottles.   141

In 1956, Bette started the Mistake Out Company. She mixed batches up   153
in her kitchen blender. Her son and his friends filled the bottles. And things   167
kept growing from there.   171

In 1968, Bette moved her company into a large factory. She sold one   184
million bottles of the paint that year alone.   192

In 1975, she moved to a larger plant. The following year, the company   205
made a profit of one and a half million dollars.   215

Bette retired. She sold her company for more than forty-seven million   226
dollars.   227

MONITOR PROGRESS • Check Fluency

Assessment

Check sequence

◉ **Sequence** Use "A Walk Through History" on p. 353m to check students' understanding of the organizational pattern provided by the sequence of events.

1. What happened first: Robert Newman held up two lanterns in the steeple of Old North Church, or Paul Revere left his house for the famous midnight ride? How do you know? (Robert Newman held up the lanterns first, even though it is described later in the text. I know because that gave Paul Revere the information he needed on the famous midnight ride.)

2. Which is the last stop on the Freedom Trail? (the Bunker Hill Monument) How do you know? (I see the clue word *finally*.)

3. Why are the sites listed in the order they are? (because that is the sequence in which you'd see them if you followed the Freedom Trail)

Corrective feedback

If... students are unable to answer the comprehension questions,
then... use the Reteach lesson in the *First Stop* book.

A Walk Through History

A good way to learn about history is to visit the places where important events happened. The Freedom Trail in Boston gives visitors a chance to find out more about how the American Revolution began. This walking path is about two and a half miles long and is made up of red bricks. A guide leads the way. The guide takes visitors to sixteen different sites that are important to the history and fate of our country.

The first stop is the Boston Common. This is one of the oldest public parks in the country. Before the war began, British soldiers camped in the park.

Another important place a visitor will find is Faneuil Hall. This was a meeting room where many speeches were given leading up to the war.

The next stop is the Paul Revere House. This is the oldest building in the downtown area. It was the home of Paul Revere. It was from this house that Paul Revere left for his famous midnight ride.

As visitors follow the red brick path, they will soon come to the Old North Church. From the steeple of this church, Robert Newman held up two lanterns. This let Paul Revere know that the British were coming by sea so he could ride and warn people.

Finally, visitors will see the Bunker Hill Monument. It marks the place of the first major battle of the war. From this amazing place, visitors can look out over the city of Boston.

MONITOR PROGRESS

• **Sequence**

Objectives
- Communicate inquiry results.
- Review verb tenses.
- Take a spelling test.

Research and Inquiry
Communicate

Present ideas   Have students share their inquiry results by presenting their information and giving a brief talk on their research. Have students display the advertisements they created. They should deliver their advertisements in a bright, enthusiastic voice. Remind students that they are trying to tell people why their invention is important.

Listening and speaking   Remind students how to be good speakers and how to communicate effectively with their audience.

- Speak clearly and loudly at a steady rate.
- Read the quotes with expression.
- Use appropriate gestures to add emphasis and clarity.
- Keep eye contact with audience members.
- Respond to questions with details from your research.

Remind students of these tips for being a good listener.

- Wait until the speaker has finished before raising your hand to ask a relevant question.
- Be polite, even if you disagree.
- Listen carefully to hear and interpret all of the speaker's verbal and non-verbal messages. In advertisements, nonverbal messages are often as important as the verbal messages.
- Pay close attention to determine the speaker's main ideas as well as the supporting ideas.

Spelling Test
Words with Schwa

Spelling test

To administer the spelling test, refer to the directions, words, and sentences on p. 327c.

Conventions
Extra Practice

Teach

Remind students that the past tense describes something that has happened and is generally formed by adding *-ed.* The present tense describes something that is happening and is generally formed by adding *-s* or *-es.* The future tense describes something that will happen and generally begins with *will* or *shall.*

Guide practice

Have students use their own plays as the basis for forming sentences with past, present, and future tense verbs. Ask students to summarize the play's events. Make some suggestions for sentence beginnings, such as the following:

> **"The play begins with…" (present tense)**
>
> **"They wanted the invention to be…" (past tense)**
>
> **"The invention will become…" (future tense)**

Daily Fix-It

Use Daily Fix-It numbers 9 and 10 in the right margin.

On their own

Write these sentences. Have students fill in the blanks with the correct form of the verb in the given tense.

> **1. Effie (*want,* past tense) _____ to show Lily and Carlos something.** (wanted)
>
> **2. She (*give,* past tense) _____ us a little hint!** (gave)
>
> **3. We (*find,* past tense) _____ the idea, not the plan, on the Internet.** (found)
>
> **4. We (*win,* future tense) _____ first prize this year.** (will win)
>
> **5. A perpetual motion machine (*run,* future tense) _____ forever.** (will run)

For additional practice, students should complete *Let's Practice It!* p. 131 on the *Teacher Resources DVD-ROM.*

Daily Fix-It

9. Spence don't want a speeking part in the play. (doesn't; speaking)

10. The stage directions say to set on the throne and rise the scepter. (sit, raise)

Let's Practice It!
TR DVD•131

Objectives
- Proofread revised drafts of short plays.
- Create and present final draft.

Writing—Play
Past, Present, and Future Tenses

Review revising

Remind students that yesterday they revised their short plays, paying particular attention to clarifying dialogue to make it sound more natural. Today they will proofread their plays.

MINI-LESSON

Proofread for Correct Tenses

Teach When we proofread, we look closely at our work, searching for errors in mechanics such as spelling, capitalization, punctuation, and grammar. Today we will focus on past, present, and future tenses.

Model Let's look at a portion of the play we started yesterday. Display Writing Transparency 11C. Explain that you will look for errors in the use of past, present, and future tenses. I see a problem in a piece of Howie's dialogue. He says "I liked Mom's speciel grilled fish." Howie is using a past tense verb "liked" when he should use a present tense verb "like." I'm going to change "liked" to "like" to make the tenses consistent. Also, "speciel" is misspelled. I'll change it to "special." Explain to students that they should reread their play a number of times, each time looking for errors in one of the following: spelling, punctuation, capitalization, and grammar.

Writing Transparency 11C, TR DVD

Proofread

Display the Proofreading Tips. Ask students to proofread their compositions, using the Proofreading Tips and paying particular attention to past, present, and future tenses. Circulate around the room answering students' questions. When students have finished editing, have pairs proofread one another's plays.

Proofreading Tips

✓ Make sure all past, present and future tenses are used correctly and consistently.

✓ Check that spelling, grammar, punctuation, and capitalization are correct.

✓ Check that dialogue for each new speaker begins on its own line.

Present Have students incorporate revisions and proofreading edits into their plays to create a final draft.

Give students the option of either presenting their plays in front of the class or reading the plays from their seats. For either option, students should find participants for their plays and should try to rehearse with everyone at least once before presenting. If performing in front of the class, students may wish to bring in props to represent the invention featured in the play. After students have finished presenting their plays, they should fill out a Writing Self-Evaluation Guide.

ROUTINE Quick Write for Fluency — Team Talk

1. **Talk** Pairs discuss what they learned about word choice in writing plays this week.

2. **Write** Students write a paragraph about what they learned.

3. **Share** Pairs read their paragraphs to each other.

Routines Flip Chart

Teacher Note

Writing Self-Evaluation Guide Make copies of the Writing Self-Evaluation Guide on p. 39 of the *Reader's and Writer's Notebook* and hand out to students.

English Language Learners

Support editing Provide practice with tenses. Have students read through their plays and mark each verb as past, present, or future tense. If they find that they're using different tenses in the same sentence, they should make sure the verb tense change is necessary.

Poster preview Prepare students for next week by using Week 2, ELL Poster 12. Read the Poster Talk-Through to introduce the concept and vocabulary. Ask students to identify and describe objects and actions in the art.

Selection summary Send home the summary of *Leonardo's Horse,* in English and the students' home languages, if available. They can read the summary with family members.

Preview NEXT WEEK

How do artists inspire future generations? Tell students that next week they will read about a famous artist whose work inspired millions of people.

Weekly Assessment

Use pp. 71–78 of *Weekly Tests* to check:

✔ **Word Analysis** Shades of Meaning

✔ ⊙ **Comprehension Skill** Sequence

✔ Review **Comprehension Skill**
Cause and Effect

✔ **Lesson Vocabulary**

applauds	inspecting
browsing	project
fabulous	

Weekly Tests

Advanced

On-Level

Differentiated Assessment

Use pp. 61–66 of *Fresh Reads for Fluency and Comprehension* to check:

✔ ⊙ **Comprehension Skill** Sequence

✔ Review **Comprehension Skill** Cause and Effect

✔ **Fluency** Words Correct Per Minute

SI

Strategic Intervention

Fresh Reads for Fluency and Comprehension

Managing Assessment

Use *Assessment Handbook* for:

✔ **Weekly Assessment Blackline Masters for Monitoring Progress**

✔ **Observation Checklists**

✔ **Record-Keeping Forms**

✔ **Portfolio Assessment**

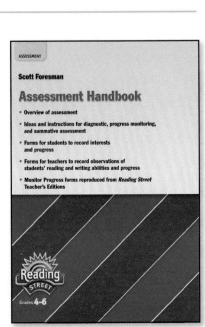

Assessment Handbook

"What's the Big Idea, Ben Franklin?"

Continued from p. 325b

Benjamin figured he knew as many how-to's as anyone else. Besides, he knew a lot of jokes. He put them all in his almanac, called it *Poor Richard's Almanack*, and published the first edition in 1733.

Small Group Time

Pacing Small Group Instruction

5-Day Plan

DAY 1	• Reinforce the concept • Read Leveled Readers Concept Literacy Below Level
DAY 2	• Sequence • Summarize • Revisit Student Edition pp. 330–337
DAY 3	• Multiple-Meaning Words • Revisit Student Edition pp. 338–343
DAY 4	• Practice Retelling • Read/Revisit Student Edition pp. 348–351
DAY 5	• Reread for fluency • Reread Leveled Readers

3- or 4-Day Plan

DAY 1	• Reinforce the concept • Read Leveled Readers
DAY 2	• Sequence • Summarize • Revisit Student Edition pp. 330–337
DAY 3	• Multiple-Meaning Words • Revisit Student Edition pp. 338–343
DAY 4	• Practice Retelling • Read/Revisit Student Edition pp. 348–351 • Reread for fluency • Reread Leveled Readers

3-Day Plan: Eliminate the shaded box.

SI Strategic Intervention — DAY **1**

Build Background

■ **Reinforce the Concept** Talk about the weekly question *How do inventors inspire our imaginations?* Discuss with students items they use every day such as televisions, computers, ballpoint pens, or backpacks. One way that we can be inspired to use our imaginations is to look at inventors and their inventions. For example, how could you improve on the things you mentioned? Or what other items do you think need to be invented? Discuss the words on the concept map on pp. 324–325 in the Teacher Edition.

■ **Connect to Reading** Point out to students that some people seem to have an endless supply of new ideas. This week you will read about famous inventors and their inventions. Benjamin Franklin, for example, was not only one of our nation's founding fathers, but he was also a very clever inventor. In the Read Aloud "What's the Big Idea, Ben Franklin?" what made Franklin come up with so many inventions? *(He came across many problems that he solved by inventing new tools or other items.)*

Objectives
• Interpret a speaker's messages (both verbal and nonverbal).

 SI · Strategic Intervention

DAY 1

For a complete literacy instructional plan and additional practice with this week's target skills and strategies, see the **Leveled Reader Teaching Guide.**

Concept Literacy Reader

- **Read** *Inspiring Wonder*

- **Before Reading** Preview the book with students, focusing on key concepts and vocabulary. Then have them set a purpose for reading.

- **During Reading** Read the first two pages of the book aloud while students track the print. Then have students finish reading the book with a partner.

- **After Reading** After students finish reading the book, connect it to the weekly question *How do inventors inspire our imaginations?*

Below-Level Reader

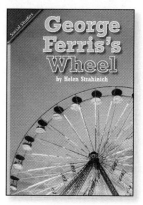

- **Read** *George Ferris's Wheel*

- **Before Reading** Have students preview the book, using the illustrations. Then have students set a purpose for reading.

- **During Reading** Do a choral reading of pp. 8–9. If students are able, have them read and discuss the remainder of the book with a partner. Have partners discuss the following questions:

  - After the Chicago Fair ended, why was the Ferris wheel a problem? *(No one knew what to do with it.)*

  - What happened to the Ferris wheel after the St. Louis World's Fair? *(It rusted out and had to be destroyed.)*

- **After Reading** Have students look at and discuss the concept map. Connect the Below-Level Reader to the weekly question *How do inventors inspire our imaginations?*

MONITOR PROGRESS

If... students have difficulty reading the selection with a partner,
then... have them follow along as they listen to the Leveled Readers DVD-ROM.

If... students have trouble understanding why Ferris's wheel was so popular,
then... reread pp. 16–17 and discuss together the wheel's view, size, and 3,000 lights.

Objectives
- Read aloud grade-level stories with fluency.

Small Group Time

Student Edition p. El•13

More Reading

Use additional Leveled Readers or other texts at students' instructional levels to reinforce this week's skills and strategies. For text suggestions, see the Leveled Reader Database or the Leveled Readers Skills Chart on pp. CL 24–CL 29.

Reinforce Comprehension

🔵 **Skill Sequence** Review with students *Envision It!* p. El•13 on sequence. Then use p. 326 to review the definition of sequence.

The sequence of events is the order in which things happen. Words such as *first, after, before,* and *later* are clues that help you understand which events came first, second, and so on. As you read, try to follow the sequence of events to understand the story better.

🔵 **Strategy Summarize** Review the definition of summarize. Discuss with students some of the main events and ideas of the drama. Remind students that they will use the main events and ideas to summarize the drama in their own words. For additional support, refer students to *Envision It!* p. El•23.

Revisit *The Fabulous Perpetual Motion Machine* on pp. 330–337 with a partner. As students read, have them apply the comprehension skill and strategy to the story.

- Before the opening scene, what have Carlos and Lily been getting ready for? *(a science fair)*

- Why don't they show the machine right away? *(Joyce hasn't arrived.)*

- After the friends see the machine, what do they want? *(a demonstration)*

- When does the machine start running? *(when Lily switches it on)*

- What does the machine do after it is started up? *(Parts start moving, and the machine starts making noises.)*

Use the During Reading Differentiated Instruction for additional support for struggling readers.

MONITOR PROGRESS

If... students have difficulty reading along with the group,
then... have them follow along as they listen to the AudioText.

Objectives
- Identify sequence of events.
- Summarize texts in ways that maintain meaning within a text.

SI Strategic Intervention | DAY **3**

Reinforce Vocabulary

◉ Multiple-Meaning Words/Context Clues
Underline the word *bank* as you write the following sentence on the board: I'm going to the bank to deposit money.

When I read the sentence, I know that the word *bank* means "a place for keeping or exchanging money," but *bank* is a multiple-meaning word. It can also mean "the ground along a river or lake" as in the sentence *We fished along the bank of the river.*

Revisit *The Fabulous Perpetual Motion Machine* on pp. 338–343. Review *Words!* on pp. W•7 and W•10.

Point out the word *sheet* on the first page of the story. I know that a sheet is "a covering for a bed" or "a piece of paper." Since it seems unlikely that a piece of paper would be draped over something large, the meaning in this sentence is probably a sheet for a bed. The context shows the meaning.

Look at the word *fair* near the bottom of this page. What is the meaning for the way it is used here? *(a show)* What are some other meanings for this word? *(honest, average, clear weather)*

As students finish reading *The Fabulous Perpetual Motion Machine*, encourage them to use context clues to figure out the meaning of any unfamiliar multiple-meaning words.

Use the During Reading Differentiated Instruction for additional support for struggling readers.

> **MONITOR PROGRESS**
>
> **If...** students need more practice with the lesson vocabulary, **then...** use *Envision It! Pictured Vocabulary Cards.*

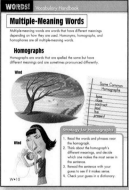

Student Edition p. W•10

More Reading

Use additional Leveled Readers or other texts at students' instructional levels to reinforce this week's skills and strategies. For text suggestions, see the Leveled Reader Database or the Leveled Readers Skills Chart on pp. CL 24–CL 29.

Objectives
• Use the context to determine the meaning of multiple-meaning words.

Practice Retelling

■ **Retell** Have students work in pairs and use the Retelling Cards to retell *The Fabulous Perpetual Motion Machine*. Monitor retelling and prompt students as needed.

• Who are the main characters?

• Tell me what this drama is about.

If students struggle, model a fluent reading.

Genre Focus

■ **Before Reading or Revisiting** "The Toy Space Shuttle Is Here!" on pp. 348–351, read aloud the genre information about persuasive text on p. 348.

Advertisements are persuasive text because their purpose is to persuade you to buy something. As you read an ad, watch for claims that are unrealistic or exaggerated.

Then have students preview "The Toy Space Shuttle Is Here!"

• Look at the illustrations. Who is using the Toy Space Shuttle? *(fifth graders or middle school-age students)*

Have students set a purpose for reading based on their preview.

■ **During Reading or Revisiting** Have students read along with you while tracking the print or do a choral reading of the advertisement. Stop to discuss any unfamiliar words, such as *orbit* and *password*.

■ **After Reading or Revisiting** Have students share their reactions to the persuasive text. Then guide them through the Reading Across Texts and Writing Across Texts activities.

MONITOR PROGRESS

If... students have difficulty retelling the selection,
then... have them review the story using the illustrations.

Objectives
• Explain the basic relationships among ideas in the argument.

SI Strategic Intervention

DAY 5

For a complete literacy instructional plan and additional practice with this week's target skills and strategies, see the **Leveled Reader Teaching Guide.**

Concept Literacy Reader

■ **Model** Model the fluency skill of expression for students. Ask students to listen carefully as you read aloud the first two pages of *Inspiring Wonder*. Have students note the way you vary your tone of voice and volume to show expression.

■ **Fluency Routine**

1. Have students reread passages from *Inspiring Wonder* with a partner.

2. For optimal fluency, students should reread three to four times.

3. As students read, monitor fluency and provide corrective feedback. Have students practice changing the tone, volume, and expression of their voices to show what the characters are feeling.

See *Routines Flip Chart* for more help with fluency.

■ **Retell** Have students retell *Inspiring Wonder*. Prompt as necessary.

Below-Level Reader

■ **Model** Ask students to listen carefully as you read aloud pp. 6–7 of *George Ferris's Wheel*, emphasizing expression.

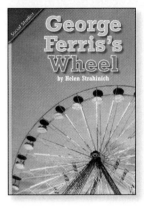

■ **Fluency Routine**

1. Have students reread passages from *George Ferris's Wheel* with a partner or individually.

2. For optimal fluency, students should reread three to four times.

3. As students read, monitor fluency and provide corrective feedback. Point out that reading with expression involves changing the tone and volume of your voice. Discuss how expression makes reading more interesting and easier to understand.

See *Routines Flip Chart* for more help with fluency.

■ **Retell** For additional practice, have students retell *George Ferris's Wheel* page-by-page, using the illustrations. Prompt as necessary.

• Summarize this part in a few sentences.

• What do you learn about Ferris wheels that surprised you?

MONITOR PROGRESS

If... students have difficulty reading fluently,

then... provide additional fluency practice by pairing nonfluent readers with fluent ones.

Objectives
• Read aloud grade-level stories with fluency.

Pacing Small Group Instruction

5-Day Plan

DAY 1	• Expand the concept • Read On-Level Reader
DAY 2	• ⊙ Sequence • ⊙ Summarize • Revisit Student Edition pp. 330–337
DAY 3	• ⊙ Multiple-Meaning Words • Revisit Student Edition pp. 338–343
DAY 4	• Practice Retelling • Read/Revisit Student Edition pp. 348–351
DAY 5	• Reread for fluency • Reread On-Level Reader

3- or 4-Day Plan

DAY 1	• Expand the concept • On-Level Reader
DAY 2	• ⊙ Sequence • ⊙ Summarize • Revisit Student Edition pp. 330–337
DAY 3	• ⊙ Multiple-Meaning Words • Revisit Student Edition pp. 338–343
DAY 4	• Practice Retelling • Read/Revisit Student Edition pp. 348–351 • Reread for fluency • Reread On-Level Reader

3-Day Plan: Eliminate the shaded box.

OL On-Level | **DAY 1**

Build Background

■ **Expand the Concept** Connect the weekly question *How do inventors inspire our imaginations?* and expand the concept. Just as inventors were inspired to develop their ideas, so can their inventions inspire us to imagine new ways of doing things. Discuss the meaning of the words on the concept map on pp. 324–325 in the Teacher Edition.

On-Level Reader

For a complete literacy instructional plan and additional practice with this week's target skills and strategies, see the **Leveled Reader Teaching Guide.**

■ **Before Reading** *The Search for a Perpetual Motion Machine,* have students preview the reader by looking at the title, cover, contents on p. 3, and pictures in the book.

• What is the topic of this book? *(the search to find a perpetual motion machine)*

• Why do you think inventors throughout history have been interested in perpetual motion machines? *(The person who actually invents one will become rich and famous.)*

Have students create a KWL chart to complete as they read.

Complete the KWL chart with what you know now about early perpetual motion machines (K column) as well as things you want to know about them (W column). As you find answers during your reading, complete the chart by filling in what you have learned (L column).

■ **During Reading** Read aloud the first three pages of the book as students follow along. Then have them finish reading the book on their own. Remind students to add things they learn to their KWL charts as they read.

■ **After Reading** Have partners compare their KWL charts.

• What similarities did you notice in the perpetual motion machines?

• How does the topic relate to the weekly question *How do inventors inspire our imaginations?*

Objectives
• Interpret a speaker's messages (both verbal and nonverbal).

OL *On-Level* **DAY 2**

Expand Comprehension

◉ Skill Sequence Use p. 326 to review the definition of sequence. For additional review, see p. EI•13 in *Envision It!* Remind students that clue words such as *first*, along with dates and phrases such as *three weeks later*, signal sequence.

◉ Strategy Summarize Review the definition of summarize. Encourage students to look for main ideas in the drama they can use to summarize the story in their own words. For additional support, use the Extend Thinking questions and refer students to *Envision It!* p. EI•23.

Revisit *The Fabulous Perpetual Motion Machine* on pp. 330–337. As they read, have them apply the comprehension skill and strategy to the story.

* What is the sequence of events that led up to Lily and Carlos deciding to build a perpetual motion machine? *(They wanted to win first prize at the science fair; they thought about and rejected a few projects; they browsed the Internet for ideas; they found the perpetual motion machine idea.)*

* What happens while Lily is saying "But first let us tell you—"? *(Joyce tugs at the sheet and reveals the machine.)*

Student Edition p. EI•13

More Reading

Use additional Leveled Readers or other texts at students' instructional levels to reinforce this week's skills and strategies. For text suggestions, see the Leveled Reader Database or the Leveled Readers Skills Chart on pp. CL 24–CL 29.

Objectives
* Identify sequence of events.
* Summarize texts in ways that maintain meaning within a text.

Small Group Time

Expand Vocabulary

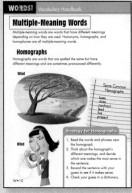

Student Edition p. W•10

More Reading

Use additional Leveled Readers or other texts at students' instructional levels to reinforce this week's skills and strategies. For text suggestions, see the Leveled Reader Database or the Leveled Readers Skills Chart on pp. CL 24–CL 29.

◉ Multiple-Meaning Words/Context Clues
Review *Words!* on p. W•10. Remind students that many words have more than one meaning. They can use context clues to figure out the correct meaning of a word in a sentence. Write the following word on the board: *jam*

- What meanings can you think of for the word *jam*? *(a preserve; a crowd; a pile up, as in "traffic jam"; in trouble; to force something into a space, as in "jam your foot into a boot")*

Write the following sentence on the board: "I never thought we'd get through that jam at the ticket counter."

- What context clues tell you the correct meaning of jam in this sentence? *("Get through" and "at the ticket counter" suggest a lot of people trying to buy tickets. So the meaning in this sentence is "a crowd.")*

Revisit *The Fabulous Perpetual Motion Machine* on pp. 338–343.

- When Mrs. Pérez uses the phrase "round of applause," does she mean that applause is "shaped like a circle" or "something a group of people do together"? Look it up in *Words!* on pp. W•7 and W•10 or in a dictionary. *(something a group does together)*

- Use *round* in a sentence to show another meaning. *(The perpetual motion machine went round and round.)*

As students finishing reading *The Fabulous Perpetual Motion Machine*, encourage them to apply the strategy to understand the correct meaning of multiple-meaning words.

Objectives
- Use the context to determine the meaning of multiple-meaning words.

OL On-Level | **DAY 4**

Practice Retelling

■ **Retell** To assess students' comprehension, use the Retelling Cards. Monitor retelling and prompt students as needed.

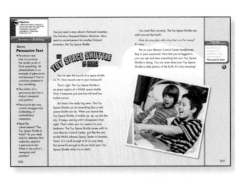

Genre Focus

■ **Before Reading or Revisiting** "The Toy Space Shuttle Is Here!" on pp. 348–351, read aloud the information about persuasive text on p. 348. Have students preview "The Toy Space Shuttle Is Here!" and set a purpose for reading.

• What text features suggest the text is an ad? *(exclamation marks, questions, pictures of a toy, a price tag)*

• Why do you think the writer uses so many exclamation points? *(to show enthusiasm and get the reader excited about the product)*

■ **During Reading or Revisiting** Have students read along with you while tracking the print.

• What exaggerated claim does the writer make about the toy in the paragraph beginning "But here's the really big news"? *(The toy can do everything that a real space shuttle can do.)*

• How do you know this is an exaggeration? *(No toy can do everything that a real space shuttle can do because the real space shuttle is far too complicated.)*

• How does the writer use other people in the ad to help persuade you to buy the toy? *(talks about how much fun you and your friend can have; uses quotes from a satisfied customer)*

■ **After Reading or Revisiting** Have students share their reaction to the persuasive text. Then have them write a short persuasive ad about something ordinary, such as a pencil or a keychain, so that it makes the reader want to buy it.

Objectives
• Explain the basic relationships among ideas in the argument.

Small Group Time

On-Level Reader

■ **Model** Model the fluency skill of expression for students. Read aloud the first two pages of *The Search for a Perpetual Motion Machine*, emphasizing expression by varying your tone of voice to reflect the struggles of the inventor. Explain to students that even expository text can be made to sound more interesting and memorable by the way it is read.

■ **Fluency Routine**

1. Have students reread passages from *The Search for a Perpetual Motion Machine* with a partner.

2. For optimal fluency, students should reread passages three to four times.

3. As students read, monitor fluency and provide corrective feedback. Have students adjust their expression, noting how tone and volume can give added meaning to the facts and events covered in the passage.

See *Routines Flip Chart* for more help with fluency.

■ **Retell** For additional practice, have students use headings, diagrams, and photographs as a guide to retell *The Search for a Perpetual Motion Machine*. Prompt as necessary.

• What is this section mostly about?

• What did you learn from reading this section?

Objectives
• Read aloud grade-level stories with fluency.

Build Background

■ **Extend the Concept** Discuss the weekly question *How do inventors inspire our imaginations?* Throughout history, people have had ideas for inventions that enrich people's lives. What do you think are the most important inventions in modern life? *(Students may say computers, television, DVDs, cell phones, or music players.)*

Advanced Reader

For a complete literacy instructional plan and additional practice with this week's target skills and strategies, see the **Leveled Reader Teaching Guide.**

■ **Before Reading** *Philo and His Invention,* tell students to recall the Read Aloud "What's the Big Idea, Ben Franklin?"

Philo and His Invention
by Pamela Dell

- What characteristics did Ben Franklin have that helped make him an accomplished inventor? *(could solve problems, conduct experiments, build new machines)*

- What modern conveniences are like Franklin's early inventions? *(step stool, ceiling fan, almanacs)*

In *Philo and His Invention* you will read about some inventors who struggled to get credit for and sell their inventions.

Have students look at the illustrations in the book and use them to predict what will happen in the text. Then have students set a purpose for reading.

■ **During Reading** Have students read the Advanced Reader independently. Encourage them to think critically. For example, ask:

- Why do you think big corporations are usually more successful than individuals in bringing new inventions to the public? *(Corporations have more money, resources, and legal help to develop a product and sell it to the public.)*

- Why do you think the author included the drawings and diagrams in the book? *(to show examples of inventors' work and patent submissions)*

■ **After Reading** Have students review the concept map and explain how *Philo and His Invention* helps students answer the weekly question *How do inventors inspire our imaginations?* Prompt as necessary.

■ **Now Try This** Assign "Now Try This" at the end of the Advanced Reader.

Objectives
- Interpret a speaker's messages (both verbal and nonverbal).

Pacing Small Group Instruction

15–20 mins.

5-Day Plan

DAY 1	• Extend the concept • Read Advanced Reader
DAY 2	• ◉ Sequence • ◉ Summarize • Revisit Student Edition pp. 330–337
DAY 3	• ◉ Multiple-Meaning Words • Revisit Student Edition pp. 338–343
DAY 4	• Persuasive Text • Read/Revisit Student Edition pp. 348–351
DAY 5	• Reread for fluency • Reread Advanced Reader

3- or 4-Day Plan

DAY 1	• Extend the concept • Advanced Reader
DAY 2	• ◉ Sequence • ◉ Summarize • Revisit Student Edition pp. 330–337
DAY 3	• ◉ Multiple-Meaning Words • Revisit Student Edition pp. 338–343
DAY 4	• Persuasive Text • Read/Revisit Student Edition pp. 348–351 • Reread for fluency • Reread Advanced Reader

3-Day Plan: Eliminate the shaded box.

More Reading

Use additional Leveled Readers or other texts at students' instructional levels to reinforce this week's skills and strategies. For text suggestions, see the Leveled Reader Database or the Leveled Readers Skills Chart on pp. CL 24–CL 29.

A Advanced

DAY 2

Extend Comprehension

⊙ Skill Sequence Review the definition of sequence. Encourage students to think about events that happen in sequence and about events that happen simultaneously, or at the same time.

⊙ Strategy Summarize Review the definition of the strategy. Remind students to think about the main ideas as they read, so they can use them to summarize the story. During reading, use the Extend Thinking questions and the During Reading Differentiated Instruction for additional support.

■ **Revisit** *The Fabulous Perpetual Motion Machine* on pp. 330–337. Have students apply the comprehension skill and strategy as they read.

• What were Vladimir Zworykin and Philo Farnsworth doing simultaneously? *(They were working on the invention of television.)*

• What did Philo do before Vladimir, and why was it so important? *(Philo patented his invention. RCA could not claim the rights to the invention, even though Vladimir and Philo completed their work at the same time.)*

■ **Critical Thinking** Encourage students to think critically as they read the selection.

• If the perpetual motion machine had been successful, what would Lily and Carlos have to do to protect their invention?

• What would happen if the perpetual motion machine gave power to other machines instead of taking power?

Objectives
• Identify sequence of events.
• Summarize texts in ways that maintain meaning within a text.

A Advanced

DAY 3

Extend Vocabulary

⊙ Multiple-Meaning Words/Context Clues Read a sentence containing a multiple-meaning word such as the following: "The race to the finish line was a close one."

• What meanings can you think of for the word *race*? *(a contest of speed; to work against a limit, such as "race the clock"; a group of people with certain physical traits such as skin color)*

• How can you figure out which meaning of a multiple-meaning word is the correct one in a sentence? *(Use context clues.)*

• Write a sentence for each of the meanings of race. Make sure your context clues make your meaning of the word clear. *(Possible answers: I beat four people to win the first race. I had to race against time to make the school bus. Our school has students from different races and cultures.)*

■ **Revisit** *The Fabulous Perpetual Motion Machine* on pp. 338–343. Remind students to use their knowledge of context clues to figure out the correct meaning of multiple-meaning words as they finish the selection.

■ **Critical Thinking** Have students recall what happened in the selection. Encourage them to think critically.

• How can a machine work without a power source?

• In what ways would you use a perpetual motion machine?

More Reading

Use additional Leveled Readers or other texts at students' instructional levels to reinforce this week's skills and strategies. For text suggestions, see the Leveled Reader Database or the Leveled Readers Skills Chart on pp. CL 24–CL 29.

Objectives
• Use the context to determine the meaning of multiple-meaning words.

Small Group Time

Genre Focus

■ **Before Reading or Revisiting** "The Toy Space Shuttle Is Here!" on pp. 348–351, read the sidebar information on persuasive text. Ask students to use the text features to set a purpose for reading.

■ **During Reading or Revisiting** Remember that persuasive text often uses exaggerated statements or statements that are possibly misleading. Let's list some of these statements. *("The Toy Space Shuttle can orbit around the Earth!" "Whatever fun you've ever had in your life, there is no way it compares to this!" "Ever since I got the Toy Space Shuttle, I have been smiling 24 hours a day.")* Discuss with students how each statement stretches the truth and what the writer's purpose was in crafting the statements. Have students evaluate the effectiveness of the statements.

■ **After Reading or Revisiting** Have students discuss Reading Across Texts. Then have them do Writing Across Texts independently.

Objectives
• Explain the basic relationships among ideas in the argument.

■ **Reread For Fluency** Have students silently reread passages from *Philo and His Invention*. Then have them reread aloud with a partner or individually. As students read, monitor fluency and provide corrective feedback. If students read fluently on the first reading, they do not need to reread three to four times. Assess the fluency of students in this group using p. 353j.

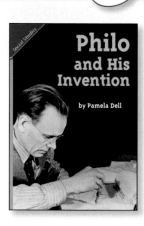

■ **Retell** Have students summarize the main idea and key details from the Advanced Reader *Philo and His Invention*.

■ **Now Try This** Have students complete their projects. You may wish to review their work before they share it with classmates.

Objectives
• Read aloud grade-level stories with fluency.

English Language Learners

The ELL lessons are organized by strands. Use them to scaffold the weekly curriculum of lessons or during small group time instruction.

Academic Language

Students will hear or read the following academic language in this week's core instruction. As students encounter the vocabulary, provide a definition or example. Ask students to suggest an example, synonym, or identify a cognate.

Skill Words	sequence summarize expression (expresión)	shades of meaning dialogue (diálogo) schwa
Concept Words	inspire (inspirar) perpetual (perpetuo)	inventors (inventor)

*Spanish cognates in parentheses.

Concept Development

How do inventors inspire our imaginations?

■ **Preteach Concept**

• **Prior Knowledge** Have students turn to pages 324-325 in the Student Edition. Call attention to the picture of the kids doing experiments. What are these students doing? What do you think they want to find out? What special tools do they use?

• **Discuss Concept** Elicit students' knowledge and experience of how inventors inspire our imaginations. Why do people want to invent new things like that car the men are sitting on? How can an inventor make us want to do new things? Supply background information as needed.

• **Poster Talk-Through** Read aloud the Poster Talk-Through on ELL Poster 11 and work through the Day 1 activities.

■ **Daily Concept and Vocabulary Development** Use the daily activities on ELL Poster 11 to build concept and vocabulary knowledge.

Objectives

• Internalize new basic and academic language by using and reusing it in meaningful ways in speaking and writing activities that build concept and language attainment.
• Listen to a variety of media to build and reinforce concept attainment.

Content Objectives

• Use concept vocabulary related to inventors.

Language Objectives

• Express ideas in response to art and discussion.

• Listen to media for concept attainment.

Daily Planner

DAY 1	• **Frontload Concept** • **Preteach** Comprehension Skill, Vocabulary, Phonics/Spelling, Conventions • **Writing**
DAY 2	• **Review** Concept, Vocabulary, Comprehension Skill • **Frontload Main Selection** • **Practice** Phonics/Spelling, Conventions/Writing
DAY 3	• **Review** Concept, Comprehension Skill, Vocabulary, Conventions/Writing • **Reread Main Selection** • **Practice** Phonics/Spelling
DAY 4	• **Review Concept** • **Read ELL/ELD Readers** • **Practice** Phonics/Spelling, Conventions/Writing
DAY 5	• **Review** Concept, Vocabulary, Comprehension Skill, Phonics/Spelling, Conventions • **Reread ELL/ELD Readers** • **Writing**

*See the ELL Handbook for ELL Workshops with targeted instruction.

Concept Talk Video

Use the Concept Talk Video Routine (*ELL Handbook*, p. 477) to build background knowledge about inventors. After students listen, have them discuss what they leaned about the concepts of inventors and inspiration.

Support for English Language Learners

Language Objectives

- Understand and use basic vocabulary.
- Learn meanings of grade-level vocabulary.

Cognates

For Spanish learners, point out that the word for *invention* is spelled *invención* in Spanish. Reinforce the concept that these languages share many words that are the same or similar.

Basic Vocabulary

■ **High-Frequency Words** Use the vocabulary routine above and the high-frequency word list on p. 451 of the *ELL Handbook* to systematically teach newcomers the first 300 sight words in English. Students who began learning ten words per week at the beginning of the year are now learning words 101–110.

Lesson Vocabulary

■ **Preteach** Introduce the Lesson Vocabulary using this routine:

1. Distribute copies of this week's Word Cards (*ELL Handbook*, p. 89).

2. Display ELL Poster 11 and reread the Poster Talk-Through.

3. Using the poster illustrations, model how a word's meaning can be expressed with other similar words: The queen is *inspecting,* or looking at, the invention.

4. Use these sentences to reveal the meanings of the other words.

   - The teacher assigned the students a *project.* (*a specific piece of work*)

   - They were *browsing* for apples in the store. (*looking for*)

   - I enjoyed the school play and thought it was *fabulous.* (*wonderful*)

   - The audience *applauds* during an exciting part in the movie. (*claps their hands together*)

Objectives

- Expand and internalize initial English vocabulary by learning and using high-frequency English words necessary for identifying and describing people, places, and objects, by retelling simple stories and basic information represented or supported by pictures, and by learning and using routine language needed for classroom communication.
- Learn relationships between sounds and letters of the English language and decode (sound out) words using a combination of skills such as recognizing sound-letter relationships and identifying cognates, affixes, roots and base words.
- Use accessible language and learn new and essential language in the process.

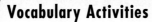

■ **Reteach** Use the following routine to check and reinforce students' understanding of the vocabulary.

• Distribute a copy of the Word Cards and five blank cards to each pair of students.

• Review the vocabulary by having one partner select a Word Card without letting the other student see it. The player with the word gives clues about the word, or other words, phrases, or gestures (Example: pantomime applause). The guesser tries to identify the word while the player with the word adds clues without showing or saying the word.

• Next, have partners work cooperatively to write a clue or draw a simple picture on a blank card for each word. (Example: inspect = "look closely")

• Have students mix the Word Cards and clue cards together and lay them face down, spread out on a table. Students can take turns choosing two cards, trying to match a word with its clue. Have students explain their choices.

■ **Writing** Place the Word Cards facedown and have each student draw one or two cards. Have students write one sentence for each word. Circulate to provide assistance as needed. When students are finished, invite them to share their sentences aloud with the class.

Beginning/Intermediate Have students express their words by drawing pictures or using gestures. They should label their pictures.

Advanced/Advanced High Have students work in pairs to write sentences.

Language Objectives

• Produce drawings, phrases, or short sentences to show understanding of the Lesson Vocabulary.

ELL Teacher Tip

Help students expand their understanding of words with multiple meanings by using card sets to illustrate word meanings. For example, contrast the illustrated sentence *He poured water from a pitcher* with *The pitcher threw the ball* to help English learners remember the two meanings of *pitcher*.

Objectives

• Use visual, contextual, and linguistic support to enhance and confirm understanding of increasingly complex and elaborated spoken language.
• Share information in cooperative learning interactions.
• Use strategic learning techniques such as concept mapping, drawing, memorizing, comparing, contrasting, and reviewing to acquire basic and grade-level vocabulary.
• Speak using grade-level content area vocabulary in context to internalize new English words and build academic language proficiency.

Listening Comprehension

Ben Franklin, Inventor

Ben Franklin was a famous American inventor. He was born in 1706 and died in 1790. Ben had lots of ideas. He was busy. But he still found time to try out new ideas. Some of Ben's ideas worked. Some did not. Ben always wanted to try.

Ben turned a lot of his ideas into inventions. He hung a cord at the end of his bed. He connected the cord to the lock on his door. He used the cord to lock the door. Ben didn't even have to get out of bed! He pulled the cord. Then he could roll over and sleep in his warm bed.

Ben invented a stepladder stool with a seat. He made a rocking chair with a fan over it. The fan kept flies away from his chair. Ben made a pole to take books down from high shelves. The pole had fingers on the end of it to grab the books. Ben cut a hole in his kitchen wall. A windmill was outside the hole. The wind blew outside. The windmill turned the meat inside! Ben also invented an iron stove with a pipe leading outside. The stove made more heat than an ordinary fireplace. It cost less money to work than a fireplace. The stove made less smoke, too. People everywhere liked it!

Ben Franklin invented many things. We use some of these things today.

Prepare for the Read Aloud The modified Read Aloud above prepares students for listening to the oral reading "What's the Big Idea, Ben Franklin?" on p. 325b.

■ **First Listening: Listen to Understand** Write the title of the Read Aloud on the board. What were some of Ben Franklin's inventions. Afterwards, ask the questions again and have students share their answers.

■ **Second Listening: Listen to Check Understanding** Using a K-W-L chart (*ELL Handbook*, p. 480), work with students to list what they know about Ben Franklin and what questions they have. Record their ideas in the K and W columns. Now listen again to check your facts and get answers for your questions. Afterwards, fill in the L column of the chart together.

Objectives

- Use visual, contextual, and linguistic support to enhance and confirm understanding of increasingly complex and elaborated spoken language.
- Demonstrate listening comprehension of increasingly complex spoken English by following directions, retelling or summarizing spoken messages, responding to questions and requests, collaborating with peers, and taking notes commensurate with content and grade-level needs.

Content Objectives

- Monitor and adjust oral comprehension.

Language Objectives

- Discuss oral passages.
- Use a graphic organizer to take notes.
- Use accessible language to learn new language.

Graphic Organizer

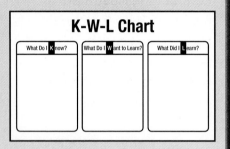

K-W-L Chart

| What Do I Know? | What Do I Want to Learn? | What Did I Learn? |

ELL Teacher Tip

Students may benefit from a third listening to confirm their answers.

Language Opportunity: New Language

Have students use the accessible language of the Read Aloud to focus on new language. Share meanings of *invent, invention, ordinary,* and *ideas,* Have students use the new language to write or speak about something they would like to create.

ELL English Language Learners

Phonics and Spelling

■ **Words with Schwa** Copy and distribute *ELL Handbook* p. 267.

• **Preteach** Point to the picture of the pretzel. As you say the word with students, have them distinguish between the short vowel sound and the schwa sound made by the same vowel. This is a pretzel. Say the two syllables: PRET-zel. The first syllable is stressed. The second is unstressed.

• **Teach/Model** In English, unstressed syllables often sound like this: /ə/. We call this the schwa sound. The schwa sound can be in the beginning, middle, or last syllable of a word: *about, animal, table.*

• **Distinguish Sounds** Raise your hand when you hear a word with the /ə/ sound: *asleep, asking, final, panel, lesson, ribbon, backbone.* Have students repeat the words and distinguish between vowel sounds. Then write the words so that students can point out the relationship between the letters and the sounds of English. Have them spell the words to focus on English spelling patterns. Students should use vowels to spell the schwa sounds in unstressed syllables with accuracy.

Word Analysis: Shades of Meaning

■ **Preteach and Model** Explain that shades of meaning refers to words that have similar meanings. Display a sentence: *Most of Mario's projects are good, but his new one is incredible.* Underline *good* and *incredible.* These words have different shades of meaning: *incredible* is stronger than *good.* Use contextual support to help students develop vocabulary. Use each word in a sentence with clear context to help students understand the difference. Have them create their own contextual sentences to show shades of meaning.

■ **Practice** Write words on the board: *curious, scrawny, dress, thin, gown, nosey.* Work with students to discuss the meaning of each word. Have them identify which words go together. Have students use the words in a sentence.

Leveled LS Support

Beginning/Intermediate Students write and illustrate a sentence.

Advanced/Advanced High Students can write sentences using each word pair to show shades of meaning.

Content Objectives

• Identify and define words with shades of meaning.

• Identify words with schwa.

Language Objectives

• Apply phonics and decoding skills to vocabulary.

• Discuss shades of meaning for words with similar meanings.

• Distinguish vowel sounds of English.

• Learn relationships between sounds and letters of English.

• Use contextual support to develop vocabulary.

• Use English spelling patterns with accuracy and spell familiar words with accuracy.

Transfer Skills

In "syllable-timed" languages, syllables are pronounced with equal stress. In English, by contrast, vowels in stressed syllables are pronounced more distinctly. Vowels in unstressed syllables often make a more neutral schwa sound, which English learners may have difficulty pronouncing and spelling.

Objectives

• Distinguish sounds and intonation patterns of English with increasing ease.
• Use visual and contextual support and support from peers and teachers to read grade-appropriate content area text, enhance and confirm understanding, and develop vocabulary, grasp of language structures, and background knowledge needed to comprehend increasingly challenging language.

Content Objectives

- Order the sequence of events in text.

Language Objectives

- Discuss sequence words.
- Use sequence words to identify the order in which events occurred.

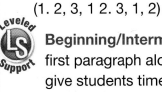

Comprehension
Sequence

■ **Preteach** Sequence refers to the order of events in nonfiction. We use sequence when we list the steps in a process. Have students turn to Envision It! on p. EI•13 in the Student Edition. Read aloud the text together. Have students identify the correct sequence by numbering the pictures of the baseball players.

■ **Reteach** Distribute copies of the Picture It! (*ELL Handbook*, p. 90). Ask students to describe the illustrations. Then read aloud the text twice. Have students listen for sequence words such as *first, then, next,* and *last.* After each reading, have students point out where they heard sequence words. Guide students in completing the practice exercises at their language proficiency levels. (1. 2, 3, 1 2. 3, 1, 2)

Beginning/Intermediate Write the sentences on sentence strips. Read the first paragraph aloud sentence by sentence. Pause after each sentence to give students time to identify if the sentence matches a sentence strip. Have students place the sentences in order as they identify them. Then have students use their sentence strips to complete the activity.

Advanced/Advanced High Have students read the sentences in the activity. Then have them underline any sequence words they see. Have students reread the paragraphs and use the sequence words to identify the sequence of the sentences.

MINI-LESSON

Social Language

Tell students that they can use sequence to organize their daily activities. As you read the following sequence, illustrate each activity with gestures. First I start the day by waking up. Then I brush my teeth. I eat breakfast. Then I go to school. In the afternoon I come home. I eat dinner. In the evening I read a book. Finally I go to bed. Write these sentence frames on the board: *In the morning I _____; In the afternoon I _____; In the evening I _____; At night I _____.* Have students describe their daily activities using the sentence frames or gestures, if necessary.

Objectives

- Demonstrate listening comprehension of increasingly complex spoken English by following directions, retelling or summarizing spoken messages, responding to questions and requests, collaborating with peers, and taking notes commensurate with content and grade-level needs.

ELL *English Language Learners*

Reading Comprehension
The Fabulous Perpetual Motion Machine

- **Frontloading** Read aloud the title and discuss what a *machine* is. I wonder what a perpetual motion machine is and why it is fabulous. Provide visual support for students to understand the lesson vocabulary by guiding students on a picture walk through *The Fabulous Perpetual Motion Machine.* Provide the language as you describe the illustrations. On the board, record their predictions in a two-column chart with headings: *What is a perpetual motion machine? Why is it fabulous?* During reading, students can adjust their predictions on their own two-column chart.

Student Edition pp. 330–331

- **Sheltered Reading** Ask questions to guide comprehension:

  • p. 333: Who are the "fabulous Pérez Twins"? (Lily and Carlos)

  • p. 336: Why did Lily and Carlos invent a perpetual motion machine? (to win first place in the Science Fair)

  • p. 336: Is perpetual motion machine a good name for this invention? Why or why not? (Yes, because it is a machine that works forever)

- **Fluency: Read with Expression** Remind students that reading with expression means to read like you are speaking to a friend. Read the dialogue on p. 335, raising your voice at the end when you read "What's up? Is this your Science Fair idea?" Point out that the question mark gives a clue how to read expressively. Do they see any other marks that give clues? (exclamation mark) Have pairs read the rest of the dialogue on p. 335. As each student reads expressively, his or her partner should listen closely and offer feedback. For more practice, use the Oral Rereading Routine (*ELL Handbook,* p. 474).

- **After Reading** Help students summarize the text with the Retelling Cards. For more practice, use the Retelling/Summarizing Routine (*ELL Handbook,* p. 476).

Content Objectives
- Monitor and adjust comprehension.
- Make and adjust predictions.

Language Objectives
- Read grade-level text with expression.
- Summarize text using visual support.
- Use visual support to confirm understanding of vocabulary.

Graphic Organizer

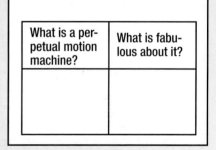

What is a perpetual motion machine?	What is fabulous about it?

Audio Support
Students can prepare for reading *The Fabulous Perpetual Motion Machine* by using the eSelection or the AudioText CD. See the AudioText CD Routine (*ELL Handbook,* p. 478).

Objectives
• Distinguish sounds and intonation patterns of English with increasing ease.

Support for English Language Learners

For additional leveled instruction, see the **ELL/ELD Reader Teaching Guide.**

Scientific Methods in Action
by D. Michael Kim
Illustrated by Bruce Day

ELL Reader   ELD Reader

Comprehension
Scientific Methods in Action

■ **Before Reading** Distribute copies of the ELL and ELD Readers, *Scientific Methods in Action*, to students at their reading level.

  • **Preview** Read the title aloud with students. This text tells how scientists do their work. Invite students to look through the pictures and name what they see. Have them predict what the scientists are doing based on the picture clues and their prior knowledge.

  • **Set a Purpose for Reading** The title is about the scientific method. Let's read to find out what that is.

■ **During Reading** Follow the Reading Routine for both reading groups.

  1. Read the entire Reader aloud slowly.

  2. Reread pp. 1–4, pausing to build background or model comprehension. Have Beginning students finger-point as you read. Use the questions in the chart below to check students' comprehension.

  3. Have students reread pp. 1–4 in pairs, taking turns reading alternate pages.

  4. Repeat steps 2–3 for pages 5–8 of the Reader.

■ **After Reading** Use the exercises on the inside back cover of each Reader and invite students to share their writing. In a whole-group discussion, ask students How did Benjamin Franklin use the scientific method? Record their answers on the board and invite them to point to pictures in the book to support their answers.

ELD Reader Beginning/Intermediate

  • **pp. 2–3** Why do scientists use the scientific method? (to answer questions; to learn things) Point to where you find the answer in the book.

  • **p. 4** What problem did Ben want to fix? (lightning burning houses)

  • **p. 7** Was lightning electricity? Point to the sentence that tells you the answers. (Lightning is electricity.)

Writing What was the first thing Benjamin Franklin did for his experiment? Find the sentence in the book that tells about the step of the experiment. Copy the sentence. Then read it aloud to your partner.

ELL Reader Advanced/Advanced High

  • **pp. 2–3** What do scientists use to learn about the physical world? (the scientific method)

  • **p. 4** What was the problem Benjamin Franklin thought about? (lightning causes damage)

  • **p. 7** What step did Benjamin Franklin skip? (writing and organizing data)

Study Guide Distribute copies of the ELL Reader Study Guide (*ELL Handbook*, page 94). Scaffold comprehension by helping students look back through the Reader in order to answer the questions. Review their answers together. (See *ELL Handbook*, pp. 209–212.)

Objectives
• Understand the general meaning, main points, and important details of spoken language ranging from situations in which topics, language, and contexts are familiar to unfamiliar.

 ELL English Language Learners

Conventions
Past, Present, and Future Tenses

■ **Preteach** Display these sentences:

We learned about scientists yesterday.

We are learning about scientists today.

We will learn about scientists tomorrow.

When a verb describes something that already happened, the verb is past tense. When the verb describes something that is happening now, it is present tense. When a verb talks about something that will happen someday, it is future tense. Read the sentences aloud and have pairs of students identify the verb tense as past, present, or future. Discuss how they identified each verb tense.

■ **Practice** List these verbs on the board: *play, look,* and *help.* Have pairs of students use sentence strips to write simple sentences. Share their sentences with the class. Have the class identify the verb and verb tense.

■ **Reteach** Write a list of verbs on the board, such as *discover, jump,* and *start.* Have students put the verbs in the past, present, and future tenses.

■ **Practice** Display a chart with empty spaces for students to fill in to practice forming verbs in the past, present, and future tenses. Have students use the words to write sentences. Students can pair up to edit sentences for tense. Sentences that take place in the past should use past tense, while those that describe future action should include future tense verbs.

Past Tense	Present Tense	Future Tense
called	help	will ask

Leveled Support

Beginning/Intermediate Have students work with a partner to fill in the chart. Choose one or two verbs to use in a sentence.

Advanced/Advanced High After students complete the chart have them create three sentences using past, present, and future tense verbs.

Objectives
- Edit writing for standard grammar and usage, including subject-verb agreement, pronoun agreement, and appropriate verb tenses commensurate with grade-level expectations as more English is acquired.
- Employ increasingly complex grammatical structures in content area writing commensurate with grade level expectations such as (i) using correct verbs, tenses, and pronouns/antecedents; (ii) using possessive case (apostrophe -s) correctly; and, (iii) using negatives and contractions correctly

Content Objectives
- Decode and use past, present, and future verb tenses.
- Correctly form past, present, and future verb tenses.

Language Objectives
- Speak using the correct verb tense.
- Write phrases and sentences with past, present, and future verb tenses.
- Edit writing for verb tense.

Transfer Skills

Spanish, Haitian Creole, and Hmong speakers may use present tense in places where English calls for future tense. Give students more practice by having partners tell each other what they will do when they get home from school or at some other time.

Grammar Jammer

For more practice with verbs, use the Grammar Jammer Routine (*ELL Handbook*, p. 478).

Support for English Language Learners

Content Objective
- Identify dialogue in a text.

Language Objectives
- Write dialogue.
- Participate in shared reading.
- Know when to use informal language.
- Speak using a variety of sentence lengths.
- Demonstrate listening comprehension.
- Narrate with detail and specificity.

Language Opportunity: Listening and Speaking

Turn to p. 346 in the Student Edition and read the prompt. Before students write, have them focus on speaking and listening. Each student can act as an inventor, explaining his or her invention. Others should retell what they hear to demonstrate listening comprehension. Then have students narrate with specificity and detail. As they say dialogue, ask questions to prompt deeper thinking and additional details. What is your invention? How does it work? What does it do? Why is it important? Have students add those details as they narrate, or tell the story, of how they created their inventions.

Write Dialogue

■ **Introduce** Display the writing model. Review that dialogue is words spoken by a character in a text. Who are the two speakers? (Juan and David)

Writing Model

> **JUAN:** What do you have for lunch?
>
> **DAVID** *(looking inside his lunchbox)*: A sandwich and some vegetables.

Point out that the sentences in the writing model are different lengths. The varying lengths make the model sound natural. Have students practice speaking with sentences both short and long to sound like natural speech. For additional practice reading dialogue, have students turn to pp. 332–333 of the Student Edition and do a shared reading. They can act as the various characters to understand that dialogue is informal language with varying sentence lengths.

■ **Practice** Write incomplete dialogue on the board. Work together to complete it.

■ **Write** Have students write a dialogue between themselves and Lily and Carlos. Students can ask Lily and Carlos questions about the perpetual motion machine and then imagine the answers they would provide.

Beginning/Intermediate Supply students with a frame with their name, *Lily, Carlos* and write-on lines. Students create dialogue with partners.

Advanced/Advanced High Have students develop dialogue independently. Then have pairs exchange papers and provide feedback for revising.

MINI-LESSON

Informal Language

Point out informal language in the model. Why does this language sound natural? It sounds the way people speak. David does not speak in complete sentences. Their language is informal. Ask students to speak using informal language and write the words as dialogue.

Objectives
- Use visual and contextual support and support from peers and teachers to read grade-appropriate content area text, enhance and confirm understanding, and develop vocabulary, grasp of language structures, and background knowledge needed to comprehend increasingly challenging language.

Common Core Standards
Weekly Planning Guide

Selection: Leonardo's Horse
Genre: Biography

Alignment of the Common Core Standards with This Week's Skills and Strategies

This Week's Common Core Standards for English Language Arts	Instructional Summary
Reading Standards for Literature/Informational Text	
Literature 2. Determine a theme of a story, drama, or poem from details in the text, including how characters in a story or drama respond to challenges or how the speaker in a poem reflects upon a topic; summarize the text.	This week, students learn to identify the **main idea** of expository text. The lesson reviews that the main idea is what the selection is mostly about and that **details** are information that tell more about the main idea. The **visualize** strategy encourages students to picture what the author is telling them about in order to better understand the selection.
Informational Text 1. Quote accurately from a text when explaining what the text says explicitly and when drawing inferences from the text.	
Informational Text 2. Determine two or more main ideas of a text and explain how they are supported by key details; summarize the text.	
Foundational Skills Standards	
Foundational Skills 4. Read with sufficient accuracy and fluency to support comprehension.	In this week's fluency activities, students focus on using an **appropriate rate** to read an informational article.
Foundational Skills 4.b. Read on-level prose and poetry orally with accuracy, appropriate rate, and expression on successive readings.	
Writing Standards	
Writing 1.a. Introduce a topic or text clearly, state an opinion, and create an organizational structure in which ideas are logically grouped to support the writer's purpose.	This week, students create a **persuasive speech** as they practice writing for tests. They evaluate their writing using a **rubric.** In the Research and Inquiry section, students write **reports** about an artist to tell how the artist or his or her work inspired others.
Writing 1.b. Provide logically ordered reasons that are supported by facts and details.	
Writing 5. With guidance and support from peers and adults, develop and strengthen writing as needed by planning, revising, editing, rewriting, or trying a new approach. (Editing for conventions should demonstrate command of Language standards 1–3 up to and including grade 5 on pages 28 and 29.)	
Speaking and Listening Standards	
Speaking/Listening 1.b. Follow agreed-upon rules for discussions and carry out assigned roles.	Students learn about **media** as a way to get information. They work with a group to prepare and present a **newscast** about Leonardo's horse. In the Research and Inquiry section, students present a review of their **reports** about an artist and may show photographs of the artist or his or her artwork to make their talk more interesting and effective.
Speaking/Listening 4. Report on a topic or text or present an opinion, sequencing ideas logically and using appropriate facts and relevant, descriptive details to support main ideas or themes; speak clearly at an understandable pace.	
Language Standards	
Language 1. Demonstrate command of the conventions of standard English grammar and usage when writing or speaking.	The Conventions section presents the principal parts of regular verbs. Students identify the differences between **present, present participle, past, and past participle verbs.**
Language 1.b. Form and use the perfect (e.g., *I had walked; I have walked; I will have walked*) verb tenses.	

Additional Support for a Common Core Standard This Week

Use the following instruction to supplement the teaching of one of this week's Common Core Standards.

Common Core Standard: Literature 2.
Display Student Edition page 382 to explore historical fiction. Point out to students that historical fiction is a made-up story but the background information is based on historical fact. Historical fiction is often written from the third-person point of view using *he, she, it,* and *they.*

• Ask students to retell the information, pointing out the historical facts and the make-believe elements of the story.

• Have students add to the story. Remind them to use historical facts about Michelangelo.

ISBN-13: 978-0-328-64415-3   ISBN-10: 0-328-64415-5

Common Core Standards and Concept Development

- Introduce and explore this unit's weekly concepts through rich, structured conversations
- Develop complex content knowledge and vocabulary
- Expand on a single concept with engaging literature and nonfiction
- Build better readers in all content areas
- Align instruction to **Common Core Anchor Standards**

Grade 5 • Unit 3 • Week 2

Leonardo's Horse

Unit 3

What do people gain from the work of inventors and artists?

Week 5

connect to SCIENCE

Special Effects in Film and Television

Question of the Week

How do artists create special effects to entertain us?

Concept Talk Guide students as they discuss questions such as:

- What examples of special effects did you discuss?
- Where have you seen special effects?

Writing Think about which form of entertainment you prefer: watching a movie or watching a television program. Compare and contrast the two, using specific details to make your point.

Week 4

connect to SOCIAL STUDIES

Mahalia Jackson

Question of the Week

How does an artist use music to inspire others?

Concept Talk Guide students as they discuss questions such as:

- What did you discuss about music as an inspiration?
- What kind of music do you like most?

Writing *Mahalia Jackson* describes the voice of a talented singer. Think about music or another unique sound. Now write a description of that sound, using vivid sensory words.

Week 3

connect to SCIENCE

The Dinosaurs of Waterhouse Hawkins

Question of the Week

How can paleontologists help us understand the past?

Concept Talk Guide students as they discuss questions such as:

- What selections or books have you read about dinosaurs?
- What do you know about paleontologists and their work?

Writing *The Dinosaurs of Waterhouse Hawkins* tells about the introduction of dinosaur models to the world. Prepare an advertisement for one of the events, enticing people to come.

Week 1

connect to SCIENCE

The Fabulous Perpetual Motion Machine

Question of the Week

How do inventors inspire our imaginations?

Concept Talk Guide students as they discuss questions such as:

- What are some important inventions we use? Why are they important?
- What books, movies, or TV shows do you know that feature inventors and inventions?

Writing In *The Fabulous Perpetual Motion Machine*, young inventors create a special machine. Think about something that could be invented. Now write a short play based on your idea.

You Are Here: Week 2

connect to SOCIAL STUDIES

Leonardo's Horse

Question of the Week

How do artists inspire future generations?

As students answer this unit's Big Question and this week's Question of the Week, they will address:

Reading 2. Determine central ideas or themes of a text and analyze their development; summarize the key supporting details and ideas. **(Also Reading 1.)**

Concept Talk Guide students as they discuss questions such as:

- What might inspire an artist to create?
- How can an artist's work inspire other people?

As students answer this week's Concept Talk questions, they will address:

Speaking/Listening 1. Prepare for and participate effectively in a range of conversations and collaborations with diverse partners, building on others' ideas and expressing their own clearly and persuasively.

Writing Think about modern inventions. Which recent invention changed people's lives the most? Write a persuasive speech that answers this question.

As students write about this week's prompt, they will address:

Writing 1. Write arguments to support claims in an analysis of substantive topics or texts, using valid reasoning and relevant and sufficient evidence. **(Also Writing 5.)**

Listening and Speaking On page 387, students learn that when they give a presentation, they should speak loudly and clearly. By doing so, they address:

Speaking/Listening 4. Present information, findings, and supporting evidence such that listeners can follow the line of reasoning and the organization, development, and style are appropriate to task, purpose, and audience. **(Also Speaking/Listening 1.)**

This Week on Reading Street!

Question of the Week

How do artists inspire future generations?

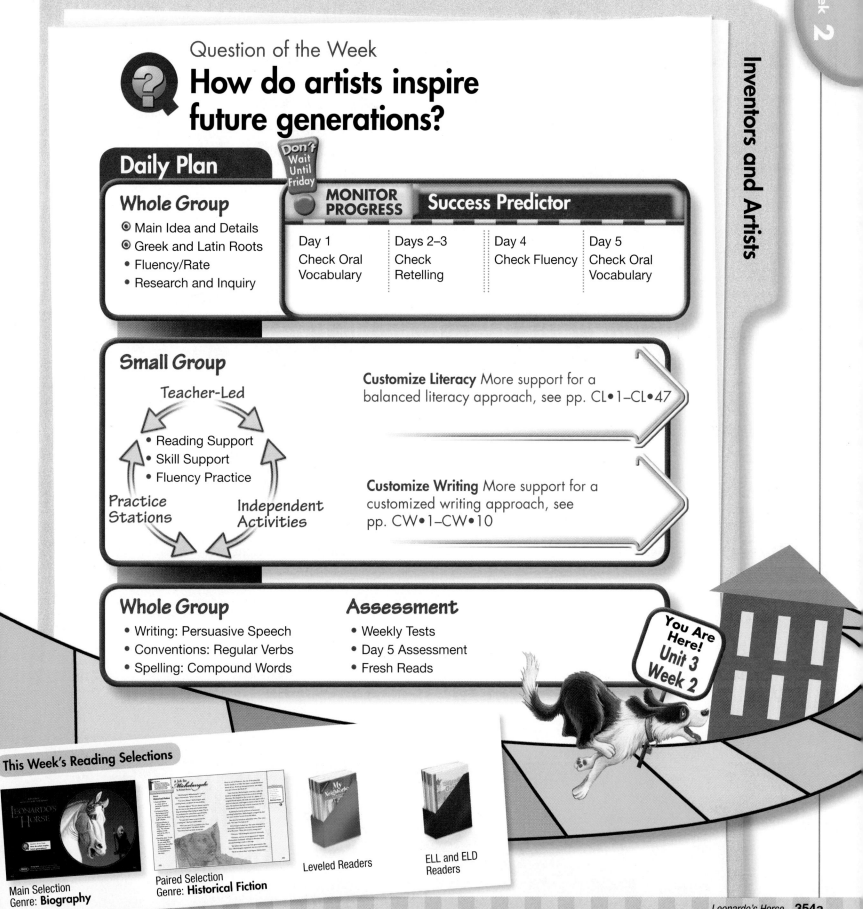

Daily Plan

Don't Wait Until Friday

Whole Group

- ◉ Main Idea and Details
- ◉ Greek and Latin Roots
- • Fluency/Rate
- • Research and Inquiry

MONITOR PROGRESS | **Success Predictor**

Day 1	Days 2–3	Day 4	Day 5
Check Oral Vocabulary	Check Retelling	Check Fluency	Check Oral Vocabulary

Small Group

Teacher-Led

- • Reading Support
- • Skill Support
- • Fluency Practice

Practice Stations

Independent Activities

Customize Literacy More support for a balanced literacy approach, see pp. CL•1–CL•47

Customize Writing More support for a customized writing approach, see pp. CW•1–CW•10

Whole Group

- • Writing: Persuasive Speech
- • Conventions: Regular Verbs
- • Spelling: Compound Words

Assessment

- • Weekly Tests
- • Day 5 Assessment
- • Fresh Reads

You Are Here! Unit 3 Week 2

This Week's Reading Selections

Main Selection
Genre: **Biography**

Paired Selection
Genre: **Historical Fiction**

Leveled Readers

ELL and ELD Readers

Resources on Reading Street!

	Build Concepts	**Comprehension**
Whole Group	 Let's Talk About pp. 354–355	Envision It! Skills/ Strategies Comprehension Skills Lesson pp. 356–357
Go Digital	• Concept Talk Video	• Envision It! Animations • eSelections
Small Group and Independent Practice	Leonardo's Horse pp. 360–361 ELL and ELD Readers Leveled Readers	Leonardo's Horse pp. 360–361 ELL and ELD Readers Leveled Readers Envision It! Skills/ Strategies Reader's and Writer's Notebook Practice Station Flip Chart
Go Digital	• eReaders • eSelections	• Envision It! Animations • eSelections • eReaders
Customize Literacy	• Leveled Readers	• Envision It! Skills and Strategies Handbook • Leveled Readers
Go Digital	• Concept Talk Video • Big Question Video • eReaders	• Envision It! Animations • eReaders

Question of the Week
How do artists inspire future generations?

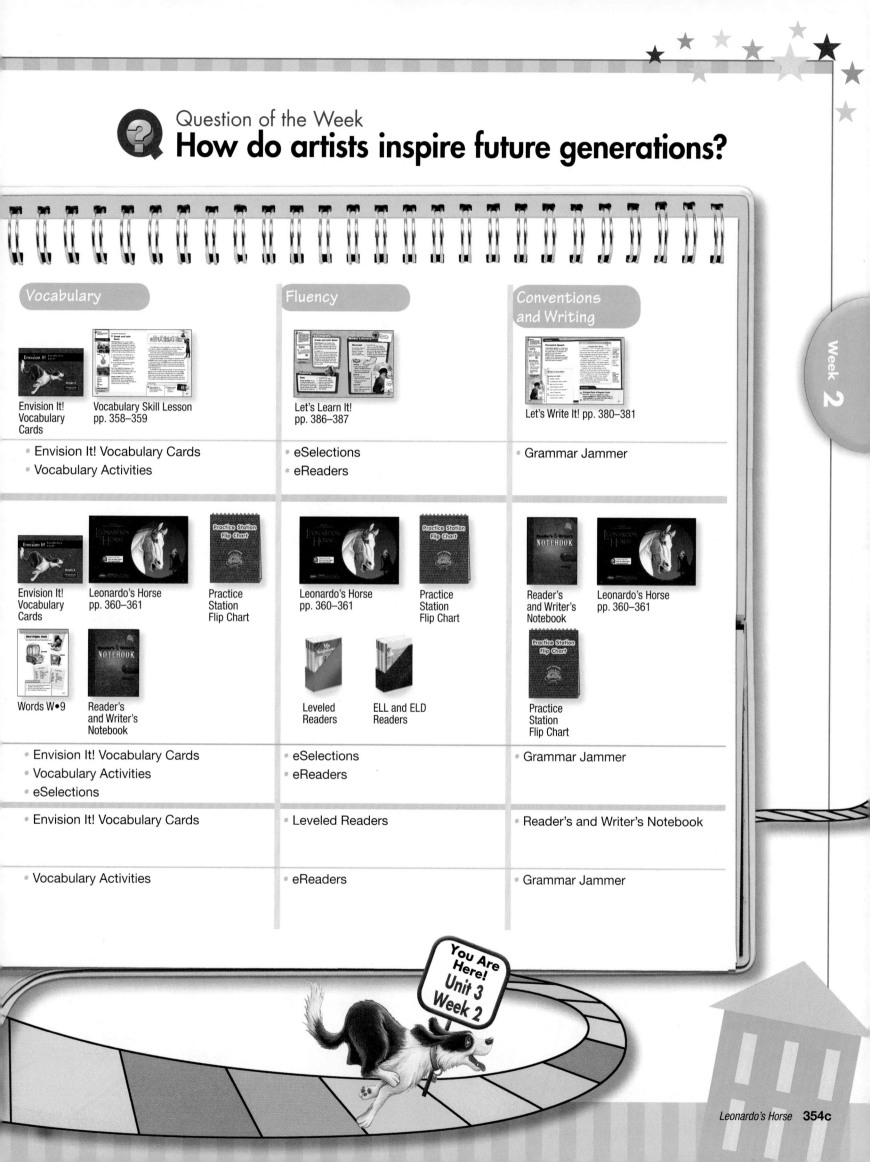

Vocabulary	Fluency	Conventions and Writing
Envision It! Vocabulary Cards	Let's Learn It! pp. 386–387	Let's Write It! pp. 380–381
Vocabulary Skill Lesson pp. 358–359		
• Envision It! Vocabulary Cards • Vocabulary Activities	• eSelections • eReaders	• Grammar Jammer
Envision It! Vocabulary Cards Leonardo's Horse pp. 360–361 Words W•9 Reader's and Writer's Notebook	Leonardo's Horse pp. 360–361 Practice Station Flip Chart Leveled Readers ELL and ELD Readers	Reader's and Writer's Notebook Leonardo's Horse pp. 360–361 Practice Station Flip Chart
Practice Station Flip Chart		
• Envision It! Vocabulary Cards • Vocabulary Activities • eSelections	• eSelections • eReaders	• Grammar Jammer
• Envision It! Vocabulary Cards	• Leveled Readers	• Reader's and Writer's Notebook
• Vocabulary Activities	• eReaders	• Grammar Jammer

You Are Here!
Unit 3
Week 2

My 5-Day Planner for Reading Street!

	Check Oral Vocabulary **Day 1** pages 354j–357f	Check Retelling **Day 2** pages 358a–371e
Get Ready to Read	**Concept Talk,** 354j **Oral Vocabulary,** 355a easel, charcoal, canvas **Listening Comprehension,** Read Aloud, 355b	**Concept Talk,** 358a **Oral Vocabulary,** 358b gallery, marble **Word Analysis,** 358c Greek and Latin Roots **Literary Terms,** 358d Tone **Story Structure,** 358d Conflict and Resolution
Read and Comprehend	**Comprehension Skill,** ⊙ Main Idea and Details, 355c **Comprehension Strategy,** ⊙ Visualize, 355c **READ Comprehension,** 356–357 **Model Fluency,** Rate, 356–357 **Introduce Lesson Vocabulary,** 357a achieved, architect, bronze, cannon, depressed, fashioned, midst, philosopher, rival	**Vocabulary Skill,** ⊙ Greek and Latin Roots, 358e **Vocabulary Strategy,** Word Structure, 358e **Lesson Vocabulary,** 358–359 achieved, architect, bronze, cannon, depressed, fashioned, midst, philosopher, rival **READ Vocabulary,** 358–359 **Model Fluency,** Rate, 358–359 **READ Main Selection,** *Leonardo's Horse,* 360–371a
Language Arts	**Research and Inquiry,** Identify Questions, 357b **Spelling,** Compound Words, 357c **Conventions,** Principal Parts of Regular Verbs, 357d **Handwriting,** Cursive Letter *j* and *J*, 357d **Writing for Tests,** Persuasive Speech, 357e–357f	**Research and Inquiry,** Navigate/Search, 371b **Conventions,** Principal Parts of Regular Verbs, 371c **Spelling,** Compound Words, 371c **Writing for Tests,** Persuasive Speech, 371d–371e

You Are Here! Unit 3 Week 2

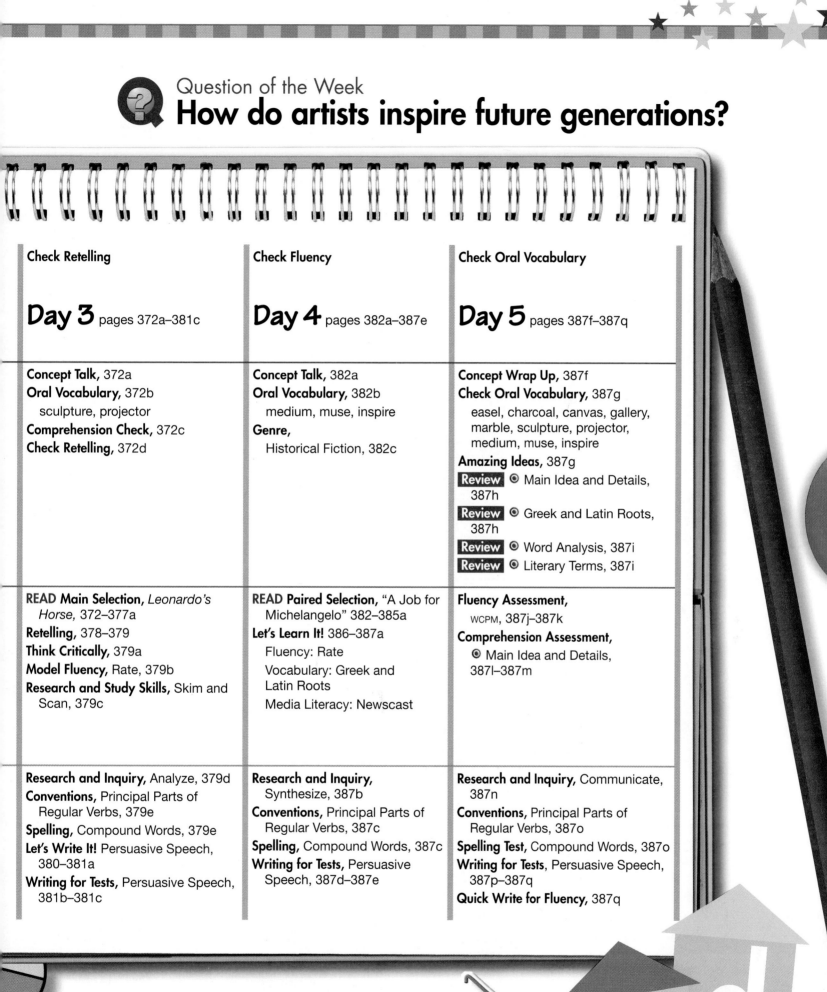

How do artists inspire future generations?

Check Retelling	Check Fluency	Check Oral Vocabulary
Day 3 pages 372a–381c	**Day 4** pages 382a–387e	**Day 5** pages 387f–387q
Concept Talk, 372a **Oral Vocabulary,** 372b sculpture, projector **Comprehension Check,** 372c **Check Retelling,** 372d	**Concept Talk,** 382a **Oral Vocabulary,** 382b medium, muse, inspire **Genre,** Historical Fiction, 382c	**Concept Wrap Up,** 387f **Check Oral Vocabulary,** 387g easel, charcoal, canvas, gallery, marble, sculpture, projector, medium, muse, inspire **Amazing Ideas,** 387g **Review** ◉ Main Idea and Details, 387h **Review** ◉ Greek and Latin Roots, 387h **Review** ◉ Word Analysis, 387i **Review** ◉ Literary Terms, 387i
READ **Main Selection,** *Leonardo's Horse,* 372–377a **Retelling,** 378–379 **Think Critically,** 379a **Model Fluency,** Rate, 379b **Research and Study Skills,** Skim and Scan, 379c	READ **Paired Selection,** "A Job for Michelangelo" 382–385a **Let's Learn It!** 386–387a Fluency: Rate Vocabulary: Greek and Latin Roots Media Literacy: Newscast	**Fluency Assessment,** WCPM, 387j–387k **Comprehension Assessment,** ◉ Main Idea and Details, 387l–387m
Research and Inquiry, Analyze, 379d **Conventions,** Principal Parts of Regular Verbs, 379e **Spelling,** Compound Words, 379e **Let's Write It!** Persuasive Speech, 380–381a **Writing for Tests,** Persuasive Speech, 381b–381c	**Research and Inquiry,** Synthesize, 387b **Conventions,** Principal Parts of Regular Verbs, 387c **Spelling,** Compound Words, 387c **Writing for Tests,** Persuasive Speech, 387d–387e	**Research and Inquiry,** Communicate, 387n **Conventions,** Principal Parts of Regular Verbs, 387o **Spelling Test,** Compound Words, 387o **Writing for Tests,** Persuasive Speech, 387p–387q **Quick Write for Fluency,** 387q

Week 2

Grouping Options for Differentiated Instruction
Turn the page for the small group time lesson plan.

Planning Small Group Time on Reading Street!

SMALL GROUP TIME RESOURCES

Look for this Small Group Time box each day to help meet the individual needs of all your students. Differentiated Instruction lessons appear on the DI pages at the end of each week.

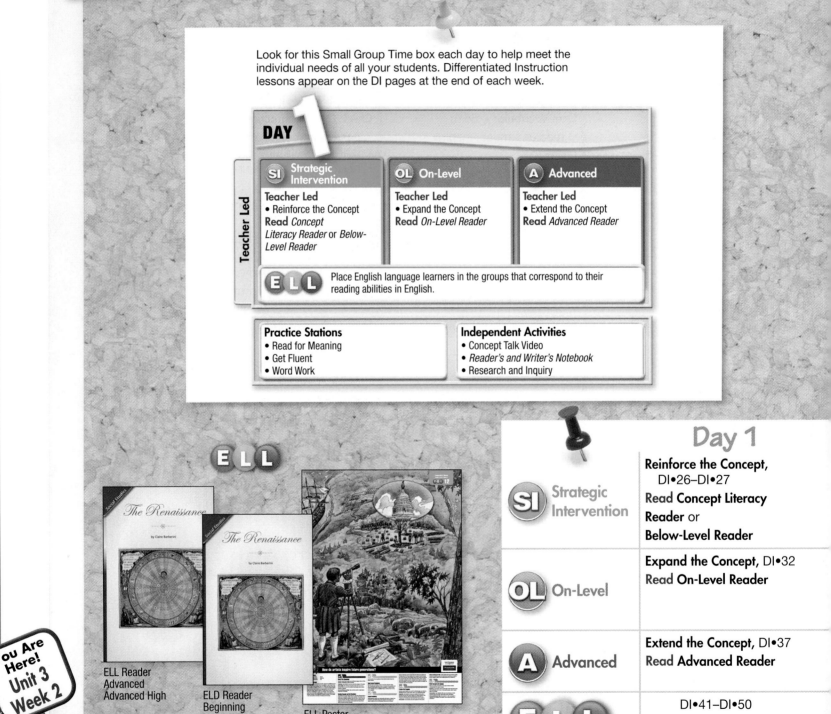

DAY 1

Teacher Led

SI Strategic Intervention	**OL** On-Level	**A** Advanced
Teacher Led • Reinforce the Concept **Read** *Concept Literacy Reader* or *Below-Level Reader*	**Teacher Led** • Expand the Concept **Read** *On-Level Reader*	**Teacher Led** • Extend the Concept **Read** *Advanced Reader*

ELL Place English language learners in the groups that correspond to their reading abilities in English.

Practice Stations
• Read for Meaning
• Get Fluent
• Word Work

Independent Activities
• Concept Talk Video
• *Reader's and Writer's Notebook*
• Research and Inquiry

ELL

ELL Reader
Advanced
Advanced High

ELD Reader
Beginning
Intermediate

ELL Poster

You Are Here!
Unit 3 Week 2

Day 1

SI Strategic Intervention	**Reinforce the Concept,** DI•26–DI•27 **Read Concept Literacy Reader** or **Below-Level Reader**
OL On-Level	**Expand the Concept,** DI•32 **Read On-Level Reader**
A Advanced	**Extend the Concept,** DI•37 **Read Advanced Reader**
ELL English Language Learners	DI•41–DI•50 **Frontload Concept** **Preteach Skills** **Writing**

Question of the Week
How do artists inspire future generations?

(SI) Strategic Intervention

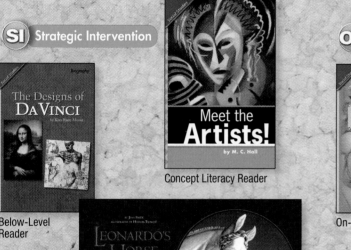

The Designs of DaVINCI
by Kara Race-Moore

Below-Level Reader

Meet the Artists!
by M. C. Hall

Concept Literacy Reader

LEONARDO'S HORSE

Question of the Week
How do artists inspire future generations?

Leonardo's Horse pp. 360–361

(OL) On-Level

The Italian Renaissance and Its Artists
by Liz Murray

On-Level Reader

(A) Advanced

Art's Inspiration
by Ellen B. Cutler

Advanced Reader

A Job for Michelangelo
by Richard Foster

A Job for Michelangelo pp. 382–383

Small Group Weekly Plan

Day 2	Day 3	Day 4	Day 5
Reinforce Comprehension, DI•28 **Revisit Main Selection**	**Reinforce Vocabulary,** DI•29 **Read/Revisit Main Selection**	**Reinforce Comprehension,** Practice Retelling DI•30 Genre Focus **Read/Revisit Paired Selection**	**Practice Fluency,** DI•31 **Reread Concept Literacy Reader** or **Below-Level Reader**
Expand Comprehension, DI•33 **Revisit Main Selection**	**Expand Vocabulary,** DI•34 **Read/Revisit Main Selection**	**Expand Comprehension,** Practice Retelling DI•35 Genre Focus **Read/Revisit Paired Selection**	**Practice Fluency,** DI•36 **Reread On-Level Reader**
Extend Comprehension, DI•38 **Revisit Main Selection**	**Extend Vocabulary,** DI•39 **Read/Revisit Main Selection**	**Extend Comprehension,** Genre Focus DI•40 **Read/Revisit Paired Selection**	**Practice Fluency,** DI•40 **Reread Advanced Reader**
DI•41–DI•50 **Review Concept/Skills** **Frontload Main Selection** **Practice**	DI•41–DI•50 **Review Concept/Skills** **Reread Main Selection** **Practice**	DI•41–DI•50 **Review Concept** **Read ELL/ELD Readers** **Practice**	DI•41–DI•50 **Reiew Concept/Skills** **Reread ELL/ELD Reader** **Writing**

Week 2

Practice Stations for Everyone on Reading Street!

Word Wise
Words with schwa

Objectives
• Spell words with schwa.

Materials
• *Word Wise* Flip Chart Activity 12
• Teacher-made word cards
• paper • pencils

Differentiated Activities

⬤ Choose five word cards. Write the words in a list. Underline the vowel that makes the schwa sound in each word. Write sentences for each of your words.

▲ Choose seven word cards, and write your words in a list. Underline the vowel in each word that has the schwa sound. Write sentences using each of the words.

⬛ Choose ten word cards, and write your words in a list. Underline the vowel in each word that has the schwa sound. Then write a fictional paragraph using as many of your words as possible.

Technology
• Online Dictionary

Word Work
Words with schwa

Objectives
• Identify words with schwa.

Materials
• *Word Work* Flip Chart Activity 12
• Teacher-made word cards
• paper • pencils

Differentiated Activities

⬤ Choose six word cards. Write the words in a list. Say each word quietly to yourself. Circle the schwa sound in each word. Think of other words you know with a schwa sound. Add them to the list.

▲ Choose eight word cards, and write the words in a list. Quietly say each word. Circle the schwa sound in each word. Think of other words you know with a schwa sound, and add them to the list.

⬛ Choose twelve word cards. Write the words in a list, and quietly say each word. Circle the schwa in each word. Add other words with a schwa sound to the list.

Technology
• Modeled Pronunciation Audio CD

Words to Know
Multiple-meaning words

Objectives
• Determine the meanings of multiple-meaning words.

Materials
• *Words to Know* Flip Chart Activity 12
• Teacher-made word cards
• dictionary • paper • pencils

Differentiated Activities

⬤ Choose three word cards. Write the words in a list. Use the dictionary to find two different meanings for each word. Write two sentences for each word to show its different meanings.

▲ Choose five word cards, and write the words in a list. Use the dictionary to find two meanings for each word. Write two sentences for each word to show its multiple meanings.

⬛ Choose seven word cards, and write the words in a list. Write at least two sentences for each word to show its multiple meanings. Write sentences with other multiple-meaning words you know.

Technology
• Online Dictionary

You Are Here!
Unit 3
Week 2

Key

- ● Below-Level Activities
- ▲ On-Level Activities
- ■ Advanced Activities

Practice Station Flip Chart

Let's Write!
Play with dialogue

Objectives
- Write a short play with dialogue.

Materials
- *Let's Write!* Flip Chart Activity 12
- paper • pens or pencils

Differentiated Activities

● Imagine two young characters are working on an invention. Write a play that tells the story of their invention. Write dialogue that shows how young inventors would really speak to each other.

▲ Write a play about two young characters working on an invention. Write realistic dialogue that tells the story of their invention. Proofread your play, and focus on word choice.

■ Imagine three young friends are working on an invention. Write a short play that tells the story of their work. Write realistic dialogue to show how young inventors might speak. Proofread for word choice.

Technology
- Online Graphic Organizers

Read for Meaning
Identify sequence of events.

Objectives
- Identify the sequence of events in a selection.

Materials
- *Read for Meaning* Flip Chart Activity 12
- Leveled Readers
- paper • pencils

Differentiated Activities

● Choose and read a book from those your teacher provided. Make a list of the events that happened. Number the events to show the sequence they occurred.

▲ Choose and read a book from those your teacher provided. Think about the order of events. Write three sentences that tell the order of events. Use words such as *first, next,* and *finally* to help show the story's sequence of events.

■ Choose and read a book from those your teacher provided. Think about the sequence of events. Write a short paragraph that tells the story's sequence of events in the order they occur. Use words such as *first, next, then,* and *finally*.

Technology
- Leveled Reader Database

Get Fluent
Practice fluent reading.

Objectives
- Read aloud with expression.

Materials
- *Get Fluent* Chart Activity 12
- Leveled Readers

Differentiated Activities

● Work with a partner. Choose a Concept Literacy Reader or Below-Level Reader. Take turns reading a page from the book. Use the reader to practice correct expression. Provide feedback as needed.

▲ Work with a partner. Choose an On-Level Reader. Take turns reading a page from the book. Use the reader to practice correct expression. Provide feedback as needed.

■ Work with a partner. Choose an Advanced Reader. Take turns reading a page from the book. Use the reader to practice correct expression. Provide feedback as needed.

Technology
- Leveled Reader Database
- Reading Street Readers CD-ROM

Name _____ Date _____

My Work Plan
Put an ⊠ next to the activities you complete.

Word Wise
☐ Underline the schwa sound.
☐ Write sentences or a paragraph.

Let's Write!
☐ Write a play.
☐ Include dialogue.

Word Work
☐ Circle the schwa sound.
☐ List words.

Words to Know
☐ Define multiple-meaning words.
☐ Write sentences.

Get Fluent
☐ Read a leveled reader.

Read for Meaning
☐ Write the sequence of events.

Wrap Up Your Week Turn your paper over. Write about what you did at school. What did you read? What did you learn about art and artists?

Unit 3 • Week 2 • *Leonardo's Horse*

My Weekly Work Plan

week 2

Objectives
- Introduce the weekly concept.
- Develop oral vocabulary.

Today at a Glance

Oral Vocabulary
easel, charcoal, canvas

Comprehension
◉ Main idea and details
◉ Visualize

Reading
"Bronze"

Fluency
Rate

Lesson Vocabulary
Tested vocabulary

Research and Inquiry
Identify questions

Spelling
Compound words

Conventions
Principal parts of regular verbs

Handwriting
Cursive *j* and *J*

Writing
Persuasive speech

Concept Talk

Question of the Week

How do artists inspire future generations?

Introduce the concept

To further explore the unit concept of Inventors and Artists, this week students will read, write, and talk about inventors and artists and how they inspire future generations. Write the Question of the Week on the board.

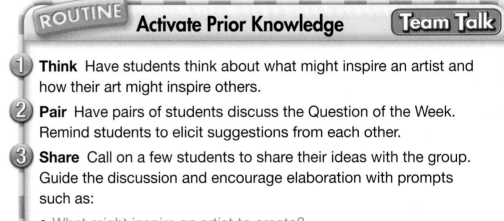

ROUTINE **Activate Prior Knowledge** **Team Talk**

1. **Think** Have students think about what might inspire an artist and how their art might inspire others.

2. **Pair** Have pairs of students discuss the Question of the Week. Remind students to elicit suggestions from each other.

3. **Share** Call on a few students to share their ideas with the group. Guide the discussion and encourage elaboration with prompts such as:
   - What might inspire an artist to create?
   - How can an artist's work inspire other people?

Routines Flip Chart

Anchored Talk

Develop oral vocabulary

Have students turn to pp. 354–355 in their Student Editions. Look at each of the photos. Then, use the prompts to guide discussion and create the *How artists inspire future generations* concept map.

- What are these students doing? (making art) What medium did they use to make their art? (paint) How might their art inspire others? (giving other artists ideas about mediums or creations) Let's add *inspiring other artists* to our concept map.

- These people are looking at the sculpture of what famous person?(Abraham Lincoln, Lincoln Memorial, Washington D.C.) How does this sculpture inspire others? (It inspires them to remember Lincoln and what he stood for and try to improve themselves.) Let's add *helping remember people* and *events* and *inspiring others to improve* to our concept map.

Objectives
• Listen to and interpret a speaker's messages and ask questions.

Oral Vocabulary

Let's Talk About

Art and Artists
• Share opinions about art and artists.
• Listen to a classmate's ideas about art.
• Ask a classmate questions about art.

READING STREET ONLINE
CONCEPT TALK VIDEO
www.ReadingStreet.com

You've learned **1 1 0** Amazing Words ★ so far this year!

354 355

Student Edition pp. 354–355

Amazing Words

You've learned **1 1 0** words so far
You'll learn **0 1 0** words this week!

easel	sculpture
charcoal	projector
canvas	medium
gallery	muse
marble	inspire

Writing on Demand

Writing Fluency
Ask students to respond to the photos on pp. 354–355 by writing as well as they can and as much as they can about the way artists inspire future generations.

ELL

English Language Learners
ELL support Additional ELL support and modified instruction is provided in the *ELL Handbook* and in the ELL Support lessons on pp. DI•41–DI•50.

Listening comprehension
English learners will benefit from additional visual support to understand the key terms in the concept map. Use the pictures on pp. 354–355 to scaffold understanding.

Frontload for Read Aloud Use the modified Read Aloud on p. DI•44 of the ELL Support lessons to prepare students to listen to "Norman Rockwell" (p. 355b).

• Why is the woman drawing the Greek ruins? (The work of the Greeks inspired her with their beauty and magnificence.) Let's add *Adding beauty to the world* to our concept map.

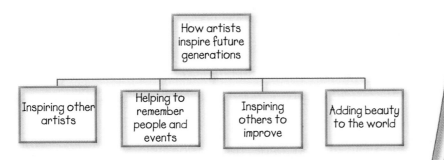

How artists inspire future generations
— Inspiring other artists
— Helping to remember people and events
— Inspiring others to improve
— Adding beauty to the world

Connect to reading
Tell students that this week they will be reading about many different artists. Throughout the week, encourage students to add concept-related words to this week's concept map.

ELL Preteach Concepts Use the Day 1 instructions on ELL Poster 12 to assess and build background knowledge, develop concepts, and build oral vocabulary.

ELL Poster 12

Leonardo's Horse **354–355**

Objectives
- Develop listening comprehension.
- Develop oral vocabulary.

Check Oral Vocabulary
SUCCESS PREDICTOR

Oral Vocabulary
Amazing Words

Introduce Amazing Words

"Norman Rockwell" on p. 355b is about the famous artist, Norman Rockwell, and how he was inspired to make an important change in his art. Tell students to listen for this week's Amazing Words—*easel*, *charcoal*, and *canvas*—as you read.

Model fluency

As you read "Norman Rockwell," model appropriate rate by reading at an appropriate speed that will improve the listener's comprehension.

Teach Amazing Words

Amazing Words Oral Vocabulary Routine

easel
charcoal
canvas

1 Introduce Write the word *easel* on the board. Have students say the word aloud with you. In "Norman Rockwell," we read that Norman Rockwell used an easel when he drew. Let's use context clues from the passage and what we already know to help define *easel.* An *easel* is a stand for holding a picture.

2 Demonstrate Break into groups. Have students elicit suggestions from other group members to demonstrate understanding. What does an easel look like? Have you ever used an easel or seen one being used by an artist? When do artists use them?

3 Apply Ask students to draw a picture of an *easel*.

See p. OV•2 to teach *charcoal* and *canvas*.

Routines Flip Chart

Apply Amazing Words

To build oral language, have students discuss the Amazing Words.

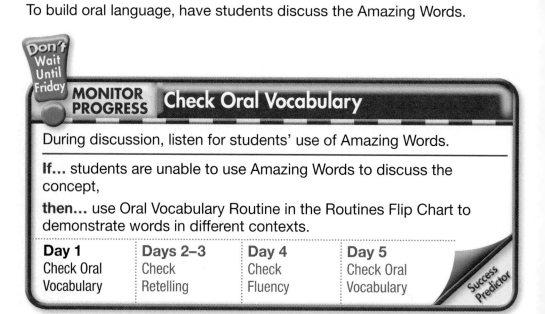

Don't Wait Until Friday

MONITOR PROGRESS Check Oral Vocabulary

During discussion, listen for students' use of Amazing Words.

If... students are unable to use Amazing Words to discuss the concept,

then... use Oral Vocabulary Routine in the Routines Flip Chart to demonstrate words in different contexts.

Day 1	Days 2–3	Day 4	Day 5
Check Oral Vocabulary	Check Retelling	Check Fluency	Check Oral Vocabulary

Success Predictor

Norman Rockwell

by Beverly Gherman

During his career, Norman Rockwell became one of the best-known artists in the country. He was especially popular for his covers for the magazine Saturday Evening Post. *In this excerpt, Rockwell is reluctantly moving from using live models to a new technology.*

By the mid-1930s, Norman Rockwell noticed that his covers were all done from the same angles because he always drew from his easel. Maybe he should try photography after all. He set up the scene for his model, arranged the props, and hired a photographer to take hundreds of shots. He discovered that it made a tremendous difference. Photographs provided him many more angles and details all at once, and he didn't have to keep a model for days when that person needed to be back on the farm or in the classroom.

Once the photographs were developed, he spread them out all over the floor and chose the ones he liked the best. Then he made a few small pencil sketches to organize his material. At last he was ready to do a full-size charcoal drawing.

He transferred the charcoal layout to a canvas, either by tracing it with a special tracing paper or by using a projector... to enlarge the image onto a canvas that might be four feet tall.

At last he was ready to start working in color. He was always nervous that he would get tense and spoil the painting, but it rarely happened. The final painting could take a few days or a few weeks, depending upon how complicated that picture was.

When he was beginning his career, people always called him "the kid with the camera eye" because he captured a scene so accurately. Now he added the actual camera lens to his own good eye, and the combination made his work richer and even more interesting.

Oral Vocabulary

Success Predictor

DAY 1 Read and Comprehend
30–35 mins.

Objectives

- Identify main ideas and details to aid comprehension.
- Use the visualize strategy to aid comprehension.
- Read grade-level text at an appropriate rate.

Skills Trace

Main Idea and Details
Introduce U3W2D1; U3W4D1; U6W2D1
Practice U3W2D2; U3W2D3; U3W4D2; U3W4D3; U6W2D2; U6W2D3
Reteach/Review U3W2D5; U3W3DXX; U3W4D5; U5W2DXX; U6W2D5; U6W4DXX
Assess/Test Weekly Tests U3W1; U3W4; U6W2 Benchmark Tests U3

KEY:
U=Unit W=Week D=Day

Skill ↔ Strategy
Main Idea and Details
Visualize

Introduce main idea and details

The main idea is the most important idea about a topic. Details are smaller pieces of information that support the main idea by telling more about it. Sometimes the author states the main idea of a text in a single sentence. When the main idea is not stated, readers must use information in the text to figure it out. Summarizing details can help you. **Have students turn to p. EI•12 in the Student Edition to review main ideas and details. Then read "Bronze" with students.**

Envision It!

Student Edition p. EI•12

Model the skill

Think Aloud Today we will read about how bronze has been used to make art. We will look for the main ideas and details in the passage as we read. In paragraph one, the main idea is that bronze has been used for thousands of years to make things. The important details that support this are: Bronze is made from copper and tin. Bronze is soft and can be hammered and bent. In molten form, bronze can be shaped into statues, pots, and bowls.

Guide practice

Have students finish reading "Bronze" on their own. After they read, have them use a graphic organizer like the one on p. 356 and identify the main ideas and details in each of the remaining paragraphs of the passage.

Strategy check

Visualize Remind students that if they have difficulty understanding "Bronze," they can use the strategy of visualizing. Model the strategy of rereading to adjust comprehension.

Model the strategy

Think Aloud Let's visualize the information in the second paragraph. First a model is made from plaster or clay. I picture a clay apple in my mind. Then the model is coated in wax. Then another layer of clay is added. Next, it is heated and the max melts away, leaving a space. I picture that in my mind, too. Then bronze is melted and poured into the space left by the wax. I can visualize and understand how a bronze apple is formed in this space. **Have students review the strategy of visualize on p. EI•25 of the Student Edition.**

Envision It!

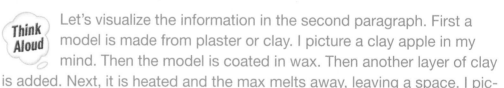

On their own

Use p. 189 in the *Reader's and Writer's Notebook* for additional practice with main idea and supporting details.

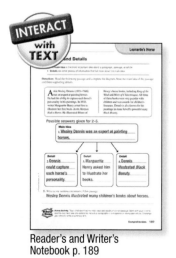

Reader's and Writer's Notebook p. 189

Visualize

Student Edition p. EI•25

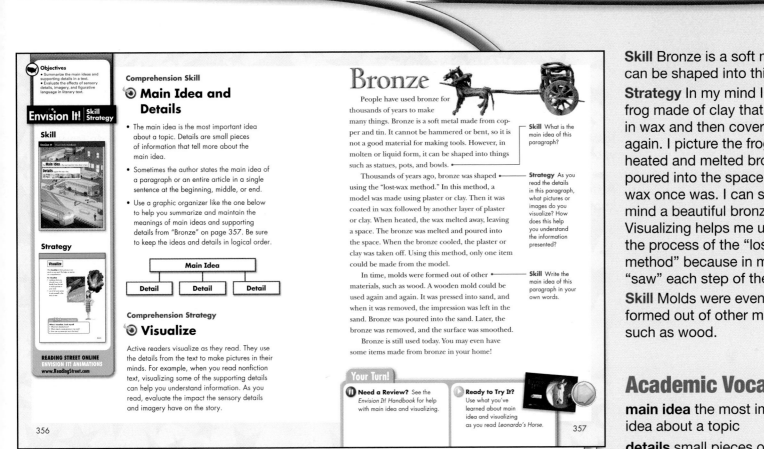

Student Edition pp.356–357

Objectives
- Summarize the main ideas and supporting details in a text.
- Evaluate the effects of sensory details, imagery, and figurative language in literary text.

Envision It! Skill Strategy

Skill

Strategy
Visualize

READING STREET ONLINE
ENVISION IT! ANIMATIONS
www.ReadingStreet.com

356

Comprehension Skill

Main Idea and Details

- The main idea is the most important idea about a topic. Details are small pieces of information that tell more about the main idea.
- Sometimes the author states the main idea of a paragraph or an entire article in a single sentence at the beginning, middle, or end.
- Use a graphic organizer like the one below to help you summarize and maintain the meanings of main ideas and supporting details from "Bronze" on page 357. Be sure to keep the ideas and details in logical order.

Main Idea		
Detail	Detail	Detail

Comprehension Strategy

Visualize

Active readers visualize as they read. They use the details from the text to make pictures in their minds. For example, when you read nonfiction text, visualizing some of the supporting details can help you understand information. As you read, evaluate the impact the sensory details and imagery have on the story.

Bronze

People have used bronze for thousands of years to make many things. Bronze is a soft metal made from copper and tin. It cannot be hammered or bent, so it is not a good material for making tools. However, in molten or liquid form, it can be shaped into things such as statues, pots, and bowls.

Skill What is the main idea of this paragraph?

Thousands of years ago, bronze was shaped using the "lost-wax method." In this method, a model was made using plaster or clay. Then it was coated in wax followed by another layer of plaster or clay. When heated, the wax melted away, leaving a space. The bronze was melted and poured into the space. When the bronze cooled, the plaster or clay was taken off. Using this method, only one item could be made from the model.

Strategy As you read the details in this paragraph, what pictures or images do you visualize? How does this help you understand the information presented?

In time, molds were formed out of other materials, such as wood. A wooden mold could be used again and again. It was pressed into sand, and when it was removed, the impression was left in the sand. Bronze was poured into the sand. Later, the bronze was removed, and the surface was smoothed.

Skill Write the main idea of this paragraph in your own words.

Bronze is still used today. You may even have some items made from bronze in your home!

Your Turn!

⏸ **Need a Review?** See the *Envision It! Handbook* for help with main idea and visualizing.

▶ **Ready to Try It?** Use what you've learned about main idea and visualizing as you read *Leonardo's Horse*.

357

Skill Bronze is a soft metal that can be shaped into things.

Strategy In my mind I picture a frog made of clay that is dipped in wax and then covered in clay again. I picture the frog being heated and melted bronze being poured into the space where the wax once was. I can see in my mind a beautiful bronze frog. Visualizing helps me understand the process of the "lost-wax method" because in my mind I "saw" each step of the process.

Skill Molds were eventually formed out of other materials, such as wood.

Academic Vocabulary

main idea the most important idea about a topic

details small pieces of information that tell more about the main idea

Model Fluency
Rate

Model fluent reading

Have students listen as you read the first paragraph of "Bronze," at an appropriate rate. Explain that you will not read too quickly because of the factual content. Point out that you will slow down particularly when the text introduces a new word or fact.

ROUTINE **Oral Reading**

① **Select a passage** For "Bronze," use paragraph one.

② **Model** Have students listen as you read with appropriate rate.

③ **Guide Practice** Have students read along with you.

④ **On Their Own** For optimal fluency, students should reread three or four times with appropriate rate.

Routines Flip Chart

English Language Learners
Main idea and details Ask students to name words and phrases which are synonyms for *main idea* (the most important point) and *details* (points that prove the main idea).

Objectives
- Activate prior knowledge of words.
- Identify questions for research.

Vocabulary
Tested Vocabulary

Lesson vocabulary

Use the following question-and-answer activity to help students improve their reading, speaking, listening, and writing vocabularies.

Activate prior knowledge

Review vocabulary words with students, asking them what they already know about each word. Then ask the following questions. Have students respond *yes* or *no* and give reasons for their choice.

- Is it an important thing to have *achieved* good grades?
- Is it important to use an *architect* when you build a new building?
- Could you use *bronze* if you were making a statue?
- Would you be more likely to see a *cannon* on an 18th century ship or on a modern ship?
- If someone smiles a lot, would you say they were *depressed*?
- Would you buy a hammer that was *fashioned* from clay?
- If you were in the *midst* of a project, would you want to leave it?
- Would a *philosopher* work at a construction site?
- Is a *rival* someone you are likely to ask to your birthday party?

Greek and Latin roots

Use the word *architect* to point out that some words are derived from Greek and Latin roots. Show students the root words *arch* (chief) and *tect* (builder) and have them identify the two roots in *architect.* Ask students to determine the meaning of *architect.* By the end of the week, students should know the vocabulary words. They can write other *yes* and *no* questions for classmates to answer.

Preteach Academic Vocabulary

ELL **Academic Vocabulary** Write the following words on the board:

main idea and details	tone
Greek and Latin roots	rate
historical fiction	problem and solution

Have students share what they know about this week's Academic Vocabulary. Use the students' responses to assess their prior knowledge. Preteach the Academic Vocabulary by providing a student-friendly description, explanation, or example that clarifies the meaning of each term. Ask students to define the Academic Vocabulary term in their own words.

Research and Inquiry
Identify Questions

Teach

Discuss the Question of the Week: *How do artists inspire future generations?* Tell students they will research the ways in which artists inspire future generations. They will use their research to prepare written reports that they will share with the class on Day 5.

Model

Think Aloud I know that many artists have inspired future generations. I'll choose just one artist: Norman Rockwell. I have seen his work before, and I think that his paintings may have inspired other American artists and the American public. Some possible questions could be *How has Norman Rockwell's art inspired other artists? How has his art inspired the American public?*

Guide practice

Have students decide on a topic and formulate open-ended inquiry questions about their artists. Explain that tomorrow they will use periodicals and reference texts to search for information. Have students generate a research plan for their search.

On their own

Have pairs of students work to write an inquiry question.

INTERNET GUY
Don Leu

21st Century Skills

Weekly Inquiry Project

Day 1 Identify Questions

Day 2 Navigate/Search

Day 3 Analyze

Day 4 Synthesize

Day 5 Communicate

Academic Vocabulary

Greek and Latin roots A Greek or Latin root is a word or part of a word from the Greek or Latin languages that is used to build many English words.

Small Group Time

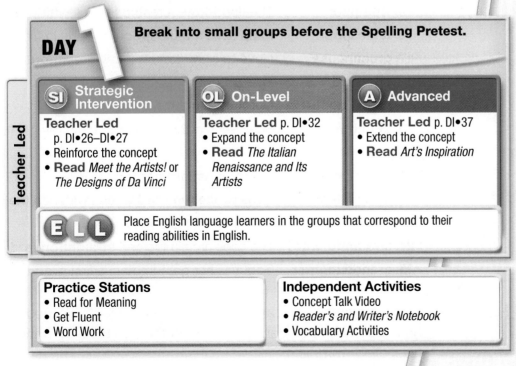

DAY 1

Break into small groups before the Spelling Pretest.

Teacher Led

SI Strategic Intervention

Teacher Led p. DI•26–DI•27
• Reinforce the concept
• **Read** *Meet the Artists!* or *The Designs of Da Vinci*

OL On-Level

Teacher Led p. DI•32
• Expand the concept
• **Read** *The Italian Renaissance and Its Artists*

A Advanced

Teacher Led p. DI•37
• Extend the concept
• **Read** *Art's Inspiration*

ELL Place English language learners in the groups that correspond to their reading abilities in English.

Practice Stations
• Read for Meaning
• Get Fluent
• Word Work

Independent Activities
• Concept Talk Video
• *Reader's and Writer's Notebook*
• Vocabulary Activities

ELL

English Language Learners

Multilingual vocabulary
Students can apply knowledge of their home languages to acquire new English vocabulary by using the Multilingual Vocabulary Lists (*ELL Handbook*, pp. 431–444).

Objectives

- Practice spelling compound words correctly.
- Use and understand the principal parts of regular verbs.
- Write cursive lowercase and capital *j* and *J* with correct letter formation.

Spelling Pretest
Compound Words

Introduce Tell students to think of words that are made of two words that function together as one *(birdhouse, mailbox)*. Students will use spelling rules and patterns to spell these words. This week we will spell compound words.

Pretest Use these sentences to administer the spelling pretest. Say each word, read the sentence, and repeat the word.

1. waterproof	My new jacket is **waterproof**.
2. teaspoon	Put one **teaspoon** of salt in the bowl.
3. grasshopper	A **grasshopper** flew out of the grass.
4. homesick	I feel **homesick** for my mother.
5. barefoot	I like to walk **barefoot** through the grass.
6. courthouse	The post office is across from the **courthouse**.
7. earthquake	California had a huge **earthquake**.
8. rowboat	Raul goes fishing in his **rowboat**.
9. scrapbook	I keep my award certificates in a **scrapbook**.
10. countryside	The sun set over the **countryside**.
11. lightweight	This book is surprisingly **lightweight**.
12. fishhook	Maya caught a pike on her **fishhook**.
13. spotlight	The **spotlight** shone on the movie stars.
14. blindfold	He wears a **blindfold** to hit the piñata.
15. whirlpool	The flood water created a small **whirlpool**.
16. tablespoon	Papa uses a **tablespoon** of garlic in his sauce.
17. greenhouse	I love to grow flowers in my **greenhouse**.
18. postcard	That **postcard** needs a special stamp.
19. hummingbird	Our **hummingbird** feeder is empty.
20. thumbtack	She needs a **thumbtack** to hang her painting.

Challenge words

21. sledgehammer	That **sledgehammer** is so loud!
22. brokenhearted	I was **brokenhearted** when I watched the movie.
23. chalkboard	Write your name on the **chalkboard**.
24. straightforward	The rules are simple and **straightforward**.
25. granddaughter	Gabby is her grandmother's first **granddaughter**.

Self-correct After the pretest, you can either display the correctly spelled words or spell them orally. Have students self-correct their pretests by writing misspelled words.

For additional practice, use *Let's Practice It!* p. 132 on the *Teacher Resources DVD-ROM*.

Let's Practice It!
TR DVD•132

Conventions
Principal Parts of Regular Verbs

Grammar Transparency 12,
TR DVD

Teach Display Grammar Transparency 12, and read aloud the explanation and examples in the box. Point out the differences between present, present participle, past, and past participle verbs.

Model Model identifying the correct regular verb principal parts to complete numbers 1 and 2. Apply the rules for identification to show how you determined the correct parts.

Guide practice Guide students to complete items 3–9. Remind them that a regular verb forms its past and past participle by adding -ed or -d to the present form. Record the correct responses on the transparency.

Daily Fix-It Use Daily Fix-It numbers 1 and 2 in the right margin.

Connect to oral language Have students read sentences 10 to 13 on the transparency and write the correct principal part to identify the underlined verbs.

Handwriting
Cursive *j* and *J*

Model letter formation Display the capital and lowercase cursive *j* and *J*. Follow the stroke instruction pictured to model letter formation.

Model legibility Explain that writing legibly means letters are the correct shape. The writing has straight or curved parts that go together to properly shape the letter. Model writing this sentence with proper letter shapes: *Jezebel jokes Josh about his job.* Make sure the letters aren't too light, dark, or jagged.

Guide practice Have students write these sentences: *Javier jingled the bells. Jaqueline loves jelly.* Circulate around the room, guiding students.

ELL

English Language Learners
Language production:
Regular verbs Review the rules for principal parts of regular verbs. Then provide support based on students' proficiency levels.

Beginning Have students identify the principal parts in these phrases: *The book describes; The girls have created.*

Intermediate Have students identify principal parts in three sentences and read them aloud.

Advanced/Advanced High Have students identify all of the principal parts from one paragraph of *Leonardo's Horse.*

Handwriting: Letter Shape Model proper letter shape by writing *Jim flies a jet* using incorrect letter shapes for the *j* and *J*. Then show students how to properly shape the letters, and have them write the sentence.

Objectives
• Identify the elements of a persuasive speech.

Writing for Tests—Persuasive Speech
Introduce

MINI-LESSON

5 Day Planner
Guide to Mini-Lessons

DAY **1**	Read Like a Writer
DAY **2**	Establish a Position
DAY **3**	Evaluation
DAY **4**	Detailed and Relevant Information
DAY **5**	Proofread for Principal Parts of Verbs

MINI-LESSON

Read Like a Writer

▌ **Introduce** This week you will write a **persuasive speech**. Persuasive speeches attempt to get others to agree with and support ideas about a topic. They include **sound reasoning**.

Genre	Persuasive Speech
Trait	Focus/Ideas
Mode	Narrative

INTERACT with TEXT

Name _____

Writing · Writing for Tests

How Cell Phones Changed Lives

1. Underline the topic sentence.
2. List two examples of details or relevant evidence that support the writer's viewpoint.
   Cell phones can send e-mail. You can call someone from almost anywhere.
3. Circle where the writer tries to get support for the idea.

190 Writing Writing for Tests

Reader's and Writer's Notebook, p. 190

▌ **Examine Model Text** Let's read an example of a persuasive speech written in response to a writing prompt on a test. This speech answers a question about which recent invention has changed people's lives the most. Have students read "How Cell Phones Changed Lives" on p. 190 of their *Reader's and Writer's Notebook.*

▌ **Key Features** Persuasive speeches **include a clear focus or idea**. This idea or argument is **stated in a topic sentence**. Find the topic sentence in the model and underline it. Have students interact by underlining the first sentence. Discuss how the idea is clear because it uses *is* instead of *is maybe* or *might be.*

Persuasive speeches **include details and relevant evidence** that support the idea. Have students locate two examples of relevant evidence in the speech.

Writers **try to gain support** for their ideas in persuasive speeches. They want the listener to agree with them. Circle where the writer tries to gain support in this speech. Help students recognize that *Don't you agree?* is a persuasive question geared toward gathering support.

Review key features

Review the key features of a persuasive speech with students. You may want to post the key features in the classroom for students to reference as they work on their compositions.

Key Features of a Persuasive Speech

- includes a clear focus or idea
- tries to get support for an idea
- has the argument or idea stated in a topic sentence
- includes details and relevant evidence to support viewpoint
- uses sound reasoning
- is written for an appropriate audience

Write Guy
Jeff Anderson

Active Verbs Snap

Writing snaps and sizzles when active, lively verbs are used. Using specific words gives writing voice, develops diction, and increases vocabulary. Note the way authors use these powerful verbs. Contrasting them with less powerful verbs can show students the difference.

ROUTINE **Quick Write for Fluency** **Team Talk**

1. **Talk** Have pairs discuss the key features of a persuasive speech.
2. **Write** Each person writes three sentences about why people write persuasive speeches.
3. **Share** Partners read one another's writing.

Routines Flip Chart

Wrap Up Your Day

✔ **Build Concepts** What did you learn about how artists inspire future generations?

✔ **Oral Vocabulary** Have students use the Amazing Words they learned in context sentences.

✔ **Homework** Send home this week's Family Times newsletter on *Let's Practice It!* pp. 133–134 on the *Teacher Resources DVD-ROM*.

Let's Practice It!
TR DVD•133–134

ELL

English Language Learners
Writing model Read aloud the writing model "How Cell Phones Changed Lives" and help students understand it. Discuss with students how they could tell this was a persuasive speech. Have students restate the important details. List them on the board.

Preview DAY 2

Tell students that tomorrow they will read about a very important man in history, one who was not only an artist, but an inventor as well.

Objectives
- Expand the weekly concept.
- Develop oral vocabulary.

Today at a Glance

Oral Vocabulary
gallery, marble

Word Analysis
Greek and Latin roots

Literary Terms
Tone

Story Structure
Conflict and resolution

Lesson Vocabulary
◉ Greek and Latin roots

Reading
"They Called It the Renaissance"

Fluency
Rate

Research and Inquiry
Navigate/Search

Spelling
Compound words

Conventions
Principal parts of regular verbs

Writing
Persuasive speech

Concept Talk

Question of the Week

How do artists inspire future generations?

Expand the concept

Remind students of the weekly concept question. Tell students that today they will begin reading *Leonardo's Horse.* As they read, encourage students to think about the ways Leonardo da Vinci's art inspired future generations.

Anchored Talk

Develop oral vocabulary

Use the photos on pp. 354–355 and the Read Aloud, "Norman Rockwell," to talk about the Amazing Words: *easel, charcoal,* and *canvas.* Add these and other concept-related words to the concept map to develop students' knowledge of the topic. Break into groups. Have students discuss the following questions, asking questions to clarify the speaker's perspective and considering suggestions from other group members.

- We have read that Norman Rockwell used *charcoal* to make his drawings. How might this inspire other artists?

- How does Norman Rockwell use *charcoal,* an *easel,* and *canvas* in his work?

- How could learning about Norman Rockwell's work and his use of *charcoal, canvas,* and an *easel* inspire other people?

- What was Norman Rockwell inspired to do instead of drawing from an easel? Why did he decide to try it? Was it successful?

Oral Vocabulary
Amazing Words

Amazing Words

easel	sculpture
charcoal	projector
canvas	medium
gallery	muse
marble	inspire

Amazing Words Oral Vocabulary Routine

Teach Amazing Words

1 **Introduce** Write the Amazing Word *gallery* on the board. Have students say it aloud with you. Relate *gallery* to the photographs on pages 352–353 and "Norman Rockwell." Where do you think you could go to see Norman Rockwell's paintings? (to a gallery) What else might you find in a gallery? (sculptures, other works of art) Have students determine the definition of the word. A gallery is a place where artwork is displayed for the public to view.

2 **Demonstrate** Have students ask and answer questions to demonstrate understanding. Can anybody display their artwork in a gallery? Why or why not? How are all galleries the same? How might galleries be different? (All galleries display art in some form, but they may differ in their size, the type of art they display, and where they are.) Have you ever been to a gallery? Could we make a gallery in our school?

3 **Apply** Have students apply their understanding. Give examples of three different types of galleries that you know of.

See p. OV•2 to teach *marble*.

Routines Flip Chart

Apply Amazing Words

As students read "They Called It the Renaissance" on p. 359, have them think about how *marble* may have been used by artists of the Renaissance, and about the importance of *galleries* at that time.

Connect to reading

Explain that today students will read about an artist and inventor named Leonardo da Vinci, who lived during the Renaissance. As they read, they should think about how the concept question *How do artists inspire future generations?* and the Amazing Words *marble* and *gallery,* apply to what they read in *Leonardo's Horse.*

ELL **Reinforce Vocabulary** Use the Day 2 instructions on ELL Poster 12 to teach lesson vocabulary and discuss the lesson concept.

Connect to Social Studies

Many famous sculptures of the Renaissance, such as Michelangelo's statue of David, were carved from Carrara marble. Carrara marble came from quarries of white and blue-gray marble located around the city of Carrara, Italy.

ELL Poster 12

Objectives
- Determine the meaning of words derived from Greek and Latin roots.
- Evaluate the author's tone in an expository text.
- Identify the story structure of conflict and resolution.

Word Analysis
Greek and Latin Roots

Teach Greek and Latin roots

Tell students that a Greek or Latin root is a word or part of a word from the Greek or Latin languages. Greek and Latin roots are often used to build English words. Have students guess the meanings of the words in the first column based on the meanings of their roots in the second column.

Model

The word *claustrophobia* comes from the Latin root *claustrum,* which means "a closed space," and the Greek root *phobia,* which means "fear." These two roots make the word *claustrophobia.* I think a person who has claustrophobia is afraid of being in closed places. When I look up the word *claustrophobia* in the dictionary, its meaning is similar to my definition.

English Word	Greek or Latin roots
claustrophobia	*claustrum* (closed space) *phobia* (fear)
fashioned	*facere* (do, make)
depressed	*depressare* (press down)

Guide practice

Have students determine the meanings of the other words based on the root words' meanings.

On their own

Have students use a printed or electronic dictionary to verify that the words' meanings are correct. Follow the Strategy for Meaningful Word Parts to teach the word *archaeology.*

> **ROUTINE** **Strategy for Meaningful Word Parts**
>
> 1. **Introduce word parts** Write the word: *archaeology*. I will circle the Greek root, *archae* and the suffix *-logy.*
>
> 2. **Connect to meaning** Define the root. The root *archae* comes from the Greek word for "ancient." I also know that the suffix *-logy* means "the science of" or "the study of."
>
> 3. **Read the word** Blend the meaningful word parts together to read *archaeology*. *Archaeology* means "the study of ancient things."
>
> Continue the Routine with the words *archaic* and *agoraphobia.*

Routines Flip Chart

Literary Terms
Tone

Teach tone

Tell students that tone is the author's attitude toward the subject or the audience. Tone in writing is like tone of voice in speaking. It shows how the author feels about the subject. For example, tone may show respect, disdain, or humor. The tone is shown through word choice, style, and the descriptions an author writes.

Model tone

Think Aloud Let's look at "They Called It the Renaissance" on page 359. What words would you use to describe the tone? (excited, admiring) Can you point out any words in the selection that define the tone? *(exciting, important, powerful, vivid)*

Guide practice

Tell students to pay attention to tone as they read *Leonardo's Horse.* Have students ask themselves what the author's attitude is toward Leonardo da Vinci and his accomplishments.

On their own

Have students describe the tone of other selections in their Student Editions and look for language that helps them to define the tone.

Story Structure
Conflict and Resolution

Teach conflict and resolution

A biography sometimes uses the story structure of conflict and resolution. A conflict can be between characters or one character's internal struggle. In expository text, the character is a real person, and the conflict is a real conflict that they faced.

Model the strategy

Think Aloud The structure of conflict and resolution makes texts interesting to read. We follow the story to see how the conflict is resolved. In *The Fabulous Perpetual Motion Machine,* the conflict arises from the characters not knowing what the machine is or how it works. The conflict builds as each incident gives rise to the next. Some incidents even foreshadow the resolution. How is the conflict resolved? (The characters figure out how the machine works and realize it is not what it seems.)

Guide practice

Have students answer this question: Where do you see the structure of conflict and resolution in other selections we've read?

On their own

Have students make a T-chart to note incidents in *Leonardo's Horse* that advance the conflict and lead to resolution as they read.

Academic Vocabulary

tone the author's attitude toward the subject or audience

Greek and Latin roots word parts derived from Greek and Latin that are combined with other affixes or roots to form new words

Objectives

◎ Use word structure to determine the meanings of words derived from Greek and Latin roots.

• Read grade-level text at an appropriate rate.

Vocabulary Strategy For
Greek and Latin Roots

Student Edition p. W•9

Teach Greek and Latin roots

Tell students that many words in English have Greek and Latin roots. For example, the Latin word *canna* means "small reed." It is found as the root of words such as *cane* and *cannon*. Explain that the strategy of looking at a word's structure—its roots and affixes—may offer clues to help determine and clarify the meaning of words. Ask students how the word *canna*, which is a small reed (a reed is a tube), helps them to understand the meaning of the word *cannon.* Refer students to *Words!* on p. W•9 in the Student Edition for additional practice.

Model the strategy

Think Aloud Write the word *philosopher* on the board. When I look up the word *philosopher* in the dictionary, I see that it comes from the Greek roots *phil* ("love") and *sophia* ("wisdom"). Underline the roots in the word. Knowing that the word *philosopher* comes from these roots can help me to figure out and understand its meaning. Someone who is a *philosopher* loves wisdom.

Guide practice

Write this sentence on the board: *The architect created a plan for the building that the construction workers followed.* Tell students that the Greek root *arkhi* means "chief" and the Greek root *tekton* means "builder." Have students use word structure to determine the meaning of *architect.* Then have them find *architect* in a dictionary and revise or confirm their definition. For additional support, use *Envision It! Pictured Vocabulary Cards* or *Tested Vocabulary Cards*.

On their own

Read "They Called it the Renaissance" on p. 359. Have students use Greek and Latin roots to find the meanings of the lesson vocabulary words. Then have them use a printed or electronic dictionary or glossary to check the meanings of the words and their Greek or Latin roots. For additional practice use *Readers and Writer's Notebook* p. 191.

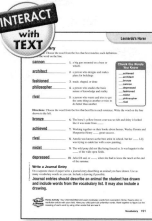

Reader's and Writer's Notebook p. 191

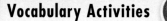

Student Edition pp. 358–359

(Objectives)
Objectives
• Determine the meaning of English words with roots from Greek, Latin, and other languages.

Envision It! Words to Know

architect

bronze

cannon

achieved
depressed
fashioned
midst
philosopher
rival

READING STREET ONLINE
VOCABULARY ACTIVITIES
www.ReadingStreet.com

358

Vocabulary Strategy for

◉ Greek and Latin Roots

Word Structure Many words in English, particularly academic vocabulary words, are based on Greek and Latin roots. For example, the Greek root *bio* means "life." The Latin word *canna* means "reed or tube." When you see a longer word you do not understand, look for a root that can help you figure out the meaning.

1. Look at the word. Try to identify its root.

2. Think of words you know where this same root appears, and then try to determine a meaning for the word.

3. Try the meaning in place of the unfamiliar word and see if it makes sense in the sentence.

Read "They Called It the Renaissance." Use your knowledge of Greek and Latin roots to help you determine the meanings of words such as *architect, philosopher,* or *achieved.*

Words to Write Reread "They Called It the Renaissance." Look at the illustrations in *Leonardo's Horse.* Write a paragraph about what you think he achieved. Use words from the *Words to Know* list in your writing.

They Called It the RENAISSANCE

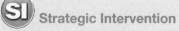

The Middle Ages ran from about 500 A.D. to about 1450 A.D. This was a time that might have depressed anyone. People in Europe looked back at the past instead of forward to the future.

But by 1450, people had stopped thinking only about the past and started looking ahead to what might be achieved in the future. This new age was known as the Renaissance.

Inventors started coming up with exciting new inventions. The title *philosopher* became important again, as thinkers explored new ways to enrich people's lives. The architect became an important figure as beautiful new buildings took shape in cities and towns across Europe. Artists fashioned powerful sculptures and painted vivid paintings that looked natural and real.

In the midst of all this growth and change, of course, there was still fighting. Art was the glory of the age, but war was the harsh reality. Bronze might be used to make a beautiful statue or a deadly cannon. People were sailing off to find new lands. A nation might become a rival of another nation, fighting for land in the Americas. In so many ways, people in the Renaissance were preparing for the modern world.

Your Turn!

Need a Review? For additional help with word structure and Greek and Latin roots, see *Words!*

Ready to Try It? Read *Leonardo's Horse* on pp. 360–377.

359

Lesson Vocabulary

achieved accomplished; did

architect person who designs buildings

bronze a dark yellow-brown alloy of copper and tin

cannon a big gun, especially one mounted on a base or wheels

depressed gloomy; low-spirited

fashioned made, shaped

midst in the middle of

philosopher person who studies in an attempt to discover and understand the basic nature of knowledge and reality

rival person or group which tries to do better than another

Differentiated Instruction

SI Strategic Intervention

Greek and Latin Roots Show students pictures of a tubular reed to help them understand the Latin root *canna.*

Reread for Fluency
Rate

Model fluent reading

Read the first paragraph of "They Called It the Renaissance" aloud, slowing your rate when reading new words and facts. Ask students to follow along as you read to see how you adjust your rate. Tell students that reading at an appropriate rate means reading at a slower pace when you are reading informational text.

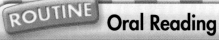

ROUTINE **Oral Reading**

1. **Select a passage** For "They Called It the Renaissance" use the whole passage.

2. **Model** Have students track the print as you read with appropriate rate.

3. **Guide Practice** Have students read along with you.

4. **On Their Own** Have the class read aloud without you. For optimal fluency, students should reread three or four times at an appropriate rate. Ask questions to be sure students comprehend the text.

ELL

English Language Learners
Build Academic Vocabulary
Use the lesson vocabulary pictured on p. 358 to teach the meanings of *architect, bronze* and *cannon.* Call on pairs to write the words on sticky notes and use them to label images of the words on the ELL Poster.

Objectives
- Understand the text features of a biography.
- Use text features to preview and predict.
- Set a purpose for reading.

BY JEAN FRITZ
ILLUSTRATED BY HUDSON TALBOTT

LEONARDO'S HORSE

Question of the Week
How do artists inspire future generations?

Genre A **biography** is a story of a person's life written by another person. As you read, notice all the major events in Leonardo da Vinci's life.

360

361

Student Edition pp. 360–361

Build Background

Discuss Leonardo da Vinci

Team Talk Have students turn to a partner and discuss the Question of the Week and these questions about Leonardo da Vinci.

- Who was Leonardo da Vinci and why is he well known?
- When did Leonardo da Vinci live?
- Where did Leonardo da Vinci live?
- How did Leonardo da Vinci's work inspire other people?

Connect to selection

Have students discuss their answers with the class. Possible responses: Leonardo da Vinci was a famous artist who lived in Italy in the 1400s during the time of the Italian Renaissance. He was not only an artist, but an inventor, architect, philosopher, musician, and astronomer. He inspired people with his knowledge, his inventions, and his art. Leonardo da Vinci's art, such as his famous painting of the Mona Lisa, is revered by people all over the world. For additional opportunities to build background, use the Background Building Audio.

Prereading Strategies

Genre
Explain that a **biography** is a story of a real person's life that is written by another person. Biographies may tell about a person's whole life, part of his or her life, or a single event. Explain to students that *Leonardo's Horse* tells the story of one of Leonardo da Vinci's inventions that proved difficult to create.

Preview and predict
Have students preview the title and illustrations of *Leonardo's Horse.* Have them predict what they will find out as they read.

Set purpose
Prior to reading, have students set their own purposes for reading this selection. To help students set a purpose, ask them to think about Leonardo da Vinci's achievements and how those achievements inspired future generations.

Strategy Response Log

Have students use their prior knowledge to visualize what they think *Leonardo's Horse* will be about. Have them write their responses on p. 18 in the *Reader's and Writer's Notebook.*

Small Group Time

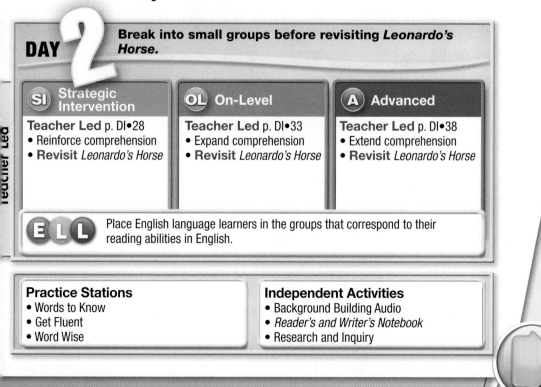

DAY 2

Break into small groups before revisiting *Leonardo's Horse.*

SI Strategic Intervention
Teacher Led p. DI•28
• Reinforce comprehension
• **Revisit** *Leonardo's Horse*

OL On-Level
Teacher Led p. DI•33
• Expand comprehension
• **Revisit** *Leonardo's Horse*

A Advanced
Teacher Led p. DI•38
• Extend comprehension
• **Revisit** *Leonardo's Horse*

ELL Place English language learners in the groups that correspond to their reading abilities in English.

Practice Stations
• Words to Know
• Get Fluent
• Word Wise

Independent Activities
• Background Building Audio
• *Reader's and Writer's Notebook*
• Research and Inquiry

Differentiated Instruction

 **A Advanced**
Have students list those who might be inspired by art, such as other artists, political leaders, or young people. Have pairs of students list five categories of people in a chart, and under each write how they might be inspired.

Double Day Read Multidraft Reading

For **Whole Group** instruction, choose one of the reading options below. For each reading, have students set the purpose indicated.

Option 1
Day 2 Read the selection. Use Guide Comprehension to monitor and clarify understanding.
Day 3 Reread the selection. Use Extend Thinking to develop higher-order thinking skills.

Option 2
Day 2 Read the first half of the selection, using both Guide Comprehension and Extend Thinking instruction.
Day 3 Read the second half of the selection, using both Guide Comprehension and Extend Thinking instruction.

ELL

English Language Learners
Build background To build background, review the selection summary in English in the (*ELL Handbook* p. 97). Use the Retelling Cards to provide visual support for the summary.

Objectives

◎ Identify the main idea and details of a text.

OPTION 1 Guide Comprehension Skills and Strategies

Teach Main Idea and Details

🔊 **Main Idea and Details** Tell students that the main idea on p. 363 is that Leonardo, even as a young man, had the makings of a great artist. Ask students to identify two details on this page that support the main idea. (Leonardo's stopping to examine everything, memorizing the landscape)

Let's Practice It!
TR DVD•135

Corrective Feedback

If... students are unable to identify two supporting details,
then... use the model to help them to identify supporting details.

Model the Skill

Think Aloud I will reread the text and ask myself which information shows why Leonardo might become a great artist. These are details which support the main idea.

362

Student Edition pp. 362–363

OPTION 2 Extend Thinking Think Critically

Higher-Order Thinking Skills

🔊 **Main Idea and Details • Analysis** Analyze the illustration on pages 362 and 363. What details can be found there which support the main idea that Leonardo da Vinci was on his way to becoming a great artist? **Possible response:** The illustration shows him sketching the landscape, carrying pens and other art supplies on his horse. It also depicts him with a look of serious concentration as he goes about his work—showing that he takes his art seriously.

Predicting • Synthesis Use what you already know about the Renaissance and the attitude toward artists at the time, along with what you have read about Leonardo's character, to make a prediction about what might happen to Leonardo as he grows up. **Possible response:** Knowing that artists had support and interest during the Renaissance, and that Leonardo had the makings of an artist, I can predict that Leonardo would have the support and environment he needed to become a great artist.

The text says that Leonardo stopped to examine everything. How does this support the idea that he might be a great artist? (Artists have to look closely at things to understand them and capture them on paper, on canvas, or as sculptures.)

ANYONE who watched the young Leonardo wander the countryside around his home in Vinci might have guessed that he would be an artist. He stopped to examine everything. He looked at the landscape as if he were memorizing it. So it was no surprise when his father took him as a young teenager to Florence to study art.

363

Author's Purpose • Evaluation Explain why the author chose to begin the text by showing what Leonardo was like when he was young. Was this an effective way to begin the story?
Possible response: The author starts the story when Leonardo is young to set up the biography in chronological order. It is effective because it establishes his character so the reader can understand Leonardo's motivations later in the story.

On Their Own

Have students reread p. 363 to find other examples of supporting details. For additional practice, use *Let's Practice It!* p. 135 on the *Teacher Resources DVD-ROM.*

Differentiated Instruction

(SI) Strategic Intervention

Graphic sources Discuss with students the advantages of graphic sources. Graphic sources can help readers get an overview of the text before they read, gain better understanding of the text as they read, and add extra information to the text. Help students identify how the illustration on this page does each of these things.

E L L

English Language Learners
Vocabulary Point to the word *landscape.* Tell students that a landscape is a view of an area of land, and also a picture or painting of that view. Discuss the details of the landscape on pp. 362–363 and ask: What do you think will be in the landscape Leonardo is drawing?

Activate prior knowledge Discuss with students the reasons why a person might want to become an artist and what they could do to become a great artist. Have students create a two-column chart titled, *Becoming an Artist,* listing their thoughts about why someone might want to become an artist *(Why)* and the things they could do to become a great artist *(How).*

Objectives

◉ Use Greek and Latin roots to determine and clarify the meaning of words.

Reader's and Writer's
Notebook p. 195

OPTION 1 Skills and Strategies, continued

Teach Greek and Latin Roots

◉ **Greek and Latin Roots** Remind students that examining the roots of words can help them determine the meaning of the words. Write these Greek roots on the board: *astr (star), ician (specialist in), arch (chief), tect (builder)*. Ask students to use the roots to help define and clarify the meanings of these words from p. 365: *architect, musician,* and *astronomer.*

Corrective Feedback

If... students have difficulty defining the words,

then... model how to use Greek and Latin roots to determine the meaning of a word.

Model the Skill

Think Aloud I can see that these words are made of different parts. In the word *astronomer* I see the root *astr* and the suffix *-er.* The Greek root *astr* means *star.* The suffix *-er* means *one who.*

Student Edition pp. 364–365

364

OPTION 2 Think Critically, continued

Higher-Order Thinking Skills

◉ **Greek and Latin Roots • Analysis** Write these Greek roots and suffixes on the board: *bio (life), geo (earth), logy (science of), logist (scientist)* Use these Greek roots and suffixes to create four words. Analyze each word based on its roots to determine its meaning. **Possible responses:** biology (science of life), biologist (scientist who studies life), geology (science of the earth), geologist (scientist who studies the earth)

Literary Language • Analysis Reread paragraph 3 on page 365. What do you notice about the sentences in this paragraph? Why do you think the author chose to use this type of language here? Possible response: The sentences are very short, and some are sentence fragments. The short sentences and fragments are startling, and the author uses them to show how surprising it is that Leonardo could write backwards and from right to left.

If I put these two meanings together, what can I learn about the word *astronomer*? (one who studies stars)

On Their Own

Have students use the root definitions on the board to determine the meanings of the words *musician* and *architect*. For additional practice use the *Reader's and Writer's Notebook* p. 195.

Connect to Social Studies

A Colonial da Vinci Many historians consider Benjamin Franklin to be the greatest Renaissance man, or universal genius, after Leonardo da Vinci. Franklin was not only a founding father, but he was also a scientist, writer, philosopher, musician, economist, and inventor. Although he was born in Boston, Philadelphia came to be known as his home. Today, visitors to the city will find his gravesite, his home, and The Franklin Institute Science Museum.

People noticed that Leonardo was different.

He dressed differently. While other young men wore long togas, Leonardo wore short, rose-colored velvet togas.

He wrote differently. Backwards. From the right side of the paper to the left. A person would have to use a mirror to read his writing.

And he wouldn't eat meat. He liked animals too much to eat anything that had once been alive. Nor could he stand the sight of caged birds. If he saw a man selling birds, he would buy them all. Then he would open the cages and watch the birds fly away. What a flurry they made! How did they do it? All his life Leonardo tried to discover their secret of flying so he could make a flying machine for himself.

For a man who liked to ask questions, Leonardo da Vinci was born at the right time—April 15, 1452. Everybody was asking questions then. The age was called the Renaissance, a time of rebirth when people who had forgotten how to be curious became curious again. They were exploring new countries, discovering, inventing, looking at old things in new ways. What was the point, Leonardo asked, in copying what had already been done? He had to bring his own experience into whatever he painted. You wouldn't catch him putting a halo around the head of a saint. How could he? He had never seen a halo.

Leonardo da Vinci turned out to be a famous artist; still, he was not just an artist. He could never be just one thing. He was an engineer, an architect, a musician, a philosopher, an astronomer. Once he fashioned a special kind of flute made of silver in the shape of a horse's head. The ruler of Florence, Lorenzo de' Medici, asked him to deliver it as a gift to the duke of Milan. This was lucky for Leonardo. He had heard that the duke of Milan wanted to honor his father with a bronze horse in front of his palace. And Leonardo wanted to be the one to make it.

365

 Visualize • Evaluation Read paragraph 4 on page 365. What words and phrases from the text can help you to form mental pictures as you read? Possible responses: open the cages, watch the birds fly away, flurry. How does visualizing the text help you monitor or adjust your comprehension? Possible response: It helps to understand how excited Leonardo must have been by the idea of flight.

English Language Learners
Understand language The next-to-last sentence on p. 365 has unclear antecedents, which may confuse some students. Read the sentence aloud, then reread the beginning: *He had heard.* Ask the students: To whom does he refer? (Leonardo) Reread more of the sentence: *The duke of Milan wanted to honor his father.* Ask the students: To whom does his refer? (The duke of Milan)

OPTION 1 Skills and Strategies, continued

Objectives
- Identify facts and opinions to improve comprehension.

Teach Fact and Opinion

Review **Fact and Opinion** Read the first paragraph of p. 366. Ask students whether what is said in this paragraph is fact or opinion, and have them support their answer. (opinion)

Corrective Feedback

If... students have difficulty answering the question,

then... model guiding students in identifying facts and opinions.

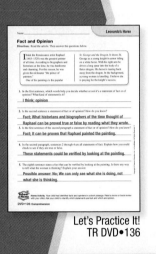

Let's Practice It!
TR DVD•136

Model the Skill

Think Aloud Who is making the statement that people would point to Leonardo's horse hundreds of years later and say "Leonardo made that"?

Temporary bridge

Eight-gun cannon

Armored tank

This would be his mark on history. Hundreds of years later people would point to the horse. "Leonardo made that," they would say.

So he wrote to the duke, listing all the things that he could do. He could make cannons, lightweight bridges, and covered chariots that couldn't be broken or harmed. On and on he went, but he saved the most important point for the last. He could make a bronze horse. In the end, he didn't send the letter. He simply left for Milan. Never mind that he was in the midst of painting a large religious picture in Florence. Let someone else finish it. He had planned the picture and that was the important part.

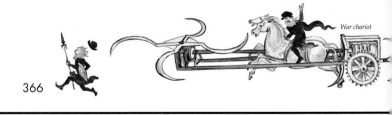

War chariot

366

Student Edition pp. 366–367

OPTION 2 Think Critically, continued

Higher-Order Thinking Skills

Review **Fact and Opinion • Synthesis** The first paragraph on page 366 shows Leonardo's opinion, his hope for the future. Pretend that Leonardo's wish came true. Rewrite the paragraph as fact, pretending that you are the author telling readers that this information is true. What changes would you make to the text? Possible response: Remove the future tense verbs, *would say, would point* and replace them with *said* and *pointed*.

Summarize • Analyze Summarize the second paragraph on page 366 by thinking about the information in the text and identifying the main idea. Use the main idea and any important details to give a short summary that maintains the meaning and order of the text. Possible response: Making the bronze horse was so important to Leonardo that he decided to leave a picture he was painting. Instead of sending a letter, he went to Milan to talk with the duke himself.

If we look back to p. 365, we can see that this statement comes from Leonardo's point of view. He is wishing that people would point to his horse and remember him. This is Leonardo's opinion, his hope about what will happen.

On Their Own

Have students look for other information in the text to identify as fact or opinion. For additional practice, use *Let's Practice It!* p. 136 on the *Teacher Resources DVD-ROM.*

Exploding cannonballs

Parachute

Cannon

Catapult

367

Inferring • Analyze Use your own experiences and what you have read in the text to make an inference about Leonardo's thoughts and feelings when he made the decision to go to Milan to see the duke. Consider any times when you wanted something badly enough to change your plans in order to pursue it.

Possible response: Leonardo was probably nervous, but he was confident that he needed to talk to the duke in person.

Differentiated Instruction

 Strategic Intervention

Fact and opinion Review with students how to use clue words to identify fact and opinion. In paragraph one, show the phrases *would point* and *they would say*. Explain that these verbs are in the future tense. This shows that Leonardo is projecting into the future about something that is not sure yet, and not a fact.

Connect to Social Studies

Da Vinci's bridge In November, 2001, a new bridge opened in Oslo, Norway. The bridge had been designed 500 years earlier by Leonardo da Vinci. Da Vinci first sketched the bridge for Sultan Bajazet II, but none of the Sultan's engineers believed it could be built. Rather than using a number of arches to hold the bridge up, da Vinci's design used only three arches.

ELL

English Language Learners

Build background Point to the picture of the catapult on p. 367. Explain that a catapult was a weapon that worked like a slingshot. It was used to throw large, heavy stones at the enemy. Point out other inventions in the illustrations and lead a discussion of other confusing terms. Then ask students to summarize the discussion in their own words.

Objectives

◎ Identify main idea and details.

OPTION 1 Skills and Strategies, continued

Teach Main Idea and Details

◉ **Main Idea and Details** Ask students to summarize the text on p. 369 by identifying and paraphrasing the main ideas of the text.

Corrective Feedback

If... students are unable to identify the main ideas of the text,

then... Use the model to guide students in identifying the main ideas.

Model the Skill

Think Aloud I can summarize the text on page 369 by restating the main idea in each paragraph. Write the following summary on the board, pointing out that each sentence states the main idea of each paragraph: *Leonardo studied live horses to learn about their muscles and bones and studied many statues of horses.*

Leonardo was thirty years old now, handsome with curly blond hair. The duke gave him the job of working on the horse, but at the same time he was expected to take charge of entertainment in the palace. He had a beautiful singing voice, he could play musical instruments, he could juggle and ask riddles, and he was also asked to stage elaborate plays for special occasions. Whenever he had a chance, he went back to the horse.

He visited the stables, studying how a horse was put together.

368

Student Edition pp. 368–369

OPTION 2 Think Critically, continued

Higher-Order Thinking Skills

◉ **Main Idea and Details • Evaluation** Reread the first paragraph on page 368. Evaluate these two summaries of the paragraph's main idea and details. Which is a better summary of the paragraph and why? 1. Leonardo got the job of making the horse and the duke also put him in charge of entertainment at the palace. 2. Leonardo was a handsome thirty-year-old, and the duke gave him many jobs at the palace.

Possible response: The first summary accurately states the main idea of the paragraph. The second focuses on details and does not express the main idea, which is about the horse.

But just as Leonardo was ready to start, the Duke of Milan decided he wanted a bigger horse. Leonardo collects the metal for the horse, but he is not sure how to proceed. Summarizing this way tells the reader the most important information from the text and keeps a logical order by following the order of the paragraphs.

On Their Own

Have students identify the supporting details on p. 369.

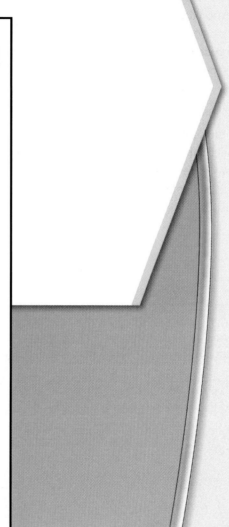

He needed to understand everything about his subject. He measured and drew pictures until he knew where all the bones and muscles of a horse were. But you couldn't show all the muscles on a statue, he said, or the horse would look like a bag of turnips. You should show only those muscles the horse was using or getting ready to use.

He visited statues of horses. Many were shown in an amble— left front leg moving at the same time as the left back leg. This was not easy for a horse; he had to be taught to do it. Leonardo saw one horse, however, that he described as free—left front leg and right back leg moving together, in a trot. Moreover, both ears were pointed forward. (Some horses pointed one ear back to hear the rider's orders.)

Leonardo was ready to begin.

But the duke wasn't quite ready. He wanted a much bigger horse than the one he had originally planned. One three times larger than life. Could Leonardo manage anything that large? the duke wondered. He wrote to Lorenzo, asking him to recommend someone who could do the job.

Lorenzo replied: Leonardo da Vinci was the only one.

On April 23, 1490, Leonardo wrote in his notebook: "I resumed work on the horse." The hardest part would be the casting. He collected 58,000 pounds of metal—tin and copper— which would be heated until it was fluid. This would be turned into bronze and used to cast the horse. But should he pour the bronze all at once? No one had tried a single pouring of anything this large.

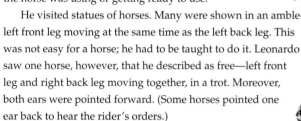

369

Inferring • Analyze On page 369, the duke asks Lorenzo de´ Medici who he should ask to make the bigger statue of the horse. Why did Lorenzo say that Leonardo da Vinci was the only one to make the statue? Make an inference, using evidence from the text to support your answer. **Possible response: Lorenzo was the ruler of Florence, a city known for art. He probably knew many artists and could make the judgment that Leonardo was the best artist for the job.**

Make Connections • Synthesis Earlier in the story, the text said that Leonardo hated to see caged birds, and that he let them free. How can you relate that idea to Leonardo's desire to build a horse that looked free, moving at a trot with its ears pointed forward? **Possible response: Leonardo must have liked animals to be free, and this stance of the horse represented freedom because it was a natural stance for the horse.**

ELL

English Language Learners
Understand language Point out the phrase on p. 369, *or the horse would look like a bag of turnips.* Explain that a turnip is a root vegetable that is round and hard, and so a bag of turnips would have lots of bulges and lumps. Ask students how a poorly made sculpture of a horse could look like a bag of vegetables.

OPTION 1 Skills and Strategies, continued

Teach Visualize

◉ **Visualize** Remind students that visualizing is when readers create pictures in their minds as they read. This helps them to enjoy what they read and monitor and adjust their comprehension of the text. Ask students which details from the text on p. 371 help them to visualize the scene.

Corrective Feedback

If... students are unable to identify the details from the text,

then... Use the model to guide students in identifying sensory details.

Model the Strategy

Think Aloud When I look for details from the text that help me create a picture in my mind, I look for sensory details. These are words that tell me sights, sounds, smells, tastes, or how something feels.

370

Student Edition pp. 370–371

OPTION 2 Think Critically, continued

Higher-Order Thinking Skills

◉ **Visualize • Evaluation** Evaluate how the illustration on pages 370–371 matches the pictures you created in your mind as you read the text. Is the scale of the horse in the picture consistent with the statement in the text that it stood 24 feet high? **Yes.** How can you tell? **Possible response: You can compare it to the height of the people.**

Text Structure • Evaluation Think about the way the text is structured on this page and throughout the book. What kind of structure does it follow? **Sequence.** Do you think this is a good way to structure the text of a biography? Why or why not? **Possible response: Yes, it is good to follow someone's life story in sequence, starting when they are younger and having the story grow with them.**

Which words or phrases on this page give me sensory information? (clay model, 24 feet high) I will use these details to visualize the scene.

On Their Own

Have students find other examples of sensory words in the text which help them visualize.

In November 1493, he had completed the clay model—twenty-four feet high. It was shown off at one of the duke's special occasions, and it was a sensation.

371

Differentiated Instruction

 Strategic Intervention

Visualize Have students think of a real life scene, such as an assembly at school, and write down words and phrases such as *crowded* and *noisy* which would help someone visualize the scene. Encourage students to use details from all of the senses (sight, sound, smell, touch, and taste).

A Advanced

Visualize Have students write a short diary entry from the point of view of a person who witnessed the unveiling of the clay model. Encourage students to include sensory details in their entries.

 ELL

English Language Learners

Access content Explain to students that a *foot* not only refers to a part of the body, but also to a customary unit of measurement. About three feet are equal to one meter. Ask students if they would describe a 24 foot horse as short or tall.

Background Knowledge • Analyze • Text to World Think about the society in which Leonardo da Vinci lived. In what ways is our society today similar or different? Possible response: Both societies appreciate art, culture, and scientific discoveries, but our American society does not have royalty, like dukes.

Check Predictions Have students look back at the predictions they made earlier and discuss whether they were accurate. Then have students preview the rest of the selection and either adjust their predictions accordingly or make new predictions.

If you want to teach this selection in two sessions, stop here.

Research and Inquiry
Navigate/Search

Teach

Have students collect information from periodicals and reference texts for information about their artist. Have them use a computer to take notes. Suggest that they keep notes for each source in a different file, font, or color. This will make it easier for them to organize their citations and create a Works Cited page.

Model

 Think Aloud

I will search through the library's database to find information about my artist. I'll start with his name, Norman Rockwell. When I search for this, I find a book with several artist biographies, including an entry on Rockwell. There is also an entry about him in the encyclopedia. When I search through the magazines, I find an article about an artist that was inspired by Rockwell. I will use all of these for my presentation.

Guide practice

Tell students to pay special attention to quotes they can use in their presentation. They may want to highlight interesting quotes in bold on their word processor so they can easily see the relationships between the ideas.

On their own

Students should use a standard format to record bibliographic information concerning author, title, and page number. They will also need to record the publisher and publication year of print sources. Write a model of the format you prefer on the board so students can use it in their notes.

Conventions
Principal Parts of Regular Verbs

Teach

Write these sentences: *She has completed her grammar test. She smiles quickly.* Point out the past participle *has completed* and the present *smiles*. Explain to students that these sentences use the active voice by having the subject perform the action. The passive voice has the subject as the receiver of the action.

Guide practice

Say these sentences. Have students tell you which principal parts of the regular verbs are being used and if the voice is active.

> **Gretchen feels happy.** (present, active)
>
> **She is asking for a new pen.** (present participle; active)

Daily Fix-It

Use Daily Fix-It numbers 3 and 4 in the right margin.

Connect to oral language

Have students look for and read aloud principal parts of regular verbs in *Leonardo's Horse*. (*was asking*, p. 357; *had planned*, p. 358; *gave*, p. 360; *was expected*, p. 360; *needed*, p. 361)

On their own

For more practice use the *Reader's and Writer's Notebook* p. 192.

Reader's and Writer's Notebook p. 192

Spelling
Compound Words

Teach

Remind students that compound words are made of shorter words. Write *waterproof*. Draw a line between *water* and *proof*. Cover *proof* and read *water* aloud. Then cover *water* and read *proof* aloud. Uncover the whole word, and explain that together the two words make the compound word *waterproof.*

Guide practice

Have students practice using this rule by taking turns saying the first word in a compound word from the spelling list and asking a partner to complete it.

On their own

For more practice use the *Reader's and Writer's Notebook* p. 193.

Reader's and Writer's Notebook p. 193

Daily Fix-It

3. Leonardo romed the countrieside, sketching and making notes. (*roamed; countryside*)

4. Did you know Leonardo invents a armored tank? (*invented; an armored*)

 ELL

English Language Learners

Conventions To provide students with practice on principal parts of regular verbs, use the modified grammar lessons in the *ELL Handbook* and Grammar Jammer online: www.ReadingStreet.com

Leveled support: Compound words Display the spelling list. Write the spelling list words in their separated forms on note cards. Provide support based on students' proficiency levels:

Beginning Have students match two cards to complete each compound word.

Intermediate Give students half the cards. Have them write the missing half of the compound word that goes with the card.

Advanced/High Advanced Give students half the cards that include the beginning of the compound words. Have them use a dictionary to write additional compound words that start the same way, such as *homework, homestead,* and *homeowner.*

DAY 2 Language Arts

Objectives
• Write a persuasive speech during a timed writing test.

Writing for Tests—Persuasive Speech
Sample Test

Introduce the prompt

Remind students that yesterday they learned about the key features of a persuasive speech. Tell them today they will practice writing for tests by creating a persuasive speech that addresses the prompt. Read aloud the writing prompt.

Writing Prompt

Think about modern inventions. Which recent invention changed people's lives most? Write a persuasive speech which answers that question.

Establish a Position

■ **Introduce** A **position** is a solid idea or opinion about a topic. The topic today is recent inventions that changed people's lives most. To help focus on a topic, let's make a list of recent inventions. Yesterday, we read about cell phones. **Have students brainstorm recent inventions and add them to the list.**

Recent Inventions

cell phones

MP3 players

handheld video games

hybrid cars

Let's discuss hybrid cars. When you choose a position, you decide how you feel about something. I feel that hybrid cars have changed people's lives the most. I feel strongly about this position for many reasons. I have established my position. Think about the invention you feel is most important. Establishing a position about it will help you to better answer the prompt you've been given.

Discuss Rubric Discuss the Scoring Rubric found on p. 194 in the *Reader's and Writer's Notebook*. Go over the criteria for each trait under each score. Remind students that this is the rubric that will be used to evaluate the persuasive speeches they write.

Sample test Ask students to get a piece of paper and a pencil ready to take a writing test. Display the writing prompt, and have students begin. Remind students to allow themselves a few minutes after writing to reread what they've written and make changes or additions.

ROUTINE **Quick Write for Fluency** **Team Talk**

1. **Talk** Have pairs discuss how they formed a position about a topic.

2. **Write** Each student writes a sentence about how they formed their position.

3. **Share** Partners read one another's writing and then ask a question about it.

Routines Flip Chart

Wrap Up Your Day

✔ **Build Concepts** What did you learn about why Leonardo da Vinci was so driven to build the bronze horse?

✔ **Main Idea and Details** What is your favorite part of *Leonardo's Horse?* What is the main idea of that part?

✔ **Visualize** How did visualizing help you understand the text?

Differentiated Instruction

SI Strategic Intervention

Reverse thought Some students may find it easier to choose a topic and establish a position based on things they *don't like.*

Reader's and Writer's
Notebook, p. 194

Teacher Tip

If students are having difficulty understanding the concept of a scoring rubric, try creating one about a familiar sport or activity with the class as an example.

Preview DAY 3

Tell students that tomorrow they will read about how Leonardo's horse inspired two Americans almost 500 years after the artist's death.

Objectives
- Expand the weekly concept.
- Develop oral vocabulary.

Today at a Glance

Oral Vocabulary
sculpture, projector

Comprehension Check/Retelling
Discuss questions

Reading
Leonardo's Horse

Think Critically
Retelling

Fluency
Rate

Research and Study Skills
Skim and scan

Research and Inquiry
Analyze

Spelling
Compound words

Conventions
Principal parts of regular verbs

Writing
Persuasive speech

Concept Talk

 Question of the Week
How do artists inspire future generations?

Expand the concept

Remind students of the Question of the Week. Discuss how the question relates to Leonardo da Vinci's building of the horse. Tell students that today in their reading, they will find out whether Leonardo finishes his great statue of the horse. Encourage students to think about how this great sculpture inspired future generations.

Anchored Talk

Develop oral vocabulary

Use text features—illustrations—to review pp. 360–371 of *Leonardo's Horse*. Discuss the Amazing Words *gallery* and *marble*. Add these and other concept-related words to the concept map. Have students break into groups and use the following questions to develop their understanding of the concept. Have students consider all group members' suggestions while discussing the questions.

- Many Renaissance artists used *marble* to make sculptures. What materials did Leonardo use to make his horse? (bronze, clay)

- The selection says that when Leonardo was young, his father took him to Florence, Italy, to study art. They may have gone to *galleries.* What kinds of art do you think they saw there? How do you think those galleries were different from galleries that you might visit today?

Oral Vocabulary
Amazing Words

Amazing Words

easel	sculpture
charcoal	projector
canvas	medium
gallery	muse
marble	inspire

Teach Amazing Words

Amazing Words Oral Vocabulary Routine

1 Introduce Write the word *sculpture* on the board. Have students say it with you. Yesterday we read about how Leonardo da Vinci wanted to make a big bronze *sculpture* of a horse. He had created a model of the *sculpture* using clay. Have students use the context to determine or clarify the definition of *sculpture*. (A *sculpture* is a work of art made by carving, modeling, or casting.)

2 Demonstrate Have students answer questions to demonstrate understanding. What are other materials which can be used to make *sculptures?* (stone, marble, clay)

3 Apply Have students apply their understanding. Think about and describe a *sculpture* that you've seen and liked.

See p. OV•2 to teach *projector.*

Routines Flip Chart

Apply Amazing Words

Have students consider how the Amazing Words *sculpture* and *projector* apply to the story of Leonardo's quest to build a horse, and perhaps to other artists' quests as well.

Connect to reading

Explain that today students will read pp. 372–377 of *Leonardo's Horse* and find out whether he was successful in achieving his dream. As they read, they should think about how this week's Question of the Week and the Amazing Words *sculpture* and *projector* apply to his experience.

ELL **Expand Vocabulary** Use the Day 3 instruction on ELL Poster 12 to help students expand vocabulary.

ELL Poster 12

Comprehension Check

Have students discuss each question with a partner. Ask several pairs to share their responses.

☑ **Genre • Analysis**

Why is *Leonardo's Horse* considered a biography? Is it the kind of biography that focuses on a whole life story or on a major event or part of a person's life? **Possible response:** *Leonardo's Horse* is considered a biography because it is the story of Leonardo da Vinci's life. It focuses on only the events surrounding his building of the bronze horse.

☑ **Main idea and details • Analysis**

Based on what you've read so far, how would you summarize the main idea of *Leonardo's Horse*? **Possible response:** Leonardo is on his way toward achieving his dream of creating a large bronze horse.

☑ **Visualize • Synthesis**

Thinking about what you've read so far, what is the most vivid image that the text has created in your mind? Use sensory details in the text to draw a picture or write a short paragraph describing the image that is in your mind. **Possible response:** The most vivid picture in my mind is of Leonardo leaving what he was doing in Florence and traveling to Milan to tell the duke that he wanted to make the horse for him. He left in a rush, and the text made me feel the urgency of his trip.

☑ **Greek and Latin roots • Synthesis**

Use what you know about Greek and Latin roots to create a word that is related to the text and derived from the Greek roots *bio* ("life") and *graph* ("to draw or write"). What other word could you make by adding the Greek root *autos*, meaning "self"? *Biography* and *autobiography*.

☑ **Connect text to world**

The world in which Leonardo da Vinci grew up was both similar and different from the world we live in now. What are two ways in which his world was similar to ours and two ways in which it was different? **Possible response:** It is similar in that art was respected then and now. It is also similar because if someone works hard, they can do great things. It is different because in America we don't work for dukes and we usually don't travel by horse.

Strategy Response Log

Have students use p. 18 in the *Reader's and Writer's Notebook* to revise and refine their mental pictures of *Leonardo's Horse* based on what they have read so far.

Check Retelling

Have students retell the part of *Leonardo's Horse* that they read yesterday. Encourage students to paraphrase the selection in their retellings in ways that maintain meaning and logical order.

Corrective feedback

If... students leave out important details,

then... have students look back through the illustrations in the selection.

Small Group Time

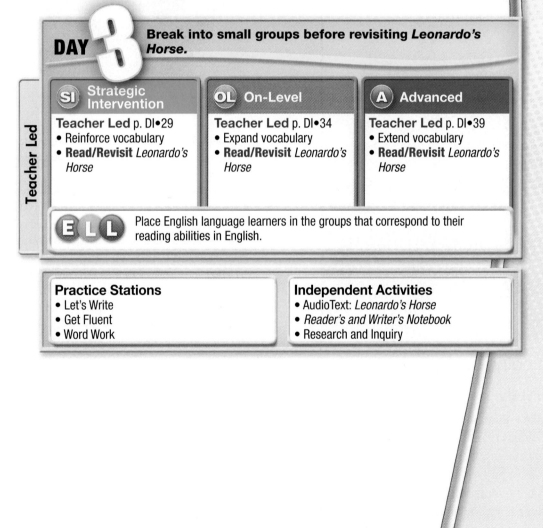

DAY 3 Break into small groups before revisiting *Leonardo's Horse.*

Teacher Led

SI Strategic Intervention

Teacher Led p. DI•29
• Reinforce vocabulary
• **Read/Revisit** *Leonardo's Horse*

OL On-Level

Teacher Led p. DI•34
• Expand vocabulary
• **Read/Revisit** *Leonardo's Horse*

A Advanced

Teacher Led p. DI•39
• Extend vocabulary
• **Read/Revisit** *Leonardo's Horse*

ELL Place English language learners in the groups that correspond to their reading abilities in English.

Practice Stations
• Let's Write
• Get Fluent
• Word Work

Independent Activities
• AudioText: *Leonardo's Horse*
• *Reader's and Writer's Notebook*
• Research and Inquiry

ELL

English Language Learners

Check retelling To support retelling, review the multilingual summary for *Leonardo's Horse* with the appropriate Retelling Cards to scaffold understanding.

Objectives
◎ Identify the main idea and details of a text.

OPTION 1 Skills and Strategies, continued

Teach Main Idea and Details

◉ **Main Idea and Details** Tell students that the main idea or ideas on a page often center around the important events happening in the text. Ask students to reread paragraphs 2 and 3 on p. 372 to find the important events. Then have students summarize the main ideas in ways that maintain meaning and logical order.

Corrective Feedback

If… students are unable to identify the main ideas,
then… model for students how to identify the main ideas.

Multidraft Reading
Double Day Read!

If you chose…

Option 1 Return to Extend Thinking instruction starting on p. 362–363.
Option 2 Read pp. 372–377.
Use the Guide Comprehension and Extend Thinking instruction.

Student Edition pp. 372–373

OPTION 2 Think Critically, continued

Higher-Order Thinking Skills

◉ **Main Idea and Details • Evaluation** You have identified the main ideas and details on page 372. Evaluate the details and accurately summarize the most important ones. Explain why they are important. **Possible responses:** Leonardo's reasoning that the metal was needed for the war was important because it shows his response to the metal being used to make a cannon. The date Leonardo and the duke fled is an important detail because it sets the event at a particular time. The fact that the French saw the horse as a perfect target is important because it tells the French's motivation for destroying it.

Model the Skill

Think Aloud I will carefully read the text to identify the important events. In the second paragraph we learn that the duke sent Leonardo's metal to be made into a cannon. Is this an important event? **(Yes.)**

But Leonardo seemed to be in no hurry to start casting. Perhaps he wasn't sure how he'd do it. Besides, he was planning a new project.

Later, in 1498, there were rumors that the French were preparing to invade Milan, and the duke wanted to be ready. And there was all the metal that Leonardo had collected. Just what the duke needed. So he sent it off to be made into cannon. Well, this is war, Leonardo reasoned. What else could they do?

When the French came in 1499, Leonardo and the duke fled. But the horse couldn't leave. There he was when the French arrived. The archers laughed. Never would they find as perfect a target, they said. Pulling back the strings on their bows, they let their arrows fly. Ping! Ping! Ping! The horse sagged. Ping!

Then it rained. And the horse became smaller and smaller. At last it was nothing but a pile of mud stuck with arrows.

372

◉ **Visualize • Analysis** Reread the text in the third paragraph on page 372 from *The archers laughed* to the end of the paragraph. Write the verbs in each sentence. Analyze how these verbs help you visualize what is happening. **Most of these verbs are action words, such as** *laughed, pulling, sagged.* **These verbs help the reader visualize what the archers are doing and how they are destroying the horse.**

Why? (It may stop Leonardo from achieving his dream.) Next, Leonardo and the duke flee, and the French invade and destroy the horse. These important events are the main ideas of the paragraphs.

On Their Own
Have students reread p. 372 to practice identifying details in the text.

373

Literary Devices • Analysis What literary device can you identify in the last line of paragraph 3 on page 372? Why do you think the author uses this literary device here? Possible response: The word *ping!* is onomatopoeia because it sounds like an arrow being shot from a bow. By using it several times in a row, the author creates the effect of many arrows hitting the horse at once.

Predicting • Synthesis Think about the events that take place on page 372. How will these events affect Leonardo's quest to make the bronze horse? Make a prediction about how this story will end. Possible response: It will be difficult for Leonardo to make another horse during wartime. I predict he will try, but he may not be successful.

Differentiated Instruction

 Strategic Intervention

Main idea and details Use a two-column chart to have students list the main ideas on p. 372 (which can also be the important events) and important details which support each main idea. Have students work in pairs to help each other compose summaries using the main ideas and important details they've written in their charts.

English Language Learners
Language transfer: Predicates
Help students identify the predicates in the third paragraph, beginning with the sentence *The archers laughed,* by acting out the verbs as you say the sentences.

Extend knowledge Point out the word *ping*. Ask students what it refers to. (The sound of archers releasing their bowstrings). Explain that using the sound something makes as the word to describe that sound is called *onomatopoeia*. Have students suggest other words or expressions that use onomatopoeia. (Possible answers: buzz, zip, splash).

Objectives
- Identify facts and opinions to improve comprehension.

OPTION 1 Skills and Strategies, continued

Teach Fact and Opinion

Review **Fact and Opinion** Tell students that it is important for them to know how to recognize facts and opinions. Tell students that Leonardo wrote in his notebook that he had wasted his time on Earth. Is this a statement of fact or opinion? Have students explain their answer.

Corrective Feedback

If... students have difficulty answering the question,

then... model how to distinguish fact from opinion.

Model the Skill

Think Aloud I ask myself if Leonardo's statement can be proved true or false. To prove the statement true, I'd have to show that the things he did in his life weren't that good, or that he could have spent his time doing better things instead.

Leonardo went back to inventing and painting, but he never forgot his horse.

He still wanted to invent a flying machine. But he still couldn't do it.

His greatest disappointment, however, was his horse.

As Leonardo became older, his hair turned white and grew down to his shoulders. His beard reached to his waist.

And he became depressed. What had he achieved? he asked himself. He complained to his notebook: "Tell me," he asked, "if anything has been achieved by me. Tell me. Tell me." It was especially hard when his rival, Michelangelo, taunted him.

"You," Michelangelo said, "who made a model of a horse you could never cast in bronze and which you gave up, to your shame."

In his notebook Leonardo mourned, "I have wasted my hours."

On May 2, 1519, Leonardo da Vinci died. It was said that even on his deathbed, Leonardo wept for his horse.

374

Student Edition pp. 374–375

OPTION 2 Think Critically, continued

Higher-Order Thinking Skills

Review **Fact and Opinion • Analysis** In the last paragraph on page 374, identify which information is factual and which information may not be factual. What clues did you use? Possible response: The date of Leonardo's death is factual. It can be proven true. That Leonardo wept for his horse on his deathbed may not be factual. The phrase *it was said* is a clue that it may be based on hearsay, but there is no way to prove whether it's true.

Character • Synthesis We learn a lot about Leonardo on page 374. What character traits are shown there? Possible responses: Ambition, high expectations of himself, being very hard on himself. Do you see any of these traits in yourself or others? Write a paragraph in which you talk about these character traits and how you see them displayed in Leonardo, yourself, and in other people you know.

But whether one thing is better than another is an opinion, which means that there is no way to prove whether Leonardo's life was wasted or not. His statement is an opinion explaining how he feels.

375

Author's Purpose • Evaluation What is the author's purpose in using direct quotations from Michelangelo and Leonardo on page 374 instead of saying things in her own words? How well did she achieve her purpose?
Possible response: The author wanted to make the story more believable. The quotations make the story and the two characters seem more real and immediate. They also signal that the information came from the characters and has not been paraphrased, which makes the text more believable.

On Their Own

Have students look for other statements in the text that can be identified as facts or opinions, and have students support their answers. Then have students verify their facts using encyclopedias or reliable Internet sources.

Differentiated Instruction

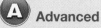

A Advanced

Fact and opinion Explain to students that both writers and readers must learn to verify facts to make sure they are true. Generate a list with students of sources which would be considered reliable in verifying facts. (encyclopedias, primary source information, .gov Web sites)

English Language Learners
Figurative language Point out the phrase *He complained to his notebook.* Hold a notebook up and look at it as you say: *I haven't accomplished a thing.* Ask if this phrase is meant to be taken literally. Then ask students to explain what the author means. (He wrote his complaints in his notebook.)

Objectives

◉ Use Greek and Latin roots to determine and clarify the meaning of words.

OPTION 1 Skills and Strategies, continued

Teach Greek and Latin Roots

◉ **Greek and Latin Roots** Have students use the Latin root word *sculp* (to carve) to determine the meaning of the word *sculptor* on p. 376.

Corrective Feedback

If... students are unable to use the root word to define the word,
then... use the model to guide students to use the Latin root word to determine the meaning of the word.

Model the Skill

Think Aloud I see that the Latin root *sculp* means "to carve." I look at the word *sculptor* and I can see the root *sculp*. I use what I already know and what I've learned from the root word to break down the word *sculptor*.

In 1977 Charles Dent, an American and a big fan of Leonardo, saw a magazine article about him. When he read that Leonardo died grieving for his horse, Charles said, "Let's give Leonardo his horse."

But Charles Dent died before work was finished. Later, a sculptor from New York City, Nina Akamu, carried on with Charles's dream. Many people contributed money to help her finish. Finally, on September 10, 1999, in Milan, Italy, in front of huge crowds, the horse was unveiled.

Student Edition pp. 376–377

376

OPTION 2 Think Critically, continued

Higher-Order Thinking Skills

◉ **Greek and Latin Roots • Analysis** Use the Greek roots, *aer* and *aero* (meaning "air, atmosphere") to determine the meaning of the words *aeronautics* and *aerodynamic*. Use a dictionary if you need help. *Aeronautics* is the science or art of flight, or going up in the air. *Aerodynamic* means to flow smoothly through the air.

Text Structure • Analysis The text on page 376 is set in italics and commonly referred to as an afterward. Why do you think the author includes this information? Possible response: The author includes this information to explain how Leonardo's goal was achieved after his death.

What does *sculptor* mean? **(someone who carves)** I can also determine the meaning of other words made from the root *sculp* such as the verb *sculpt*, which means to carve, and the word *sculpture*, which is something that is carved.

On Their Own

Have students consider the words *finish* and *finally* from p. 376, breaking down each to find the root, analyzing similarities in the meanings and guessing at the meaning of the root word. (Latin *fīnīre*, from *fīnis*, "end")

Differentiated Instruction

SI **Strategic Intervention**

Greek and Latin roots Help students look up words in a dictionary, either online or in print. Show them where to look for root words in the definition. Have students use a dictionary to look up the words *sympathy*, *audible*, and *dictionary* and write the meanings and roots.

A **Advanced**

Inferring Have students write a brief paragraph describing a time that, like Leonardo da Vinci, they were disappointed with being unable to accomplish something that was important to them.

At last Leonardo's horse was home.

377

ELL

English Language Learners
Professional development strategy: Monitor language production
"For second-language learners, it is perhaps most valuable to stage exposure to new vocabulary items in related groups, since many words are more meaningful when they are understood in connection with other words related to the same general topic." —L. Wong Fillmore and Catherine E. Snow

Comprehension Check

Spiral Review

Questioning • Evaluation Form three questions to help you evaluate the text. For example, you might ask, *What was the author's purpose in writing the book and did she achieve it?* Answers will vary.

Inferring • Evaluation Do you consider Leonardo da Vinci to have been successful as an artist and as a person?

Make an inference based on Leonardo's experiences as described in the text. **Possible answer:** Leonardo was successful as an artist and a person because he continued to paint and invent despite facing disappointments.

Check Predictions Have students return to the predictions they made earlier and confirm whether they were accurate.

Objectives

◉ Visualize to aid in comprehension.

◉ Identify the main idea and details to enhance comprehension.

Check Retelling
SUCCESS PREDICTOR

Objectives
• Provide evidence from text to support understanding. • Read independently for a sustained period of time and paraphrase the reading, including the order in which events occur.

Envision It! Retell

READING STREET ONLINE
STORY SORT
www.ReadingStreet.com

378

Think Critically

1. Imagine that you are an artist like Leonardo. How would you feel if you were unable to complete a challenging project? Why do you think you would feel this way? **Text to Self**

2. Jean Fritz's biographies put readers right there with the subject of each book. Identify examples from the selection that made you feel as if you were right beside da Vinci. **Think Like an Author**

3. What is the author's main idea in this selection? She shows how da Vinci was brilliant, but what else does she show about the kind of person he was? Look back at the text to answer the question. **Main Idea**

4. Think about what happened to the clay model of Leonardo's horse. Describe how the visual details helped you understand what happened. Look back at page 364 to help you. **Visualize**

5. **Look Back and Write** Look back at pages 376–377. Did Leonardo da Vinci's greatest dream ever come true? Provide evidence to support your answer.
TEST PRACTICE Extended Response

Meet the Author

JEAN FRITZ

Jean Fritz writes books about history because she enjoys doing research. She says, "For every book I write, I have to read a great deal and usually travel to the place where that person lived. It's like being a detective. I want to find the truth, so I never make up anything in these books, not even conversation. If you see quotation marks, you can be sure I have a source for them."

While writing *Leonardo's Horse*, Ms. Fritz went to Italy. She was there when the twenty-four-foot bronze horse was presented as a gift from the people of the United States to the people of Italy. She says, "It was one of my most exciting adventures."

Although Ms. Fritz today lives along the Hudson River in New York, she spent her childhood in China. She heard her parents' stories about the United States and felt a need to know all she could about the United States, both past and present. Many of her biographies are about people important in U.S. history, such as George Washington, Benjamin Franklin, and Harriet Beecher Stowe.

Ms. Fritz says, "I get letters from readers sometimes who say they like the way I add 'fun' to history. I don't add anything. It's all true, because past times were just as filled with exciting events and 'fun' stories as are present times."

Here are other books by Jean Fritz.
Bully for You, Teddy Roosevelt!

Can't You Make Them Behave, King George?

Use the Reader's and Writer's Notebook to record your independent reading.

379

Student Edition pp. 378–379

Retelling

Envision It!

Have students work in pairs to retell the selection, using the Envision It! Retelling Cards as prompts. Remind students that they should accurately describe the topic and main ideas and use key vocabulary in their retellings. Encourage students to use sensory images to monitor and adjust their comprehension of the selection.

Scoring rubric

Top-Score Response A top-score response makes connections beyond the text, describes the topic and main ideas using accurate information, evaluates facts and opinions, and draws conclusions from the text.

Plan to Assess Retelling

☑ **Week 1** Assess Strategic Intervention students.

☑ **This week assess Advanced students.**

☐ **Week 3** Assess Strategic Intervention students.

☐ **Week 4** Assess On-Level students.

☐ **Week 5** Assess Any students you have not yet checked during this unit.

Don't Wait Until Friday
MONITOR PROGRESS **Check Retelling**

Retelling Cards

If... students have difficulty retelling,

then... use the Retelling Cards to scaffold their retellings.

Day 1	**Days 2–3**	**Day 4**	**Day 5**
Check Oral Vocabulary	Check Retelling	Check Fluency	Check Oral Vocabulary

Success Predictor

Think Critically

Text to self

1. Possible response: An ambitious artist like Leonardo would feel frustrated and angry, especially if this project had long been the artist's dream. I would feel this way if I were such an artist because I would put all of my energy and passion into my project. Not being able to share it with the world would make me feel like a failure.

Think like an author

2. Possible response: One example of a time when I felt as if I were right there with Leonardo is when the text said that he let birds out of their cages so they could fly away in a flurry.

Main idea

3. She shows that Leonardo was also passionate and sensitive. He put a lot of emotion into his work and became very upset with himself when he felt that he had failed.

Visualize

4. There are many details to help readers visualize that scene. For example, the horse sagged as the arrows hit it, and then the horse became smaller and smaller in the rain until it was only a pile of mud stuck with arrows. These details made the scene more realistic.

5. **Look Back and Write** To build writing fluency, assign a 10–15 minute time limit.

Suggest that students use a prewriting strategy, such as brainstorming or using a graphic organizer, to organize their ideas. Remind them to establish a topic sentence and support it with facts, details, or explanations. As students finish, encourage them to reread their responses, revise for organization and support, and proofread for errors in grammar and conventions.

Scoring rubric

> **Top-Score Response** A top-score response uses details from the text to support a position as to whether or not Leonardo's greatest dream ever came true.
>
> **A top-score response should include:**
>
> - Although Leonardo did not complete the horse, it was completed by other artists after him.
>
> - The horse would never have been made if it were not for Leonardo's work and vision.
>
> - The question about whether an artist's dream can come true after the artist's death.

Differentiated Instruction

SI Strategic Intervention

Have partners retell the ending of the story. Ask them to explain why they believe Leonardo's dream may or may not have come true.

Meet the Author

Have students read about author Jean Fritz on page 379. Ask them how she acted like a detective when she researched *Leonardo's Horse.*

Independent Reading

After students enter their independent reading information into their Reading Logs, have them summarize what they have read. Remind students that a summary should be no more than a few sentences about the main idea of a text.

ELL

English Language Learners
Retelling Use the Retelling Cards to discuss the selection with students. Arrange the cards in order and ask volunteers to explain what they show. Then, challenge students to describe what happens between what is shown on the cards.

Retelling

Success Predictor

Objectives

- Read grade-level text at an appropriate rate.
- Reread for fluency.
- Use scanning and skimming techniques to locate information and gain an overview of the contents of texts.

Model Fluency
Rate

Model fluent reading

Have students turn to p. 368 of *Leonardo's Horse.* Have students follow along as you read the page. Tell students that you will read at a slower rate because this is an informational text. Reading at a slower rate allows you to take in and think about the information you are learning from the text.

Guide practice

Have the students follow along as you read the page again. Then have them reread the page as a group without you until they read at the appropriate rate and with no mistakes. Ask questions to be sure students comprehend the text. Continue in the same way on p. 369.

Reread for Fluency

Corrective feedback

If... students are having difficulty reading at the correct rate, then... prompt:

- Do you think you need to slow down or read more quickly?
- Read the sentence more quickly. Now read it more slowly. Which helps you understand what you are reading?
- Tell me the sentence. Read it at the rate that would help me understand it.

> ROUTINE **Oral Reading**
>
> 1) **Select a passage** Read aloud p. 368 in *Leonardo's Horse.*
> 2) **Model** Have students track the print as you read at a slow, steady rate.
> 3) **Guide Practice** Have students read along with you.
> 4) **On Their Own** Have the class read aloud without you. For optimal fluency, students should reread three or four times.

Routines Flip Chart

Research and Study Skills
Skim and Scan

Teach

Discuss with students how to deal with a large number of encyclopedia entries and/or magazine articles when doing research. Let's say I've collected twenty-five articles about Michelangelo. I read the first one, but it's entirely about his childhood in Florence. It doesn't have any information that will help me write about his influence on later generations. How can I tell if the remaining articles will be of any help without having to take the time to read each one? (Glance over each one or read through it quickly to see what type of information it might contain.) Tell students that two techniques for prereading an article to see if it will be helpful are skimming and scanning. Show students an informational article to demonstrate how to skim and scan.

- To **skim** text is to read the first and last paragraphs; text features such as headings, subheadings, and titles; and to review any graphics or visuals in the text. The goal of skimming is to gain an overview of the contents of text.

- To **scan** text is to move your eyes quickly down the page, looking for specific words or phrases. Scanning the text and multiple text features can help you locate information.

Take students to the media center so they may utilize magazines and encyclopedias to research the topic of their inquiry project.

Guide practice

Discuss these questions:

How do you know what to look for when you are skimming or scanning? (Think of a few keywords or phrases to look for to help you locate the information you want to find.)

What are ways to help me learn to skim and scan quickly? (Try using your finger as a pointer over the text.)

After students have spent some time skimming and scanning their articles, ask specific questions about what information they found.

On their own

Have students complete pp. 196–197 of the *Reader's and Writer's Notebook.*

Reader's and Writer's Notebook pp. 196–197

English Language Learners
Skim and scan Have students write down the keywords or phrases they are searching for in a text so they can more easily remember and recognize them.

Objectives
- Ask questions to refine the research question.
- Recognize the principal parts of regular verbs and the active voice.
- Spell frequently misspelled words.

Research and Inquiry
Analyze

Teach

Tell students that today they will analyze their findings. Have them ask themselves questions to refine their inquiry topics.

Model

Think Aloud Originally, my inquiry question asked about how Norman Rockwell influenced other artists and the American public. My research led me to an article in the Boston Globe, a respected newspaper. It tells about how Norman Rockwell's political art inspired an exhibit where sixty other artists were invited to create works of art about democracy. I ask myself, How can I change my inquiry question to fit what I have found? I am going to focus on Rockwell's political art and the exhibit so I can talk about the newspaper article. Now my question will be: How did Norman Rockwell's political art influence the artists involved in this exhibit?

Guide practice

Have students work in groups to narrow the focus of their research question. They may want to focus on how their artist inspired a particular person or group of people, or they may want to focus on a special work of art.

On their own

Ask students to review their notes and sources. Then have students meet with a partner to share their inquiry questions and summarize their research. Students should offer each other help in evaluating the reliability, relevance, and validity of their sources. Make sure students understand why it is important that their sources be reliable and valid.

Conventions
Principal Parts of Regular Verbs

Review

Remind students that this week they learned about principal parts of regular verbs and about the active voice:

- A verb's tenses are formed from its **principal parts:** present, present participle, past, and past participle.
- **A regular verb** forms its past and past participle by adding *-ed* or *-d* to the present form.
- **Active voice** has the subject performing the action.

Daily Fix-It

Use Daily Fix-It numbers 5 and 6 in the right margin.

Connect to oral language

Have students create oral phrases by choosing parts from the list. Then have them say what principal part they used.

The leaves	**have fallen** (past participle)
The season	**is changing** (present participle)

On their own

For additional practice, use *Let's Practice It!* p. 137 on the *Teacher Resources DVD-ROM.*

Spelling
Compound Words

Frequently misspelled words

The words *everybody, everyone,* and *something* are compound words that are often misspelled. The smaller words that form these do not change when they are joined together. I'm going to read a sentence. Write the correct compound word to complete each sentence. Then check your answers with a dictionary.

1. I think there's _____ under the sand. (something)

2. Don't worry, there's plenty for _____. (everyone or everybody)

3. _____ knows the truth about the missing book. (everyone or everybody)

On their own

For more practice, use the *Reader's and Writer's Notebook* p. 198.

Differentiated Instruction

SI Strategic Intervention

Active voice Create a sample chart to display in the classroom. Write these sentences for students to reference:

Active voice: Amelia <u>flew</u> the airplane.

Passive voice: The plane <u>was flown</u> by Amelia.

Daily Fix-It

5. Leonardos fame put him in the public spot light. (*Leonardo's; spotlight*)

6. Does his parachute desine look practical. (*design; practical?*)

Let's Practice It!
TR DVD•137

Reader's and Writer's Notebook p. 198

Objectives

- Understand the criteria for writing an effective persuasive speech.
- Use a rubric to evaluate writing.

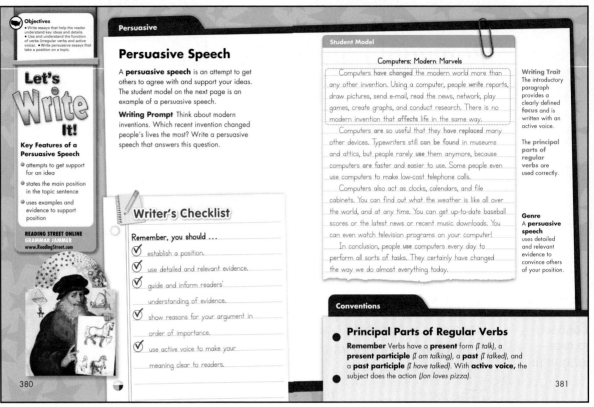

Student Edition pp. 380–381

Let's Write It!
Persuasive Speech

Teach

Use pp. 380–381 in the Student Edition. Direct students to read the key features of a persuasive speech which appear on p. 380. Remind students that they can refer to the information in the Writer's Checklist as they write their own persuasive speeches.

Read the student model on p. 381. Point out that the introductory paragraph has a clear focus in the model.

Connect to conventions

Remind students that regular verbs have principal parts. Point out the correct use of principal parts of regular verbs and the function of the active voice in the model.

Writing for Tests
Evaluation

Display rubric

Have students return to the scoring rubric on p. 194 from the *Reader's and Writer's Notebook* that they discussed yesterday. Then explain to students that they will use this rubric to evaluate the persuasive speeches they wrote yesterday.

Reader's and Writer's Notebook p. 194

Differentiated Instruction

A Advanced

Evaluating a famous speech
Challenge students to evaluate a famous speech, such as one by Martin Luther King Jr. or John F. Kennedy, based on the Persuasive Speech Rubric. Encourage them to find places where the speechwriter could have improved.

Scoring Rubric: Persuasive Speech

	④	③	②	①
Focus/Ideas	Has a clear focus, idea, and position; uses sound reasoning	Has a mostly clear focus, idea, and position; uses some sound reasoning	Lacks a clear idea, focus, and position; lacks sound reasoning	Has no clear idea, focus, or position; has no sound reasoning
Organization	Has the argument stated in a topic sentence with strong supporting details	Includes an argument and some supporting details	Lacks an argument or supporting details	Has no argument or supporting details
Voice	Uses clear persuasive language and an active voice	Uses mostly persuasive language and an active voice	Uses very little persuasive language; very little active voice	Uses no persuasive language or active voice
Word Choice	Strong persuasive language	Language persuasive	Language sometimes unpersuasive	Language unpersuasive
Sentences	Smooth, varied, rhythmic sentences	Some variety in sentences	Many sentences lacking variety	Choppy or rambling sentences
Conventions	Correct use of principal parts of regular verbs	Mostly correct use of principal parts of regular verbs	Little correct use of principal parts of regular verbs	No correct use of principal parts of regular verbs

English Language Learners

Oral practice English language learners may find it helpful to "tell" their persuasive speech to another student before they begin drafting. Once students have explored their ideas orally, encourage them to write using the same details and features as they used in telling the persuasive speech.

Writing for Tests–Evaluation

MINI-LESSON

Evaluation

■ **Introduce** Tell students that they will evaluate their sample writing tests based on 1 of the 6 traits in the rubric. We will focus on trait 4, word choice.

■ Remind students that word choice can make the difference between a truly persuasive speech and one that has no effect on the listener. According to the rubric, we want to make sure that we use clear, persuasive language and an active voice. You will want to check that the sentences you wrote encourage the audience to agree with you. You will also check the presence of the active voice by making sure the subjects of your sentences perform the actions. For example, *I have fixed your bicycle* uses active voice. *Your bicycle has been fixed* does not.

Have students review their persuasive speech and circle all the persuasive language. They should also underline places where they used the active voice. Then, using the rubric as a guide, have them assess their use of word choice on a scale from 4 to 1.

■ **Apply Scoring** Direct students to continue evaluating their persuasive speeches based on the other 5 traits in the rubric. Remind students that they may receive different number scores for each of the different traits, but that is all right. Lower or higher scores for different traits can help them see where their strengths lie, and where they might need to focus more attention and effort.

ROUTINE **Quick Write for Fluency** **Team Talk**

1) **Talk** Have pairs discuss one trait at which they excel.

2) **Write** Each student writes a brief paragraph explaining why they feel they excel at that trait.

3) **Share** Partners read their own writing to their partner and then check their partner's writing for correct use of the principal parts of regular verbs.

Routines Flip Chart

Differentiated Instruction

SI **Strategic Intervention**

Persuasive words Have students brainstorm a list of phrases that could be used to persuade people, such as *you know* and *of course*. Display the list in the room.

Wrap Up Your Day

✔ **Build Concepts** What did you learn about the people who wanted to see Leonardo's dream accomplished?

✔ **Main Idea and Details** What is the main idea of *Leonardo's Horse*?

✔ **Visualize** How did visualizing help you understand the main idea of *Leonardo's Horse*?

Preview DAY 4

Tell students that tomorrow they will read about another great artist of the Renaissance.

Objectives
- Expand the weekly concept.
- Develop oral vocabulary.

Today at a Glance

Oral Vocabulary
medium, muse, inspire

Genre
Historical fiction

Reading
"A Job for Michelangelo"

Let's Learn It!
Fluency: Rate

Vocabulary: Word structure

Media Literacy: Newscast

Research and Inquiry
Synthesize

Spelling
Compound words

Conventions
Principal parts of regular verbs

Writing
Persuasive speech

Concept Talk

 Question of the Week
How do artists inspire future generations?

Expand the concept

This week we have read about artists, the mediums they use, and how they create their work. Today we are going to read a historical fiction story about another artist and his journey toward creating masterpieces that have inspired many future generations.

Anchored Talk

Develop oral vocabulary

Use the illustrations to review pp. 372–377 of *Leonardo's Horse*. Then discuss the Amazing Words *sculpture* and *projector* and add these and other concept-related words to the concept map. Use the following questions to guide discussion and broaden students' understanding of the concept.

- Think about where you've seen sculptures. What have these *sculptures* added to the places where you've seen them?

- Artists use tools to help them in their work. One tool that some artists, such as Norman Rockwell, use is a *projector*. Explain how a *projector* can help an artist with his or her work. What can they achieve with a *projector* that would be difficult to achieve otherwise?

Strategy Response Log

Have students complete p. 18 in *Reader's and Writer's Notebook.* Then have students write a descriptive summary of the selection.

Oral Vocabulary
Amazing Words

Amazing Words

easel	sculpture
charcoal	projector
canvas	medium
gallery	muse
marble	inspire

Teach Amazing Words

Amazing Words Oral Vocabulary Routine

1 Introduce Write the concept word *medium* on the board. Have students say it aloud with you. In reading *Leonardo's Horse,* we know that to make his sculpture Leonardo planned to use many *mediums,* including modeling with clay and then casting in bronze. Can you use context clues to tell me the meaning of the word *medium*? (A *medium* is a material or technique that an artist uses.)

2 Demonstrate Have students answer questions to demonstrate understanding. What are some other mediums that artists use to create works of art? (paint and canvas, charcoal, marble, beads)

3 Apply Have students apply their understanding. Make a list of the mediums you have used in creating art.

See p. OV•2 to teach *muse* and *inspire*.

Routines Flip Chart

Apply Amazing Words

As students read "A Job for Michelangelo" on pp. 382–385, have them think about the things that *inspired* Michelangelo to want to be an artist. Think about the obstacles that stood in his way. What mediums did Michelangelo use for his sketches in the story? What other mediums did he use for his later works of art?

Connect to reading

As students read today's selection about Michelangelo, have them think about how Question of the Week and the Amazing Words *medium, muse* and *inspire* apply to what they've read.

E L L Produce Oral Language Use the Day 4 instruction on ELL Poster 12 to extend and enrich language.

E L L Poster 12

Objectives
• Introduce historical fiction.

Let's Think About Genre

Historical Fiction

Introduce historical fiction

Remind students that what we read is structured differently depending on the author's reasons for writing and what he or she wishes to convey. Tell them that historical fiction is one type of genre.

Discuss the genre

Explain that historical fiction is realistic fiction set in the past. It is a combination of both fact and fiction. Ask: In historical fiction, what elements are usually based on fact? (Possible response: The setting is a real historical setting and the background and major characters and events are usually based on fact.)

On the board, draw a T-chart and label it *Historical Fiction.* Label the sides *Fact* and *Fiction.* Ask the following questions:

• What parts of the setting in historical fiction are real? Possible response: time and place; technology and objects; clothing; some of the characters; and peoples' names, jobs, and popular opinions.

• Is it possible to include real characters in historical fiction? Possible response: Yes. Even though sometimes the main character is fictional, real people can play a part in historical fiction.

• Is it possible to include real events in historical fiction? Possible response: Yes. Because historical fiction is set in a real time and place, authors use historical events to influence the characters and form the story's theme.

Historical Fiction	
Fact	**Fiction**
Historic setting	Some characters
Technology/fashion from past	Most dialogue
Names, occupations, and worldviews fit the past	Fictional plot
Some real characters	
Some real events	

Guide practice

Have students work in pairs to evaluate a historical fiction story they have read in class, listing examples of fact and fiction in a T-chart.

Connect to reading

Tell students that they will now read a historical fiction story about a real person named Michelangelo. Ask students to think about what is real and what is made up in the story as they read.

Small Group Time

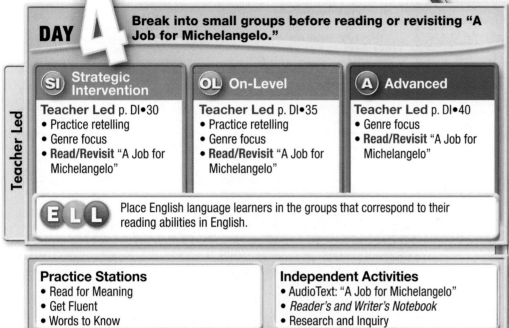

DAY 4 Break into small groups before reading or revisiting "A Job for Michelangelo."

Teacher Led

(SI) Strategic Intervention

Teacher Led p. DI•30
- Practice retelling
- Genre focus
- **Read/Revisit** "A Job for Michelangelo"

(OL) On-Level

Teacher Led p. DI•35
- Practice retelling
- Genre focus
- **Read/Revisit** "A Job for Michelangelo"

(A) Advanced

Teacher Led p. DI•40
- Genre focus
- **Read/Revisit** "A Job for Michelangelo"

ELL

Place English language learners in the groups that correspond to their reading abilities in English.

Practice Stations
- Read for Meaning
- Get Fluent
- Words to Know

Independent Activities
- AudioText: "A Job for Michelangelo"
- *Reader's and Writer's Notebook*
- Research and Inquiry

Objectives
- Understand the elements of historical fiction.

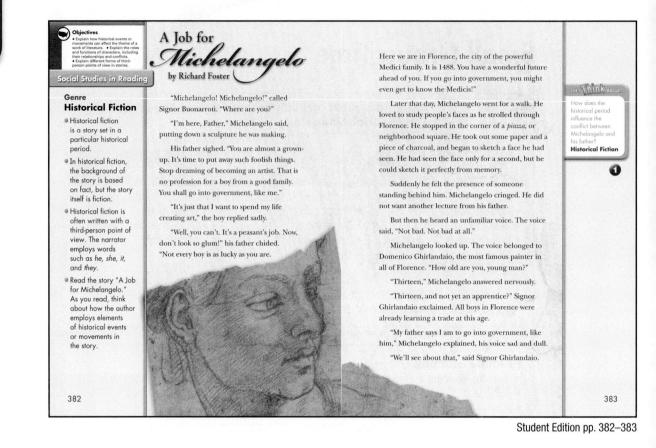

Student Edition pp. 382–383

Guide Comprehension

Teach the genre

Historical Fiction Have students preview "A Job for Michelangelo" on pp. 382–385. Have them discuss what might be real in this story and what might be fictional.

Corrective feedback

If... students are unable to predict the real and fictional elements, **then...** use the model to guide students in understanding these elements of historical fiction.

Model the genre

Think Aloud I know that Michelangelo is a person who truly existed, so I'm guessing that the other important characters are based on real people. I know that in historical fiction, the setting is based on a real historical setting. So I can say that the year 1488 and the location, Florence, are historically correct in relation to the characters and events. However, the dialogue between Michelangelo and his father is probably fictional. We don't know if they really said what was written.

On their own

Have students work in pairs to make a T-Chart listing what they think is fact and fiction in the story as they read.

Extend Thinking
Think Critically

Higher-order thinking skills

Draw Conclusions • Analysis What conclusions can you draw about Michelangelo's character and his father's character based on their conversation on page 382? Summarize each of their characters in one or two lines. **Possible response:** Michelangelo loves art and wants to follow this passion. Michelangelo's father is concerned with status and money and stubbornly wants to force Michelangelo to do what he wants him to do.

Visualize • Evaluation Reread the scene between Michelangelo and Ghirlandaio on page 383. What details does the author use to help you to visualize the scene? How well does the author accomplish this visualization? **Possible response:** The sentence *Michelangelo cringed* and the dialogue bring the scene to life. The author does a good job because it feels natural. I would like more physical details, though. For example, what did Ghirlandaio look like and what was his facial expression?

Let's **Think** About...

1 Michelangelo's father is concerned about money and status. If the Medicis were not such big patrons of the arts, Ghirlandaio might not have been able to change Michelangelo's father's mind.

Differentiated Instruction

 **Strategic Intervention**

Historical Fiction Being "true to the time" in historical fiction not only means that Michelangelo wouldn't ride in a car or use a computer. It also means that he and his father would have opinions and points of view true to the historical period in which they lived. Discuss and have students list the ways in which Michelangelo's father's viewpoint is "true to the time." List other elements of the story that are true to the time.

A **Advanced**

Historical Fiction Have students use encyclopedias or other informational sources to gather information on Michelangelo's childhood to better understand the context of the story.

ELL

English Language Learners
Cognates Point out to students that the word *historical* comes from the root word, *history*, which has a Spanish cognate, *historia*.

Objectives

• Understand the elements of historical fiction.

Michelangelo led Ghirlandaio to his family's home. He told a servant to ask his father to come outside.

When Michelangelo's father saw Signor Ghirlandaio, he looked surprised. After greeting the artist, he said, "It is an honor to have a visit from Florence's greatest artist. But what brings you here, good sir?"

"Your son's talent," explained Ghirlandaio. "I should like him to become my apprentice."

Signor Buonarroti was surprised. "*Your* apprentice?"

The artist nodded. "Your son has a tremendous gift. One day, he may be even a better artist than me."

"You are too kind," his father said. "But I am afraid it is quite impossible. My son will go into government or law, just as I have done. I want him to move among great men. This is a time of great wealth for Florence. I want my son to have part of that for himself."

Signor Ghirlandaio smiled at Michelangelo's father. "In times past, being an artist was the job of a peasant. That is true. But times have changed. The great Medicis are spending huge amounts of money on art. Why, I work directly with members of the Medici family. If your son works with me, so will he."

Michelangelo's father looked stunned. The Medici family was the wealthiest family in Florence. They built marvelous churches and palaces. "Did you say that my son will meet the Medici family?"

"Of course. And in time, perhaps they will sponsor him as they have sponsored me!"

"Father, please. To sculpt, to draw, to paint. It is my dream," Michelangelo pleaded.

His father took a deep breath. "Very well. You may apprentice with Signor Ghirlandaio for three years."

Things worked out very well for Michelangelo. After just one year working for Ghirlandaio, he had learned everything the master artist could teach him. After that, Lorenzo de Medici paid Michelangelo to create art. Lorenzo had a wonderful ancient art collection. Looking at ancient Roman statues gave Michelangelo many ideas. He used these ideas to create a renaissance, or a rebirth, of art.

Michelangelo became a famous and wealthy artist. More importantly, he spent his life doing what he loved: creating beautiful works of art.

Let's Think About

How is the historical movement Ghirlandaio talks about important to the story? **Historical Fiction**

❷

Let's Think About

What kind of third-person narrator is used in this story? How can you tell? **Historical Fiction**

❸

Let's Think About

Reading Across Texts List some traits that made Leonardo da Vinci and Michelangelo different from other artists.

Writing Across Texts Use your list to write a paragraph that describes why da Vinci and Michelangelo were such unique artists.

384

385

Student Edition pp. 384–385

Guide Comprehension

Teach the genre

Historical Fiction Explain that when authors write historical fiction, they include details in the story to help the historical setting seem real. Ask students to name some details on pp. 384–385 that make the historical setting realistic.

Corrective feedback

If... students are unable to point out historical details,
then... use the model to guide students in recognizing historical details in historical fiction.

Model the genre

Think Aloud

There are many details here that tell me this story takes place in the past. Michelangelo's father says, "But what brings you here, good sir?" That is a historical way of speaking. Another historical detail I see includes Michelangelo's father describing Ghirlandaio as "Florence's greatest artist."

On their own

Have students look for and list other details in the story that add to the realism of the historical setting.

Extend Thinking
Think Critically

Higher-order thinking skills

 **Main Idea and Details • Analysis** How would you summarize the main idea of "A Job for Michelangelo"? Possible response: Michelangelo's career as an artist begins when one of his sketches catches the attention of Florence's greatest artist, who convinces Michelangelo's reluctant father to allow Michelangelo to become his apprentice.

Author's Purpose • Evaluation Do you think that the author's decision to use the third-person point of view in the story was a good choice? Why or why not? Possible response: Yes, because it allows the reader to see what the characters are thinking and feeling.

2 Because this movement is one where greater money and recognition are given to artists, Michelangelo's father changes his mind and allows Michelangelo to become an apprentice.

3 The narrator is omniscient third person because it uses "he" and knows what the characters are thinking.

Reading Across Texts

Have students think about other artists as they list Leonardo's and Michelangelo's traits.

Writing Across Texts

Paragraphs should contain information from the lists, along with descriptions of other artists' traits. Students should use information from both texts to support why Leonardo and Michelangelo were unique.

Connect to Social Studies

Michelangelo Michelangelo is one of the most well-known artists of the Italian Renaissance. He is best known for his statues *David* and the *Pietà*, and for his paintings, such as those on the ceiling of the Sistine Chapel in Rome.

ELL

English Language Learners
Point of View Tell students that stories usually use first-person or third-person point of view. Describe a scene in both first-person and third-person points of view. For example: "I sat down at my desk to eat my lunch when I heard a loud sound." or "Mr./Ms. Jones sat down at his/her desk to eat his/her lunch when he/she heard a loud sound." Have students practice describing a scene from both first-person and third-person points of view.

Objectives

- Use Greek and Latin roots to determine and clarify the meanings of words.
- Read grade-level text at an appropriate rate.
- Present a newscast.

Check Fluency

SUCCESS PREDICTOR

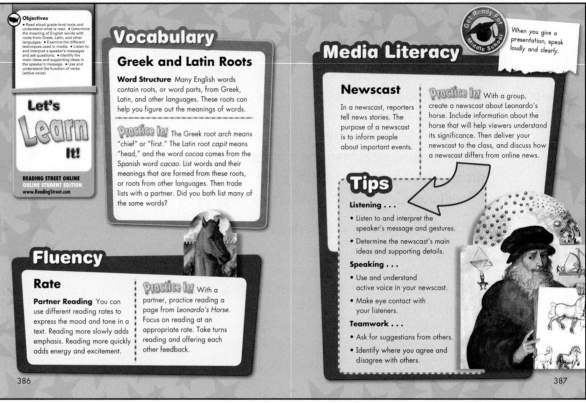

Student Edition pp. 386–387

Fluency
Rate

Guide Practice

Use the Student Edition activity as an assessment tool. Make sure the reading passage is at least 200 words in length. As students read aloud with partners, walk around to make sure they are reading at an appropriate rate, adjusting their rate when they share new information from the text.

Don't Wait Until Friday

MONITOR PROGRESS — Check Fluency

As students reread, monitor their progress toward their individual fluency goals.
Current Goal: 115–122 words correct per minute
End-of-Year Goal: 140 words correct per minute

If... students cannot read fluently at a rate of 115–122 words correct per minute,

Then... make sure students practice with text at their independent levels.

Day 1	Days 2–3	Day 4	Day 5
Check Oral Vocabulary	Check Retelling	Check Fluency	Check Oral Vocabulary

Success Predictor

Vocabulary
Greek and Latin Roots

Teach Greek and Latin roots

Word Structure Write the Greek roots *arch* (chief, first), *phil* (love) and the Latin root *ject* (throw) on the board. Explain to students that knowing about word structure can help them build and decode words. Ask students to explain how it affects the meaning when the prefix *inter* (between) is added to the root word *ject* (throw) to form the word *interject.*

Guide practice

Have students write as many words as they can using these roots and more. Tell them they can use a dictionary to help them find words and look up meanings.

On their own

Walk around the room and assist students as needed in thinking of words that are built from the roots and then comparing their lists with a partner.

Media Literacy
Newscast

Teach

Tell students that they will work in groups to create a newscast about the 1999 unveiling of Leonardo's Horse. Discuss with students the elements of a newscast, including the roles that each student can play (newscasters, writers, teleprompters) and the writing of a newscast, emphasizing the idea that news should be presented from a neutral point of view. Have students consider how the messages conveyed and the techniques used in a news broadcast differ from those used in commercials and other media.

Guide practice

Remind students that as they work, they should be paying attention to the following speaking and listening skills: Speaking clearly and loudly so they are understood; choosing their words carefully so they express their ideas well; listening carefully when a group member is speaking to be able to interpret their verbal and nonverbal messages; using teamwork and including suggestions and ideas from all members of the group.

On their own

Have groups write their newscasts and present them to the class in an organized manner.

Presenting a Newscast

Remind students that when they present their newscasts to the class, they should focus on the following things to make their presentations seem professional and realistic:

- Enunciate words clearly.
- Use standard English and appropriate vocabulary.
- Make the presentation clear and to the point.
- Be organized.
- Use natural gestures.

Academic Vocabulary

Greek and Latin roots Word parts that have their origin in the ancient Greek or Latin languages.

Fluency

Success Predictor

Objectives
- Find pertinent information from online sources.
- Recognize the principal parts of regular verbs and use active voice.
- Practice correctly spelling compound words.

Research and Inquiry
Synthesize

Teach

Have students synthesize their research findings and results and write their reports. Students should read over their notes and synthesize the research into a written presentation that compiles important information from multiple sources and that develops a topic sentence, summarizes findings, uses quotations to support ideas, and uses an appropriate form of documentation to acknowledge the sources. Review how to choose relevant information from a number of sources and organize it logically.

Guide practice

Have students organize their reports carefully, including topic sentences, supporting evidence, and quotations. Have students make sure that quotations include citations and that their works cited page is complete. Discuss the difference between paraphrasing and plagiarism and the importance of citing valid, reliable sources.

Once the written reports are completed, have students work with a partner to review and critique the reports, focusing on helping students to make suggestions in a positive and constructive way. You may also encourage students to find and print out a picture of the artist or the artist's work which they are researching.

On their own

Have students write a brief explanation of their research findings. Then have them organize and combine information for presenting their research findings to the class.

Conventions
Principal Parts of Regular Verbs

Test practice

Remind students that grammar skills, such as principal parts of regular verbs and the active voice, are often assessed on important tests.

- A verb's tenses are formed from its **principal parts.**
- The four principal parts are the present, present participle, past, and past participle.
- **A regular verb** forms its past and past participle by adding *-ed* or *-d* to the present form.
- **Active voice** has the subject performing the action.

Reader's and Writer's Notebook, p. 199

Daily Fix-It

Use Daily Fix-It numbers 7 and 8 in the right margin.

On their own

For more practice, use the *Reader's and Writer's Notebook,* p. 199.

Spelling
Compound Words

Practice spelling strategy

Have pairs of students write each part of each list word on a separate note card. Tell students to turn the cards face down and then take turns turning up two cards at a time. If the two revealed words together form a list word, the student who chose the words keeps the cards. Play continues until all cards are paired.

On their own

For additional practice, use *Let's Practice It!* p. 138 on the *Teacher Resources DVD-ROM.*

Let's Practice It!
TR DVD•138

Daily Fix-It

7. Renaissance Artists learned how to create the illusion of deapth. (*artists; depth*)
8. These technique made there pictures seem more realistic. (*This; their*)

ELL

English Language Learners
Leveled support: Active voice
Provide support based on students' proficiency levels.

Beginning: Write *I learned new words* and *The new words were learned by me*. Explain the difference to students and have them read the sentences aloud.

Intermediate: Write four sentences on the board—two with active and two with passive voice. Have students read them aloud and orally identify which sentences are active.

Advanced/Advanced High Have students write two sentences using the active voice and two using the passive voice. Have students orally explain what makes them different.

Objectives
- Write a persuasive speech in response to a prompt.
- Practice timed test writing.

Writing for Tests
Persuasive Speech

Review the key features of a persuasive speech. Stress the importance of establishing a position or a clear focus and stating it in a topic sentence, using sound reasoning. A persuasive speech also includes details and relevant evidence and information that support the main focus.

Detailed and Relevant Information

■ Yesterday we wrote persuasive speeches about recent important inventions. Today we will write again for additional practice in answering test questions.

■ Persuasive speeches include **detailed and relevant information** that supports the author's position. This information relates to the topic in a very clear way. Focus on what information needs to be included in your speech. Leave out information that is unnecessary.

Help students understand the difference between relevant and irrelevant information. Create a simple T-chart about what could be included in a persuasive speech about why the school needs a swimming pool. Then make a list of information as a sample *(exercise; competitions; it's fun; there is a good pool in the neighboring town, etc.)*. Help students sort the list into *Relevant* and *Irrelevant* columns. Before they choose which list the information belongs in, have students ask themselves: *Does my audience need to know this?*

Sample test

Direct students to get paper and pencil ready to take a writing test. Display the new writing prompt for students and allow them appropriate time to write to the prompt. Tell students to spend some time thinking about the key features of a persuasive speech before beginning to write. Remind students to allow themselves a couple of minutes after writing to reread what they've written and make changes or additions.

Prompt   Write a speech that persuades people to go to a new art exhibit. What is in the exhibit, and why is it important?

Write Guy
Jeff Anderson

Topic Sentence? Really?

Topic sentences are excellent, but many good paragraphs actually don't have topic sentences. That's right. We want students to learn how to craft a topic sentence and a paragraph. We also want students to know that not all paragraphs consist of five sentences, beginning with a topic sentence. Those kinds of limitations smother writers sooner or later.

ROUTINE   Quick Write for Fluency   Team Talk

1 **Talk** Have pairs discuss Leonardo's many inventions.

2 **Write** Each student writes a short paragraph about which invention they find most interesting.

3 **Share** Partners read one another's writing and then check their partner's writing for the correct use of principal parts of regular verbs.

Routines Flip Chart

Wrap Up Your Day

✔ **Build Concepts** What did you learn about how Michelangelo became a great artist?

✔ **Oral Vocabulary** Monitor students' use of oral vocabulary as they respond: How did looking at people's faces inspire Michelangelo?

✔ **Story Structure** Discuss how understanding conflict and resolution helped students to understand Michelangelo's conflict with his father.

Differentiated Instruction

SI Strategic Intervention

Irrelevant information If students are having difficulty determining what is relevant, begin a discussion about school lunch. Then insert random thoughts into the conversation, such as which book you are reading. Explain that this is irrelevant information.

Preview DAY 5

Remind students to think about how artists inspire future generations.

Objectives
- Review the weekly concept.
- Review oral vocabulary.

Today at a Glance

Oral Vocabulary

Comprehension
⊙ Main idea and details

Lesson Vocabulary
⊙ Greek and Latin roots

Word Analysis
Greek and Latin roots

Literary Terms
Tone

Assessment
Fluency

Comprehension:

Research and Inquiry
Communicate

Spelling
Compound words

Conventions
Principal parts of regular verbs

Writing
Persuasivespeech

Check Oral Vocabulary
SUCCESS PREDICTOR

Concept Wrap Up

Question of the Week

How do artists inspire future generations?

Review the concept

Have students look back at the reading selections to find examples that best demonstrate the the way that artists inspire future generations.

Review Amazing Words

Display and review this week's concept map. Remind students that this week they have learned ten Amazing Words related to art and artists. Have students break into groups and use the Amazing Words and the concept map to answer the question *How do artists inspire future generations?* Encourage students to consider suggestions from other group members.

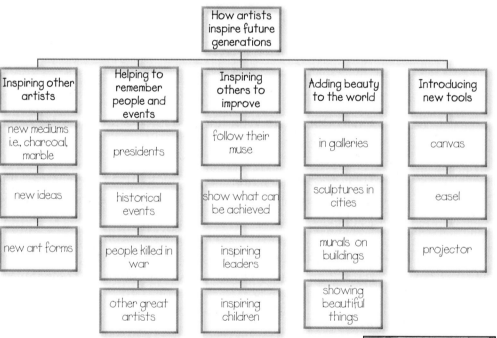

E L L Visual Learning: Check Concepts and Language Use the Day 5 instructions on ELL Poster 12 to monitor students' understanding of the lesson concept.

 Poster 12

Amazing Ideas

Amazing Words

easel	sculpture
charcoal	projector
canvas	medium
gallery	muse
marble	inspire

Connect to the Big Question

Have pairs of students discuss how the Question of the Week connects to the Big Question: *What do people gain from the work of inventors and artists?* Tell students to use the concept map and what they have learned from this week's Anchored Talks and reading selections to form an Amazing Idea – a realization or "big idea" about Inventors and Artists. Then ask each pair to share their Amazing Idea with the class.

Amazing Ideas might include these key concepts:

• Inventors and artists inspire people and help society in many ways.

• It's important for people to recognize the work of inventors and artists.

• It's important for everyone, including inventors and artists, to realize that what they do may inspire others.

Write about it

Have students write a few sentences about their Amazing Idea that begins with "This week I learned…"

It's Friday

MONITOR PROGRESS | **Check Oral Vocabulary**

Have individuals use this week's Amazing Words to describe art and artists. Monitor students' abilities to use the Amazing Words and note which words you need to reteach.

If… students have difficulty using the Amazing Words,

then… reteach using the Oral Vocabulary Routine, pages pp. 355a, 358b, 372b, 382b, OV•2.

Day 1	**Days 2–3**	**Day 4**	**Day 5**	
Check Oral vocabulary	Check Summarizing	Check Fluency	Check Oral Vocabulary	Success Predictor

ELL

English Language Learners
Concept Map Work with students to add new words to the concept map.

 Oral Vocabulary
Success Predictor

Objectives
- Review main idea and details.
- Review Greek and Latin roots.
- Review tone.

Comprehension Review
Main Idea and Details

Teach main idea and details

Envision It!

Review the definitions of main idea and details on p. 356. Remind students that the main idea is the most important idea in a piece of writing and that details give more information about the main idea. For additional support have students review p. EI•12 on main idea and details.

Student Edition p. EI•12

Guide practice

Have partners write 1–2 sentences that summarize the main idea of *Leonardo's Horse* and maintain meaning and logical order. Have them summarize, while maintaining meaning and logical order, at least three details that support the main idea.

On their own

For additional practice with main idea and details use *Let's Practice It!* p. 139 on the *Teacher Resources DVD-ROM.*

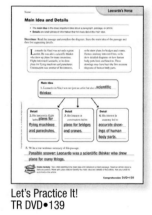

Let's Practice It!
TR DVD•139

Vocabulary Review
Greek and Latin Roots

Teach Greek and Latin roots

Remind students that knowing the meaning of Greek and Latin roots can help them analyze words and determine their meanings.

Guide practice

Have students use a dictionary to determine the meaning of the Greek root words *astro* (star) and *nomia* (knowledge). Then ask them to figure out the meaning of the word *astronomy.* (knowledge of stars)

On their own

Have students work in small groups and use a dictionary to determine the meaning of the Latin root *vis* (to see). Have them use the dictionary to make a list of words that have the Latin root *vis.* (visible, vision, visionary, visit, visor, vista) Remind them to read the definitions of the words to be certain their meanings have some association with the root *vis.*

Word Analysis Review
Greek and Latin Roots

Teach Greek and Latin roots

Review Greek and Latin roots as words or parts of words from Greek or Latin that are used to build many English words. Use prefixes and root words to discuss the meanings of the words *bicycle, tricycle,* and *unicycle.*

Guide practice

Display the following word: *philanthropy.* Use the Strategy for Meaningful Parts to teach *philanthropy.*

ROUTINE Strategy for Meaningful Word Parts

1 **Introduce word parts** Write the word *philanthropy*. Circle the Greek roots, *phila* and *anthro*.

2 **Connect to meaning** Define each smaller word. The root *phila* means "love/friendship." *Anthro* means "human."

3 **Read the word** Blend the word parts together to read *philanthropy*. Then use the meanings of the smaller words to determine the meaning of the new word. *Philanthropy* means "love for humankind."

Routines Flip Chart

On their own

Have students work in pairs to come up with words made from these roots: *scrib* (to write) and *tele-* (far, distant)

Literary Terms Review
Tone

Teach tone

Have students reread "A Job for Michelangelo" on pp. 382–385. Remind students that tone is the attitude of the writer toward the subject. Identifying the tone allows the reader to see how the author feels about the subject. The tone can be found in the author's word choice, descriptions, and general style.

Guide practice

Read the sentence, "More importantly, he spent his life doing what he loved…" How does this sentence reveal the tone, or the author's attitude about the subject? (The author finds it important to follow your passions.) Have students find other words and phrases in the selection that reveal the tone.

On their own

Have students list words that describe the tone of the selection.

E L L

English Language Learners
Word Analysis: Greek and Latin Roots To give students practice in finding Greek and Latin roots, explain the meanings of the prefixes *pre-* (before) and *post-* (after). Have students use a dictionary to find words using these prefixes. Discuss how the meanings of the prefixes affect the meanings of the words.

Leonardo's Horse **387i**

Objectives
- Read grade-level text with fluency.

Assessment

Check words correct per minute

Fluency Make two copies of the fluency passage on p. 387k. As the student reads the text aloud, mark mistakes on your copy. Also mark where the student is at the end of one minute. To check the student's comprehension of the passage, have him or her retell what was read. To figure words correct per minute (WCPM), subtract the number of mistakes from the total number of words read in one minute.

Corrective feedback

If... students cannot read fluently at a rate of 115–122 WCPM, **then...** make sure they practice with text at their independent reading level. Provide additional fluency practice by pairing nonfluent readers with fluent readers. Check to be sure students are reading with comprehension.

If... students already read at 140 WCPM, **then...** have them read a book of their choice independently.

Plan to Assess Fluency

☑ **Week 1** Assess Advanced students.

☑ **This week assess Strategic Intervention students.**

☐ **Week 3** Assess On-Level students.

☐ **Week 4** Assess Strategic Intervention students.

☐ **Week 5** Assess Any students you have not yet checked during this unit.

Set individual goals for students to enable them to reach the year-end goal.

- Current Goal: 115–122 WCPM
- Year-End Goal: 140 WCPM

Small Group Time

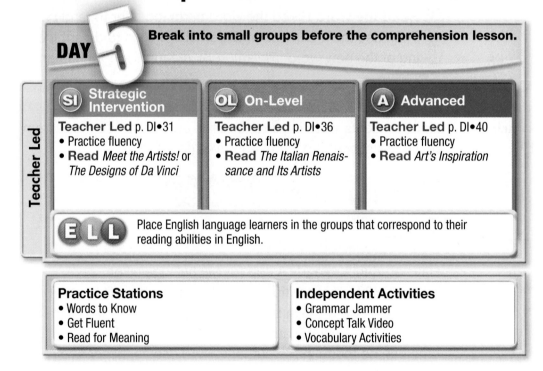

DAY **5** Break into small groups before the comprehension lesson.

Teacher Led

SI Strategic Intervention
Teacher Led p. DI•31
- Practice fluency
- **Read** *Meet the Artists!* or *The Designs of Da Vinci*

OL On-Level
Teacher Led p. DI•36
- Practice fluency
- **Read** *The Italian Renaissance and Its Artists*

A Advanced
Teacher Led p. DI•40
- Practice fluency
- **Read** *Art's Inspiration*

ELL Place English language learners in the groups that correspond to their reading abilities in English.

Practice Stations
- Words to Know
- Get Fluent
- Read for Meaning

Independent Activities
- Grammar Jammer
- Concept Talk Video
- Vocabulary Activities

See How They Survive

A painting by a great artist can sell for millions of dollars. If you own one   16
of these original paintings, it could be worth a lot of money. Some people   30
who don't own an original painting want to make a lot of money anyway. So   45
they make fake paintings. A fake painting is called a forgery.   56

There are two aspects to a forgery. The first is artistic. You want people   70
to believe your painting was painted by a great artist. So you have to paint   85
very well. What's more, you have to paint in the style of that artist. You can   101
practice by copying real paintings. But eventually, you are going to have to   114
make up one of your own. (After all, you cannot paint a copy of, say, the   130
Mona Lisa and expect anyone to believe it's real. Everyone knows the real   143
Mona Lisa is in the Louvre.)   149

The second aspect of forgery is technical. Let's say you want to paint   162
a fake Rembrandt. Rembrandt lived 400 years ago. So you have to find a   176
canvas that is 400 years old. Then you have to make your paints the same   191
way people made paint 400 years ago. You might even have to find a   205
400-year-old brush.   207

After you paint the fake, you have to age it. Over hundreds of years,   221
paint dries up, shrinks, and cracks. Dirt and dust settles in the cracks. But you   236
don't want to wait hundreds of years. You have to find a way to make real-   252
looking cracks in the paint. You have to get real-looking dust and dirt into the   266
cracks.   267

Art forgery is a lot of work.   274

MONITOR PROGRESS   • Check Fluency

Objectives
• Read grade-level text with comprehension.

Assessment

Check main idea and details

Main Idea and Details Use "Do What You Want to Do" on p. 387m to check students' understanding of main idea and details. Check to be sure students maintain the meaning and logical order of the main idea and details in their summaries in questions 2 and 3.

1. What kinds of paintings did John Constable most like to paint? **Realistic landscape paintings** Were these kinds of paintings popular at the time he lived? **No**

2. Summarize the main idea of this passage. **Possible response: John Constable was an English landscape painter who painted the kinds of pictures he loved, though he did not become famous until after his death.**

3. Summarize three important details that support the main idea. **Possible response: John Constable loved painting landscapes, but landscape paintings were not popular in England during the time when he lived. He sold few paintings and was not successful. John Constable is now considered an important painter.**

Corrective feedback

If... students are unable to answer the comprehension questions, **then...** use the Reteach lesson in the *First Stop* book.

Do What You Want to Do

John Constable was one of the greatest English painters of all time. Sadly, he never achieved great success while he was alive.

John was born in 1776. His father made a lot of money in the wheat business. The plan was for John to take over the family business. But John wanted to paint.

In 1799 John began to study art. He took classes at the Royal Academy School. The school is run by The Royal Academy of Arts. The academy is like a club. Only the greatest English artists are members and you have to be invited to join.

Also at the school was a young man named J.M.W. Turner. He was only a year older than John. But the two never became friends. In fact, Turner became John's great rival.

Like most painters of the time, Turner painted mythological and biblical scenes. John painted fields and trees. Artists and critics loved Turner's work, but they ignored John's. In 1802 Turner was elected to the Royal Academy, but John wasn't asked to join until 1829. Turner achieved great success during his life, and yet John only sold twenty paintings in England while he was alive.

John could have painted things that other people liked. In fact, he sometimes painted portraits just to make some money. But he loved painting landscapes. At the time, other artists painted strange, imaginary landscapes. John painted real, actual landscapes. John thought that what he was painting was important. And history has proven him right.

MONITOR PROGRESS

• **Main Idea and Details**

Research and Inquiry
Communicate

Present Ideas   Have students give a brief talk on their research. Have students share their inquiry question and give highlights from their written reports. They may want to display a visual aid such as a photograph of the artist or the artist's work.

Listening and speaking   Remind students how to be good speakers and how to communicate effectively with their audience.

- Speak clearly and loudly, at an appropriate rate.
- Use natural gestures to enhance the presentation.
- Keep eye contact with audience members.
- Use language that shares your thoughts clearly.
- Respond to questions with details from your research.

Remind students to follow these tips for being a good listener.

- Listen to and interpret all of the speaker's messages, both verbal and nonverbal.
- If necessary, ask questions to clarify the speaker's purpose or perspective.
- Wait until the speaker has finished before raising your hand to ask a question.
- Be polite, even if you disagree.

Spelling Test
Compound Words

Spelling test   To administer the spelling test, refer to the directions, words, and sentences on p. 357c.

Conventions
Principal Parts of Regular Verbs

Teach   Remind students that regular verbs have principal parts: present, present participle, past, and past participle.

Guide practice   Have students work with a partner to underline the verbs in these sentences. Then have them identify which principal part of each regular verb is being used.

> Teachers <u>have told</u> me that I am a good student. (past participle)
>
> He <u>plays</u> drums after school. (present)

Daily Fix-It   Use Daily Fix-It numbers 9 and 10 in the right margin.

On their own   Write these sentences. Have students look back in *Leonardo's Horse* to find the correct principal parts of regular verbs to complete the sentences.

1. He _____ to examine everything. (stopped)

2. Everybody _____ questions then. (was asking)

3. He _____ the picture and that was the important part. (had planned)

4. He _____ to understand everything about his subject. (needed)

5. No one _____ a single pouring of anything this large. (had tried)

For additional practice, use *Let's Practice It!* p. 140 on the *Teacher Resources DVD-ROM.*

Daily Fix-It

9. Leonardo was sed to be a very strong and handsom man. *(said; handsome)*

10. He were also a talented musican with a fine singing voice. *(was; musician)*

Let's Practice It!
TR DVD•140

Objectives
- Proofread for the correct use of the principal parts of verbs and active voice.
- Evaluate a timed-writing sample.

Writing for Tests—Persuasive Speech

Review
evalulating

Remind students that yesterday they learned more about including detailed and relevant evidence in persuasive speech writing. Today they will review and evaluate their speeches for correct use of verbs.

Proofread for Principal Parts of Verbs

■ Yesterday we wrote persuasive speeches about why people should attend a new art exhibit. Today we will proofread our speeches for correct use of verbs. The goal is to make sure we are using the principal parts of verbs correctly.

■ First, look for and circle all the verbs in your speech. Now, evaluate your use of verbs. Do your sentences have the subject perform the action? This will ensure that you have used the active voice. Did you form the principal parts of verbs correctly? **Remind students that a regular verb forms its past and past participle by adding *-ed* or *-d* to the present form.**

Have students continue to assess their writing based on correct use of verbs. Then ask them to evaluate their speeches using the other traits of the Scoring Rubric from their *Reader's and Writer's Notebook* p. 194.

Remind students that they may receive different number scores for each of the different traits, but that is all right. Lower or higher scores for different traits can help them see where their strengths lie, and where they might need to focus more attention and effort.

Evaluate Have students spend a few minutes revising the sample test-writing, paying particular attention to the use of verbs. When students have finished, have them use the scoring rubric to evaluate their work.

ROUTINE Quick Write for Fluency Team Talk

1 Talk Have pairs discuss what they learned about persuasive speech writing this week.

2 Write Each student writes a few sentences about how they can use persuasive speeches in the future.

3 Share Each student reads aloud their own writing to their partner.

Routines Flip Chart

Teacher Note

Writing Self-Evaluation Guide Make copies of the Writing Self-Evaluation Guide on p. 39 of the *Reader's and Writer's Notebook* and hand out to students.

English Language Learners

Support revising Provide practice with using the rubric. Visit briefly with each student to ensure they know how to use it correctly.

Poster preview Prepare students for next week by using Week 3, ELL Poster 13. Read the Poster Talk-Through to introduce the concept and vocabulary. Ask students to identify and describe objects and actions in the art.

Selection summary Send the summary of *Waterhouse Hawkins,* in English and the students' home languages, if available, home with students. They can read the summary with family members.

Preview NEXT WEEK

How can paleontologists help us understand the past? Tell students that next week they will read about how dinosaur bones can help us learn about the past.

Weekly Assessment

Use pp. 79–86 of *Weekly Tests* to check:

✔ **Word Analysis** Greek and Latin Roots

✔ 🎯 **Comprehension Skill** Main Idea and Details

✔ Review **Comprehension Skill** Fact and Opinion

✔ **Lesson Vocabulary**

achieved	fashioned
architect	midst
bronze	philosopher
cannon	rival
depressed	

Weekly Tests

A

Advanced

OL

On-Level

SI

Strategic Intervention

Differentiated Assessment

Use pp. 67–72 of *Fresh Reads for Fluency and Comprehension* to check:

✔ 🎯 **Comprehension Skill** Main Idea and Details

✔ Review **Comprehension Skill** Fact and Opinion

✔ **Fluency** Words Correct Per Minute

Fresh Reads for Fluency and Comprehension

Managing Assessment

Use *Assessment Handbook* for:

✔ **Weekly Assessment Blackline Masters for Monitoring Progress**

✔ **Observation Checklists**

✔ **Record-Keeping Forms**

✔ **Portfolio Assessment**

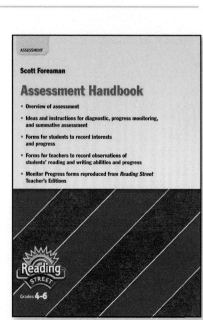

Assessment Handbook

Teacher Notes

Small Group Time

SI *Strategic Intervention*

DAY 1

5-Day Plan

DAY 1	• Reinforce the concept • Read Leveled Readers Concept Literacy Below Level
DAY 2	• Main Idea and Details • Visualize • Revisit Student Edition pp. 360–371
DAY 3	• Greek/Latin Roots • Revisit Student Edition pp. 372–377
DAY 4	• Practice Retelling • Read/Revisit Student Edition pp. 382–385
DAY 5	• Reread for fluency • Reread Leveled Readers

3- or 4-Day Plan

DAY 1	• Reinforce the concept • Read Leveled Readers
DAY 2	• Main Idea and Details • Visualize • Revisit Student Edition pp. 360–371
DAY 3	• Greek/Latin Roots • Revisit Student Edition pp. 372–377
DAY 4	• Practice Retelling • Read/Revisit Student Edition pp. 382–385 • Reread for fluency • Reread Leveled Readers

3-Day Plan: Eliminate the shaded box.

Build Background

■ **Reinforce the Concept** Discuss the weekly question *How do artists inspire future generations?* Ask students if they have seen a picture, sculpture, or other work of art that they liked. Discuss what they liked about it and how it made them feel. One way we can be inspired by artists is to look at the artwork they have created. Great artwork can make us see the world in different ways. For example, Greek and Roman art inspired artists in Italy to see the human form more realistically. Have students add new words to the concept map.

■ **Connect to Reading** Explain to students that artists today can also inspire others. Norman Rockwell, for example, is still popular today for his vivid portraits of ordinary people. This week you will read about artists and the art they create. Norman Rockwell is a famous American artist whose pictures appeared on the covers of many magazines. In the Read Aloud "Norman Rockwell," why did the artist start using photographs of his subjects? *(He wanted to paint people more realistically, but he couldn't ask models to stay in his studio for days at a time.)*

Objectives
• Interpret a speaker's messages (both verbal and nonverbal).

For a complete literacy instructional plan and additional practice with this week's target skills and strategies, see the **Leveled Reader Teaching Guide.**

Concept Literacy Reader

- **Read** *Meet the Artists!*

- **Before Reading** Preview the selection with students, focusing on key concepts and vocabulary. Then have them set a purpose for reading.

- **During Reading** Read the first two pages of the selection aloud while students track the print. Then have students finish reading the selection with a partner.

- **After Reading** After students finish reading the selection, connect it to the weekly question *How do artists inspire future generations?*

Below-Level Reader

- **Read** *The Designs of Da Vinci*

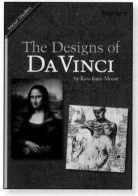

- **Before Reading** Have students preview the selection, using the illustrations. Then have students set a purpose for reading.

- **During Reading** Do a choral reading of the first two pages. If students are able, have them read and discuss the remainder of the book with a partner. Discuss the following questions:

  - Why was da Vinci's handwriting so hard to read? *(He wrote from right to left.)*

  - Why was Leonardo da Vinci a true Renaissance man? *(He had many interests, he studied nature, and he was an artist.)*

- **After Reading** Have students look at and discuss the concept map. Connect the Below-Level Reader to the weekly question *How do artists inspire future generations?*

MONITOR PROGRESS

If... students have difficulty reading the selection with a partner,

then... have them follow along as they listen to the Leveled Readers DVD-ROM.

If... students have trouble understanding why da Vinci studied living horses,

then... reread p. 9 and discuss da Vinci's dream together.

Objectives
- Read aloud grade-level stories with fluency.

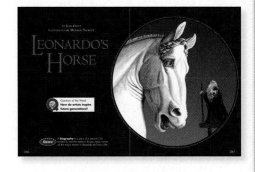

Reinforce Comprehension

◉ **Skill Main Idea and Details** Review with students *Envision It!* p. E1•12 on Main Idea and Details. Then use p. 356 to review the definitions of main idea and details.

◉ **Strategy Visualize** Review the definition of visualize. Remind students to picture the images as they read the story. What details does the author use to help the reader "see" the action? For additional support, refer students to *Envision It!* p. EI•25.

Revisit *Leonardo's Horse* on pp. 360–371. Have students begin reading aloud with a partner. As they read, have them apply the comprehension skill and strategy to the story.

- What is the main idea of the paragraph on p. 363? *(Even as a boy, da Vinci was interested in art.)*

- What details support this main idea? *(He looked carefully at everything in the countryside near his home. When he was a teenager, he studied art in Florence.)*

- As a young artist, Leonardo pursued a dream. What was his dream? *(He wanted to create a sculpture of a bronze horse.)*

- What details caused the failure of Leonardo's dream? *(Leonardo was slow to cast the bronze. When the French invaded, he fled. Then rain washed away his clay model.)*

- Why did Leonardo become sad and depressed near the end of his life? *(He felt he had wasted his life and failed because he hadn't finished the bronze horse.)*

Use the During Reading Differentiated Instruction for additional support for struggling readers.

MONITOR PROGRESS

If... students have difficulty reading along with the group,

then... have them follow along as they listen to the AudioText.

Student Edition, p. EI•12

More Reading

Use additional Leveled Readers or other texts at students' instructional levels to reinforce this week's skills and strategies. For text suggestions, see the Leveled Reader Database or the Leveled Readers Skills Chart on pp. CL 24–CL 29.

Objectives
- Summarize the main idea and supporting details in text.
- Evaluate the impact of sensory details in literary text.

SI Strategic Intervention   **DAY 3**

Reinforce Vocabulary

◉ **Greek and Latin Roots/Word Structure** Say the word *artist* as you write it on the board. Circle the Latin root *art* and point out that it means "skill."

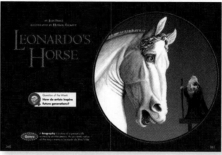

If I know a root word, I can figure out the meaning of words formed from these roots, or word parts. Many English words come from Greek and Latin roots. The words *artist, artful,* and *artisan* all have the Latin root *art.*

Revisit *Leonardo's Horse* on pp. 372–377. Review *Words!* on p. W•9.

• Write the word *astronomer* on the board. How does knowing that the Greek root *astron* means "star" help you figure out the meaning of *astronomer? (An* astronomer *is a person who studies the stars.)*

• Then write the word *philosopher* on the board. *Phil* means "love of" and *sophos* means "wise." What does *philosopher* mean? *(A* philosopher *is a person who loves wisdom.)*

As students finish reading the selection, help them use Greek and Latin roots to figure out the meanings of unfamiliar words.

Use the During Reading Differentiated Instruction for additional support for struggling readers.

Student Edition, p. W•9

More Reading

Use additional Leveled Readers or other texts at students' instructional levels to reinforce this week's skills and strategies. For text suggestions, see the Leveled Reader Database or the Leveled Readers Skills Chart on pp. CL 24–CL 29.

MONITOR PROGRESS

If... students need more practice with the lesson vocabulary, **then...** use *Envision It! Pictured Vocabulary Cards.*

Objectives
• Determine the meaning of grade-level academic English words derived from Latin roots.
• Use word structure to analyze and decode new words.

Small Group Time

Practice Retelling

■ **Retell** Have students work in pairs and use the Retelling Cards to retell *Leonardo's Horse.* Monitor retelling and prompt students as needed. For example, ask:

- Who is the main character in the selection?

- Tell me what this selection is about in a few sentences.

If students struggle, model a fluent retelling.

Genre Focus

■ **Before Reading or Revisiting** "A Job for Michelangelo" on pp. 382–385, read aloud the genre information about historical fiction on p. 382. Explain to students that historical fiction is based on facts from a period in history, but the story itself is made up.

Then have students preview "A Job for Michelangelo." Ask:

- What do the pictures show? *(examples of art)*

- Scan the first page and find a date. What does this tell you about the historical period? *(It is around 1488, during the Renaissance.)*

Then have students set a purpose for reading based on their preview.

■ **During Reading or Revisiting** Have students read along with you while tracking the print or do a choral reading of the story. Stop to discuss any unfamiliar words.

■ **After Reading or Revisiting** Have students share their reactions to the historical fiction. Then guide them through the Reading Across Texts and Writing Across Texts activities.

MONITOR PROGRESS

If... students have difficulty retelling the selection,
then... have them review the story using the illustrations.

Objectives
- Explain the effect of a historical event or movement on the theme of a work of literature.

 Strategic Intervention

DAY **5**

For a complete literacy instructional plan and additional practice with this week's target skills and strategies, see the **Leveled Reader Teaching Guide.**

Concept Literacy Reader

- **Model** Model the fluency skill, rate, for students. Ask students to listen carefully as you read aloud the first two pages of *Meet the Artists!* Have students note how varying the rate helps you express different moods and tones in the story.

- **Fluency Routine**

  1. Have students reread passages from *Meet the Artists!* with a partner.

  2. For optimal fluency, students should reread three to four times.

  3. As students read, monitor fluency and provide corrective feedback. Have students note that reading slowly gives emphasis and reading more quickly shows excitement.

  See *Routines Flip Chart* for more help with fluency.

- **Retell** Have students retell *Meet the Artists!* Prompt as necessary.

Below-Level Reader

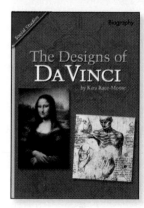

- **Model** Ask students to listen carefully as you read aloud the first two pages of *The Designs of Da Vinci,* varying the rate to show differences in the mood and tone of the story.

- **Fluency Routine**

  1. Have students reread passages from *The Designs of Da Vinci* with a partner or individually.

  2. For optimal fluency, students should reread three to four times.

  3. As students read, monitor fluency and provide corrective feedback. Point out that reading slowly helps emphasize the seriousness of the text, and reading quickly helps express excitement or suspense.

  See *Routines Flip Chart* for more help with fluency.

- **Retell** For additional practice, have students retell *The Designs of Da Vinci* page-by-page, using the illustrations. Prompt as necessary.

  - What happens in this part?

  - What is the main idea in this part?

  - What are the details that support the main idea?

MONITOR PROGRESS

If... students have difficulty reading fluently,

then... provide additional fluency practice by pairing nonfluent readers with fluent ones.

 Objectives
- Read aloud grade-level stories with fluency.

Small Group Time

Pacing Small Group Instruction

15~20 mins.

5-Day Plan

DAY 1	• Expand the concept • Read On-Level Reader
DAY 2	• ⊚ Main Idea and Details • ⊚ Visualize • Revisit Student Edition pp. 360–371
DAY 3	• ⊚ Greek and Latin Roots • Revisit Student Edition pp. 372–377
DAY 4	• Practice Retelling • Read/Revisit Student Edition pp. 382–385
DAY 5	• Reread for fluency • Reread On-Level Reader

3- or 4-Day Plan

DAY 1	• Expand the concept • On-Level Reader
DAY 2	• ⊚ Main Idea and Details • ⊚ Visualize • Revisit Student Edition pp. 360–371
DAY 3	• ⊚ Greek and Latin Roots • Revisit Student Edition pp. 372–377
DAY 4	• Practice Retelling • Read/Revisit Student Edition pp. 382–385 • Reread for fluency • Reread On-Level Reader

3-Day Plan: Eliminate the shaded box.

 OL On-Level **DAY 1**

Build Background

■ **Expand the Concept** Connect the weekly question *How do artists inspire future generations?* and expand the concept. Works of art can spark the imaginations of many people long after the artist is gone. These works can teach generations how to see the world in different ways. Add new words to the concept map.

On-Level Reader

For a complete literacy instructional plan and additional practice with this week's target skills and strategies, see the **Leveled Reader Teaching Guide.**

The Italian Renaissance *and* Its Artists
by Liz Murray

■ **Before Reading** *The Italian Renaissance and Its Artists,* have students preview the reader by looking at the title, cover, and pictures. Ask:

• What is the topic of this book? *(a time of great artists and artistic work in Italy)*

• What types of art do you see in the illustrations? *(paintings, sculpture, buildings)*

Have students create a graphic organizer like the one on p. 356 of the Student Edition to help them identify the main ideas and supporting details in the selection.

As you read, look for main ideas and record them on your graphic organizer. Think about the details that support the main ideas and add them as well.

■ **During Reading** Read aloud the first three pages of the book as students follow along. Then have them finish reading the book with a partner. Remind students to note the main ideas and supporting details as they read.

■ **After Reading** Have students compare their main idea graphic organizers.

• What is the main idea about artists of the Italian Renaissance?

• How does the main idea relate to the weekly question *How do artists inspire future generations?*

Objectives
• Interpret a speaker's messages (both verbal and nonverbal).

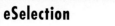

OL On-Level   DAY 2

Expand Comprehension

Skill Main Idea and Details Use p. 356 to review the definitions of main idea and details. For additional review, see p. EI•12 in *Envision It!* The main idea is the most important idea about the topic, such as this sentence from the Read Aloud "Norman Rockwell": *After Rockwell began painting from photographs, his work became richer and better.*

Strategy Visualize Review the definition of visualize. Encourage students to use the images and sensory details to visualize the action and characters as they read. During reading, use the Extend Thinking questions for additional support. For additional support, refer students to *Envision It!* p. EI•25.

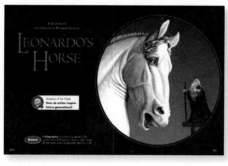

Revisit *Leonardo's Horse* on pp. 360–371. As they read, have them apply the comprehension skill and strategy to the story.

- Which of the following best states the main idea of the selection?

  (a) Leonardo believed he was a failure because he didn't complete the bronze horse.

  (b) Leonardo made a large clay model of the horse.

  (c) Leonardo wanted to help the duke by making the horse.
     (a)

- What details does the author use to support the main idea? *(Leonardo wanted to become famous for the horse, he never forgot the horse, and he wrote that he had "wasted" his time.)*

Student Edition, p. EI•12

More Reading

Use additional Leveled Readers or other texts at students' instructional levels to reinforce this week's skills and strategies. For text suggestions, see the Leveled Reader Database or the Leveled Readers Skills Chart on pp. CL 24–CL 29.

Objectives

- Summarize the main idea and supporting details in text.
- Evaluate the impact of sensory details in literary text.

Small Group Time

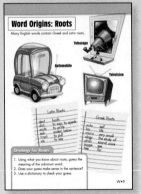

Student Edition, p. W•9

More Reading

Use additional Leveled Readers or other texts at students' instructional levels to reinforce this week's skills and strategies. For text suggestions, see the Leveled Reader Database or the Leveled Readers Skills Chart on pp. CL 24–CL 29.

Expand Vocabulary

Greek and Latin Roots/Word Structure Review *Words!* on p. W•9. Remind students that many words in English are formed from Greek and Latin roots. Knowing the meaning of these roots can help them figure out the meanings of unfamiliar words. Write the word *variety* as you say it aloud and use it in a sentence: "Leonardo was talented in a variety of ways."

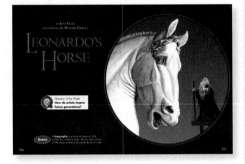

- The root in *variety* is *var,* which means "different." What does this tell you about the meaning of *variety* in this sentence? *(Leonardo was talented in many different ways.)*

- What others words can you think of that are related to *variety*? *(various, vary, variation, varied)*

Revisit *Leonardo's Horse* on pp. 372–377. Write the following Greek and Latin roots and their meanings on the board:

cert = sure   scri = write

clar = clear   sci = know

Match the following words with their roots and give their definitions: *certify, declare, describe, science* (certify *(cert)* = "to make certain"; declare *(clar)* = "to state clearly"; describe *(scri)* = "to say or write about something"; science *(sci)* = "branch of knowledge about the physical world")

As students finish reading *Leonardo's Horse,* help them apply the strategy to the selection. Then have students recall what they have read so far. Ask: What do da Vinci's feelings at the end of his life suggest about this character? *(He was ambitious, modest, and unable to please himself.)*

Objectives
- Determine the meaning of grade-level academic English words derived from Latin roots.
- Use word structure to analyze and decode new words.

OL On-Level   DAY **4**

Practice Retelling

■ **Retell** To assess students' comprehension, use the Retelling Cards. Monitor retelling and prompt students as needed.

Genre Focus

■ **Before Reading or Revisiting** "A Job for Michelangelo" on pp. 382–385, read aloud the genre information about historical fiction on p. 382. Have students preview the selection and set a purpose for reading. Ask:

• What do the illustrations show about Michelangelo's work? *(He was a painter and a sculptor.)*

• Why do you think the writer used dialogue in this story? *(to show what Michelangelo might have been like and to bring his story to life)*

■ **During Reading or Revisiting** Have students read along with you while tracking the print.

• Read aloud the last sentence in the selection. Why is this the main idea? *(It expresses the most important idea about the topic: Michelangelo spent his life creating art.)*

• What supporting details tell you this is the main idea? *(Michelangelo told his father he wanted to spend his life creating art; he begged to become an apprentice; de Medici paid him to create art.)*

■ **After Reading or Revisiting** Have students share their reaction to the historical fiction selction. Then have them write the first page of a historical fiction story about one of their favorite people from history.

Objectives
• Explain the effect of a historical event or movement on the theme of a work of literature.

On-Level Reader

■ **Model** Model the fluency skill of rate for students. Read aloud p. 7 of the On-Level Reader *The Italian Renaissance and Its Artists,* varying your reading rate to show how to express different moods and tones.

■ **Fluency Routine**

1. Have students reread passages from *The Italian Renaissance and Its Artists* with a partner.

2. For optimal fluency, students should reread passages three to four times.

3. As students read, monitor fluency and provide corrective feedback. Encourage students to read slowly to show a serious tone and quickly to show excitement. Discuss how varying the rate makes the reading more interesting.

See *Routines Flip Chart* for more help with fluency.

■ **Retell** For additional practice, have students use the heads as a guide to retell *The Italian Renaissance and Its Artists.* Prompt as necessary.

- What did you learn from reading this section?

- Why do you think the author wrote this selection?

Objectives
- Read aloud grade-level stories with fluency.

A Advanced **DAY 1**

Build Background

- **Extend the Concept** Discuss the weekly question *How do artists inspire future generations?* Throughout history, artists have created sculptures and paintings that we have today as a reminder of their talents. For example, think of a painting or sculpture you have seen. What makes it memorable for you?

Advanced Reader

For a complete literacy instructional plan and additional practice with this week's target skills and strategies, see the **Leveled Reader Teaching Guide.**

- **Before Reading** *Art's Inspiration,* tell students to recall the Read Aloud "Norman Rockwell." What did Norman Rockwell do to improve his paintings? *(He had a photographer take pictures of his subjects before he painted them.)*

Have students look at the illustrations in *Art's Inspiration* and use them to predict ways that artists are inspired to create. Then have students set a purpose for reading.

- **During Reading** Have students read the Advanced Reader independently. Encourage them to think critically. For example, ask:

  • Why had Michelangelo spent many hours looking at the art of ancient Greece and Rome? *(The Greek and Roman artists inspired him to be an artist; he wanted to create lasting works as they did; he was studying their craft and materials.)*

  • Why did artists from all over Europe travel to Rome during the Renaissance? *(They wanted to be part of the great explosion of art happening there.)*

- **After Reading** Have students review the concept map and explain how *Art's Inspiration* helps them answer the weekly question *How do artists inspire future generations?* Prompt as necessary.

  • Why have artists always studied the artworks of earlier times?

  • How does copying a work of art help preserve artistic styles?

- **Now Try This** Assign "Now Try This" at the end of the Advanced Reader.

Objectives
• Interpret a speaker's messages (both verbal and nonverbal).

Pacing Small Group Instruction
15–20 mins.

5-Day Plan

DAY 1	• Extend the concept • Read Advanced Reader
DAY 2	• ⓦ Main Idea and Details • ⓦ Visualize • Revisit Student Edition pp. 360–371
DAY 3	• ⓦ Greek and Latin Roots • Revisit Student Edition pp. 372–377
DAY 4	• Historical Fiction • Read/Revisit Student Edition pp. 382–385
DAY 5	• Reread for fluency • Reread Advanced Reader

3- or 4-Day Plan

DAY 1	• Extend the concept • Advanced Reader
DAY 2	• ⓦ Main Idea and Details • ⓦ Visualize • Revisit Student Edition pp. 360–371
DAY 3	• ⓦ Greek and Latin Roots • Revisit Student Edition pp. 372–377
DAY 4	• Historical Fiction • Read/Revisit Student Edition pp. 382–385 • Reread for fluency • Reread Advanced Reader

3-Day Plan: Eliminate the shaded box.

Small Group Time

More Reading

Use additional Leveled Readers or other texts at students' instructional levels to reinforce this week's skills and strategies. For text suggestions, see the Leveled Reader Database or the Leveled Readers Skills Chart on pp. CL 24–CL 29.

Extend Comprehension

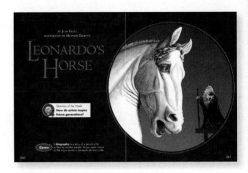

Skill Main Idea and Details To broaden students' understanding of main idea and details, encourage students to look for main ideas that are implied rather than directly stated. Explain that when the author does not state the main idea, readers must use details from the text to infer the main idea.

Think of the book *Art's Inspiration* that you just read. What main idea do all of the details support? *(Possible answer: Inspiration can come from many sources; when artists work and live closely together, they inspire one another; great art never loses its power to inspire generations of artists.)*

Strategy Visualize Review the definition of the strategy. Remind students to visualize the details and images as they read the rest of *Leonardo's Horse.* During reading, use the Extend Thinking questions and the During Reading Differentiated Instruction for additional support.

Revisit *Leonardo's Horse* on pp. 360–371. Tell students to apply the comprehension skill and strategy as they read.

- What main idea about Leonardo's character does the story suggest? *(Possible answer: Leonardo wanted to have lasting fame.)*

- What details support your answer? *(Students should be able to point to specific details from the text.)*

Critical Thinking Encourage students to think critically as they look for main ideas in the selection.

- Why do you think the horse was so important to da Vinci? *(Possible answer: it was a huge challenge and would mark his place in history forever.)*

- What if someone wanted the work done today? Do you think people would make it? Explain. *(Possible answers: probably not, because it would be too large and require too many resources; someone might make it because of the fame it would bring them.)*

Objectives
- Summarize the main idea and supporting details in text.
- Evaluate the impact of sensory details in literary text.

A Advanced

DAY 3

Extend Vocabulary

Greek and Latin Roots/Word Structure
Write the word *innovative* and circle the root *nov*.

- The root *nov* means "new." What might the word *innovate* mean? *("make something that is new and different")*

- What other words can you think of that have *nov* as their root? *(novel, novelty, nova, innovate, innovator)*

Write the following roots and their meanings on the board. Have students think of words that have these roots.

pol = "people" *(politics, political, police)*

scri = "write" *(scribe, describe, inscribe)*

sat = "enough" *(satisfy, satisfaction, saturate)*

Revisit *Leonardo's Horse* on pp. 372–377. Help students apply the strategy as they read. Discuss how understanding Greek and Latin roots can be helpful in figuring out the meanings of unfamiliar words.

Critical Thinking Have students recall what happened in the selection. Encourage them to think critically. For example, ask:

- Why does the author say that Leonardo da Vinci was born at the right time in history?

- Describe Leonardo as he is portrayed by Jean Fritz.

More Reading

Use additional Leveled Readers or other texts at students' instructional levels to reinforce this week's skills and strategies. For text suggestions, see the Leveled Reader Database or the Leveled Readers Skills Chart on pp. CL 24–CL 29.

Objectives
- Determine the meaning of grade-level academic English words derived from Latin roots.
- Use word structure to analyze and decode new words.

Small Group Time

Genre Focus

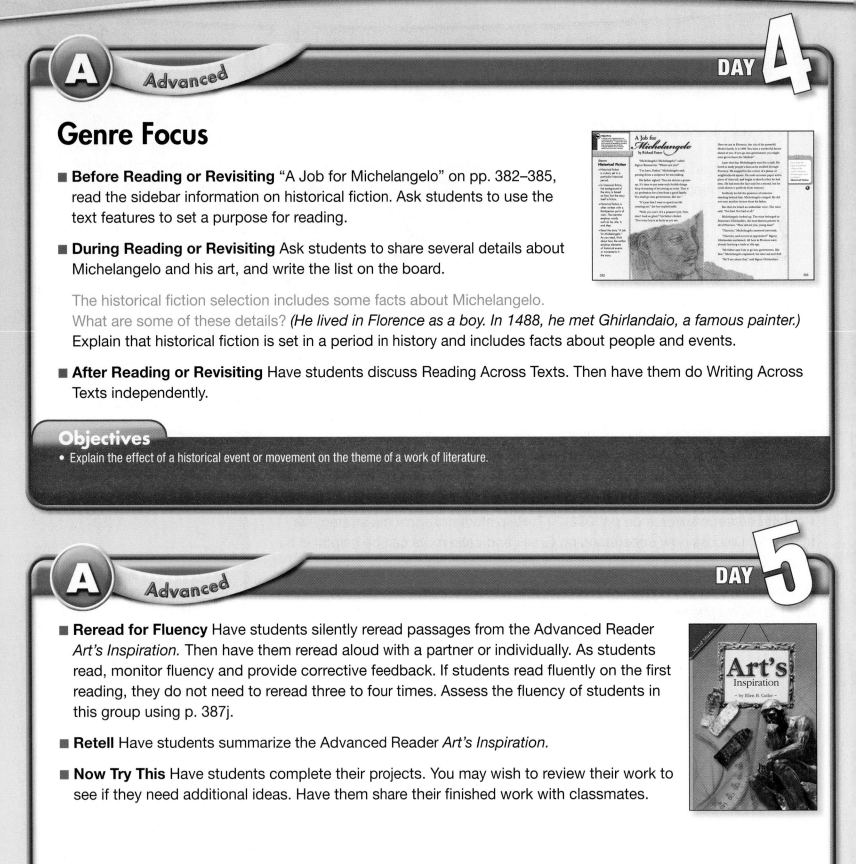

- **Before Reading or Revisiting** "A Job for Michelangelo" on pp. 382–385, read the sidebar information on historical fiction. Ask students to use the text features to set a purpose for reading.

- **During Reading or Revisiting** Ask students to share several details about Michelangelo and his art, and write the list on the board.

  The historical fiction selection includes some facts about Michelangelo. What are some of these details? *(He lived in Florence as a boy. In 1488, he met Ghirlandaio, a famous painter.)* Explain that historical fiction is set in a period in history and includes facts about people and events.

- **After Reading or Revisiting** Have students discuss Reading Across Texts. Then have them do Writing Across Texts independently.

Objectives
- Explain the effect of a historical event or movement on the theme of a work of literature.

- **Reread for Fluency** Have students silently reread passages from the Advanced Reader *Art's Inspiration.* Then have them reread aloud with a partner or individually. As students read, monitor fluency and provide corrective feedback. If students read fluently on the first reading, they do not need to reread three to four times. Assess the fluency of students in this group using p. 387j.

- **Retell** Have students summarize the Advanced Reader *Art's Inspiration.*

- **Now Try This** Have students complete their projects. You may wish to review their work to see if they need additional ideas. Have them share their finished work with classmates.

Objectives
- Read aloud grade-level stories with fluency.

ELL *English Language Learners*

The ELL lessons are organized by strands. Use them to scaffold the weekly curriculum of lessons or during small group time instruction.

Academic Language

Students will hear or read the following academic language in this week's core instruction. As students encounter the vocabulary, provide a simple definition or concrete example. Then ask students to suggest an example or synonym of the word and identify available cognates.

Skill Words	main idea	details
	compound	problem
	word rate	solution
Concept Words	artist	generations

Concept Development

How do artists inspire future generations?

■ **Preteach Concept**

• **Prior Knowledge** Have students turn to pp. 354–355 in the Student Edition. Call attention to the picture of the kids painting and tap into students' knowledge of artwork. What are these kids making? What kinds of things do you like to paint? Do you have a favorite artist? What kind of artwork do you like best?

• **Discuss Concept** Elicit students' knowledge and experience of how artists inspire future generations. That building is very old! The woman is copying it in her book. Why do you think she is doing that? Being inspired is being excited about something and wanting to do it yourself. If an artist made some great art, do you think other people could be inspired by it? Why? Supply background information as needed.

• **Poster Talk-Through** Read aloud the Poster Talk-Through on ELL Poster 12 and work through the Day 1 activities.

■ **Daily Concept and Vocabulary Development** Use the daily activities on ELL Poster 12 to build concept and vocabulary knowledge.

Content Objectives

• Use concept vocabulary related to artists and their achievements.

Language Objectives

• Express ideas in response to art and discussion.

Daily Planner	
DAY 1	• **Frontload Concept** • **Preteach** Comprehension Skill, Vocabulary, Phonics/Spelling, Conventions • **Writing**
DAY 2	• **Review** Concept, Vocabulary, Comprehension Skill • **Frontload Main Selection** • **Practice** Phonics/Spelling, Conventions/Writing
DAY 3	• **Review** Concept, Comprehension Skill, Vocabulary, Conventions/Writing • **Reread Main Selection** • **Practice** Phonics/Spelling
DAY 4	• **Review Concept** • **Read ELL/ELD Readers** • **Practice** Phonics/Spelling, Conventions/Writing
DAY 5	• **Review** Concept, Vocabulary, Comprehension Skill, Phonics/Spelling, Conventions • **Reread ELL/ELD Readers** • **Writing**

See the ELL Handbook for ELL Workshops with targeted instruction.

Concept Talk Video

Use the Concept Talk Video Routine (*ELL Handbook*, p. 477) to build background knowledge about artists. For more listening practice, see *Use Classroom Resources* (*ELL Handbook*, pp. 408–409).

Support for English Language Learners

Language Objectives

- Understand and use basic vocabulary.
- Learn meanings of grade-level vocabulary.
- Use drawing to learn basic vocabulary.

Cognates

For Spanish learners, point out that the Spanish word for *artist* is *artista*, which is very similar to the English word. Reinforce the concept that these languages share many words that are the same or similar.

Basic Vocabulary

■ **High-Frequency Words** Use the vocabulary routine above and the high-frequency word list on page 450 of the *ELL Handbook* to systematically teach newcomers the first 300 sight words in English. Students who began learning ten words per week at the beginning of the year are now learning words 111–120. Have students use strategies to learn the new basic vocabulary, such as drawing. Students can create graphic representations of the words *little, world, nation, hand,* and *write*.

Lesson Vocabulary

■ **Preteach** Introduce the Lesson Vocabulary using this routine:

1. Distribute copies of this week's Word Cards (*ELL Handbook*, p. 95).

2. Display ELL Poster 12 and reread the Poster Talk-Through.

3. Using the poster illustrations, model how a word's meaning can be expressed with other similar words: The workers began building the city in the *midst,* or middle, of the forest.

4. Use these sentences to reveal the meanings of the other words.

- Lara *achieved* her goal of finishing her homework. **(finished or completed)**

- Carlos *fashioned* a tool from wood. **(made)**

- The *philosopher* thought people would be happier if they rode bicycles more often. **(person who thinks about people's beliefs and actions)**

- The bell is made of *bronze.* **(a type of metal)**

- The *architect* wanted to build a house like the one on the hill. **(builder)**

- The *cannon* was used during the war. **(a type of weapon)**

- My *rival* and I both want to win the game. **(opponent)**

- After his dog ran away, Joseph was *depressed.* **(feeling very sad)**

Objectives

- Use strategic learning techniques such as concept mapping, drawing, memorizing, comparing, contrasting, and reviewing to acquire basic grade-level vocabulary.

ELL English Language Learners

■ **Reteach** Distribute a copy of the Word Cards to each student. Have students choose a partner.

• Partners will pick a card, read the word, and think of clues to give the other student. The other student has to guess the word based on given clues.

Example:

architect (a person who designs)

bronze (metal)

rival (person, enemy)

midst (middle, center)

• Encourage students to vary the clues they give. Students can give oral clues, use gestures, or provide drawings. They can also make a home language connection using a clue from their native language. Students should provide clues for as many words as they can.

• Have pairs and partners take turns. Make sure all students have time to play and identify words.

■ **Writing** Place students into small groups. Put the Word Cards facedown in the center of each group. Have each group draw one or two cards. Assign each group to create a word web of the words they picked. Before students begin, model using the graphic organizer: Word: bronze; web entries: metal; brown in color; hard. Circulate to provide assistance as needed throughout the activity. Have students use the new basic language to write. Once they have created their webs, they can choose several words from the web to use in a sentence.

Beginning/Intermediate Ask students to draw or write an example of each web entry.

Advanced/Advanced High Assign students to write a short sentence connecting the main word to one web entry. Provide a sentence frame if necessary, such as _____ is _____. *(Bronze* is *metal.)*

Language Objectives
• Produce drawings, phrases, and short sentences to show an understanding of Lesson Vocabulary.

• Use new basic language in writing activities.

ELL Teacher Tip
According to the ELL program author team, including "topics about students' cultures and experiences helps engage and motivate English learners." For this week's vocabulary, you might help students make connections to home by naming family members who are *artists* or are creative.

Objectives
• Internalize new basic and academic language by using and reusing it in meaningful ways in speaking and writing activities that build concept and language attainment.

Content Objectives
- Monitor and adjust oral comprehension.

Language Objectives
- Discuss oral passages.
- Use a graphic organizer to take notes.

Graphic Organizer

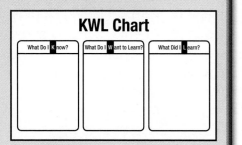

KWL Chart

What Do I **K**now?	What Do I **W**ant to Learn?	What Did I **L**earn?

ELL Teacher Tip
Students may benefit from a third listening to confirm their answers.

Listening Comprehension

A New Way

Norman Rockwell was a famous artist in the 1920s. He painted pictures for the cover of a magazine. Some artists copied their paintings from photographs. Norman did not work that way. He gave money to models to pose for him. They sat still for a long time while Norman drew.

In the 1930s, Norman Rockwell decided to try using a camera. He thought it might make the pictures more interesting. He hired a photographer to take pictures of his models. The photographer took hundreds of pictures.

Norman looked at the pictures and picked his favorite ones. He used charcoal to draw the people in the pictures. He finally painted the people in the pictures. He was nervous at first!

Soon he saw that his new work was just as good as his old work. Norman Rockwell was glad he used a camera. He could get pictures from any angle. Norman painted many people details in his pictures. People called him "the kid with the camera eye." Now, the camera would make his pictures even better.

Prepare for the Read Aloud The modified Read Aloud above prepares students for listening to the oral reading "Norman Rockwell" on page 355b.

■ **First Listening: Listen to Understand** Write the title of the Read Aloud on the board. This text is about an artist who is learning to use a new tool in his work. Listen to find out what tool he is using. How do you think it will help him? Afterwards, ask the questions again and have students share their answers.

■ **Second Listening: Listen to Check Understanding** Using a KWL chart (ELL Handbook, p. 480), work with students to list what they know about how artists create paintings using photographs and what questions they have. Record their ideas in the K and W columns. Now listen again to check your facts and get answers for your questions. Afterwards, fill in the L column of the chart together.

Objectives
- Demonstrate listening comprehension of increasingly complex spoken English by following directions, retelling or summarizing spoken messages, responding to questions and requests, collaborating with peers, and taking notes commensurate with content and grade-level needs.

ELL **English Language Learners**

Phonics and Spelling

■ **Compound Words**

• **Preteach** On two separate index cards, write *scrap* and *book.* Ask students to define each word. Then hold the cards side by side. Ask students what *scrapbook* means. A *scrapbook* is a book in which people put scraps.

• **Teach** Write the following pairs of words on separate index cards: *grass, hopper; green, house; row, boat; thumb, tack.* Discuss the meaning of each, and then show how each pair of can form a compound word. When you make a compound word, you put two words together to make a new word. Usually, there isn't any change to the spellings of the two smaller words.

• **Assess** Write the following pairs of words on separate index cards: *water, proof; tea, spoon; bare, foot.* Challenge students to match the cards to create a complete set of compound words. Have them put cards together and say the words aloud to see if they sound like real words.

Word Analysis: Greek and Latin Roots

■ **Teach/Model** On the board write *autograph, phonograph, photograph,* and *paragraph.* What do these words have in common? They all contain *graph. Graph* comes from the Greek language. It means written. Other English words have Greek roots. Learning these roots can help you learn more words.

■ **Practice** Write the chart of Greek roots from p. 304 in the *ELL Handbook* on the board. Then have students combine the word parts to find the meanings of the following words: *autobiography, phonology, geography,* and *telescope.* Have students notice the language structures of words with Greek roots that are used in the classroom. Many of the words with Greek roots name classes or disciplines. Have students use these words to tell about something they have learned in class.

Beginning/ Intermediate Read the words aloud and emphasize the roots as you read. Have students circle the roots.

Advanced/Advanced High Challenge students to use the parts from the chart to create one other English word and write its meaning.

Objectives
• Learn new language structures, expressions, and basic and academic vocabulary heard during classroom instruction and interactions.
• Monitor oral and written language production and employ self-corrective techniques or other resources.
• Use accessible language and learn new and essential language in the process.

Content Objectives
• Identify Greek and Latin roots in words.
• Identify words in compound words.

Language Objectives
• Apply phonics and decoding skills to vocabulary.
• Discuss meanings of Greek and Latin roots.
• Learn language structures heard during classroom interactions.
• Monitor oral language production.
• Develop sight words for basic classroom vocabulary.
• Use teacher support to learn vocabulary.

Language Opportunity: Classroom Words

Use p. W•9 in the Student Edition to reinforce understanding of root words. As you study root words, have students discuss how they use the word *Earth,* featured in the poster, in class. Then have them identify other words in the classroom that are base words, or cannot be broken into smaller parts.

Support for English Language Learners

Content Objectives

- Identify the main idea and details.

Language Objectives

- Write the main idea of familiar stories.

- Use the new academic language: *main idea* and *details.*

- Expand the basic reading skill of determining main idea and details.

- Understand main points of spoken language.

- Express ideas.

Language Opportunity: Listening and Speaking

Have students listen for main ideas in spoken language as an extension to reading for main ideas. Read aloud p. 365 of the Student Edition as students listen for main points about Leonardo. Consider stopping after reading each paragraph for students to list main points. Then have students express their ideas about Leonardo. What made him interesting? What made him unique? Would they have liked to know Leonardo? Why or why not? Provide a sentence frame for expressing ideas: *I think Leonardo was _____ because _____.* Extend discussion with students.

Comprehension
Main Idea and Details

■ **Preteach** The main idea of a piece of writing is the most important idea about a topic. Have students turn to Envision It! on page EI•12 in the Student Edition. Read aloud the text together. Students should be able to identify a main idea: the way people from move place to place. Have them expand by naming details: different ways in which people move.

■ **Reteach** Distribute copies of the Picture It! (*ELL Handbook,* p. 96). Ask students to describe the illustration. Then read aloud the text twice. Prepare students for the first reading by asking them to listen for the main idea. For the second reading, done chorally, have students listen for details. After each reading, have students tell the main idea and details. Guide students in completing the practice exercises at their language proficiency levels. (Main Idea: Brass is not a metal that comes from nature. Details: It is a mixture of two metals and uses the good qualities from each; To make brass, copper and zinc are melted.)

Beginning Have students use the following sentence frame to write a sentence about the main idea: *The terms* main idea *and* most important *are connected because _____.*

Intermediate/Advanced/Advanced High Have students write two or more sentences explaining their understanding of main idea. They can use this sentence frame: *The main idea is _____.*

MINI-LESSON

Academic Language

Main idea and *details* are academic language used in various classes and subjects in schools. Have students use the academic language to talk about a topic in social studies or science, such as earthquakes (main idea) and fault lines, tremor, and Richter scale. Have students use sentence frames to write about main ideas: *The main idea is _____. Ideas that support it are _____.*

Objectives

- Use visual, contextual, and linguistic support to enhance and confirm understanding of increasingly complex and elaborated spoken language.

ELL English Language Learners

Reading Comprehension
Leonardo's Horse

■ **Frontloading** Have students look through *Leonardo's Horse*, pp. 360–377 in the Student Edition, and tell what they think makes it look like nonfiction. Distribute copies of the English summary of *Leonardo's Horse* (*ELL Handbook*, p. 97). Have students read the summary aloud with you and ask questions about any ideas or unfamiliar words. If you have sent copies of the summary home, have students read it again. Preview the selection by having students look at the pictures. Provide students with a two-column chart to fill out with details as they read. Supply these headings: *Who was Leonardo? What did Leonardo do?*

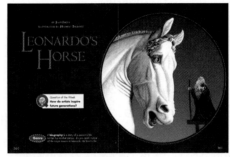
Student Edition pp. 360–361

■ **Sheltered Reading** Ask questions to guide students' comprehension:

• p. 365: Why was the time Leonardo lived called the Renaissance? (It was a time of rebirth and exploring new ideas.)

• p. 365: What were some of the jobs Leonardo did? (He was an architect, an artist, a musician, a philosopher, and an astronomer.)

• p. 372: What happened to Leonardo's horse? (The French destroyed it.)

To delve more deeply into the content, use the Critical Thinking questions on Student Edition p. 378. Have students answer the questions to deepen their understanding of the content-based topic, the Renaissance.

■ **Fluency: Rate** Remind students that rate is the speed at which they read. Read the first paragraph on p. 369, modeling the correct rate. Reading too fast leads to errors, and reading too slow makes it hard to get the gist of the passage. Have pairs choose a paragraph on page 372. Have students read aloud as their partners listen and offer feedback about their rate.

■ **After Reading** Divide students into groups. Have pairs use the Retelling Cards on p. 378 to retell important ideas as they collaborate with peers. As one student in the pair retells, the other can take notes to demonstrate listening comprehension. Then students switch roles.

Objectives
• Distinguish sounds and intonation patterns of English with increasing ease.
• Develop and expand repertoire of learning strategies such as reasoning inductively or deductively, looking for patterns in language, and analyzing sayings and expressions commensurate with grade-level learning expectations.

Content Objectives
• Monitor and adjust comprehension.
• Make and adjust predictions.

Language Objectives
• Read grade-level text at an appropriate rate.
• Summarize text using visual support.
• Respond to questions commensurate with content-area needs.
• Collaborate with peers to show listening comprehension.

Graphic Organizer

Two-Column Chart	
Who was Leonardo?	What did Leonardo do?

Audio Support

Students can prepare for reading *Leonardo's Horse* by using the eSelection or the AudioText CD. See the AudioText CD Routine. (*ELL Handbook,* p. 477)

ELL Reader   ELD Reader

ELL English Language Learners

For additional leveled instruction, see the **ELL/ELD Reader Teaching Guide.**

Comprehension
The Renaissance

■ **Before Reading** Distribute copies of the ELL and ELD Readers, *The Renaissance*, to students at their reading level.

  • **Preview** This is a nonfiction text about a special time in Europe called the Renaissance. Have students look through the pictures and predict what made the time special. Focus on directionality. Have students place their fingers on the text where they would start reading and trace the text from left to right, top to bottom to reinforce directionality.

  • **Set a Purpose for Reading** Let's read to figure out what made the Renaissance so special.

■ **During Reading** Follow the Reading Routine for both reading groups.

1. Read the entire Reader aloud slowly.

2. Reread pp. 2–5, pausing to build background or model comprehension. Use the questions in the chart to check students' comprehension.

3. Have students reread pp. 2–5 in pairs.

4. Repeat the steps for pp. 6–8.

■ **After Reading** Use the exercises on the inside back cover of each Reader and invite students to speak and write about the concepts. Have them respond orally to questions based on both the print and the illustrations to build understanding of the concepts and the language in the readers. Ask questions to gauge understanding of concepts. Have students retell to gauge understanding of language. In a whole-group discussion, ask students What made the Renaissance such a special time? Record their answers on the board.

ELD Reader Beginning/Intermediate

  • **p. 3** What does *Renaissance* mean? (a time when things are found again) Read aloud the sentence that gives you the answer. ("It means . . .)

  • **p. 5** Who traveled to the Americas? (Christopher Columbus) Read aloud the sentence that gives you the answer. ("In Spain, the king and queen sent Christopher Columbus across the ocean.")

Writing Which person from the Renaissance is most interesting to you? Find the sentence in the book that tells what that person did. Copy the sentence. Then read it aloud to your partner.

ELL Reader Advanced/Advanced High

  • **p. 3** What was life in Europe like just before the Renaissance? (People had forgotten many ancient ideas and practices.)

  • **p. 4** How did Descartes contribute to the Renaissance? (He wrote about right and wrong.) Read aloud the sentence that gives you the answer.

Study Guide Distribute copies of the ELL Reader Study Guide (*ELL Handbook*, p. 100). Scaffold comprehension of the main point by helping students look back through their reader. Review the responses together. (See *ELL Handbook*, pp. 209–212.)

Objectives
  • Use visual, contextual, and linguistic support to enhance and confirm understanding of increasingly complex and elaborated spoken language.
  • Understand the general meaning, main points, and important details of spoken language ranging from situations in which topics, language, and contexts are familiar to unfamiliar.

ELL English Language Learners

Conventions
Principal Parts of Regular Verbs

■ **Preteach** Tell me what I do. Clap your hands. Write *clap* on the board. What if I did it yesterday? How would I write the verb? Listen to student suggestions and then write *clapped* on the board. Continue with examples to show *clapping* and *have clapped.*

■ **Practice** Write the following chart on the board and have students complete it with the correct form of each verb.

Past Tense	Present Participle	Past	Past Participle
		stopped	
	is playing		have played
			have cried
pass	is passing		
		jumped	
turn			

Beginning /Intermediate Have students choose one verb and use two different forms of it to write two sentences. Provide the following sentence frames: *She is _____. They _____ yesterday.*

Advanced/Advanced High Have students choose a new verb and write two sentences using different forms of the verb.

■ **Reteach** Display and review the following chart on the board:

Past Tense	Present Participle	Past	Past Participle
the verb without an ending	the verb with an -ing ending + am/is/are	the verb with an -ed ending	the verb with an -ed ending + have/has
share	is sharing	shared	have shared

■ **Practice** Have students review the chart above. Remind students of the differences between the verb tenses for regular verbs. Then have students select a verb from the following list and use it to complete a new row in the chart. Review the answers for all the words. Regular verbs: *invite, create, inspire, fill,* and *compare.*

Objectives
• Edit writing for standard grammar and usage, including subject-verb agreement, pronoun agreement, and appropriate verb tenses commensurate with grade-level expectations as more English is acquired.

Content Objectives
• Identify principal parts of regular verbs.

Language Objectives
• Speak using correct forms of regular verbs.

Transfer Skills

Verb Tenses Speakers of several languages, including Arabic, may find the English distinction between the past and present perfect tenses unfamiliar. Show contrasting examples, and explain how the sense of time differs.

Grammar Jammer

Use the Grammar Jammer for more practice with verbs. See the Grammar Jammer Routine (*ELL Handbook*, p. 478) for suggestions on using this learning tool.

Detailed and Relevant Evidence

Content Objectives

- Identify evidence to support the main idea in writing.

Language Objectives

- Write complete paragraphs.

- Express ideas.

- Know when to use formal English and adapt language for formal purposes.

- Use teacher support to grasp language structures.

- Take notes to demonstrate listening comprehension.

Mini-Lesson: Formal Language

Ask students what kind of English is used in a report: formal English or informal? The language is formal: it uses complete sentences and sounds like a reference book rather than spoken English with a friend. Have students create detail sentences for the writing model in formal English.

Language Opportunity: Listen for Details

Have students listen for important details. Read the prompt on p. 380 of the Student Edition. Have students express their ideas about important inventions. While one group member expresses ideas, others can take notes to show listening comprehension.

■ **Introduce** Display the paragraph model and read it aloud. Review that a paragraph gives evidence to support one main idea. What is the main idea of the paragraph? (Renaissance inventors changed the world.) Which sentences give evidence, or proof, that the main idea is true? (the second, third, and fourth sentences) Underline the first sentence and explain how each of the other sentences give detailed proof that the first sentence is correct.

Writing Model

Renaissance artists and inventors changed the world. They made new discoveries about the sun and the planets. They created great artistic works. They even discovered new lands. It was a time of new and great things for the people of Europe.

■ **Practice** Provide support to help students understand the language structure of the paragraph. The first paragraph tells an important idea. Each sentence after it gives a detail about the idea. Support students with a paragraph-starter frame: *Leonardo wanted the horse to be perfect. He _____. He also _____.* Work together to create detailed sentences.

■ **Write** Tell students that they are giving a formal talk about the Renaissance. They should use formal language as they speak, including complete sentences and other language structures of formal English. First, students write a paragraph about an interesting part of the Renaissance they studied this week. For ideas, they can use *Leonardo's Horse*, The Renaissance, or the class concept map. After writing, they can deliver that speech to the class.

Beginning Have students write the name of one Renaissance artist or inventor at the top of their papers. Then have them draw details about the topic and dictate to you one sentence for each drawing. Write out their sentences and have them read them aloud to you.

Intermediate Provide this sentence frame for a topic sentence: _____ *was a Renaissance _____.* Have partners work together to write supporting details in the form of a paragraph.

Advanced/Advanced High Have students complete their paragraphs independently and exchange papers to provide feedback for revising.

Objectives

- Demonstrate an increasing ability to distinguish between formal and informal English and an increasing knowledge of when to use each one commensurate with grade-level learning expectations.
- Narrate, describe, and explain with increasing specificity and detail to fulfill content area writing needs as more English is acquired.

This Week's ELL Overview

ELL Handbook

- Maximize Literacy and Cognitive Engagement
- Research Into Practice
- Full Weekly Support for Every Selection

Leonardo's Horse
  - Multi-Lingual Summaries in Five Languages
  - Selection-Specific Vocabulary Word Cards
  - Frontloading/Reteaching for Comprehension Skill Lessons
  - ELD and ELL Reader Study Guides

- Transfer Activities
- Professional Development

Daily Leveled ELL Notes

ELL notes appear throughout this week's instruction and ELL Support is on the DI pages of your Teacher's Edition. The following is a sample of an ELL note from this week.

English Language Learners

Beginning Have students identify the principal parts in these phrases: *The book describes; The girls have created.*

Intermediate Have students identify principal parts in three sentences and read them aloud.

Advanced Have students identify all of the principal parts from one paragraph of *Leonardo's Horse.*

Advanced High Have students choose three regular verbs and write them in their present form in sentences. Then have them change each verb to either its past or past participle form.

ELL by Strand

The ELL lessons on this week's Support for English Language Learners pages are organized by strand. They offer additional scaffolding for the core curriculum. Leveled support notes on these pages address the different proficiency levels in your class. See pages DI•41–DI•50.

ELL Guy
Dr. Jim Cummins

The Three Pillars of ELL Instruction

ELL Strands	Activate Prior Knowledge	Access Content	Extend Language
Vocabulary pp. DI•42–DI•43	Preteach	Reteach	Leveled Writing Activities
Reading Comprehension p. DI•47	Frontloading	Sheltered Reading	After Reading
Phonics, Spelling, and Word Analysis p. DI•45	Preteach	Teach/Model	Leveled Practice Activities
Listening Comprehension p. DI•44	Prepare for the Read Aloud	First Listening	Second Listening
Conventions and Writing pp. DI•49–DI•50	Preteach	Leveled Practice Activities	Practice
Concept Development p. DI•41	Activate Prior Knowledge	Discuss Concept	Daily Concept and Vocabulary Development

This Week's Practice Stations Overview

Six Weekly Practice Stations with Leveled Activities can be found at the beginning of each week of instruction. For this week's Practice Stations, see pp. 354h–354i.

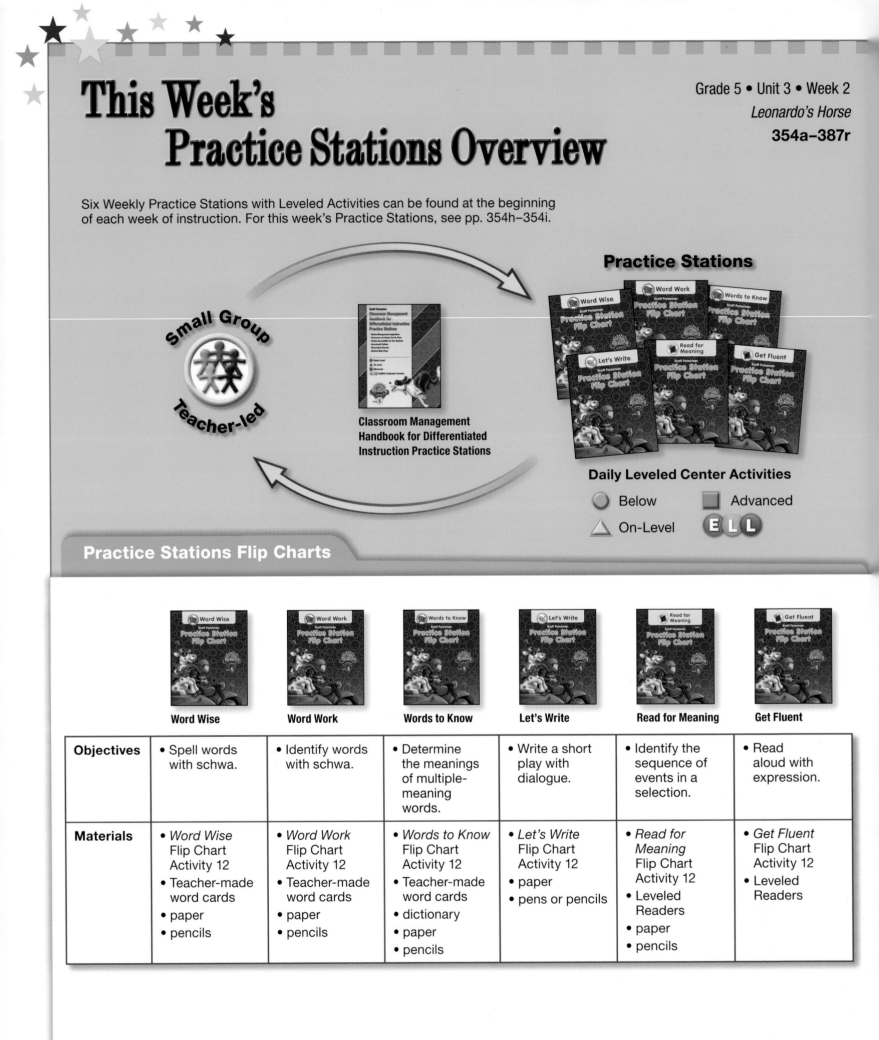

Small Group — Teacher-led

Classroom Management Handbook for Differentiated Instruction Practice Stations

Practice Stations

Daily Leveled Center Activities

○ Below   ▢ Advanced

△ On-Level   **ELL**

Practice Stations Flip Charts

	Word Wise	Word Work	Words to Know	Let's Write	Read for Meaning	Get Fluent
Objectives	• Spell words with schwa.	• Identify words with schwa.	• Determine the meanings of multiple-meaning words.	• Write a short play with dialogue.	• Identify the sequence of events in a selection.	• Read aloud with expression.
Materials	• *Word Wise* Flip Chart Activity 12 • Teacher-made word cards • paper • pencils	• *Word Work* Flip Chart Activity 12 • Teacher-made word cards • paper • pencils	• *Words to Know* Flip Chart Activity 12 • Teacher-made word cards • dictionary • paper • pencils	• *Let's Write* Flip Chart Activity 12 • paper • pens or pencils	• *Read for Meaning* Flip Chart Activity 12 • Leveled Readers • paper • pencils	• *Get Fluent* Flip Chart Activity 12 • Leveled Readers

Common Core Standards
Weekly Planning Guide

Selection: The Dinosaurs of Waterhouse Hawkins
Genre: Biography

Alignment of the Common Core Standards with This Week's Skills and Strategies

This Week's Common Core Standards for English Language Arts	Instructional Summary
Reading Standards for Informational Text	
Informational Text 1. Quote accurately from a text when explaining what the text says explicitly and when drawing inferences from the text.	This week's comprehension lesson helps students distinguish between **facts and opinions.** The guided instruction and questions help students identify facts and opinions in the selections. Students learn to use the **predict and set a purpose** strategy to help them predict what the selection might be about and set a purpose to help them understand what they read.
Informational Text 3. Explain the relationships or interactions between two or more individuals, events, ideas, or concepts in a historical, scientific, or technical text based on specific information in the text.	
Foundational Skills Standards	
Foundational Skills 3.a. Use combined knowledge of all letter-sound correspondences, syllabication patterns, and morphology (e.g., roots and affixes) to read accurately unfamiliar multisyllabic words in context and out of context.	This week's Word Analysis instruction provides information about adding **suffixes** to words and reviews how meaning is changed when a suffix is added. The fluency activities help students use punctuation to read sentences with **appropriate phrasing.**
Foundational Skills 4.b. Read on-level prose and poetry orally with accuracy, appropriate rate, and expression on successive readings.	
Writing Standards	
Writing 1.b. Provide logically ordered reasons that are supported by facts and details.	This week, students write an **advertising brochure** to encourage readers to come see an exhibit of dinosaur models. After drafting their brochure, students revise to be sure that the purpose of their advertisement is clear. In the Research and Inquiry section, students prepare a **chart** and a **schedule** for a seminar.
Writing 1.d. Provide a concluding statement or section related to the opinion presented.	
Writing 5. With guidance and support from peers and adults, develop and strengthen writing as needed by planning, revising, editing, rewriting, or trying a new approach. (Editing for conventions should demonstrate command of Language standards 1–3 up to and including grade 5 on pages 28 and 29.)	
Speaking and Listening Standards	
Speaking/Listening 1.b. Follow agreed-upon rules for discussions and carry out assigned roles.	In the Listening and Speaking section, students prepare an **introduction** of Waterhouse's dinosaur display. In the Research and Inquiry section, students develop a **schedule** for an imaginary **seminar** on dinosaurs and orally present topics and features from the charts they created.
Speaking/Listening 4. Report on a topic or text or present an opinion, sequencing ideas logically and using appropriate facts and relevant, descriptive details to support main ideas or themes; speak clearly at an understandable pace.	
Language Standards	
Language 1. Demonstrate command of the conventions of standard English grammar and usage when writing or speaking.	The Conventions section presents the principal parts of irregular verbs. Students identify the differences between **present, present participle, past, and past participle verbs.** The Vocabulary section has students use **context clues** to determine the meaning of **homonyms.**
Language 1.b. Form and use the perfect (e.g., *I had walked; I have walked; I will have walked*) verb tenses.	
Language 4.a. Use context (e.g., cause/effect relationships and comparisons in text) as a clue to the meaning of a word or phrase.	

Additional Support for a Common Core Standard This Week

Use the following instruction to supplement the teaching of one of this week's Common Core Standards.

Common Core Standard: Language 1.b.
Write this line from *Waterhouse Hawkins* on the board: "Like many artists, he had grown up sketching the world around him."

- Underline the verb *had grown,* and explain that it is made up of a helping verb *(had)* and the past participle of the main verb *(grown).*
- Have students choose one of the verb forms to complete each sentence.
    Raul has _____ six inches this year. (grow, grew, grown, growing)
    The hikers will have _____ 14 miles by nightfall. (walk, walked, walking)
- Ask students to write their own sentence using an irregular or regular past participle verb with the helping verb *have, has, had,* or *will have.*

ISBN-13: 978-0-328-64415-5   ISBN-10: 0-328-64415-3

Week 5

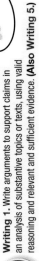

connect to **SCIENCE**

Special Effects in Film and Television

? Question of the Week

How do artists create special effects to entertain us?

Concept Talk Guide students as they discuss questions such as:

• What examples of special effects did you discuss?
• Where have you seen special effects?

Writing Think about which form of entertainment you prefer: watching a movie or watching a television program. Compare and contrast the two, using specific details to make your point.

Week 4

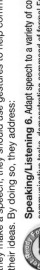

connect to **SOCIAL STUDIES**

Mahalia Jackson

? Question of the Week

How does an artist use music to inspire others?

Concept Talk Guide students as they discuss questions such as:

• What did you discuss about music as an inspiration?
• What kind of music do you like most?

Writing *Mahalia Jackson* describes the voice of a talented singer. Think about music or another unique sound. Now write a description of that sound, using vivid sensory words.

Grade 5 • Unit 3 • Week 3

The Dinosaurs of Waterhouse Hawkins

Unit 3

THE BIG ? **What do people gain from the work of inventors and artists?**

Common Core Standards and Concept Development

• Introduce and explore this unit's weekly concepts through rich, structured conversations
• Develop complex content knowledge and vocabulary
• Expand on a single concept with engaging literature and nonfiction
• Build better readers in all content areas

Align instruction to **Common Core Anchor Standards**

connect to **SCIENCE**

Writing *The Dinosaurs of Waterhouse Hawkins* tells about the introduction of dinosaur models to the world. Prepare an advertisement for one of the events, enticing people to come.

As students write about this week's prompt, they will address:

Writing 1. Write arguments to support claims in an analysis of substantive topics or texts, using valid reasoning and relevant and sufficient evidence. **(Also Writing 5.)**

Listening and Speaking On page 423, students learn that when they make a speech, they should use gestures to help communicate their ideas. By doing so, they address:

Speaking/Listening 6. Adapt speech to a variety of contexts and communicative tasks, demonstrating command of formal English when indicated or appropriate. **(Also Speaking/Listening 1.)**

You Are Here: Week 3

The Dinosaurs of Waterhouse Hawkins

? Question of the Week

How can paleontologists help us understand the past?

As students answer this unit's Big Question and this week's Question of the Week, they will address:

Reading 1. Read closely to determine what the text says explicitly and to make logical inferences from it; cite specific textual evidence when writing or speaking to support conclusions drawn from the text. **(Also Reading 3.)**

Concept Talk Guide students as they discuss questions such as:

• What selections or books have you read about dinosaurs?
• What do you know about paleontologists and their work?

As students answer this week's Concept Talk questions, they will address:

Speaking/Listening 1. Prepare for and participate effectively in a range of conversations and collaborations with diverse partners, building on others' ideas and expressing their own clearly and persuasively.

Week 1

The Fabulous Perpetual Motion Machine

? Question of the Week

How do inventors inspire our imaginations?

connect to **SCIENCE**

Concept Talk Guide students as they discuss questions such as:

• What are some important inventions we use? Why are they important?
• What books, movies, or TV shows do you know that feature inventors and inventions?

Writing In *The Fabulous Perpetual Motion Machine*, young inventors create a special machine. Think about something that could be invented. Now write a short play based on your idea.

Week 2

Leonardo's Horse

? Question of the Week

How do artists inspire future generations?

connect to **SOCIAL STUDIES**

Concept Talk Guide students as they discuss questions such as:

• What might inspire an artist to create?
• How can an artist's work inspire other people?

Writing Think about modern inventions. Which one changed people's lives the most? Write a persuasive speech that answers this question.

This Week's ELL Overview

ELL Handbook

- Maximize Literacy and Cognitive Engagement
- Research Into Practice
- Full Weekly Support for Every Selection

The Dinosaurs of Waterhouse Hawkins

- Multi-Lingual Summaries in Five Languages
- Selection-Specific Vocabulary Word Cards
- Frontloading/Reteaching for Comprehension Skill Lessons
- ELD and ELL Reader Study Guides

- Transfer Activities
- Professional Development

Daily Leveled ELL Notes

ELL notes appear throughout this week's instruction and ELL Support is on the DI pages of your Teacher's Edition. The following is a sample of an ELL note from this week.

English Language Learners

Beginning Have students draw an illustration to accompany a brochure for a product.

Intermediate Have students write a bulleted list of reasons for buying a product they like.

Advanced Have students role-play a conversation between a salesperson and a customer.

Advanced High Have students explain what in an advertisement makes them pay attention and what seems uninteresting. Then have them write a list of ways to attract interest in something they want the public to know about.

ELL by Strand

The ELL lessons on this week's Support for English Language Learners pages are organized by strand. They offer additional scaffolding for the core curriculum. Leveled support notes on these pages address the different proficiency levels in your class. See pages DI•66–DI•75.

ELL Guy
Dr. Jim Cummins

The Three Pillars of ELL Instruction

ELL Strands	Activate Prior Knowledge	Access Content	Extend Language
Vocabulary pp. DI•67–DI•68	Preteach	Reteach	Leveled Writing Activities
Reading Comprehension p. DI•72	Frontloading	Sheltered Reading	After Reading
Phonics, Spelling, and Word Analysis p. DI•70	Preteach	Teach and Model	Leveled Practice Activities
Listening Comprehension p. DI•69	Prepare for the Read Aloud	First Listening	Second Listening
Conventions and Writing pp. DI•74–DI•75	Preteach	Leveled Practice Activities	Leveled Writing Activities
Concept Development p. DI•66	Activate Prior Knowledge	Discuss Concept	Daily Concept and Vocabulary Development

This Week's Practice Stations Overview

Six Weekly Practice Stations with Leveled Activities can be found at the beginning of each week of instruction. For this week's Practice Stations, see pp. 388h–388i.

Practice Stations

Small Group
Teacher-led

Classroom Management Handbook for Differentiated Instruction Practice Stations

Daily Leveled Center Activities

◯ Below   ▢ Advanced

△ On-Level   Ⓔ Ⓛ Ⓛ

Practice Stations Flip Charts

	Word Wise	Word Work	Words to Know	Let's Write	Read for Meaning	Get Fluent
Objectives	• Spell compound words.	• Identify and write compound words.	• Determine the meaning of words with Greek and Latin roots.	• Write a persuasive speech.	• Identify the main idea and supporting details in a nonfiction selection.	• Read aloud at an appropriate rate.
Materials	• *Word Wise* Flip Chart Activity 13 • Teacher-made word cards • paper • pencils	• *Word Work* Flip Chart Activity 13 • Teacher-made word cards • paper • pencils	• *Words to Know* Flip Chart Activity 13 • Teacher-made word cards • List of Greek and Latin roots and their meanings • paper • pencils	• *Let's Write* Flip Chart Activity 13 • paper • pens or pencils	• *Read for Meaning* Flip Chart Activity 13 • Leveled Readers • paper • pencils	• *Get Fluent* Flip Chart Activity 13 • Leveled Readers

This Week on Reading Street!

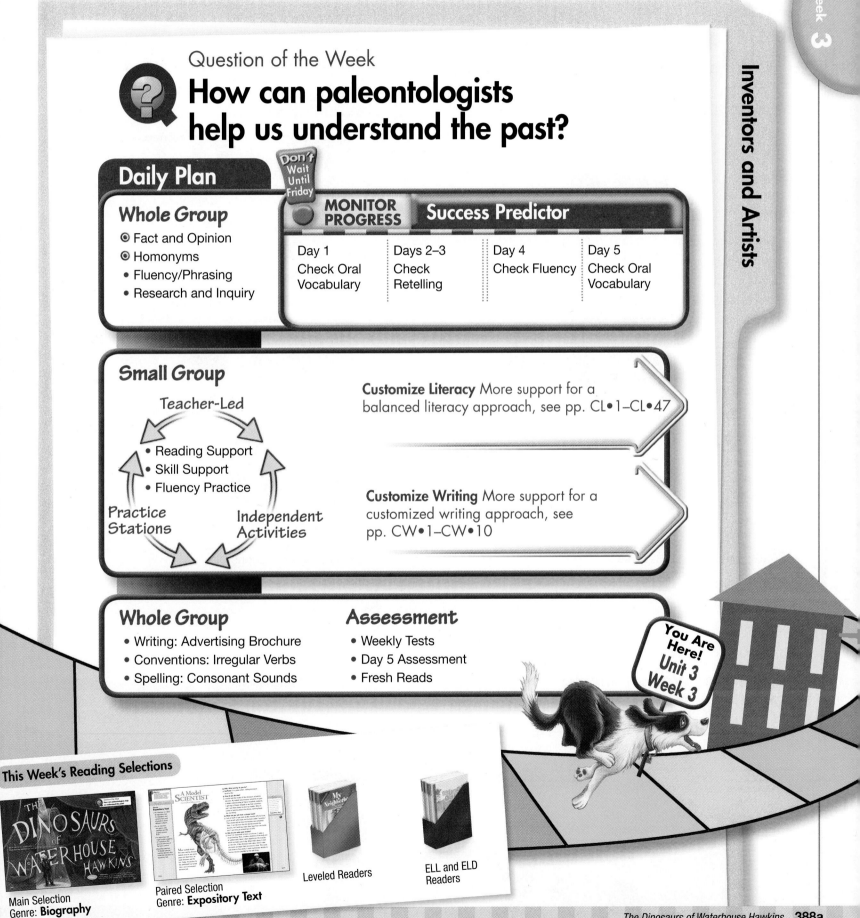

Question of the Week

How can paleontologists help us understand the past?

Daily Plan

Don't Wait Until Friday

Whole Group

- ◉ Fact and Opinion
- ◉ Homonyms
- • Fluency/Phrasing
- • Research and Inquiry

MONITOR PROGRESS | **Success Predictor**

| Day 1 Check Oral Vocabulary | Days 2–3 Check Retelling | Day 4 Check Fluency | Day 5 Check Oral Vocabulary |

Small Group

Teacher-Led

- • Reading Support
- • Skill Support
- • Fluency Practice

Practice Stations

Independent Activities

Customize Literacy More support for a balanced literacy approach, see pp. CL•1–CL•47

Customize Writing More support for a customized writing approach, see pp. CW•1–CW•10

Whole Group

- • Writing: Advertising Brochure
- • Conventions: Irregular Verbs
- • Spelling: Consonant Sounds

Assessment

- • Weekly Tests
- • Day 5 Assessment
- • Fresh Reads

You Are Here! Unit 3 Week 3

This Week's Reading Selections

Main Selection
Genre: **Biography**

Paired Selection
Genre: **Expository Text**

Leveled Readers

ELL and ELD Readers

Resources on Reading Street!

	Build Concepts	Comprehension
Whole Group	 Let's Talk About pp. 388–389	Envision It! Skills/ Strategies Comprehension Skills Lesson pp. 390–391
Go Digital	• Concept Talk Video	• Envision It! Animations • eSelections
Small Group and Independent Practice	The Dinosaurs of Waterhouse Hawkins pp. 394–395 ELL and ELD Readers Leveled Readers	The Dinosaurs of Waterhouse Hawkins pp. 394–395 ELL and ELD Readers Leveled Readers Envision It! Skills/ Strategies Reader's and Writer's Notebook Practice Station Flip Chart
Go Digital	• eReaders • eSelections	• Envision It! Animations • eSelections • eReaders
Customize Literacy	• Leveled Readers	• Envision It! Skills and Strategies Handbook • Leveled Readers
Go Digital	• Concept Talk Video • Big Question Video • eReaders	• Envision It! Animations • eReaders

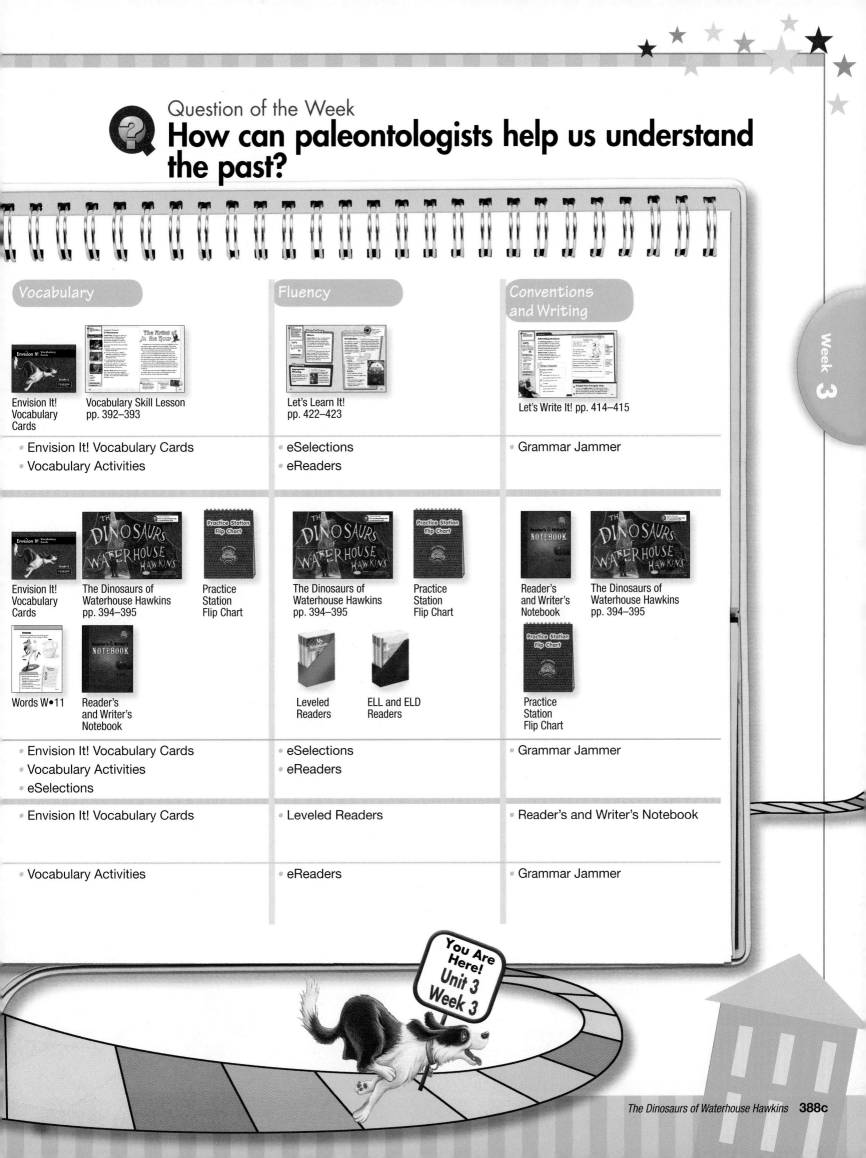

How can paleontologists help us understand the past?

Vocabulary

Envision It!
Vocabulary
Cards

Vocabulary Skill Lesson
pp. 392–393

- Envision It! Vocabulary Cards
- Vocabulary Activities

Fluency

Let's Learn It!
pp. 422–423

- eSelections
- eReaders

Conventions and Writing

Let's Write It! pp. 414–415

- Grammar Jammer

Envision It!
Vocabulary
Cards

The Dinosaurs of
Waterhouse Hawkins
pp. 394–395

Practice
Station
Flip Chart

Words W•11

Reader's
and Writer's
Notebook

The Dinosaurs of
Waterhouse Hawkins
pp. 394–395

Practice
Station
Flip Chart

Leveled
Readers

ELL and ELD
Readers

Reader's
and Writer's
Notebook

The Dinosaurs of
Waterhouse Hawkins
pp. 394–395

Practice
Station
Flip Chart

- Envision It! Vocabulary Cards
- Vocabulary Activities
- eSelections

- eSelections
- eReaders

- Grammar Jammer

- Envision It! Vocabulary Cards

- Leveled Readers

- Reader's and Writer's Notebook

- Vocabulary Activities

- eReaders

- Grammar Jammer

You Are Here!
Unit 3
Week 3

My 5-Day Planner for Reading Street!

	Check Oral Vocabulary **Day 1** pages 388j–391f	Check Retelling **Day 2** pages 392a–401e

Get Ready to Read	**Concept Talk,** 388j
	Oral Vocabulary, 389a
	   fossils, paleontologists, sandstone, uncanny
	Listening Comprehension, Read Aloud, 389b
		Concept Talk, 392a
		Oral Vocabulary, 392b
		   remains, model
		Word Analysis, 392c
		   Suffixes -tion, -sion
		Literary Terms, 392d
		   Flashback
		Text Structure, 392d
		   Sequence

Read and Comprehend	**Comprehension Skill,**
	   ◉ Fact and Opinion, 389c
	Comprehension Strategy,
	   ◉ Predict and Set Purpose, 389c
	READ Comprehension, 390–391
	Model Fluency, Phrasing, 390–391
	Introduce Lesson Vocabulary, 391a
	   erected, foundations, mold, occasion, proportion, tidied, workshop
		Vocabulary Skill, ◉ Homonyms, 392e
		Vocabulary Strategy, Context Clues, 392e
		Lesson Vocabulary, 392–393
		   erected, foundations, mold, occasion, proportion, tidied, workshop
		READ Vocabulary, 392–393
		Model Fluency, Phrasing, 392–393
		READ Main Selection, *The Dinosaurs of Waterhouse Hawkins,* 394–401a

Language Arts	**Research and Inquiry,** Identify Questions, 391b **Spelling,** Words with Consonant Sounds /j/, /ks/, /sk/, and /s/, 391c **Conventions,** Principal Parts of Irregular Verbs, 391d **Handwriting,** Cursive Letter *p* and *P,* 391d **Writing,** Advertising Brochure, 391e–391f	**Research and Inquiry,** Navigate/Search, 401b **Conventions,** Principal Parts of Irregular Verbs, 401c **Spelling,** Words with Consonant Sounds /j/, /ks/, /sk/, and /s/, 401c **Writing,** Advertising Brochure, Word Choice, 401d

You Are Here!
Unit 3
Week 3

Question of the Week
How can paleontologists help us understand the past?

Check Retelling	Check Fluency	Check Oral Vocabulary
Day 3 pages 402a–415c	**Day 4** pages 416a–423e	**Day 5** pages 423f–423q
Concept Talk, 402a **Oral Vocabulary**, 402b illustration, extinct **Comprehension Check**, 402c **Check Retelling**, 402d	**Concept Talk**, 416a **Oral Vocabulary**, 416b replica, archaic **Genre**, Expository Text: Interview, 416c	**Concept Wrap Up**, 423f **Check Oral Vocabulary**, 423g fossils, paleontologists, sandstone, uncanny, remains, model, illustration, extinct, replica, archaic **Amazing Ideas**, 423g `Review` ◉ Fact and Opinion, 423h `Review` ◉ Homonyms, 423h `Review` Word Analysis, 423i `Review` Literary Terms, 423i
READ Main Selection, *The Dinosaurs of Waterhouse Hawkins*, 402–411a **Retelling**, 412–413 **Think Critically**, 413a **Model Fluency**, Phrasing, 413b **Research and Study Skills**, Schedules, 413c	**READ Paired Selection,** "A Model Scientist" 416–421a **Let's Learn It!** 422–423a Fluency: Phrasing Vocabulary: Idioms Listening and Speaking: Introduction	**Fluency Assessment,** WCPM, 423j–423k **Comprehension Assessment,** ◉ Fact and Opinion, 423l–423m
Research and Inquiry, Analyze, 413d **Conventions,** Principal Parts of Irregular Verbs, 413e **Spelling,** Words with Consonant Sounds /j/, /ks/, /sk/, and /s/, 413e **Let's Write It!** Advertising Brochure, 414–415a **Writing,** Advertising Brochure, Sound Reasoning, 415b–415c	**Research and Inquiry,** Synthesize, 423b **Conventions,** Principal Parts of Irregular Verbs, 423c **Spelling,** Words with Consonant Sounds /j/, /ks/, /sk/, and /s/, 423c **Writing,** Advertising Brochure, Revising, 423d–423e	**Research and Inquiry,** Communicate, 423n **Conventions,** Principal Parts of Irregular Verbs, 423o **Spelling Test,** Words with Consonant Sounds /j/, /ks/, /sk/, and /s/, 423o **Writing,** Advertising Brochure, Principal Parts of Irregular Verbs, 423p **Quick Write for Fluency,** 423q

Week 3

Grouping Options for Differentiated Instruction
Turn the page for the small group time lesson plan.

Planning Small Group Time on Reading Street!

SMALL GROUP TIME RESOURCES

Look for this Small Group Time box each day to help meet the individual needs of all your students. Differentiated Instruction lessons appear on the DI pages at the end of each week.

DAY 1

Teacher Led

SI Strategic Intervention	OL On-Level	A Advanced
Teacher Led • Reinforce the Concept **Read** *Concept Literacy Reader* or *Below-Level Reader*	**Teacher Led** • Expand the Concept **Read** *On-Level Reader*	**Teacher Led** • Extend the Concept **Read** *Advanced Reader*

ELL Place English language learners in the groups that correspond to their reading abilities in English.

Practice Stations
• Read for Meaning
• Get Fluent
• Word Work

Independent Activities
• Concept Talk Video
• *Reader's and Writer's Notebook*
• Research and Inquiry

ELL

DINOSAUR TIME LINE
by Carl Escobedo
Illustrated by Gary Torrisi

ELL Reader
Advanced
Advanced High

DINOSAUR TIME LINE
by Carl Escobedo
Illustrated by Gary Torrisi

ELD Reader
Beginning
Intermediate

ELL Poster

You Are Here!
Unit 3
Week 3

Day 1

SI Strategic Intervention	**Reinforce the Concept,** DI•51–DI•52 **Read Concept Literacy Reader** or **Below-Level Reader**
OL On-Level	**Expand the Concept,** DI•57 **Read On-Level Reader**
A Advanced	**Extend the Concept,** DI•62 **Read Advanced Reader**
ELL English Language Learners	DI•66–DI•75 **Frontload Concept** **Preteach Skills** **Writing**

Question of the Week
How can paleontologists help us understand the past?

SI Strategic Intervention

Picturing the Past
by Renee Carver
Concept Literacy Reader

Paleontology:
Digging for Dinosaurs and More
by Laura Johnson
Below-Level Reader

OL On-Level

SEARCHING FOR **DINOSAURS**
by Anne Cembal
On-Level Reader

A Advanced

What's New with Dinosaur Fossils?
by Laura Johnson
Advanced Reader

THE **DINOSAURS** OF **WATERHOUSE HAWKINS**
by BARBARA KERLEY, illustrated by BRIAN SELZNICK
The Dinosaurs of Waterhouse Hawkins pp. 394–395

A Model **SCIENTIST**
FROM OWL MAGAZINE
A Model Scientist pp. 416–417

Small Group Weekly Plan

Day 2	Day 3	Day 4	Day 5
Reinforce Comprehension, DI•53 **Revisit Main Selection**	**Reinforce Vocabulary,** DI•54 **Read/Revisit Main Selection**	**Reinforce Comprehension,** Practice Retelling DI•55 Genre Focus **Read/Revisit Paired Selection**	**Practice Fluency,** DI•56 **Reread Concept Literacy Reader** or **Below-Level Reader**
Expand Comprehension, DI•58 **Revisit Main Selection**	**Expand Vocabulary,** DI•59 **Read/Revisit Main Selection**	**Expand Comprehension,** Practice Retelling DI•60 Genre Focus **Read/Revisit Paired Selection**	**Practice Fluency,** DI•61 **Reread On-Level Reader**
Extend Comprehension, DI•63 **Revisit Main Selection**	**Extend Vocabulary,** DI•64 **Read/Revisit Main Selection**	**Extend Comprehension,** Genre Focus DI•65 **Read/Revisit Paired Selection**	**Practice Fluency,** DI•65 **Reread Advanced Reader**
DI•66–DI•75 **Review Concept/Skills** **Frontload Main Selection** **Practice**	DI•66–DI•75 **Review Concept/Skills** **Reread Main Selection** **Practice**	DI•66–DI•75 **Review Concept** **Read ELL/ELD Readers** **Practice**	DI•66–DI•75 **Review Concept/Skills** **Reread ELL/ELD Reader** **Writing**

Week 3

Practice Stations for Everyone on Reading Street!

Word Wise
Compound words

Objectives
• Spell compound words.

Materials
• *Word Wise* Flip Chart Activity 13
• Teacher-made word cards
• paper • pencils

Differentiated Activities

⬤ Choose five word cards. Write your words in a list, Next to each word, write the two words that form the compound word. Write a sentence for each compound word.

▲ Choose eight word cards. Write your words in a list. Next to each word, write the two words that form the compound word. Write sentences using each of the compound words.

◼ Choose ten word cards, and write the words in a list. Next to each word, write the two words that form the compound word. Write sentences using each of the compound words.

Technology
• Online Dictionary

Word Work
Compound words

Objectives
• Identify and write compound words.

Materials
• *Word Work* Flip Chart Activity 13
• Teacher-made word cards
• paper • pencils

Differentiated Activities

⬤ Choose eight word cards. Write your words in a list. Quietly say each word. Circle the two words that form each compound word. Add other compound words you know to the list.

▲ Choose ten word cards, and write your words in a list. Quietly say each word. Circle the two words that form each compound word. Add other compound words you know to the list.

◼ Choose twelve word cards, and write the words in a list. Quietly say each word, and circle the two words that form each compound word. Add other compound words to the list.

Technology
• Modeled Pronunciation Audio CD

Words to Know
Greek and Latin roots

Objectives
• Determine the meaning of words with Greek and Latin roots.

Materials
• *Words to Know* Flip Chart Activity 13
• Teacher-made word cards
• List of Greek and Latin roots and their meanings.
• paper • pencils

Differentiated Activities

⬤ Choose five word cards. Write the words in a list. Circle the Greek or Latin root in each word. Write a sentence for each word. List other words you know with these Greek and Latin roots.

▲ Choose seven word cards, and list the words on paper. Circle the Greek or Latin root in each word. Write sentences using each of your words. Add other words with Greek and Latin roots to the list.

◼ Choose eight word cards, and list the words on paper. Underline the Greek or Latin root in each word. Write sentences using each of your words. Add other words with Greek and Latin roots to the list.

Technology
• Online Dictionary

You Are Here!
Unit 3
Week 3

Key

● Below-Level Activities

▲ On-Level Activities

■ Advanced Activities

Practice Station Flip Chart

Let's Write!
Persuasive speech

Objectives
• Write a persuasive speech.

Materials
• *Let's Write!* Flip Chart Activity 13
• paper • pens or pencils

Differentiated Activities

● Think about an improvement that should be made to your school. Write a persuasive speech convincing others that this improvement is a good idea. Give details to persuade others to agree with you.

▲ Write a persuasive speech about an improvement that should be made to your school. Include details about how the school would be better. Provide reasons why the improvement is a good idea.

■ Think about change you'd like to see in your school. Write a speech persuading others why this change is a good idea. Give detailed evidence about how your school would benefit from the change.

Technology
• Online Graphic Organizers

Read for Meaning
Main idea and supporting details

Objectives
• Identify the main idea and supporting details in a nonfiction selection.

Materials
• *Read for Meaning* Flip Chart Activity 13
• Leveled Readers
• paper • pencils

Differentiated Activities

● Choose and read a book provided by your teacher. Think about what the selection is mostly about. Write a sentence that tells the selection's main idea. Write one sentence with a detail that tells more about the main idea.

▲ Choose and read a book provided by your teacher. Think about the selection's main idea. Write a sentence that tells the main idea of the selection. Write two sentences with details that tell more about the main idea.

■ Choose and read a book provided by your teacher. As you read, think about the selection's main idea. Write a short paragraph that tells the main idea. Include at least three details from the selection that tell more about this idea.

Technology
• Leveled Reader Database

Get Fluent
Practice fluent reading.

Objectives
• Read aloud at an appropriate rate.

Materials
• *Get Fluent* Flip Chart Activity 13
• Leveled Readers

Differentiated Activities

● Work with a partner. Choose a Concept Literacy Reader or Below-Level Reader. Take turns reading a page from the book. Use the reader to practice appropriate rate. Provide feedback as needed.

▲ Work with a partner. Choose an On-Level Reader. Take turns reading a page from the book. Use the reader to practice appropriate rate. Provide feedback as needed.

■ Work with a partner. Choose an Advanced Reader. Take turns reading a page from the book. Use the reader to practice appropriate rate. Provide feedback as needed.

Technology
• Leveled Reader Database
• Reading Street Readers CD-ROM

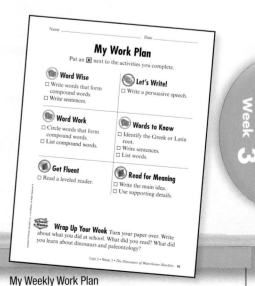

My Weekly Work Plan

Week 3

Objectives
- Introduce the weekly concept.
- Develop oral vocabulary.

Today at a Glance

Oral Vocabulary
fossils, paleontologists, sandstone, uncanny

Comprehension
◉ Fact and opinion
◉ Predict and set purpose

Reading
Dinosaurs

Fluency
Appropriate phrasing

Lesson Vocabulary
Tested Vocabulary

Research and Inquiry
Identify questions

Spelling
Words with consonant sounds /j/, /ks/, /sk/, /s/

Conventions
Principal parts of irregular verbs

Handwriting
Cursive letters *p* and *P*

Writing
Advertising brochure

Concept Talk

Question of the Week

 How can paleontologists help us understand the past?

Introduce the concept

To further explore the unit concept of Inventors and Artists, this week students will read, write, and talk about how people learn about the past. Write the Question of the Week on the board.

ROUTINE **Activate Prior Knowledge** **Team Talk**

1. **Think** Have students think about the different ways that people have studied and learned about the past.

2. **Pair** Have pairs of students discuss the Question of the Week. Encourage students to consider each other's suggestions.

3. **Share** Call on a few students to share their ideas with the group. Guide the discussion and encourage elaboration with prompts such as:

   - What selections or books have you read about dinosaurs?

   - What do you know about paleontologists and their work?

Anchored Talk

Develop oral vocabulary

Have students turn to pp. 388–389 in their Student Editions. Look at each of the photos. Then use the prompts to guide discussion and create the *How can paleontologists help us understand the past?* concept map.

- What are the scientists looking at? (fossils and dinosaur bones)
  Paleontologists are scientists who use fossils to learn about the past. Let's add *Study fossils* to our concept map.

- What is the boy looking at? (a dinosaur model) How do you think the model was created? (An artist probably used information and research provided by paleontologists to make the model.)

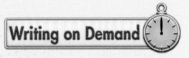

Objectives
• Listen to and interpret a speaker's messages and ask questions.
• Identify the main ideas and supporting ideas in the speaker's message.

Oral Vocabulary

Let's Talk About

Dinosaurs and Paleontology

• Share what you know about dinosaurs and paleontology.

• Listen to and interpret a classmate's knowledge of dinosaurs and paleontology.

• Determine main and supporting ideas in your classmate's messages.

READING STREET ONLINE
CONCEPT TALK VIDEO
www.ReadingStreet.com

388

You've learned
1 2 0
Amazing Words ⭐
so far this year!

389

Student Edition pp. 388–389

Connect to reading

• Paleontologists' research probably played an important role in making the model. Let's add *Help create dinosaur models* to our concept map.

• After discussing the photos, ask: How do paleontologists help us to understand the past?

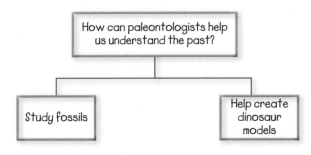

How can paleontologists help us understand the past?

Study fossils

Help create dinosaur models

ELL **Preteach Concepts** Use the Day 1 instruction on ELL Poster 13 to assess and build background knowledge, develop concepts, and build oral vocabulary.

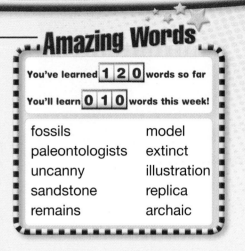

⭐ **Amazing Words** ⭐

You've learned **1 2 0** words so far

You'll learn **0 1 0** words this week!

fossils	model
paleontologists	extinct
uncanny	illustration
sandstone	replica
remains	archaic

Writing on Demand ⏱

Writing Fluency
Ask students to respond to the photos on pp. 388–389 by writing as well as they can and as much as they can about how paleontologists learn about the past.

ELL

English Language Learners
ELL support Additional ELL support and modified instruction is provided in the *ELL Handbook* and in the ELL Support lessons on pp. DI•66–DI•75.

Listening comprehension
English learners will benefit from additional visual support to understand the key terms in the concept map. Use the pictures on pp. 388–389 to scaffold understanding.

Frontload for Read Aloud Use the modified Read Aloud on p. DI•69 of the *ELL Handbook* to prepare students to listen to "Graveyards of the Dinosaurs" (p. 389b).

ELL Poster 13

The Dinosaurs of Waterhouse Hawkins **388–389**

Objectives
- Develop listening comprehension.
- Develop oral vocabulary.

Check Oral Vocabulary
SUCCESS PREDICTOR

Oral Vocabulary
Amazing Words

Introduce Amazing Words

"Graveyards of the Dinosaurs" on p. 389b is about the work of Paul Sereno, a dinosaur expert. Tell students to listen for this week's Amazing Words—*fossils, paleontologists, uncanny,* and *sandstone*—as you read.

Model fluency

As you read "Graveyards of the Dinosaurs," model appropriate phrasing by grouping words in a meaningful way and paying attention to punctuation cues.

Amazing Words Oral Vocabulary Routine

fossils
paleontologists
uncanny
sandstone

Teach Amazing Words

1 **Introduce** Write the word *paleontologists* on the board. Have students say the word aloud with you. In "Graveyards of the Dinosaurs" we learn that *paleontologists* are dinosaur experts. Does the author include context clues that give additional information about the meaning of this word? Supply a student-friendly definition.

2 **Demonstrate** Break into groups. Have students elicit suggestions from other group members to demonstrate understanding. What are some challenges for *paleontologists*?

3 **Apply** Ask students to describe what *paleontologists* do.

See p. OV•3 to teach *fossils, uncanny,* and *sandstone*.

Routines Flip Chart

Apply Amazing Words

To build oral language, lead the class in a discussion about the Amazing Words' meanings.

Don't Wait Until Friday

MONITOR PROGRESS **Check Oral Vocabulary**

During discussion, listen for students' use of the Amazing Words.

If... students are unable to use the Amazing Words to discuss the concept,

then... use Oral Vocabulary Routine in the Routines flip chart to demonstrate words in different contexts.

Day 1	Days 2–3	Day 4	Day 5
Check Oral Vocabulary	Check Retelling	Check Fluency	Check Oral Vocabulary

Success Predictor

Graveyards of the Dinosaurs

by Shelley Tanaka

Paul Sereno is a university professor who has discovered dinosaur fossils on five continents. He is one of the most respected dinosaur experts in the world.

One of Sereno's most dramatic discoveries came near the beginning of his career, starting with the earliest dinosaur yet known—Herrerasaurus. Although a number of Herrerasaurus fossils had been found, there weren't enough bones to tell him exactly what the creature had looked like. Most important, no one had ever discovered a complete skull.

Sereno decided to look for a complete skeleton himself. That is how he ended up in the Valley of the Moon [in Argentina], the place where the other Herrerasaurus fossils had been found.

And just how was he going to find this rare skeleton? As [someone] has said, finding fossils is painfully simple. You walk, and you look.

It was like looking for a needle in a haystack.

Sereno and his team were combing the area piece by piece, gradually making their way along the valley. As they drove away from one spot, he realized there was a small ravine that they had missed. They moved on anyway, but that small triangle of land nagged at him. He couldn't sleep. So, a few weeks later, they drove back to it.

Most paleontologists will tell you that there are some field workers who have a special knack for finding fossils. Some call it accident or luck. Some say it's a sixth sense, an uncanny instinct.

Whatever it is, Sereno had it that day. He laid his backpack on a rock and headed down into the little valley. He walked a dozen paces, straight to where a fossil was poking out of a sandstone ledge.

He was too experienced to get excited right away. The fossil most likely belonged to a rhynchosaur. The bones of those ancient owl-faced lizards had been popping out of the rock so often that the team had stopped collecting them.

Then Sereno looked more closely. A few neck bones had started to roll down the slope. Sereno rolled them back into place. And he realized that the neck bones led to the back of a skull. A Herrerasaurus skull.

(Continued on p. 423s)

Oral Vocabulary

Success Predictor

Objectives
- Identify facts and opinions to aid comprehension.
- Use the predict and set purposes strategy to aid comprehension.
- Read grade-level text with appropriate phrasing.

Skills Trace

Fact and Opinion

Introduce U1W4D1; U3W3D1; U6W4D1

Practice U1W4D2; U1W4D3; U3W3D2; U3W3D3; U6W4D2; U6W3D3

Reteach/Review U1W4D5; U3W2D2; U3W2D3; U3W3D5; U3W4D3; U6W4D5

Assess/Test Weekly Tests U1W4; U3W3; U6W4 Benchmark Tests U3

KEY:
U=Unit   W=Week   D=Day

Skill ↔ Strategy
Fact and Opinion
Predict and Set Purpose

Student Edition p. EI • 7

Introduce fact and opinion

Envision It!

A statement of fact can be proven to be true or false. How can I prove that a statement is true? (Possible responses: look in a reference book, ask an expert, or rely on my own knowledge) How can I identify an opinion when I read? (look for words that signal a judgment or a belief) Have students turn to page EI•7 in the Student Edition to review fact and opinion. Then read "Dinosaurs" with students.

Model the skill

Think Aloud Today we're going to read about dinosaurs. Have students follow along as you read the first paragraph of "Dinosaurs." The first paragraph of "Dinosaurs" has one statement of fact: the word *dinosaurs* has Greek roots. I can check in a reference book or a valid online resource to verify that this statement is true. The first sentence says "the most fascinating." When I see the word *most*, I know that this is often a signal word of an opinion or judgment.

Guide practice

Have students finish reading "Dinosaurs" on their own. After they read, have them use a graphic organizer like the one on p. 390 and identify statements of fact and opinion from the selection.

Strategy check

Predict and Set Purpose Remind students that if they have difficulty understanding "Dinosaurs," they can use the strategy of predict and set a purpose. Model the strategy of predicting and setting a purpose to adjust understanding.

Model the strategy

Envision It!

Think Aloud I can use text features to predict what an article will be about. I see the title and two headings. These features help me predict what information will be in the article. Now I can set a purpose for reading: I'll read to learn more about types and characteristics of dinosaurs. Set a purpose for students as they read "Dinosaurs," and have them set their own purposes as well. Then have students review the strategy of predict and set purpose on p. EI•20 of the Student Edition.

Student Edition p. EI • 20

On their own

Use p. 200 in the *Reader's and Writer's Notebook* for additional practice with fact and opinion.

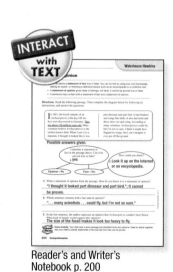

Reader's and Writer's Notebook p. 200

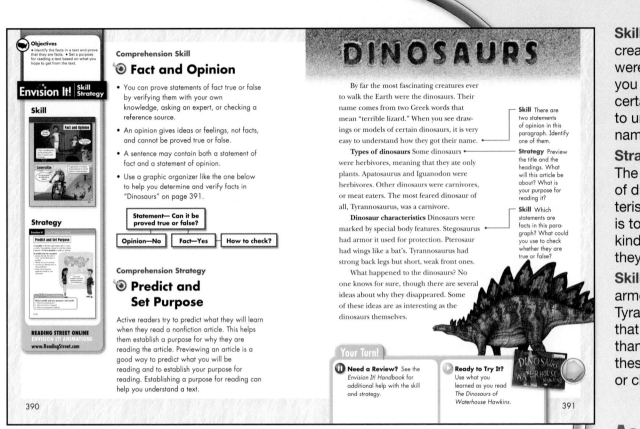

Student Edition pp. 390–391

Model Fluency
Appropriate Phrasing

Model fluent reading

Have students listen as you read paragraph 1 of "Dinosaurs" with appropriate phrasing. Explain that you will pay particular attention to the grouping of words, or phrasing, as you read.

ROUTINE — Paired Reading

1. **Read** Have partners read paragraphs 3 and 4 of "Dinosaurs."

2. **Reader 1** Students read the entire passage, switching readers at the end of each paragraph.

3. **Reader 2** Partners reread the passage. This time, the other student begins.

4. **Reread** For optimal fluency, have partners reread aloud three or four times.

5. **Corrective Feedback** Provide feedback about students' phrasing.

Routines Flip Chart

Skill "By far the most fascinating creatures ever to walk the Earth were the dinosaurs" or "When you see drawings or models of certain dinosaurs, it is very easy to understand how they got their name."

Strategy Possible response: The article will be about types of dinosaurs and their characteristics. My purpose for reading is to learn more about different kinds of dinosaurs and what they were like.

Skill Stegosaurus had armor; Pterosaur had wings; Tyrannosaurus had front legs that were shorter and weaker than the back legs. I could verify these facts by asking an expert or checking a reference source.

Academic Vocabulary

predict and set purpose a comprehension strategy in which the reader makes a prediction about what they are about to read and sets a purpose for reading

ELL

English Language Learners
Fact and opinion Provide oral practice by asking students to state facts and opinions about dinosaurs. Then write these sentences on the board and read them together. Have students identify whether each statement is a fact or an opinion. Have them explain their answers.

• Everyone enjoys learning about dinosaurs. (opinion)

• Dinosaurs lived millions of years ago. (fact)

Objectives
- Activate prior knowledge of words.
- Identify questions for research.

Vocabulary
Tested Vocabulary

Lesson vocabulary

Use the following categorizing activity to help students acquire word knowledge that improves reading, speaking, listening, and writing vocabularies.

Activate prior knowledge

Display the lesson words. Give oral clues to help students think about the categories in which the words belong. Have students check their glossary or a printed or electronic dictionary to determine the meanings, syllabications, pronunciations, and part of speech of any unknown words. Read aloud each three-item category below. Ask students to name the vocabulary word that fits each category and discuss their reasons.

- built, created, produced (erected – all name ways something is made)
- container, frame, shape (mold – all can be used to create a figure)
- birthday, holiday, party (occasion – all name a special event)
- dusted, swept, mopped (tidied – all name ways to clean)
- office, classroom, factory (workshop – all name a place to do work)
- base, groundwork, underpinning (foundation – all name the basis or supporting part of a building or other structure)
- quantity, relationship, ratio (proportion – all name a relationship between amounts)

Suffixes -tion, -sion

Use the words *proportion* and *occasion* to discuss the suffixes *-tion* and *-sion.* These suffixes form nouns of action or condition. Have students determine the meaning of these words based on these Latin-based suffixes.

Preteach Academic Vocabulary

ELL **Academic Vocabulary** Write the following words on the board:

predict and set purpose	**sound reasoning**
interview	**morpheme**
flashback	**schedule**

Have students share what they know about this week's Academic Vocabulary. Use students' responses to assess their prior knowledge. Preteach the Academic Vocabulary by providing a student-friendly description, explanation, or example that clarifies the meaning of each term. Then ask students to restate the meaning of the Academic Vocabulary term in their own words.

Research and Inquiry
Identify Questions

Teach

Discuss the Question of the Week: *How can paleontologists help us to understand the past?* Tell students they will research how paleontologists help us understand the past. Students will also plan the schedule for an imaginary seminar that presents paleontologists and their work with dinosaurs. Students will present their schedules for the seminar on Day 5.

Model

Think Aloud I am interested in the fact that dinosaurs lived for millions of years, and then completely disappeared. I start by thinking of open-ended questions to address the major research topic. So, an inquiry question might be *According to paleontologists, how did dinosaurs become extinct?* This helps me form a research plan for gathering information about my question. Now I can follow my research plan to collect data from a print and electronic resources.

Guide practice

After students have brainstormed inquiry questions, explain that tomorrow they will conduct an online research of their questions. Help students identify keywords that will guide their search.

On their own

Have students work individually, in pairs, or in small groups to write an inquiry question.

INTERNET GUY
Don Leu

21st Century Skills

Weekly Inquiry Project
Day 1 Identify Questions
Day 2 Navigate/Search
Day 3 Analyze
Day 4 Synthesize
Day 5 Communicate

Small Group Time

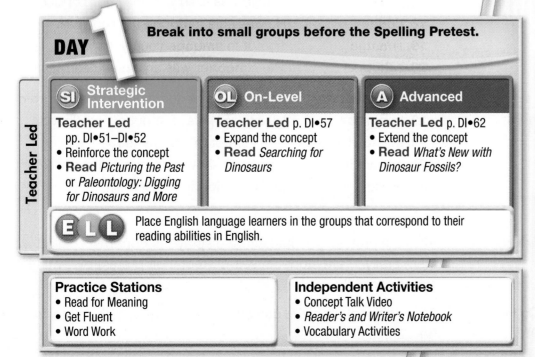

Break into small groups before the Spelling Pretest.

DAY 1

Teacher Led

SI Strategic Intervention

Teacher Led pp. DI•51–DI•52
• Reinforce the concept
• **Read** *Picturing the Past* or *Paleontology: Digging for Dinosaurs and More*

OL On-Level

Teacher Led p. DI•57
• Expand the concept
• **Read** *Searching for Dinosaurs*

A Advanced

Teacher Led p. DI•62
• Extend the concept
• **Read** *What's New with Dinosaur Fossils?*

ELL Place English language learners in the groups that correspond to their reading abilities in English.

Practice Stations
• Read for Meaning
• Get Fluent
• Word Work

Independent Activities
• Concept Talk Video
• *Reader's and Writer's Notebook*
• Vocabulary Activities

ELL

English Language Learners
Multilingual vocabulary
Students can apply knowledge of their home languages to acquire new English vocabulary by using the Multilingual Vocabulary Lists (*ELL Handbook*, pp. 431–444).

Objectives

- Spell words with consonant sounds /j/, /ks/, /sk/, /s/.
- Use and understand principal parts of irregular verbs.
- Write cursive capital letter *P* and lowercase *p* in words.

Spelling Pretest
Words with Consonant Sounds /j/, /ks/, /sk/, /s/

Introduce   Tell students: this week we will work on spelling words with the consonant sounds /j/, /ks/, /sk/, and /s/.

Pretest   Use these sentences to administer the spelling pretest. Say each word, read the sentence, and repeat the word.

1. excuse	Vonda had an **excuse** for her absence.
2. scene	The first **scene** is set in Venice.
3. muscle	The heart is a **muscle.**
4. explore	We decided to **explore** the museum.
5. pledge	The soldier made a **pledge** to return.
6. journal	For how long have you kept your **journal?**
7. science	I plan to study **science** in college.
8. schedule	Don't forget to bring your new school **schedule!**
9. gigantic	The **gigantic** statue stood in the harbor.
10. scheme	The police foiled the criminal's **scheme.**
11. Japan	The capital of **Japan** is Tokyo.
12. excellent	Mr. Ramirez makes **excellent** dumplings.
13. exclaim	Audiences sometimes **exclaim** "Bravo!"
14. fascinate	Choose a topic that will **fascinate** you.
15. ginger	Anita prepared the salmon with **ginger.**
16. scholar	The **scholar** gave a talk on French history.
17. scent	The air was filled with the **scent** of lilacs.
18. dodge	He was able to **dodge** the snowball.
19. smudge	Try not to **smudge** your writing.
20. schooner	The **schooner** was anchored nearby.

Challenge words

21. extraordinary	The athlete's performance was **extraordinary.**
22. reminisce	I like to **reminisce** about my childhood.
23. acknowledge	Don't forget to **acknowledge** the gifts.
24. prejudice	The judge showed no **prejudice** toward either side.
25. allergic	Eddie is **allergic** to penicillin.

Self-correct   After the pretest, you can either display the correctly spelled words or spell them orally. Have students self-correct their pretest by writing misspelled words correctly.

On their own   For additional practice, use *Let's Practice It!* p. 141 on the *Teacher Resources DVD-ROM.*

Let's Practice It!
TR DVD•141

Conventions
Principal Parts of Irregular Verbs

Teach
Display Grammar Transparency 13, and read aloud the explanation and examples in the box. Point out the principal part of the irregular verb *see.*

Model
Model writing the complete form of the irregular verb to complete items 1 and 2. Explain how you use the chart to determine the part of the irregular verb that occurs in the sentences.

Guide practice
Guide students to complete item 3. Remind them to use the chart to determine which part of the verb is used. Record the correct responses on the transparency.

Daily Fix-It
Use Daily Fix-It numbers 1 and 2 in the right margin.

Connect to oral language
Have students read sentences 4 and 5 on the transparency and use the correct principal part of an irregular verb to complete each sentence.

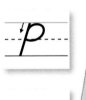

Grammar Transparency 13, TR DVD

Handwriting
Cursive Letters *p* and *P*

Model letter formation
Display the cursive letters *p* and *P.* Follow the stroke instructions pictured to model letter formation.

Model spacing
Explain that writing legibly means letters are correctly spaced. They are placed neither too closely together nor too far apart. Model writing this sentence smoothly: *Paul picked the palest apple.* Make sure the letters are spaced properly.

Guide practice
Have students write these sentences: *Put pineapple in the cup. Petra keeps a popcorn popper.* Circulate around the room, guiding students.

1. Have you saw the dinosaur exhibit. *(seen; exhibit?)*
2. It's displays include every dinosaur I ever knowed about. *(Its; knew)*

E L L

English Language Learners
Conventions Have students practice the difference between past tense and past participle in mixed ability pairs. Have one partner say a sentence using the past tense form of an irregular verb, and the other say a corresponding sentence using the past participle. Ask students to practice the following verbs: *become, do, know, think.*

Objectives
- Identify the elements of an advertising brochure.

Writing—Advertising Brochure
Introduce

5 Day Planner
Guide to Mini-Lessons

DAY 1	Read Like a Writer
DAY 2	Developing a Word Web
DAY 3	Using Sound Reasoning
DAY 4	Revising Strategy: Subtracting
DAY 5	Proofread for Principal Parts of Irregular Verbs

MINI-LESSON
Read Like a Writer

■ **Introduce** This week you will write an advertising brochure. An advertising brochure is a short document that tries to persuade people to purchase a product or attend an event.

Prompt *The Dinosaurs of Waterhouse Hawkins* tells about the introduction of dinosaur models to the world. Prepare an advertisement for one of the events, enticing people to come.

Trait Word choice

Mode Persuasive

Reader's and Writer's
Notebook p. 201

■ **Examine Model Text** Let's read an example of an advertising brochure that tries to persuade people to attend an event. Have students read "Come Visit the Oak Lake Music Festival!" on p. 201 of their *Reader's and Writer's Notebook.*

■ **Key Features** Advertising brochures are organized around persuading the reader to do something. Underline the first place in the brochure that invites the reader to do something. Have students underline the title of the brochure. Point out that the persuasive point of the brochure is clear from the title.

An advertising brochure contains a list of reasons for taking the action that the author recommends. Have students identify the four listed reasons for attending the festival.

Advertising brochures often contain text features, such as illustrations or bulleted lists. What text features are used in "Come Visit the Oak Lake Music Festival!"? (subheads, bulleted list) Discuss how the text features help to make the brochure more appealing. Text features, such as bulleted lists, help readers locate important information.

Review
key features

Review the key features of an advertising brochure with students. You may wish to post the key features in the classroom so students can refer to them while working on compositions.

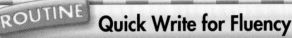

Key Features of an Advertising Brochure

- persuades readers to do something, such as buy a product or attend an event
- includes persuasive words or artwork to draw in readers
- may appeal to a specific audience, such as teens, women, or fathers
- often includes text features, such as graphics or bulleted lists

ROUTINE **Quick Write for Fluency** **Team Talk**

1. **Talk** Have pairs take two or three minutes to talk about the features of an advertising brochure.

2. **Write** Each person writes a few sentences describing the features of an advertising brochure.

3. **Share** Partners read each others' sentences.

Routines Flip Chart

Wrap Up Your Day

✔ **Build Concepts** Have students discuss how paleontologists help us understand the past.

✔ **Oral Vocabulary** Have students use the Amazing Words they learned in context sentences.

✔ **Homework** Send home this week's Family Times newsletter in *Let's Practice It!* pp. 142–143 on the *Teacher Resources DVD-ROM.*

Let's Practice It!
TR DVD•142–143

Write Guy
Jeff Anderson

Life in a Fishbowl

A "fishbowl conference" allows other students to observe how to appropriately respond to others' writing. It's important to reflect what the student is doing well and how a draft might be improved.

ELL

English Language Learners
Point out that "Come Visit the Oak Lake Music Festival!" uses graphics and bullets to convince readers to attend.

Beginning Have students draw an illustration to accompany a brochure for a product.

Intermediate Have students write a bulleted list of reasons for buying a product they like.

Advanced/Advanced High Have students role-play a conversation between a salesperson and a customer.

Preview DAY 2

Tell students that tomorrow they will read about one of the first people to study dinosaurs.

Objectives
- Expand the weekly concept.
- Develop oral vocabulary.

Today at a Glance

Oral Vocabulary
remains, model

Word Analysis
Suffixes *-tion, -sion*

Literary Terms
Flashback

Text Structure
Sequence

Lesson Vocabulary
◉ Homonyms

Reading
"The Artist of the Hour"

The Dinosaurs of Waterhouse Hawkins

Fluency
Appropriate phrasing

Research and Inquiry
Navigate/Search

Spelling
Words with consonant sounds /j/, /ks/, /sk/, and /s/

Conventions
Principal parts of irregular verbs

Writing
Persuasive text: Advertising brochure

Concept Talk

Question of the Week

How can paleontologists help us understand the past?

Expand the concept

Remind students of the Question of the Week. Tell students that today they will begin reading *The Dinosaurs of Waterhouse Hawkins.* As they read, encourage students to think about why it is important to learn about the past.

Anchored Talk

Develop oral vocabulary

Use the photos on pp. 388–389 and the Read Aloud, "Graveyards of the Dinosaurs," to talk about the Amazing Words: *fossils, paleontologists, sandstone,* and *uncanny.* Add these and other concept-related words to the concept map to develop students' knowledge of the topic.

Break students into groups. Have students use the following questions to consider suggestions from each group member and develop their understanding of the concept.

- How do *paleontologists* discover information about dinosaurs?
- What are *fossils*?
- How would *uncanny* instincts help a paleontologist?

Whole Group

Oral Vocabulary
Amazing Words

Amazing Words

fossils	model
paleontologists	illustration
sandstone	extinct
uncanny	replica
remains	archaic

Amazing Words — Oral Vocabulary Routine

Teach Amazing Words

1 Introduce Write the Amazing Word *remains* on the board. Have students say it aloud with you. Relate *remains* to the photographs on pp. 388–389 and "Graveyards of the Dinosaurs." The word *remains* refers to what the paleontologists found. Have students use context clues to determine the definition of the word. (*Remains* means "what is left over.")

2 Demonstrate Have students answer questions to demonstrate understanding. What types of *remains* might a paleontologist find? How could *remains* help us to learn about the past?

3 Apply Have students apply their understanding. What are some *remains* that might be left over from lunch?

See p. OV•3 to teach *model*.

Routines Flip Chart

Apply Amazing Words

Help students establish a purpose for reading as they read "The Artist of the Hour" on p. 393. Have them think about how *remains* might help the artist with the *model* for the project.

Connect to reading

Explain that today students will read about the artist Waterhouse Hawkins. As they read, they should think about how the Question of the Week and the Amazing Words *remains* and *model* apply to *The Dinosaurs of Waterhouse Hawkins*.

ELL Reinforce Vocabulary Use the Day 2 instruction on ELL Poster 13 to teach lesson vocabulary and the lesson concept.

ELL Poster 13

The Dinosaurs of Waterhouse Hawkins **392b**

Objectives
- Understand suffixes *-tion, -sion*.
- Use sequence to aid comprehension.
- Understand how a flashback is used in fiction.

Word Analysis
Suffixes *-tion, -sion*

Teach suffixes -tion, -sion

Remind students that suffixes *-tion* and *-sion* are added to verbs to form nouns of action or condition. Have students choose a base word from the first column and a suffix from the second column to form a noun.

Model the skill

Think Aloud I'll choose the word *confuse* from the first column and figure out which suffix will make a noun. I know the word *confusion.* I can use a dictionary to check the spelling and meaning.

Base Word	Suffix
confuse	*-tion*
found	*-sion*
distribute	
create	

Guide practice

Explain that a morpheme is the smallest unit of language that carries meaning, such as a suffix or base word. Have students combine a base words with suffixes to form nouns. Then have students determine the meaning of these words based on these Latin-based suffixes.

On their own

Then have students use a dictionary to confirm that their spellings and meanings are correct. They should also determine the syllabications, pronunciations, and part of speech of any unknown words. Then have students use the new words in sentences. Follow the Strategy for Meaningful Word Parts to teach the word *foundation.*

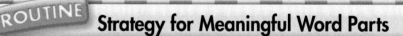

ROUTINE Strategy for Meaningful Word Parts

1. **Introduce word parts** Circle the suffix *-tion* and underline the base word *found.* These are morphemes. (The *a* is a connecting letter that makes pronunciation easier.)

2. **Connect to meaning** One meaning of the morpheme *found* is to "setup or establish." *Foundation* means something that is or has been set up or established.

3. **Blend** Blend the meaningful word parts together to read *foundation.* Continue the Routine with the words *distribution* and *creation.*

Routines Flip Chart

Literary Terms
Flashback

Teach flashbacks

Tell students that a flashback is an interruption in the narrative to explain an event that happened earlier. A flashback is a literary device used to give background or to show how a past event affects a character's actions or feelings in the present.

Model flashbacks

 Think Aloud Sometimes an author chooses to begin a story at an exciting moment. The author might use a flashback to give the reader necessary background information. I'm going to be aware of how the author presents major events in *The Dinosaurs of Waterhouse Hawkins.* I'll look to see if the author uses flashbacks.

Guide practice

Help students to find an example of a flashback as they begin to read the selection.

On their own

Have students look for examples of flashback in other selections of their Student Edition.

Text Structure
Sequence

Teach sequence

Remind students that sequence is the order of events in fiction and nonfiction. Chronological order, or time order, is one way that authors can organize text. This organizational pattern influences the relationships among the ideas.

Model the Strategy

Think Aloud Noting the sequence can help me understand and remember the events in a biography. The sequence is one way the authors present the major events in a person's life.

Guide practice

Have students read pages 396–397. Have students tell if the portion of the story on these pages is told chronologically or if it uses flashbacks. Then have them analyze how this organizational pattern and literary language influence the flow of the story and their understanding of the major event's in Waterhouse Hawkins's life.

On their own

Have students determine the sequence of steps in "The Artist of the Hour" and tell how the structure helps you understand how to make a sculpture.

Academic Vocabulary

morpheme smallest unit of language that carries meaning

flashback when an event is recounted, out of chronological order, to show how it impacts a current situation

Objectives

◎ Use context clues to determine and clarify the meanings of homonyms.

• Read grade-level text with appropriate phrasing.

Vocabulary Strategy for
🎯 Homonyms

Student Edition p. W•11

Teach homonyms

Envision It!

Remind students that homonyms are words with the same pronunciation and spelling but different origins and meanings. Tell students that they can use the strategy of context clues — other words and phrases around the homonym — to figure out its meaning. Refer students to *Words!* on p. W•11 in the Student Edition for additional practice.

Model the strategy

Think Aloud

Write on the board: *Jenny checked the mail every day, but the letter did not arrive.* I want to clarify the meaning of the word *mail*. *Mail* is a homonym because it has different meanings. I know that *mail* can mean "letters," and it can also mean "armor made of metal plates or rings," like a knight would wear. The context clues "checked," "letter," and "arrive," help me clarify that *mail* means "letters" in this sentence.

Guide practice

Write on the board: *The artist poured plaster into the mold.* Have students determine the meaning of the homonym *mold* using context clues. ("hollow shape") For additional support, use *Envision It! Pictured Vocabulary Cards* or *Tested Vocabulary Cards.*

On their own

Read "The Artist of the Hour" on p. 393. Have students use context clues to determine and clarify the meanings of the Words to Know. For additional practice, use *Reader's and Writer's Notebook* p. 202.

Reader's and Writer's Notebook p. 202

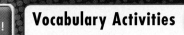
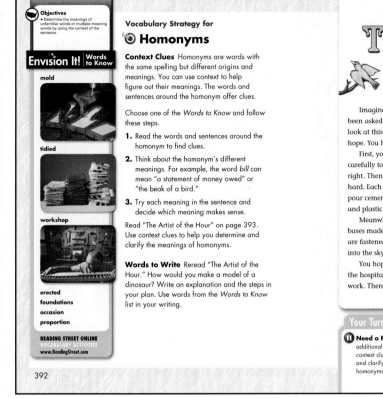

Objectives
● Determine the meanings of unfamiliar words or multiple-meaning words by using the context of the sentence.

Envision It! Words to Know

mold

tidied

workshop

erected
foundations
occasion
proportion

READING STREET ONLINE
VOCABULARY ACTIVITIES
www.ReadingStreet.com

392

Vocabulary Strategy for

🔵 Homonyms

Context Clues Homonyms are words with the same spelling but different origins and meanings. You can use context to help figure out their meanings. The words and sentences around the homonym offer clues.

Choose one of the *Words to Know* and follow these steps.

1. Read the words and sentences around the homonym to find clues.

2. Think about the homonym's different meanings. For example, the word *bill* can mean "a statement of money owed" or "the beak of a bird."

3. Try each meaning in the sentence and decide which meaning makes sense.

Read "The Artist of the Hour" on page 393. Use context clues to help you determine and clarify the meanings of homonyms.

Words to Write Reread "The Artist of the Hour." How would you make a model of a dinosaur? Write an explanation and the steps in your plan. Use words from the *Words to Know* list in your writing.

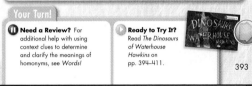

The Artist of the Hour

Imagine that you are an artist at work in your workshop. You have been asked to make a sculpture for the new hospital. When people look at this sculpture, they are supposed to think about freedom and hope. You have decided to make a group of birds in flight.

First, you make a clay shape of each bird. You must measure carefully to be sure the proportion of the wings to the body is just right. Then you cover the shapes with melted plastic and let it get hard. Each mold has the exact shape of the bird you made. Next, you pour cement into each mold. After it hardens, any crumbs of cement and plastic must be tidied up. Then you have a whole bird shape.

Meanwhile, you have to build foundations for the birds. These are bases made of wood or cement, with iron pipes sticking up. When they are fastened to the rods, the birds will look as though they are sailing into the sky.

You hope your work of art will be erected in the flower garden at the hospital. When it is put in place, you will be honored for your work. There will be a party to celebrate the occasion.

Your Turn!

⏸ **Need a Review?** For additional help with using context clues to determine and clarify the meanings of homonyms, see *Words!*

▶ **Ready to Try It?** Read *The Dinosaurs of Waterhouse Hawkins* on pp. 394–411.

393

Student Edition pp. 392–393

Reread for Fluency
Appropriate Phrasing

Model fluent reading

Read paragraph 1 of "The Artist of the Hour" with appropriate phrasing. Tell students that you are watching for the groupings of words as you read, using punctuation marks as a guide.

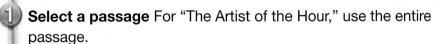 **ROUTINE** **Paired Reading**

① **Select a passage** For "The Artist of the Hour," use the entire passage.

② **Reader 1** Students read the passage, switching readers at the end of each paragraph.

③ **Reader 2** Partners reread the passage. This time, the other student begins.

④ **Reread** For optimal fluency, have partners continue to read three or four times.

⑤ **Corrective Feedback** Provide feedback about their phrasing.

Routines Flip Chart

Lesson Vocabulary

erected put up; built

foundations parts on which other parts rest for support; bases

mold a hollow shape in which things are formed, cast, or solidified

occasion a special event

proportion proper relation between parts

tidied put in order; made neat

workshop shop or building where work is done

Differentiated Instruction

SI Strategic Intervention

Context clues Have students find the word *mold* in the fourth sentence of paragraph 2. Guide them to find context clues to help them find the meaning of the word. Then use a dictionary to check the meaning of the homonym.

ELL

English Language Learners
Build Academic Vocabulary
Use the lesson vocabulary pictured on p. 392 to teach the meanings of *mold, tidied,* and *workshop.* Call on pairs to write the words on sticky notes and use them to label images of the words on the ELL Poster.

Objectives
- Discuss a biography.
- Identify statements of fact and opinion to improve comprehension.
- Use the predict and set purpose strategy to aid comprehension.

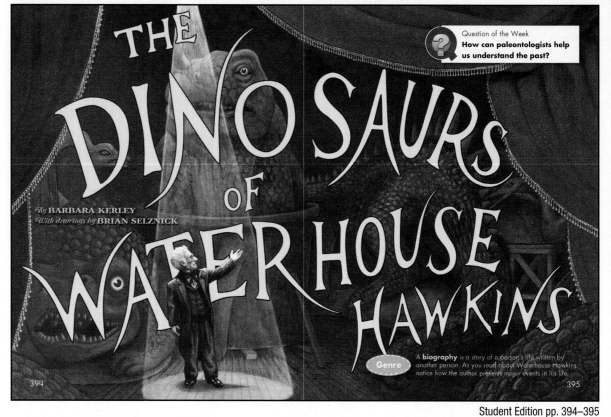

Question of the Week
How can paleontologists help us understand the past?

THE DINOSAURS OF WATERHOUSE HAWKINS

By BARBARA KERLEY
With drawings by BRIAN SELZNICK

Genre A **biography** is a story of a person's life written by another person. As you read about Waterhouse Hawkins, notice how the author presents major events in his life.

394 395

Student Edition pp. 394–395

Build Background

Discuss learning about the past

[Team Talk] Have students turn to a partner and discuss the Question of the Week and these questions about the past. Encourage students to find points of agreement.

- Why is it important to learn about the past?
- How do people learn about dinosaurs?
- What dinosaurs have you learned about?

Connect to selection

Have students discuss their answers with the class. Possible responses: When scientists make discoveries about the past, they can make connections and understand more about the present. Today, scientists and paleontologists work with fossils that help us learn about early mammals, birds, and reptiles. Stegosaurus and Apatosaurus are two types of dinosaurs. For additional opportunities to build background, use the Background Building Audio.

Go Digital! | eSelection

Prereading Strategies

Genre
Explain that a **biography** tells the story of a person's life that is written by another person. Authors present major events about a person's whole life, or a particular period in the person's life.

Preview and predict
Have students preview the title, illustrations, and diagrams in *The Dinosaurs of Waterhouse Hawkins.* Have them predict what they will find out as they read.

Set purpose
Prior to reading, have students set their own purposes for reading this selection based on their own desired outcomes. To enhance comprehension, help students set a purpose.

INTERACT with TEXT

Strategy Response Log

Have students use p. 19 in the *Reader's and Writer's Notebook* to set a purpose for reading and to make predictions about *The Dinosaurs of Waterhouse Hawkins.*

Small Group Time

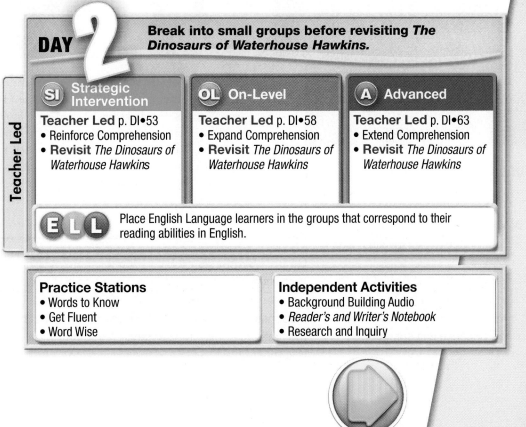

DAY 2

Break into small groups before revisiting *The Dinosaurs of Waterhouse Hawkins.*

Teacher Led

SI Strategic Intervention
Teacher Led p. DI•53
• Reinforce Comprehension
• **Revisit** *The Dinosaurs of Waterhouse Hawkins*

OL On-Level
Teacher Led p. DI•58
• Expand Comprehension
• **Revisit** *The Dinosaurs of Waterhouse Hawkins*

A Advanced
Teacher Led p. DI•63
• Extend Comprehension
• **Revisit** *The Dinosaurs of Waterhouse Hawkins*

ELL Place English Language learners in the groups that correspond to their reading abilities in English.

Practice Stations
• Words to Know
• Get Fluent
• Word Wise

Independent Activities
• Background Building Audio
• *Reader's and Writer's Notebook*
• Research and Inquiry

Differentiated Instruction

A Advanced
Ask students to find out more about paleontologists. Have students write a short report to share their information.

Double Day Read Multidraft Reading

For **Whole Group** instruction, choose one of the reading options below. For each reading, have students set the purpose indicated.

Option 1
Day 2 Read the selection. Use Guide Comprehension to monitor and clarify understanding.
Day 3 Reread the selection. Use Extend Thinking to develop higher-order thinking skills.

Option 2
Day 2 Read the first half of the selection, using both Guide Comprehension and Extend Thinking instruction.
Day 3 Read the second half of the selection, using both Guide Comprehension and Extend Thinking instruction.

English Language Learners
Build Background
Take a picture walk to front-load the selection, then review the selection summary (*ELL Handbook*, p. 103). Use the Retelling Cards to provide visual support for the summary.

Objectives
⊙ Identify facts and opinions to improve comprehension.

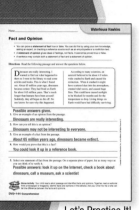

Let's Practice It!
TR DVD•144

Student Edition pp. 396–397

OPTION 1 Guide Comprehension Skills and Strategies

Teach Fact and Opinion

⊙ **Fact and Opinion** Ask students to read the first sentence on page 396 and decide if it is a statement of fact or opinion.

Corrective Feedback

If... students are unable to distinguish between statements of fact and statements of opinion,

then... use the model to guide students in identifying facts and opinions.

Model the Skill

Think Aloud If a statement is a fact, then I have to be able to prove it is true. How could I find out if there were horse-drawn carriages in London in 1853?

ORSE-DRAWN carriages clattered down the streets of London in 1853. Gentlemen tipped their hats to ladies passing by. Children ducked and dodged on their way to school.

But Benjamin Waterhouse Hawkins had no time to be out and about. Waterhouse, as he liked to call himself, hurried toward his workshop in a park south of town. He was expecting some very important visitors. He didn't want to be late.

396

OPTION 2 Extend Thinking Think Critically

Higher-Order Thinking Skills

⊙ **Fact and Opinion • Analysis** A statement can include a fact and an opinion, such as: Waterhouse Hawkins, who lived in London, was one of the world's best sculptors. Which part of the statement is a fact? What part of the statement is an opinion? Why? The first part of the statement is a fact because it can be proven. The second part of the statement is an opinion because it is someone's belief. It cannot be proven.

Genre • Synthesis How can you tell that *The Dinosaurs of Waterhouse Hawkins* is a biography and not an autobiography? Give an example from the text to support your answer. Possible response: The story is told from the third-person point of view, not the first. On p. 396, the sentence "He didn't want to be late" shows that the author is writing in the third person.

(find pictures of London at that time to see if there were carriages on the street; do research to prove it.) So, the statement is a fact.

As he neared his workshop, Waterhouse thought of the hours he'd spent outside as a boy. Like many artists, he had grown up sketching the world around him. By the time he was a young man, he'd found his true passion: animals. He loved to draw and paint them. But what he really loved was sculpting models of them. Through his care and hard work, they seemed to come to life.

397

Literary Terms • Analysis A flashback, a literary device sometimes used in a biography, is an interruption in the narrative to show an event that happened earlier. Reread pages 396–397. When does the author use a flashback? Why do you think the author used a flashback? The story takes place in 1853. The author uses a flashback on p. 397 when she describes Waterhouse's childhood. The author uses the flashback to give the reader important background information about Hawkins.

On Their Own

Have students find a statement of opinion on p. 397. For additional practice with fact and opinion, see *Let's Practice It!* p. 144 on the *Teacher Resources DVD-ROM*.

Differentiated Instruction

 Strategic Intervention

Fact and Opinion Work together to make a list of words that often signal an opinion, such as *most, always, best, all, everyone*. Then provide a topic, such as weather, food, or school. Ask one student to give a fact about the topic, and then have the partner give an opinion.

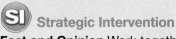

English Language Learners
Activate Prior Knowledge Create a two-column chart to record students' prior knowledge of reptiles and dinosaurs. We're going to read about an artist who learned about dinosaurs. What do you know about dinosaurs? What do you know about reptiles, such as crocodiles and lizards? How are they the same? How are they different?

OPTION 1

OPTION 1 Skills and Strategies, continued

Objectives
- Identify main idea and details to aid comprehension.

Teach Main Idea

Review Main Idea and Details

Remind students that summarizing the main idea in a way that maintains meaning can help a reader understand and remember important points in a story. Have students read page 398. Then ask them to identify the main idea of the text.

Corrective Feedback

If... students have difficulty identifying the main idea,

then... model how to identify the main idea.

Let's Practice It!
TR DVD•145

Model the Skill

Think Aloud The first three paragraphs tell me that although scientists were not sure what dinosaurs looked like, Waterhouse created models of them.

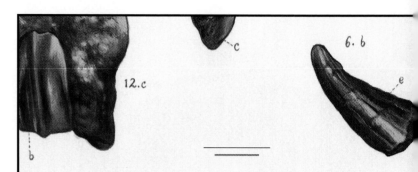

Now Waterhouse was busy with a most exciting project: He was building dinosaurs! His creations would prowl the grounds of Queen Victoria and Prince Albert's new art and science museum, the Crystal Palace.

Even though the English had found the first known dinosaur fossil many years before—and the bones of more dinosaurs had been unearthed in England since then—in 1853, most people had no idea what a dinosaur looked like.

Scientists weren't sure either, for the only fossils were some bits and pieces—a tooth here, a bone there. But they thought that if they studied a fossil and compared it to a living animal, they could fill in the blanks.

And so, with the help of scientist Richard Owen, who checked every muscle, bone, and spike, that's exactly what Waterhouse was doing. He wanted to create such perfect models that anyone—a crowd of curious children, England's leading scientists, even the Queen herself!—could gaze at his dinosaurs and see into the past.

398

Student Edition pp. 398–399

OPTION 2 Think Critically, continued

Higher-Order Thinking Skills

Review Main Idea and Details • **Synthesis** A newspaper headline usually summarizes the main idea, or topic, of an article. A headline also uses exciting language to persuade someone to read the article. Write a headline that gives the main idea and maintains the meaning of the text on page 398. Possible response: Artist Builds Dinosaurs for the Crystal Palace!

Text Features • Analysis Do you think the illustrator's style adds to your understanding of the story? Explain your thinking. Possible response: Yes. The illustrations on pages 398–399 show what pieces of fossil might look like, and I get a sense of how Waterhouse labeled them and created diagrams.

I think this is the main idea of the text. What does the third paragraph explain? (how scientists filled in blanks from the bits of fossils) This is a detail that supports the main idea and maintains the meaning of the text.

On Their Own

Have students use *Let's Practice It!* p. 145 on the *Teacher Resources DVD-ROM* for additional practice.

Differentiated Instruction

(SI) Strategic Intervention

Main idea Ask students to reread the last paragraph on p. 398. Ask what the paragraph is mostly about, and identify that statement as the main idea. Use an idea support map to show the main idea and details.

Connect to Science

Scientists have different theories to explain why dinosaurs died out over 60 million years ago. Some believe that dinosaurs disappeared slowly over time or died from disease. Others believe an asteroid or comet crashed into Earth, causing destruction.

E L L

English Language Learners

Vocabulary Reread the last sentence in the first paragraph on p. 398. Explain that *prowl* means "move slowly and quietly." Have students suggest examples of people or animals that might prowl.

Main idea Write the following statement and read it together: *Waterhouse and Owen created realistic dinosaur models.* Tell students that this sentence gives a main idea of a paragraph on p. 398. Help them find the matching paragraph.

Draw Conclusions • Synthesis How did Waterhouse help people "see into the past"? Draw a conclusion supported by information in the text. Possible response: He used fossils to create models of dinosaurs at a time when no one knew what they looked like. People could imagine what life on earth may have been like millions of years ago.

Objectives
◎ Identify homonyms.

OPTION 1 Skills and Strategies, continued

Teach Homonyms

👁 **Homonyms** Remind students that homonyms are words that have the same pronunciation and spelling, but different origins and meanings. Ask students to clarify the meaning for the homonym *spike* on p. 400.

Corrective Feedback

If... students are unable to understand a homonym,

then... model using the context to determine the correct meaning for a homonym.

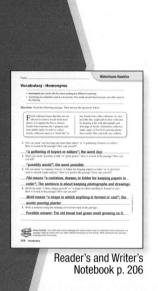

Reader's and Writer's
Notebook p. 206

Model the Skill

Think Aloud I can use a dictionary to find the correct meaning for the homonym *spike*. When I look in a dictionary, I see that the word *spike* is listed twice.

Waterhouse threw open the doors to his workshop. Nervously, he tidied up here and there. His assistants came, then Richard Owen.

At last, the visitors arrived: Queen Victoria and Prince Albert!

The Queen's eyes grew wide in surprise. Waterhouse's creatures were extraordinary! How on earth had he made them?

He was happy to explain: The iguanodon, for instance, had teeth that were quite similar to the teeth of an iguana. The iguanodon, then, must surely have looked like a giant iguana. Waterhouse pointed out that the few iguanodon bones helped determine the model's size and proportion. And another bone—almost a spike—most likely sat on the nose, like a rhino's horn.

Just so for the megalosaurus. Start with its jawbone. Compare it to the anatomy of a lizard. Fill in the blanks. And voilà! A dinosaur more than forty feet long.

Waterhouse was also making ancient reptiles and amphibians. While Richard Owen could imagine their shapes, it took an artist to bring the animals to life.

400

Student Edition pp. 400–401

OPTION 2 Think Critically, continued

Higher-Order Thinking Skills

👁 **Homonyms • Analysis** Look back at page 398. What context clues on this page can help you to clarify the meaning of *spike*? The word *spike* appears in the context of an explanation of how Waterhouse and Owen checked fossils. I know that fossils are hard, so this helps me clarify that *spike* means something that resembles a long heavy nail.

Draw Conclusions • Synthesis Do you think Waterhouse's models were as accurate as dinosaur models today? Draw a conclusion based on information presented by the author. Possible response: Probably not; paleontology was a new science at the time, and there was still a lot to learn. Scientists today know much more about dinosaurs, so models are more accurate.

Each word is shown with a superscript, or small number written above the entry word. The first definition is "a long, heavy nail," or something like a long, heavy nail. The second definition is "an ear of grain." In paragraph 4, I can use the context clue "another bone" to determine the meaning. I think the author compared the dinosaur's bone to a "long, heavy nail." That definition makes sense.

401

Background Knowledge • Evaluation • Text to
Text Compare this selection to another biography that you have read. How were the authors' purposes and viewpoints the same or different? Answers will vary.

On Their Own

Ask students to look up the word *spike* in a dictionary. Have them use each homonym in a sentence. For additional practice use p. 206 in the *Reader's and Writer's Notebook*.

Check Predictions Have students look back at the predictions they made earlier and discuss whether they were accurate. Then have students preview the rest of the selection and either adjust their predictions accordingly or make new predictions.

Differentiated Instruction

SI **Strategic Intervention**

Homonyms Write the word *bank* on the board and explain that it is a homonym because it has two different meanings. Help students find the word in the dictionary. Read each definition together and use each word in a sentence.

A **Advanced**

Ask students to analyze Waterhouse's process for building his models. Have students make a list of problems that could occur during each step of the process.

English Language Learners
Cognates Read the following phrase: *Waterhouse was also making ancient reptiles.* Point out that *reptiles* is a Spanish cognate. Ask students if any other words on page 400 have cognates in their home language. (amphibians/anfibios)

 If you want to teach this selection in two sessions, stop here.

Objectives
- Find pertinent information from various sources.
- Differentiate between primary and secondary sources.
- Recognize and correctly use principal parts of irregular verbs.
- Practice correctly spelling words with consonant sounds /j/, /ks/, /sk/, /s/.

Research and Inquiry
Navigate/Search

Teach

Have students identify keywords for their search and discuss their choices. Write good keywords on the board. Then have students enter their keywords into a student-friendly search engine. Have them use a similar search technique when looking for information in reference books and magazines.

Model

Think Aloud I want to find out what important dinosaur discoveries have been made this year, so I will use the keywords *dinosaur discovery* and the year. When I search, I find an article about how a university has discovered two new carnivorous dinosaurs. I think this would be a good seminar topic, so I will use this article as a source. I also will look for a primary source. I wonder if there is someone at my local university that studies dinosaurs. I will try to find a local expert.

Guide practice

Students should look for both primary and secondary sources as they collect information from Web sites. With students, discuss the difference between a primary source and a secondary source. They should understand that a secondary source is information gathered by other people. For example, a newspaper or journal article is a secondary source. A primary source is an original source. For example, if students talk to someone who studies dinosaurs, they will have a primary source for their report. Other primary sources may include blogs or papers written by paleontologists.

On their own

Circulate around the classroom to verify that students are pursuing research plans and viewing Web sites that are appropriate for their topics. Make sure students have at least one primary source, and give suggestions on how to find and interview a local expert. Students may want to work together to find and interview paleontologists.

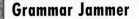
Conventions
Principal Parts of Irregular Verbs

Teach — Remind students of the four principal parts of verbs: present, past, present participle, and past participle.

Guide practice — Point out to students that the past form of an irregular verb is not used with a helping verb, but the past participle form is.

> He *has gone* to the store is correct. (past participle)
>
> He *went* to the store is also correct. (past)

Daily Fix-It — Use Daily Fix-It numbers 3 and 4 in the right margin.

Connect to oral language — Have students look for principal parts of irregular verbs in *The Dinosaurs of Waterhouse Watkins.* (thought, spent, had grown, p. 397; had found, p. 398; threw, sat, p. 400; built, p. 402; was set, were strung, p. 404)

On their own — For more practice use the *Reader's and Writer's Notebook* p. 203.

Spelling
Words with Consonant Sounds /j/, /ks/, /sk/, and /s/

Teach — Remind students that the sounds /j/, /ks/, /sk/, and /s/ can each be spelled in more than one way. Write *pledge, journal,* and *gigantic.* These three words all have the /j/ sound. Underline *dge, j,* and the first *g* in *gigantic.* Say each word.

Guide practice — Have students identify other spelling words that contain the /j/ sound and name the letter or letters that spell the sound. Then repeat the process with /ks/, /sk/, and /s/.

On their own — For more practice use the *Reader's and Writer's Notebook* p. 204.

Reader's and Writer's Notebook p. 204

Daily Fix-It
3. The sientist speaked about dinosaur bones and fossils. (*scientist; spoke*)
4. Them bones are bigger than any I have seed. (*Those; seen*)

Reader's and Writer's Notebook p. 203

English Language Learners
Conventions To provide students with practice on principal parts of irregular verbs, use the modified grammar lessons in the *ELL Handbook* and Grammar Jammer online at:
www.ReadingStreet.com

Writing—Advertising Brochure
Writing Trait: Word Choice

Introduce the prompt

Review the key features of an advertising brochure. Remind students that they should think about these features as they plan their writing. Then explain that today they will begin the writing process for an advertising brochure. Read aloud the writing prompt.

Writing Prompt

The Dinosaurs of Waterhouse Hawkins tells about the introduction of dinosaur models to the world. Prepare an advertisement for one of the events, enticing people to come.

Select a topic

Think Aloud When writing an advertising brochure about an event, our purpose is to convince readers to attend the event. You will have to decide whether to advertise for the dinner party on New Year's Eve or for the grand opening of the Crystal Palace which you will read about tomorrow. We can make a chart of reasons why readers might attend one of the events and include details that support those reasons. Display a T-chart. One reason someone might attend the dinner party Hawkins planned is that it is educational. A detail that supports this is that people will learn more about dinosaurs. Add this information to the T-chart. Invite students to suggest other reasons for attending the event, along with supporting details, in order to generate ideas for the first draft.

Gather information

Remind students that they can read *The Dinosaurs of Waterhouse Hawkins* to help them find more information about Hawkins's events. Remember to keep this chart as the students will refer back to it tomorrow as they draft.

Reason for attending dinner party	Supporting detail
educational	learn more about dinosaurs
entertaining	see exciting exhibits
social	talk until the new year comes

Corrective feedback

Circulate around the room as students use the chart to select persuasive details. Talk briefly with students who are having difficulty filling in the chart. Ask struggling students to think about reasons why they might want to attend such an event.

MINI-LESSON

Developing a Word Web

■ Using precise words will make your brochure more interesting and persuasive. You can use a word web to think about precise words. I want to say that the dinosaur exhibit is special. Write *special* in the center of the web.

■ Then I fill in the outer circles with synonyms. I might use a thesaurus to look up *special* and find more precise words. Write *unusual, extraordinary, distinguished,* and *peculiar* in the outer circles. The best choice would be *extraordinary.* It conveys the idea that this exhibit is definitely worth attending.

Have students fill out their own word web using the form on p. 205 of their *Reader's and Writer's Notebook.* Explain that they should use their web to select precise words.

ROUTINE — Quick Write for Fluency — Team Talk

1 **Talk** Have pairs discuss their reasons for attending Hawkins's event.

2 **Write** Each student writes a paragraph summarizing his or her partner's reasons.

3 **Share** Students read their paragraphs to each other.

Routines Flip Chart

Wrap Up Your Day

✔ **Build Concepts** Why did Waterhouse Hawkins want to build dinosaur models?

✔ **Fact and Opinion** Write a statement of fact and a statement of opinion about the selection.

✔ **Predict and Set Purpose** How can predicting help you set a purpose for reading the rest of *The Dinosaurs of Waterhouse Hawkins?*

Differentiated Instruction

SI Strategic Intervention

Synonyms Have students practice using a thesaurus to make their word choices more precise. Ask them to select an appropriate synonym for the underlined words in the following sentences:
The task was hard.
The necklace was pretty.
The weather was warm.

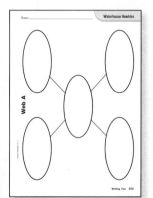

Reader's and Writer's Notebook p. 205

Teacher Tip

Post images of dinosaur models in the classroom to reinforce the theme of *The Dinosaurs of Waterhouse Hawkins.*

Preview DAY 3

Tell students that tomorrow they will read about the public's reaction to Waterhouse Hawkins.

Objectives
- Expand the weekly concept.
- Develop oral vocabulary.

Today at a Glance

Oral Vocabulary
extinct, illustration

Comprehension Check/Retelling
Discuss Questions

Reading
The Dinosaurs of Waterhouse Hawkins

Think Critically
Retelling

Fluency
Appropriate phrasing

Research and Study Skills
Schedules

Research and Inquiry
Analyze

Spelling
Words with consonant sounds /j/, /ks/, /sk/, /s/

Conventions
Principal parts of irregular verbs

Writing
Advertising brochure

Concept Talk

Question of the Week

How can paleontologists help us understand the past?

Expand the concept

Remind students of the weekly concept question. Discuss how the question relates to Waterhouse Hawkins's work. Tell students that today they will read more about Waterhouse's dinosaur sculptures. Encourage students to think about how people benefited from his work.

Anchored Talk

Develop oral vocabulary

Use the illustrations to review pp. 394–401 of *The Dinosaurs of Waterhouse Hawkins*. Discuss the Amazing Words *remains* and *model*. Add these and other concept-related words to the concept map. Break into groups. Have students discuss the following questions and identify points of agreement among group members and develop their understanding of the concept.

- Waterhouse used fossils and *remains* in his work. How do present day paleontologists also use fossils and *remains*?

- Waterhouse used different types of *models*. How are present day museum *models* different than *models* used in movies?

Oral Vocabulary
Amazing Words

Amazing Words

fossils | model
paleontologists | extinct
uncanny | illustration
sandstone | replica
remains | archaic

Teach Amazing Words

Amazing Words Oral Vocabulary Routine

1. **Introduce** Write the Amazing Word *extinct* on the board. Have students say it aloud with you. Yesterday we read about Waterhouse's models of dinosaurs that were extinct. Have students use context clues to clarify the meaning of *extinct*. (*Extinct* means to have died out or no longer exist.)

2. **Demonstrate** Have students answer questions to demonstrate understanding. How did Waterhouse learn about animals that were *extinct*? (He compared fossils to other animals.)

3. **Apply** Have students apply their understanding. Why might some animals become *extinct*?

See p. OV•3 to teach *illustration*.

Routines Flip Chart

Apply Amazing Words

As students read pp. 402–411 of *The Dinosaurs of Waterhouse Hawkins*, have them consider how the Amazing Words *extinct* and *illustration* apply to Waterhouse's models.

Connect to reading

Explain that today students will read about how Waterhouse presented his models to the public. As they read, students should think about how this week's concept question and the Amazing Words *extinct* and *illustration* apply to Waterhouse's models.

E L L Expand Vocabulary Use the Day 3 instruction on ELL Poster 13 to help students expand vocabulary.

Objectives

◎ Identify fact and opinion to aid comprehension.

◎ Use the predict and set purpose strategy to aid comprehension.

◎ Use context clues to determine and clarify the meanings of homonyms.

Comprehension Check

Have students discuss each question with a partner. Ask several pairs to share their responses.

☑ Genre • Analysis

How did the author use literary language and devices to describe the events in Waterhouse Hawkins's life? Possible response: The author used imagery and a flashback to present the events in Waterhouse's life.

☑ Fact and opinion • Analysis

Why do you think the author included facts and opinions about Waterhouse Hawkins? Possible response: A biography needs to give facts about a person's life that can be proven. The author also includes opinions about the person's actions and accomplishments. These opinions often let us know how the author feels about the person he or she is writing about.

☑ Predict and set purpose • Analysis

How did you use predictions to set purposes for reading this selection and what is your purpose for reading? Possible response: I used illustrations and diagrams to predict what the text might be about. Based on that information, my purpose for reading is to learn how Waterhouse made large dinosaurs.

☑ Homonyms • Synthesis

Use what you learned about homonyms to determine the meaning of the word *mold* in this sentence: *I set the clay in a mold to form a figure of a bird.* Use the word in a new sentence. Possible response: I can use context clues to figure out that *mold* means "a container that gives a shape." I poured the hot wax into a mold to make a candle.

☑ Connect text to text

Compare this biography to another biography that you have read. How were the selections the same? How were they different? Possible response: Both *Leonardo's Horse* and *The Dinosaurs of Waterhouse Hawkins* took place in the past and are about artists who used science in their art. Leonardo's horse was not meant to be exactly like a real horse, but Waterhouse wanted his dinosaur models to be replicas.

Strategy Response Log

Have students revise their predictions and set a new purpose for reading on p. 19 in the *Reader's and Writer's Notebook.*

Check Retelling

Have students retell the first part of *The Dinosaurs of Waterhouse Hawkins,* paraphrasing the text in a way that maintains its meaning and logical order. Encourage students to use the text features in their retellings.

Corrective feedback

If... the students leave out important details,
then... have students look back through the illustrations and diagrams in the selection.

Small Group Time

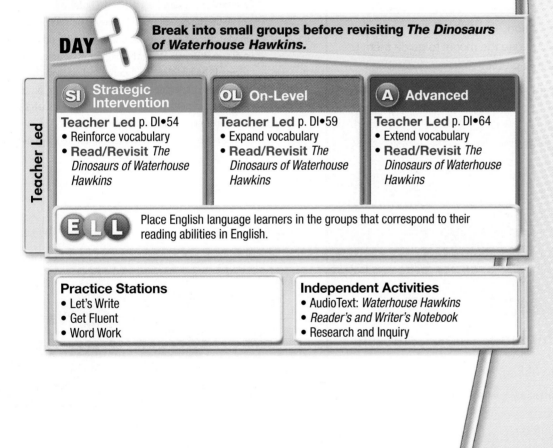

DAY 3 Break into small groups before revisiting *The Dinosaurs of Waterhouse Hawkins.*

Teacher Led

SI Strategic Intervention

Teacher Led p. DI•54
• Reinforce vocabulary
• **Read/Revisit** *The Dinosaurs of Waterhouse Hawkins*

OL On-Level

Teacher Led p. DI•59
• Expand vocabulary
• **Read/Revisit** *The Dinosaurs of Waterhouse Hawkins*

A Advanced

Teacher Led p. DI•64
• Extend vocabulary
• **Read/Revisit** *The Dinosaurs of Waterhouse Hawkins*

ELL Place English language learners in the groups that correspond to their reading abilities in English.

Practice Stations
• Let's Write
• Get Fluent
• Word Work

Independent Activities
• AudioText: *Waterhouse Hawkins*
• *Reader's and Writer's Notebook*
• Research and Inquiry

English Language Learners
Check retelling To support retelling, review the multilingual summary for *The Dinosaurs of Waterhouse Hawkins* with the appropriate Retelling Cards to scaffold understanding.

Objectives
◎ Use the predict and set purpose strategy to aid comprehension.

OPTION 1 Guide Comprehension Skills and Strategies

Teach Predict and Set Purpose

◉ **Predict and Set Purpose** Explain that good readers make predictions about text as they read. Tell students that after making a prediction, they can set the purpose of finding out if their predictions were correct. By confirming and revising their predictions, they can check their comprehension of the text. Have students examine the illustrations and text features on pp. 402–403. Ask them to make a prediction before they read.

Corrective Feedback

If... students are unable to make a prediction,
then... use the model to guide them to make a prediction using illustrations.

Multidraft Reading

If you chose...

Option 1 Return to Extend Thinking instruction starting on p. 396–397.
Option 2 Read pp. 402–411. Use the Guide Comprehension and Extend Thinking instruction.

Student Edition pp. 402–403

OPTION 2 Extend Thinking Think Critically

Higher-Order Thinking Skills

◉ **Predict and Set Purpose • Anaylsis** Turn to page 405 and examine the illustration. Make a prediction about what will happen next in the story. Possible response: Waterhouse Hawkins will unveil his dinosaur model to an audience. Set your own purpose for reading the next page. Possible response: to find out where and to whom Hawkins will unveil his model

Model the Strategy

Think Aloud Before I begin reading the page, I notice that there is an illustration. What information does the illustration show? (six steps to build a dinosaur model)

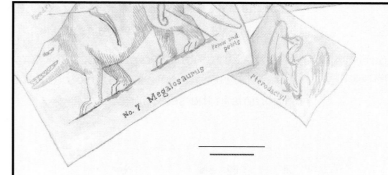

Designing the creatures was only the first step. There was still the monumental task of building them.

Waterhouse showed his guests the small models he'd made, correct in every detail, from scales on the nose to nails on the toes. With the help of his assistants, he had formed the life-size clay figures and created the molds from them. Then he erected iron skeletons, built brick foundations, and covered the whole thing with cement casts from the dinosaur-shaped molds.

"It is no less," Waterhouse concluded, "than building a house upon four columns."

Context Clues • Analysis Reread the last sentence in the second paragraph on page 402. What context clues in the paragraph can help you determine the meaning of the word *erected*? Possible response: The words *formed* and *built* help me to figure out that *erected* means "constructed."

Using this information, I can predict that the text on this page will explain the process of making a dinosaur model.

On Their Own

Have students read pp. 402–403 with the purpose of finding out if their predictions were correct.

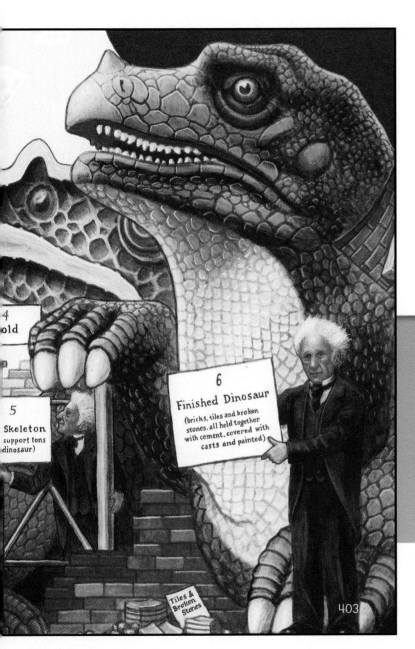

Summarize • Synthesis Summarize the details of Waterhouse's process for building the dinosaur models. Make sure your summary maintains the meaning of the text. Possible response: Waterhouse and his assistants made cement casts from molds shaped like dinosaurs. He built a support structure and covered it in the cement casts.

Differentiated Instruction

 **Strategic Intervention**

Set purposes for reading Ask questions to help students set purposes for reading. What do you want to find out after you read these two pages? What questions do you have about the illustration?

English Language Learners
Vocabulary Point out the word *dinosaur-shaped* on p. 402. Explain that it is a hyphenated word. A hyphenated word joins two words together to make a new word that is an adjective, or describing word. Ask students what the adjective describes. Then have students find another hyphenated word on this page and explain what it is describing. *(life-size)*

Objectives

- Identify main ideas and details to aid comprehension.

Student Edition pp. 404–405

OPTION 1   Skills and Strategies, continued

Teach Main Idea and Details

Review **Main Idea and Details**
Explain to students that sometimes the main idea can be found in details spread over several paragraphs. Ask students to find the main idea of the last four paragraphs on p. 404.

Corrective Feedback

If... students have difficulty answering the question,
then... model how to identify the main idea.

Model the Skill

Think Aloud I can use the details in the text to help me identify the main idea. The fourth paragraph tells me that Waterhouse worked hard on the invitations and the menus for his party.

In the weeks to follow, Waterhouse basked in the glow of the Queen's approval. But he would soon face a much tougher set of critics: England's leading scientists. Waterhouse wanted to be accepted into this circle of eminent men. What would they think of his dinosaurs?

There was only one way to find out. Waterhouse would show them. But why not do it with a little style?

A dinner party. On New Year's Eve, no less. And not just any dinner party. Waterhouse would stage an event that no one would ever forget!

He sketched twenty-one invitations to the top scientists and supporters of the day, the words inscribed on a drawing of a pterodactyl wing. He pored over menus with the caterer.

The iguanodon mold was hauled outside. A platform was built. A tent erected.

As the hour drew near, the table was elegantly set, and names of famous scientists—the fathers of paleontology—were strung above the tent walls. All was ready.

With great anticipation, Waterhouse dressed for the occasion in his finest attire. He was ready to reveal his masterpiece!

404

OPTION 2   Think Critically, continued

Higher-Order Thinking Skills

Review **Main Idea and Details • Analysis** The main idea of the first paragraph on page 404 is that Waterhouse wanted his work to be accepted by scientists. Summarize the details in the paragraph that support this main idea.
Possible response: Waterhouse had the Queen's approval, but the scientists were tougher critics. He had doubts that this group of distinguished men would accept him.

Draw Conclusions • Analysis How does the author want us to perceive Waterhouse's character? Draw a conclusion from the information on page 404. Possible responses: The author wants us to know that Waterhouse craved approval; he enjoyed being in the spotlight; he was creative; he enjoyed his life.

What does the sixth paragraph describe? **(the elegant table)** What does the seventh paragraph describe? **(Waterhouse's fine clothes)** All of these details support the main idea that Waterhouse was going to great lengths to prepare for his party.

On Their Own

Ask students to reread the third paragraph on p. 404 and identify the main idea.

405

Literary Language • Synthesis What question does the author ask in the first paragraph on page 404? **"What would they think of his dinosaurs?"** What kind of mood does this question create and how does it affect the presentation of Waterhouse's life? Explain.

Possible response: It creates a mood of anticipation because we know how important the scientists' opinions are to Waterhouse. The mood helps us understand how important Waterhouse's work is to him.

Differentiated Instruction

 Advanced

Have students use the library or Internet to find out more about Waterhouse's work during his life.

English Language Learners
Formal and informal language
Point out the question in paragraph 2 on page 404: *But why not do it with a little style?* Explain that sometimes an author asks a question that is not expected to be answered. What kind of mood is the author creating with this question? **(playful, curious)**

OPTION 1 Skills and Strategies, continued

Objectives

◉ Identify facts and opinions to improve comprehension.

Teach Fact and Opinion

◉ **Fact and Opinion** Ask students to reread the first sentence on p. 407. Have them decide if it is a statement of fact or opinion.

Corrective Feedback

If... If students have difficulty answering the question,

then... model how to distinguish between statements of fact and opinion.

Student Edition pp. 406–407

OPTION 2 Think Critically, continued

Higher-Order Thinking Skills

◉ **Fact and Opinion • Analysis** Sometimes a reader can notice words, such as adjectives, that may signal an opinion. Find a statement of opinion on page 407 that uses a signal word. **Possible response:** *All the guests agreed: The iguanodon was a marvelous success.*

Model the Skill

Think Aloud The sentence shares two pieces of information: the dinner lasted for eight hours and it was held on New Year's Eve. Can you prove both of these pieces of information? (Yes.)

When the guests arrived, they gasped with delight! Waterhouse smiled as he signaled for dinner to begin. With solemn formality, the footmen served course after course from silver platters. Up and down the steps of the platform they carried the lavish feast: rabbit soup, fish, ham, and even pigeon pie. For dessert, there were nuts, pastries, pudding, and plums.

406

Graphic Sources • Evaluation What information does the illustration on pages 406–407 provide that is not directly stated in the text? How does this illustration help you interpret the text? **Possible response:** Waterhouse and his guests ate their dinner inside the model of an iguanodon. This illustration shows that Waterhouse had great creativity and a sense of humor.

How? **(through research)** Since I can prove the two pieces of information are true, the sentence is a statement of fact.

For eight hours, the men rang in the New Year. They laughed and shouted. They made speech after speech, toasting Waterhouse Hawkins. All the guests agreed: The iguanodon was a marvelous success. By midnight they were belting out a song created especially for the occasion:

THE JOLLY OLD BEAST IS NOT DECEASED
THERE'S LIFE IN HIM AGAIN!

407

Unfamiliar Words • Analysis Use context clues to determine the meaning of the word *lavish* on page 406. Use a printed or electronic dictionary to check the meaning. Possible response: The text describes many plates of different types of food. There was probably more food than was needed. When I looked the word up in a dictionary, I found that it means "given in excess."

On Their Own

Have students find another statement of fact and a statement of opinion on pp. 406–407.

Differentiated Instruction

SI **Strategic Intervention**

Fact and Opinion Reread the first sentence on p. 407 with students. Ask if the statement could be proven. Then help students to formulate an opinion about Waterhouse's party.

English Language Learners

Build Fluency Have students read aloud the verse of the song on p. 407. Help them place emphasis on rhythm: *The jolly old beast/is not deceased/there's life in him again.* Ask students to find the rhyming words. Explain that *beast* means "a large or dangerous animal" and *deceased* is another word for "dead."

Objectives

◉ Use the strategy of predict and set purpose to aid comprehension.

OPTION 1 Skills and Strategies, continued

Teach Predict and Set Purpose

👁 **Predict and Set Purpose** Explain to students that sometimes statements of fact and opinion can be used to make a prediction. Ask students to use the opinions of the Queen and the scientists to make a prediction about what the public will think of the dinosaur models.

Corrective Feedback

If... students are unable to make a prediction,

then... help students make a prediction using facts and opinions.

Student Edition pp. 408–409

OPTION 2 Think Critically, continued

Higher-Order Thinking Skills

👁 **Predict and Set Purpose • Analysis** Based on this selection, what prediction could you make about what Waterhouse did later in his life? How could you check your prediction? **Possible response: I would predict that he continued his work with dinosaur models and then went on to do other types of sculptures. I could check my prediction by doing research about Waterhouse's life.**

Model the Strategy

Think Aloud The text on pages 404–407 describes the Queen's and the scientists' reactions to the dinosaur models. What opinions are given in the text?

The next months passed by in concrete, stone, and iron, as Waterhouse put the finishing touches on his dinosaurs. Inside the iguanodon's lower jaw he signed the work: B. HAWKINS, BUILDER, 1854. The models were now ready for the grand opening of the Crystal Palace at Sydenham Park.

Forty thousand spectators attended the regal ceremony. In the sun-filled center court, Waterhouse mingled with scientists and foreign dignitaries. At last, the Queen arrived! The crowd cheered, "Hurrah!"

408

👁 **Fact and Opinion • Analysis** How does the author use facts to show the impact of the grand opening on the public? Support your answer with examples from the text. **The author tells us that there were forty thousand people at the opening and one thousand singers. The Queen and Prince Albert were there, and cannons were shot. These facts show us that the opening had a huge impact.**

The Queen was amazed by the models and the scientists thought the iguanodon was a success. Based on these opinions, I predict that the public will also be amazed by the models.

Cannons boomed, music swelled, and a choir of one thousand voices sang. Waterhouse bowed before the Queen. Then she and Prince Albert invited the spectators to enjoy the amazing sights.

Waterhouse hurried to the lake and waited for the crowd to arrive.

First two, then ten, then a dozen more . . . Gasped! Shrieked! Laughed and cried: So this was a dinosaur!

409

On Their Own

Before they read the text, have students set the purpose of finding out if this prediction is correct.

Figurative Language • Analysis On page 408, paragraph 1, what does the author mean by this literary language: "The next months passed by in concrete, stone, and iron ..."? Possible response: Waterhouse spent the next months doing nothing but working with concrete, stone, and iron to put the finishing touches on his dinosaurs.

Differentiated Instruction

 Strategic Intervention

Fact and Opinion Say a factual statement about today's weather, such as: *The temperature is 42 degrees.* Have students identify the statement as a fact and discuss how the fact could be verified. (Check the weather report on the Internet, TV news, or in a newspaper.)

Connect to Science

The Crystal Palace was built in Hyde Park in 1851 for the Great exhibition, a World's Fair that was intended to show off the great industrial achievements of Britain. After the Exhibition closed, the Crystal Palace was moved to Sydenham, and rebuilt and enlarged. The new Crystal Palace was an art museum, an exhibition hall, and a theme park. Part of the park included a dinosaur exhibit.

ELL

English Language Learners
Understand Language On p. 408, reread the third sentence in the first paragraph. Write the word *spectators*. Explain that it comes from a Latin word meaning "watch" or "view." Ask students what they think *spectator* means.

Objectives
• Identify main ideas and details to aid comprehension.

OPTION 1 Skills and Strategies, continued

Teach Main Idea and Details

Review **Main Idea and Details**
Explain that an Afterword is a short section after a selection that often gives a conclusion or commentary. Have students find the main idea of the Afterword on p. 411.

Corrective Feedback

If... students cannot state the main idea,
then... help them infer the main idea and find supporting details.

Model the Skill

Think Aloud I don't see a sentence in the Afterword that gives the main idea. I notice many facts that explain what Waterhouse did later in his life.

410

Student Edition pp. 410–411

OPTION 2 Think Critically, continued

Higher-Order Thinking Skills

Review **Main Idea and Details • Synthesis** How would you use the main ideas in the text to summarize this selection? Possible response: Waterhouse Hawkins used his talents as an artist and sculptor to create the first dinosaur models in England.

Fact and Opinion • Analysis Find a sentence in the Afterword on page 411 that gives a statement of fact and opinion. Possible response: "The model went on display to amazed visitors of Philadelphia's Academy of Natural Sciences."

I can use these details as clues to figure out the main idea: Waterhouse continued his work by making dinosaur sculptures in the United States.

On Their Own

Have students identify details from the Afterword or p. 411 that support the main idea.

Differentiated Instruction

SI **Strategic Intervention**

Main Idea and Details Remind students that they often need to use clues to find the main idea. Have partners use a word web to show details in the Afterword. Then guide them to figure out the main idea by using the details in the web.

A **Advanced**

Have students find out more about the two places that are mentioned in the Afterword.

Afterword

In 1868, Waterhouse traveled to the United States to create the first-ever model of a complete dinosaur skeleton. The model went on display to amazed visitors of Philadelphia's Academy of Natural Sciences. Waterhouse also worked on making more dinosaur sculptures for a museum in New York City's Central Park. But before he could finish, vandals broke into his workshop, smashed the models to pieces, and buried them in the park. Today, pieces of the dinosaurs of Waterhouse Hawkins are still buried somewhere in Central Park.

411

Comprehension Check

Spiral Review

Draw Conclusions • Analysis Draw a conclusion about the impact of Waterhouse Hawkins' work on our knowledge of dinosaurs today. **Possible response:** Hawkins inspired people to become more interested in dinosaurs and study them.

Author's Purpose • Evaluation What do you think the author's purpose was in writing this selection? Do you think she succeeded in meeting her purpose? **Possible response:** I think the author wrote this selection to share information about Waterhouse's work and inspire her readers to use their talents. I think she succeeded because I learned new things. I realized that people can believe in themselves and their ideas when they try something new.

Check Predictions Have students return to the predictions they made earlier and confirm whether they were accurate.

English Language Learners

Reread the next to last sentence on p. 411 with students. Help them use context clues to determine the meaning of the word *vandals*. Help them use the words and phrases that come before and after the word to figure out its meaning.

Objectives

◉ Identify facts and opinions to aid in comprehension.

◉ Predict and set purposes to help comprehension.

Check Retelling

SUCCESS PREDICTOR

Objectives
• Provide evidence from text to support understanding. • Write responses to literary or expository texts and provide evidence from the text to show that you understand the text.

Envision It! Retell

READING STREET ONLINE
STORY SORT
www.ReadingStreet.com

412

Think Critically

1. Waterhouse Hawkins's dinosaurs were considered a remarkable artistic and scientific achievement in the 1800s. What modern-day artistic or scientific achievement might be considered remarkable? How does it compare to Waterhouse Hawkins's dinosaurs? Text to World

2. This biography is about an artist and his art. It does not give personal information, such as whether Hawkins had children or likes to swim. Do you think this kind of information should be in the story or not? What do you think needs to be told in a biography? Think Like an Author

3. Turn to pages 402 and 403. What facts did you learn about Waterhouse's method of constructing the dinosaur figure? Why do you think he expresses the opinion "It is no less than building a house upon four columns"? Fact and Opinion

4. Look back at page 398. What might lead readers to predict that Hawkins would one day amaze the people of Victorian England? Predict and Set Purpose

5. **Look Back and Write** Look back at the story. Describe the way Waterhouse Hawkins introduced the world to a new kind of creature. Provide evidence from the text to support your answer.

TEST PRACTICE Extended Response

Meet the Author and the Illustrator

BARBARA KERLEY and BRIAN SELZNICK

Barbara Kerley

Barbara Kerley says she got the idea for writing *The Dinosaurs of Waterhouse Hawkins* when her daughter asked how big a T. rex was. "I had no idea, so we got a book on dinosaurs from the library. In it was this incredible drawing of a dinner party, with formal waiters, candlesticks on the table, and all these elegant gentlemen stuffed into a dinosaur. I was hooked—I just had to find out the story behind that picture."

Brian Selznick

Once Ms. Kerley had written the manuscript, Brian Selznick got a call from his editor. She described *The Dinosaurs of Waterhouse Hawkins*. Mr. Selznick said the story left his head spinning, and all he could say was "I'll do it!" Mr. Selznick has also written and illustrated his own books.

Here are other books by Barbara Kerley and Brian Selznick.

A Week in the Woods by Andrew Clements, illustrated by Brian Selznick

Songs of Papa's Island by Barbara Kerley

Use the *Reader's and Writer's Notebook* to record your independent reading.

413

Student Edition pp. 412–413

Retelling

Plan to Assess Retelling

☑ **Week 1** Assess Strategic Intervention students.

☑ **Week 1** Assess Advanced students.

☑ **This week assess Strategic Intervention students.**

☐ **Week 4** Assess On-Level students.

☐ **Week 5** Assess any students you have not yet checked during this unit.

Envision It!

Have students work in pairs to retell the selection, using the Envision It! Retelling Cards as prompts. Remind students that they should accurately summarize the main topic and important ideas in a way that maintains meaning and logical order. Monitor students' retellings.

Scoring rubric

Top-Score Response A top-score response makes connections beyond the text, describes the main topic and important ideas using accurate information, evaluates facts and opinions, and draws conclusions from the text.

Don't Wait Until Friday

Grade 5 Retelling Cards

MONITOR PROGRESS Check Retelling

If... students have difficulty retelling,

then... use the Retelling Cards to scaffold their retellings.

Day 1	Days 2–3	Day 4	Day 5	
Check Oral Vocabulary	Check Retelling	Check Fluency	Check Oral Vocabulary	Success Predictor

Think Critically

Text to world

1. The development of the Internet is a remarkable modern-day achievement. The Internet is similar to Hawkins' achievement because scientists have used both to envision the world in a different way.

Think like an author

2. I think a biography needs facts to provide an accurate picture. Details about a person's life add interest. I would enjoy knowing more details about Waterhouse's life.

Fact and opinion

3. I learned how Waterhouse used models, molds, brick foundations, and cement casts to build his dinosaur models. He might have given this opinion to point out the challenges of building the dinosaur models.

Predict and set purpose

4. Waterhouse had a great desire and motivation to build the dinosaur models, and many people did not know what a dinosaur looked like.

 **Writing on Demand**

5. **Look Back and Write** To build writing fluency, assign a 10–15 minute time limit.

Suggest that students use a prewriting strategy, such as brainstorming or using a graphic organizer, to organize their ideas. Remind them to establish a topic sentence in response to the text and support it with facts, details, or explanations from the text. As students finish, encourage them to reread their responses, revise for organization and support, and proofread for errors in grammar and conventions.

Scoring rubric

Top-Score Response A top-score response uses details to explain how Waterhouse presented the dinosaur models to the public.

A top-score response should include:

• Waterhouse planned an elegant dinner party to show the models to scientists.

• After the successful dinner, Waterhouse completed other dinosaur models.

• The Queen joined thousands of people to see the models at the opening at the Crystal Palace.

Differentiated Instruction

SI Strategic Intervention

Have partners summarize the events that Waterhouse planned that led to the presentation of his dinosaurs.

Meet the Author

Have students read about author Barbara Kerley on p. 413. Discuss what inspired her to write a biography.

Meet the Illustrator

Have students read about illustrator Brian Selznick on p. 413. Ask them to think about how the illustrations influence their reading of the text.

Independent Reading

After students enter their independent reading information into their Reading Logs or a journal, have them summarize what they have read. Remind students that a summary should be a few sentences about the main idea of a text, maintaining meaning and logical order.

English Language Learners
Retelling Have students use the retelling strip on p. 412 in the Student Edition to describe the people, places, and objects in the selection.

Retelling

Success Predictor

Model Fluency
Appropriate Phrasing

Model fluency Have students turn to p. 398 of *The Dinosaurs of Waterhouse Hawkins.* Have students follow along as you read this page. Tell them to listen to your phrasing as you read about Waterhouse's project. Point out that you are using punctuation marks as guides for phrasing.

Guide practice Have the students follow along as you read the page again. Then have them reread the page as a group without you until they read with appropriate phrasing and with no mistakes. Ask questions to be sure students comprehend the text. Continue in the same way on p. 400.

Reread for Fluency

Corrective feedback

If... students are having difficulty reading with correct phrasing,
then... prompt:

- Where can we break up this sentence? Which words are related?
- Read the sentence again. Pause after each group of words.
- Tell me the sentence. Now read it with pauses after each group of words.

ROUTINE   Paired Reading

1. **Select a passage** For *The Dinosaurs of Waterhouse Hawkins,* have partners read p. 398.
2. **Reader 1** Students read the entire passage, switching readers at the end of each paragraph.
3. **Reader 2** Partners reread the passage. This time, the other student begins.
4. **Reread** For optimal fluency, have partners continue to read three or four times.
5. **Corrective Feedback** Listen as students read. Provide feedback about their phrasing and encourage them to adjust their voices to stress important word and phrases.

Routines Flip Chart

Research and Study Skills
Schedules

Teach

Ask students when they use schedules. Students may mention school schedules, television or movie schedules, or bus schedules. Show an example of a schedule and use it to discuss these terms:

- A **schedule** is a kind of chart. Most schedules have a title.

- A single box in a chart is called a **cell**.

- Schedules contain words arranged in a row or column. Corresponding numbers or times are also arranged in a row or column.

- Sometimes a schedule will have boxes or lines to clearly show information.

Provide groups with different types of schedules. Have each group show the schedule to the class, tell what it shows, and explain how to read it.

Guide practice

Discuss these questions:

How do you know what the schedule shows? (The title as well as the column and row heads tell what the schedule shows.)

How can you use the schedule to find a specific time? (Look at the column and row heads, and then look down and across to find the information.)

After groups describe their schedules, ask specific questions about the information contained in them. Have students convert the information into written notes.

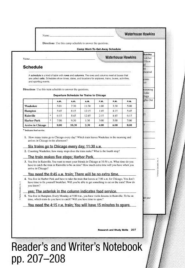

Reader's and Writer's Notebook pp. 207–208

On their own

Have students complete pp. 207–208 of the *Reader's and Writer's Notebook.*

Academic Vocabulary

schedule a kind of chart that lists starting and ending times for various events

ELL

English Language Learners Professional Development

What ELL experts say about content material "Before students read content material, provide them with hands-on or visual experiences directly related to the content. Then have them use a graphic organizer to map what they have learned or seen about the topic."–Dr. Georgia Earnest García

Objectives
- Analyze data to focus the research.
- Identify and correctly use principal parts of irregular verbs.
- Spell frequently misspelled words.

Research and Inquiry
Analyze

Teach

Tell students that today they will analyze their findings. They should ask themselves questions to improve the focus of their schedules.

Model

Think Aloud I have found a lot of useful information that answers my original inquiry question. In fact, I have more information than I can use! I ask myself, What am I trying to use this research for? Since I am going to create a schedule for a paleontologist seminar, I only need to know a little bit about each topic. But I might need to find more topics.

Have students create a chart to help them analyze their findings. Write a model on the board with the headings Seminar Topic, Description, and Source. Then show them how to fill out one row.

Seminar Topic	Description	Source
New carnivorous dinosaurs found	Paleontologists who found the dinosaurs will talk about their discoveries.	Newspaper article

Guide practice

Have students continue to fill out their charts. Have them examine schedules and meeting agendas as a model for their own schedules. Some students may want to add columns for speakers and times.

As they work, students should also evaluate the reliability, validity, and relevance of each source. Some of the information may answer their original inquiry question but not help them create a seminar topic.

On their own

Have students survey each other about what topics they are going to add to their schedule. This may help them generate new keywords if they need to do further research.

Conventions
Principal Parts of Irregular Verbs

Review

Remind students that this week they learned about the principal parts of irregular verbs.

- An irregular verb does not form its past or past participle by adding *-ed* or *-d* to the present form.

Daily Fix-It

Use Daily Fix-It numbers 5 and 6 in the right margin.

Connect to oral language

Have the class complete these sentence frames by replacing the underlined words with the correct past tense verb and past participle.

I <u>go</u> to the exhibit. I <u>write</u> an essay about dinosaurs.

On their own

For additional practice, use *Let's Practice It!* p. 146 on the *Teacher Resources DVD-ROM.*

Spelling
Words with Consonant Sounds /j/, /ks/, /sk/, and /s/

Frequently misspelled words

The words *except, excited, excellent, fascinate,* and *school* are often misspelled. I'm going to read a sentence. Choose the right word to complete each sentence, and then write it correctly.

1. I'm _____ about my trip to the city. (excited)

2. Janelle leaves for _____ at 7:00 A.M. (school)

3. Everyone was there _____ Ted. (except)

4. The lives of ancient animals _____ paleontologists. (fascinate)

5. Al's teacher said his oral report was _____ . (excellent)

On their own

For more practice, use the *Reader's and Writer's Notebook* p. 209.

Objectives
- Write a draft of an advertising brochure.
- Use sound reasoning to persuade readers to take action.

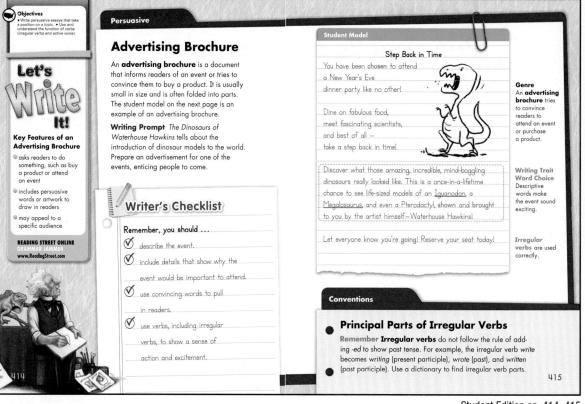

Student Edition pp. 414–415

Let's Write It!
Advertising Brochure

Teach

Use pp. 414–415 in the Student Edition. Direct students to read the key features of an advertising brochure which appear on p. 414. Remind students that they can refer to the information in the Writer's Checklist as they write their own advertising brochure.

Read the student model on p. 415. Point out the persuasive purpose as well as the reasons given in the model.

Connect to conventions

Remind students that irregular verbs do not use -ed or -d to form the past tense and past participle. Point out the correct use of the verbs *choose, show,* and *bring* in the model.

Writing—
Advertising Brochure
Writer's Craft: Sound Reasoning

Display rubric

Display Scoring Rubric 10 from the *Teacher Resources DVD* and go over the criteria for each trait under each score. Then, using the model in the Student Edition, choose students to explain why the model should score a 4 for one of the traits. If a student offers that the model should score below 4 for a particular trait, the student should offer support for that response. Remind students that this is the rubric that will be used to evaluate the advertising brochure they write.

Scoring Rubric: Advertising Brochure

	4	3	2	1
Focus/Ideas	Clear, focused brochure with many supporting details	Most ideas are clear and well supported	Some ideas are unclear or lack development	Brochure with no clear ideas or development
Organization/ Reasoning	Organized logically and displays sound reasoning throughout	Organized logically and mostly displays sound reasoning	Organizational pattern attempted but not clear; some sound reasoning	No clear organizational pattern; reasoning is unsound
Voice	Engaging and persuasive voice	Mostly engaging and persuasive voice	Weak voice	Flat and unpersuasive writing
Word Choice	Vivid, precise word choice	Mostly precise word choice	Limited or repetitive word choice	Incorrect or very limited word choice
Sentences	graphics, subheadings, and bulleted lists used to organize information	Some use of sentences and text features such as graphics and bulleted lists	Sentences and/or text features are present but incomplete/ineffective	No use of sentences and/or text features
Conventions	Excellent control and accuracy; principal parts of irregular verbs used correctly	Good control, few errors; principal parts of irregular verbs generally used correctly	Weak control; principal parts of irregular verbs used incorrectly	Serious errors that obscure meaning

T-chart

Have students get out the T-charts that they worked on yesterday. If their charts are not complete, have them reread *The Dinosaurs of Waterhouse Hawkins* to gather information, take notes, and compete their charts.

Write

You will be using your chart as you write the first draft of your advertising brochure. When you are drafting, don't worry if your brochure does not come out exactly the way you want it to. You will have a chance to revise it tomorrow.

The Dinosaurs of Waterhouse Hawkins **415a**

Objectives
- Write a first draft of an advertising brochure.
- Develop a persuasive argument that reflects sound reasoning.

Writing, continued
Writer's Craft: Sound Reasoning

MINI-LESSON

Using Sound Reasoning

■ **Introduce** Explain to students that sound reasoning involves giving logical reasons to support their claims. Sound reasoning is persuasive because the reasons given will make sense to the reader. Display the Drafting Tips to students. Remind them that the purpose of drafting is getting their ideas onto paper in an organized way. Then display Writing Transparency 13A. Point out the bulleted list of reasons to attend the event.

Come See the Dinosaur Models!

Would you like to see something incredible? Have you ever saw what a real live dinosaur looked like? Come to Waterhouse Hawkins' New Year's Eve celebration to see a model iguanadon!

When and Where
The event will be at the home of Waterhouse Hawkins, on December 31.

What to Expect
Waterhouse Hawkins was born in England. He learned how to draw and paint when he was a boy. Now he makes model dinosaurs. Dinosaurs roamed the earth millions of years ago. Waterhouse has been working on his giant model of an iguanadon for years. Now it is ready to be viewed.
- See a creature that walked the earth long ago!
- Be the first of your friends to see Hawkins's new work!
- Eat a delicious New Year's Eve feast!
- Enjoy the company of England's finest scientists!
- Waterhouse Hawkins knows the Queen!
Please respond by December 24th to reserve your place at the grand celebration.

Unit 3 The Dinosaurs of Waterhouse Hawkins   Writing: Model **13A**

Writing Transparency 13A,
TR DVD

Drafting Tips

✔ To get started, review your chart.

✔ Include reasons that will persuade your audience to attend the event.

✔ Don't worry about mechanics and grammar when drafting. You will take care of these issues during proofreading.

Think Aloud I'm going to include a list of reasons in my advertising brochure, "Come See the Dinosaur Models!" When I draft, I develop my ideas. I don't worry about proofreading or revising. Those are later steps in the writing process. I use my chart to choose logical reasons that will make my reader want to attend the event.

Direct students to use the drafting tips to guide them in developing their drafts. Remind them to use sound reasoning, making sure that the reasons they give are connected to their purpose.

ROUTINE **Quick Write for Fluency** **Team Talk**

1. **Talk** Pairs talk about the events that Waterhouse Hawkins held.

2. **Write** Each student writes a brief paragraph about the events Hawkins held. Students use irregular verbs in their paragraphs.

3. **Share** Partners check each other's paragraphs for correct use of irregular verbs.

Routines Flip Chart

A Advanced

Dramatize the event Work with students to recreate Waterhouse Hawkins's New Year's Eve event. Plan a field trip to a natural history museum, or use a toy dinosaur model in the classroom. Then have students role-play the famous scientists of England, discussing the dinosaurs while they eat lunch.

✔ **Build Concepts** What did you learn about the public's reaction to Waterhouse's dinosaur models?

✔ **Fact and Opinion** How did checking for facts and opinions help you understand the dinner party Waterhouse Hawkins gave for the scientists?

✔ **Predict and Set Purpose** Predict what would have happened if vandals had not destroyed Waterhouse's models in New York City.

Preview DAY 4

Tell students that tomorrow they will read about a paleo-artist, someone who makes models of dinosaurs today.

Objectives
• Expand the weekly concept.
• Develop oral vocabulary.

Today at a Glance

Oral Vocabulary
replica, archaic

Genre
Expository Text: Interview

Reading
"A Model Scientist"

Let's Learn It!
Fluency: Appropriate phrasing
Vocabulary: context clues
Listening/Speaking: Introduction

Research and Inquiry
Synthesize

Spelling
Words with consonant sounds /j/, /ks/, /sk/, /s/

Conventions
Principal parts of irregular verbs

Writing
Advertising brochure

Concept Talk

Question of the Week
How can paleontologists help us understand the past?

Expand the concept

Remind students that this week they have learned about a sculptor who created the first dinosaur sculptures. Tell students that today they will learn about another scientist who creates dinosaur models.

Anchored Talk

Develop oral vocabulary

Use the illustrations and diagrams to review pp. 402–411 of *The Dinosaurs of Waterhouse Hawkins*. Discuss the Amazing Words *extinct* and *illustration*. Add these words and other concept-related words to the concept map. Use the following questions to develop students' understanding of the concept.

• Why do you think dinosaurs became *extinct*?

• *Illustrations* can have many purposes. How did the illustrations add to your enjoyment of the selection about Waterhouse Hawkins?

Strategy Response Log

Have students complete p. 19 in *Reader's and Writer's Notebook*. Then have students summarize the selection.

Oral Vocabulary
Amazing Words

Words

fossils | model
paleonto- | extinct
logists | illustration
uncanny | replica
sandstone | archaic
remains

Amazing Words Oral Vocabulary Routine

Teach Amazing Words

1 Introduce Write the Amazing Word *replica* on the board. Have students say it aloud with you. Yesterday we read about how the queen and other scientists reacted to Waterhouse's *replica* of a dinosaur. Have students use context clues to determine a definition of *replica*. (A *replica* is an accurate copy of an object.)

2 Demonstrate Have students answer questions to demonstrate understanding. Why do you think so many people came to see Waterhouse's *replica* of a dinosaur? (People had never seen what a dinosaur looked like.)

3 Apply Have students apply their understanding. Where could you see a *replica* of a dinosaur today?

See p. OV•3 to teach *archaic*.

Routines Flip Chart

Apply Amazing Words

As students read "A Model Scientist," have them think about why his *replica* is probably different than Waterhouse's *archaic* model.

Connect to reading

As students read today's selection about another scientist, have them think about how this week's concept question and the Amazing Words *replica* and *archaic* apply to "A Model Scientist."

ELL Produce Oral Language Use the Day 4 instruction on ELL Poster 13 to extend and enrich language.

ELL Poster 13

Objectives
• Introduce interviews.

Let's Think About Genre
Expository Text: Interview

Introduce the genre

Explain to students that expository text is nonfiction writing that may be organized in a number of ways and for a variety of purposes. Ask students to share what they already know about kinds of expository texts. Inform students that an interview is one kind of expository text.

Discuss the genre

Remind students that an interview is a written record of a conversation, often between two people—usually a reporter and someone who is considered an expert in something. Ask: Where have you read interviews? (Possible responses: magazines, newspapers, the Internet) Let's take a closer look and compare interviews to biographies. Let's make connections between the themes of these texts.

On the board, draw a Venn diagram like the one below. Label the sides *Interview* and *Biography.* Ask the following questions:

- What is the purpose of an interview? What is the purpose of a biography? The purpose of an interview is to learn about a person or a subject and the purpose of a biography is to learn about a person.

- Who writes an interview and who writes a biography? An author or a reporter could write either an interview or a biography.

- How is information given in an interview versus in a biography? word-for-word and third person, respectively

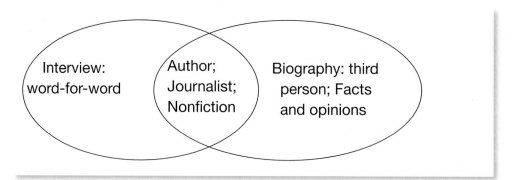

Interview: word-for-word | Author; Journalist; Nonfiction | Biography: third person; Facts and opinions

Guide practice

Have pairs of students make similar logical connections among interviews and biographies they have read. After students synthesize their ideas, have them share their results with the class.

Connect to reading

Tell students that they will read an interview about a scientist who makes dinosaur models. Have the class think about when reading an interview might be interesting or informative.

Small Group Time

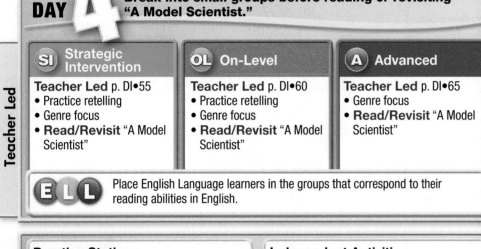

DAY 4 Break into small groups before reading or revisiting "A Model Scientist."

Teacher Led

SI Strategic Intervention

Teacher Led p. DI•55
- Practice retelling
- Genre focus
- **Read/Revisit** "A Model Scientist"

OL On-Level

Teacher Led p. DI•60
- Practice retelling
- Genre focus
- **Read/Revisit** "A Model Scientist"

A Advanced

Teacher Led p. DI•65
- Genre focus
- **Read/Revisit** "A Model Scientist"

ELL Place English Language learners in the groups that correspond to their reading abilities in English.

Practice Stations
- Read for Meaning
- Get Fluent
- Words to Know

Independent Activities
- AudioText: "A Model Scientist"
- *Reader's and Writer's Notebook*
- Research and Inquiry

Academic Vocabulary

Interview a meeting between a reporter or writer and a person from whom information is sought.

Objectives
◎ Use illustrations to predict and set purposes for reading an interview.
• Ask questions to aid comprehension.

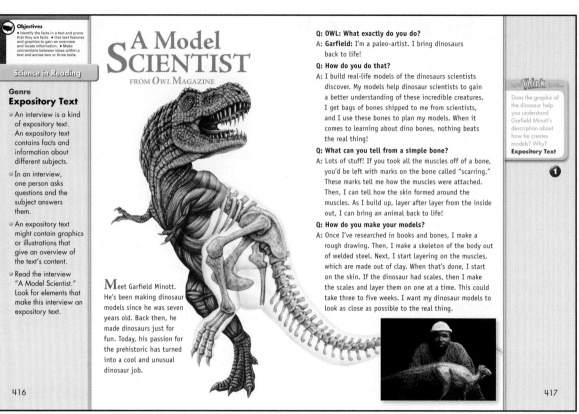

Student Edition pp. 416–417

Guide Comprehension
Skills and Strategies

Teach the genre

Expository Text: Interview Have students preview "A Model Scientist" on pp. 416–421. Remind students that good readers look at pictures and ask questions to help them predict and set purposes for reading. Students may ask and answer questions about the interview before, during and after reading it. Types of questions they might ask include literal (right there), interpretive and evaluative (on your own), and universal (theme related).

Corrective feedback

If... students cannot ask questions to help them set their reading purpose, **then...** guide students in questioning as they read.

Model the skill

Think Aloud — One of my purposes for reading was to learn about Garfield's work. Garfield says, *I bring dinosaurs back to life.* What does that mean? The illustration shows Garfield working on a dinosaur model. I can answer my question: He means that he makes lifelike dinosaur models.

On their own

Have partners ask questions about information in the interview to help them set their own purposes for reading.

Extend Thinking
Think Critically

Higher-order thinking skills

 **Predict and Set Purpose • Synthesis** Based on the information you have read in the first two pages, set a purpose for reading the rest of the interview. What do you want to learn? Possible response: I want to find out more about how Mr. Minott became interested in dinosaurs.

Draw Conclusions • Analysis Why does Garfield Minott base his work on dinosaur bones rather than on drawings or paintings of whole dinosaurs? Possible response: The marks on the bones tell him how the muscles were attached and how the skin formed and help him better understand the body structure of a dinosaur.

 Let's **Think** About...

1 Yes, the graphic helps me to understand how Garfield's drawing relates to the actual model and how Garfield builds his models from the inside out in layers.

Differentiated Instruction

SI **Strategic Intervention**

Ask partners to reread the third question and answer on p. 417. Guide students to think of a question they have about the information. Help them to find an answer to their question.

A **Advanced**

Point out that the term *paleo-artist* is a word that was created to describe a special career. Ask students to create and define another word that begins with *paleo.* Then have partners exchange words and try to define each other's word.

English Language Learners
Activate prior knowledge
Based on context and what they already know about the word *scar,* help students to define the word *scarring* as it is used on p. 417. Discuss how the words *scar* and *scarring* are related.

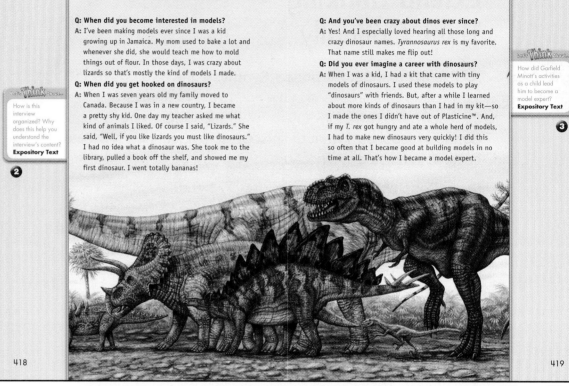

Q: When did you become interested in models?
A: I've been making models ever since I was a kid growing up in Jamaica. My mom used to bake a lot and whenever she did, she would teach me how to mold things out of flour. In those days, I was crazy about lizards so that's mostly the kind of models I made.

Q: When did you get hooked on dinosaurs?
A: When I was seven years old my family moved to Canada. Because I was in a new country, I became a pretty shy kid. One day my teacher asked me what kind of animals I liked. Of course I said, "Lizards." She said, "Well, if you like lizards you must like dinosaurs." I had no idea what a dinosaur was. She took me to the library, pulled a book off the shelf, and showed me my first dinosaur. I went totally bananas!

Q: And you've been crazy about dinos ever since?
A: Yes! And I especially loved hearing all those long and crazy dinosaur names. *Tyrannosaurus rex* is my favorite. That name still makes me flip out!

Q: Did you ever imagine a career with dinosaurs?
A: When I was a kid, I had a kit that came with tiny models of dinosaurs. I used these models to play "dinosaurs" with friends. But, after a while I learned about more kinds of dinosaurs than I had in my kit—so I made the ones I didn't have out of Plasticine™. And, if my *T. rex* got hungry and ate a whole herd of models, I had to make new dinosaurs very quickly! I did this so often that I became good at building models in no time at all. That's how I became a model expert.

Let's Think About...
How is this interview organized? Why does this help you understand the interview's content?
Expository Text
❷

Let's Think About...
How did Garfield Minott's activities as a child lead him to become a model expert?
Expository Text
❸

418   419

Student Edition pp. 418–419

Guide Comprehension
Skills and Strategies

Teach the genre

Expository Text: Interview Explain that a person who is interviewed may answer questions with facts or opinions. As students read, ask: How can you tell when the person being interviewed is giving an opinion?

Corrective feedback

If... students cannot recognize an opinion,
then... model how to use clues to find opinions.

Model the skill

Think Aloud In the second question, Garfield explains why he was shy. I don't see any clue words that signal an opinion. But I can use clues to figure out that the information is Garfield's personal belief. I can prove that Garfield moved to Canada, but I can't prove that the move actually caused him to be shy. He may have been shy if he still lived in Jamaica.

On their own

Have students find a fact and another opinion on pp. 418–419.

Extend Thinking
Think Critically

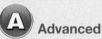 **Fact and Opinion • Evaluation** Do you think an interview will always have both facts and opinions? Why or why not? Possible response: Yes. When people are explaining their lives or their work, they will share their thoughts and beliefs in addition to giving facts.

Compare and Contrast • Synthesis Suppose you read an article about Garfield and his work. How might an article and an interview be the same? How might they be different? Possible response: Both would give facts and opinions. Both would probably have photos or illustrations. An interview gives information word for word, but an article is usually written in third person. An interview may also give more personal information.

Compare and Contrast • Analysis Synthesize and make logical connections between ideas from "A Model Scientist" and *The Dinosaurs of Waterhouse Hawkins.* Provide textual evidence in your answer. Possible response: Both are about real people with a passion for recreating dinosaurs in a way that is scientific as well as artistic. The genres are different because the account of Waterhouse is a biography and this is an interview. Also, Waterhouse lived long ago, but Garfield is alive today, which helps explain the differences in their methods.

2 The article begins by describing Garfield's job. Then there is a flashback that describes Garfield's childhood. It was helpful for me to know the information about Garfield's work before I read about his childhood because then I could understand how the ideas were connected.

3 Garfield's work with molds and kits and his fascination with dinosaurs inspired him to become a model expert.

Differentiated Instruction

SI Strategic Intervention

Fact and opinion Reread each sentence that answers the first question on p. 418. Ask students to decide if each statement is a fact or an opinion. Have them explain their answers.

A Advanced

Have students use the Internet to find out more information about Garfield Minott and his work. Have small groups share their information.

English Language Learners
Vocabulary: Idioms Direct students to look at the phrase *I went totally bananas* on p. 418. Explain that the phrase is an idiom that means "got really excited." Ask students what gets them excited.

Objectives
- Use graphic sources in an interview to aid comprehension.
- Synthesize ideas across multiple texts of different genres.

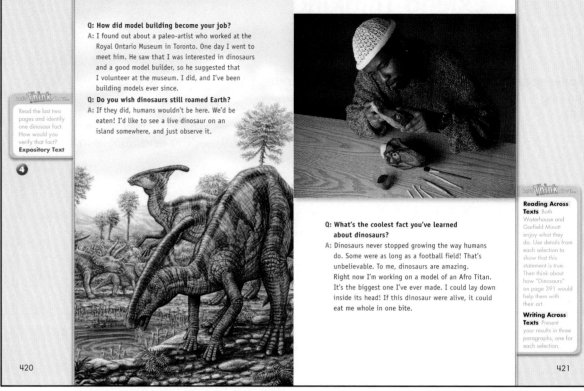

Think about...

Read the last two pages and identify one dinosaur fact. How would you verify that fact?
Expository Text

Q: **How did model building become your job?**
A: I found out about a paleo-artist who worked at the Royal Ontario Museum in Toronto. One day I went to meet him. He saw that I was interested in dinosaurs and a good model builder, so he suggested that I volunteer at the museum. I did, and I've been building models ever since.

Q: **Do you wish dinosaurs still roamed Earth?**
A: If they did, humans wouldn't be here. We'd be eaten! I'd like to see a live dinosaur on an island somewhere, and just observe it.

Q: **What's the coolest fact you've learned about dinosaurs?**
A: Dinosaurs never stopped growing the way humans do. Some were as long as a football field! That's unbelievable. To me, dinosaurs are amazing. Right now I'm working on a model of an Afro Titan. It's the biggest one I've ever made. I could lay down inside its head! If this dinosaur were alive, it could eat me whole in one bite.

Think about...

Reading Across Texts Both Waterhouse and Garfield Minott enjoy what they do. Use details from each selection to show that this statement is true. Then think about how "Dinosaurs" on page 391 would help them with their art.

Writing Across Texts Present your results in three paragraphs, one for each selection.

420

421

Student Edition pp. 420–421

Guide Comprehension
Skills and Strategies

Teach the genre

Expository Text: Interview Point out that an interview will often use photos, diagrams, and illustrations to show information. As students read the interview, ask: How do the graphics help you to gain an overview of the contents of the interview? How do the illustrations and photos help you understand Garfield's work?

Corrective feedback

If... students are unable to use graphic sources,
then... guide them to see how graphic sources aid understanding.

Model the skill

Think Aloud — As I look at the photo on page 421, I get a clearer understanding of what Garfield's models actually look like. I can also see some of the tools that he uses.

On their own

Have partners talk about what they learned from the graphic sources in the interview and how they helped them gain an overview of the text and locate specific information.

Extend Thinking
Think Critically

Higher-order thinking skills

Graphic Sources • Synthesis What other graphic sources might help you understand this article? Possible response: photos of the dinosaur bones, or an example of Garfield's rough drawings

Summarize • Synthesis Summarize Garfield's opinion of dinosaurs in a way that maintains his meaning? Possible response: He thinks they are exciting and fascinating animals, but also dangerous.

Genre • Synthesis How does the genre change the way information is presented in "Dinosaurs" on page 391, "A Model Scientist," and *The Dinosaurs of Waterhouse Hawkins?* Possible response: In "Dinosaurs," the information is factual and straightforward. "A Model Scientist" is less formal but more structured because it is an interview and follows the question-and-answer format. The biography is more like a story and uses narration to give information.

 Dinosaurs never stopped growing the way humans do. I could check that fact in a reference book.

Reading Across Texts

Have students use a three-column chart to organize their comparisons and make connections between the selections. Encourage students to reread each selection quickly and look for words such as *enjoy, like,* or *love.*

Writing Across Texts

Have students use their charts as they develop their paragraphs. Circulate among students and offer suggestions when necessary.

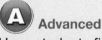

Objectives

- Read with fluency and comprehension.
- Use context clues to clarify meaning of idioms.
- Make an introduction.

Check Fluency: WCPM
SUCCESS PREDICTOR

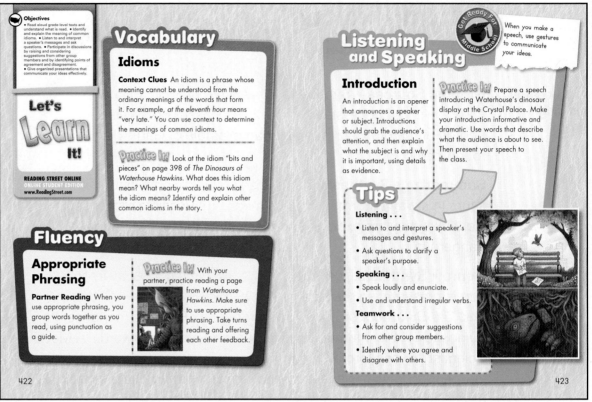

Student Edition pp. 422–423

Fluency
Appropriate Phrasing

Guide practice

Use the Student Edition activity as an assessment tool. Make sure the reading passage is at least 200 words in length. As students read aloud with partners, walk around to make sure their phrasing is appropriate and guided by punctuation marks.

Don't Wait Until Friday

MONITOR PROGRESS Check Fluency: WCPM

As students reread, monitor their progress toward their individual fluency goals.
Current Goal: 115–122 words correct per minute
End-of-Year Goal: 140 words correct per minute

If... students cannot read fluently at a rate of 115–122 words correct per minute,

then... have students practice with text at their independent levels.

Day 1	Days 2–3	Days 4	Day 5
Check Oral Vocabulary	Check Summarizing	Check Fluency	Check Oral Vocabulary

Success Predictor

Vocabulary
Idioms

Teach context clues

Context Clues Write this sentence on the board: *Waterhouse basked in the glow of the Queen's approval.* Point out that this sentence contains an idiom. Context clues can help determine the idiom's meaning.

Guide practice

Have students use context clues to determine and explain the meaning of the unfamiliar idiom.

On their own

Walk around the room as students work with partners to make sure they are finding helpful context clues to clarify the meaning of the words in the idiom. If necessary, have students use a dictionary to check the word's meaning. Then have students identify other common idioms in their reading selections.

Listening and Speaking
Introduction

Teach

Explain that a speaker may use facts and opinions as he or she organizes the material for the introduction of a special person. Remind students to think about why Waterhouse's exhibit was important, and why it would be interesting to others. Point out that the tone of an introduction and gestures of the speaker can "set the stage" for an audience's reaction. Encourage students to use exciting, powerful language.

Guide practice

Make sure that students include relevant information in their introductions. Remind students that good speakers maintain eye contact with listeners, speak at an appropriate rate and volume with clear enunciation, make natural gestures with their hands and body, and use proper conventions of language while speaking. Also remind the students to listen attentively to the speaker and to take notes to help them accurately interpret the speaker's verbal and nonverbal message.

On their own

Have students present their organized introductions to the class.

Introduction

Remind students to speak in complete sentences. Students should also choose vocabulary based on their audience and the topic. Explain that the speaker can also vary volume to make a point or add interest.

English Language Learners
Idioms Encourage students to use a dictionary or glossary to determine the meaning of words in idioms. Explain that, when used in an idiom, the meaning of words sometimes changes.

Success Predictor

DAY 4 Language Arts
30–35 mins.

Research and Inquiry
Synthesize

Teach

Have students use their chart from Day 3 to create a schedule for an imaginary seminar. Tell them that their final version should have seminar topics that will catch a person's attention. For example, instead of calling a seminar *New Carnivorous Dinosaurs Found*, they may want to use facts from their research, such as how one of the dinosaurs looks like a shark. *Discover the Shark Dinosaur!* may be a more interesting name for the seminar. Additionally, the descriptions should be clear and to the point. Make sure students use complete sentences.

Guide practice

Have students use a word processing program and a poster board to prepare for their presentation on Day 5. They will need to make up a time and a location for each seminar. Make sure that the schedules show the necessary information about times, topics, descriptions, and locations in a clear, easy-to-understand chart. Each column should be labeled clearly. Remind students that their audience needs to be able to interpret the information in the chart without their help.

On their own

Have students work in groups to prepare their presentations. Their partners should give constructive advice and ideas on how to make the schedule clearer.

Go Digital! **Grammar Jammer**

Conventions
Principal Parts of Irregular Verbs

7. Scientists have wrote many books on dinosaurs! *(written; dinosaurs.)*

8. They have telled how new discoverys were made. *(told; discoveries)*

Test practice

Remind students that grammar skills such as principal parts of irregular verbs are often assessed on important tests.

- Verbs have four principal parts: present, past, present participle, and past participle.
- Irregular verbs may have different forms for the past tense and the past participle.

Daily Fix-It

Use Daily Fix-It numbers 7 and 8 in the right margin.

On their own

For additional practice, use the *Reader's and Writer's Notebook* p. 210.

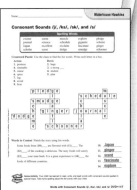

Reader's and Writer's Notebook p. 210

Spelling
Words with Consonant Sounds /j/, /ks/, /sk/, /s/

Practice spelling strategy

On index cards or slips of paper, have students write each of the spelling words, replacing the letter or group of letters that spell the /j/, /ks/, /sk/, and /s/ sound with a single blank. Have them place all the cards or slips of paper in a bag. The first partner then chooses one from the bag and spells the word. If the spelling is correct, he or she keeps the paper. If not, it goes back into the bag. Play alternates until all the words have been spelled correctly.

On their own

For more practice, use *Let's Practice It!* p. 147 on the *Teacher Resources DVD-ROM*.

Let's Practice It!
TR DVD • 147

Objectives
- Revise a draft of an advertising brochure.
- Apply the revising strategy of subtracting.
- Support a persuasive purpose with relevant details.

Writing—Advertising Brochure
Revising Strategy

MINI-LESSON

Revising Strategy: Subtracting

■ Yesterday we wrote an advertising brochure about an important event. Today we will revise our drafts to make our writing clearer, more interesting, and more informative.

■ Display Writing Transparency 13B. Remind students that revising does not include corrections of grammar and mechanics. Tell them that this will be done later when they proofread their work. Then introduce the revising strategy of subtracting.

■ Remember, your purpose is to persuade readers to attend the event. Ask yourself: *Are there any sentences that are not relevant to my topic?* For instance, when Waterhouse Hawkins learned to draw and paint isn't relevant for my purpose, so I subtract it from my draft.

Writing Transparency 13B, TR DVD

Tell students that as they revise, they should not only look for places where sentences could be removed to make the brochure more focused but also consider how strongly the reasons support the main purpose.

Revising Tips

✔ Make sure that the details support the main idea with sound reasoning.

✔ Review writing to make sure that it is well-organized and uses precise words.

✔ Take out any sentences that are not directly related to the purpose of the brochure.

Peer conferencing

Peer Revision Have pairs of students exchange brochures for peer reviewing. Ask students to indicate any sentences that do not fit the focus of the brochure. Remind them that they are looking for places where the author of the brochure could improve it by subtracting unnecessary details. Refer to the *First Stop* book for more information about peer conferencing.

Have students revise their brochure using the suggestions made by their partner as well as thinking about the key features of advertising brochures. Be sure that students are using the revising strategy subtracting.

Corrective feedback

Circulate around the room to monitor students and have conferences with them as they revise. Remind students that they will have time to edit tomorrow. They should be working on content and organization today.

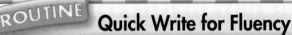

ROUTINE   Quick Write for Fluency   Team Talk

1. **Talk** Pairs discuss what they read about Waterhouse Hawkins in *The Dinosaurs of Waterhouse Hawkins.*

2. **Write** Each person writes a brief paragraph about Waterhouse Hawkins.

3. **Share** Partners check each other's paragraphs to make sure that all details are relevant.

Routines Flip Chart

Wrap Up Your Day

✔ **Build Concepts** What did you learn about how modern paleo-artists make models?

✔ **Oral Vocabulary** Monitor students' use of oral vocabulary as they respond to this question: How does a paleo-artist use fossils to make replicas of dinosaurs?

✔ **Text Features** Discuss how the question-and-answer text features helped students understand the interview with Garfield Minott.

Write Guy
Jeff Anderson

Conferencing Is Listening

Conferring about student's writing is more about teachers *listening* than teachers speaking. What is the student trying to say? We can ask questions: "What do you want your reader to know? Wow, how did you think of this vivid phrase?"

English Language Learners
Professional Development: What experts say about process writing
"Several researchers have suggested that process writing within school settings can help bridge the gap between home and school for elementary students from linguistically diverse backgrounds. Allowing students to choose their own topics, modeling writing skills, providing feedback on students' drafts, and encouraging students to share their writing with others can be a powerful means for English language learners to develop their writing abilities." –Georgia Earnest García and Sarah J. McCarthey

Preview DAY 5

Remind students to think about what people gain from the work of paleo-artists.

Objectives
- Review the weekly concept.
- Review oral vocabulary.

Today at a Glance

Oral Vocabulary

Comprehension
◉ Fact and opinion

Lesson Vocabulary
◉ Homonyms

Word Analysis
Suffixes *-tion, -sion*

Literary Terms
Flashback

Assessment
Fluency

Comprehension

Research and Inquiry
Communicate

Spelling
Words with consonant sounds /j/, /ks/, /sk/, /s/

Conventions
Principal parts of irregular verbs

Writing
Advertising brochure

Check Oral Vocabulary
SUCCESS PREDICTOR

Concept Wrap Up

 Question of the Week

How can paleontologists help us understand the past?

Review the concept

Have students look back at the reading selections to find examples that best demonstrate how paleontologists help us understand the past.

Review Amazing Words

Display and review this week's concept map. Remind students that this week they have learned ten Amazing Words related to learning about the past. Have students break into groups and use the Amazing Words and the concept map to answer the question *How can paleontologists help us understand the past?* Encourage students to elicit suggestions from one another.

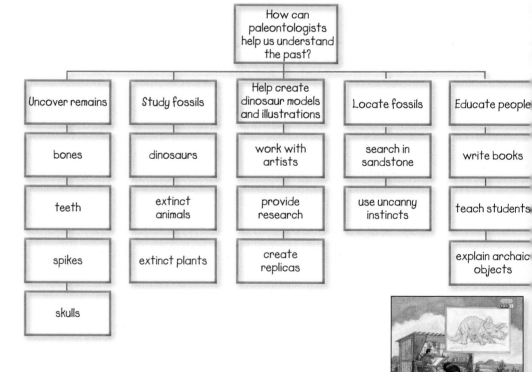

ELL Check Concepts and Language Use the Day 5 instructions on ELL Poster 13 to monitor students' understanding of the lesson concept.

ELL Poster 13

Amazing Ideas

Connect to the Big Question

Have pairs of students discuss how the Question of the Week connects to the Big Question: *What do people gain from the work of inventors and artists?* Tell students to use the concept map and what they have learned from this week's Anchored Talks and reading selections to form an Amazing Idea — a realization or "big idea" about inventors and artists. Then ask each pair to share their Amazing Idea with the class.

Amazing Ideas might include these key concepts:

- Inventors and artists use creative ideas to help us learn new things.

- The models and illustrations of some artists and paleo-artists help us learn about the past.

- Examining the remains of extinct animals reveals information about what life was like millions of years ago.

Write about it

Have students write a few sentences about their Amazing Idea beginning with "This week I learned …" Encourage students to provide evidence from the reading selections to support their ideas.

Amazing Words

fossils	model
paleontologists	extinct
uncanny	illustration
sandstone	replica
remains	archaic

It's Friday

MONITOR PROGRESS | **Check Oral Vocabulary**

Have individuals use this week's Amazing Words to describe what people gain from the work of artists and inventors. Monitor students' ability to use the Amazing Words and note which words you need to reteach.

If… students have difficulty using the Amazing Words,

then… reteach using the Oral Vocabulary Routine, pp. 389a, 392b, 402b, 416b, OV•3.

Day 1	**Days 2–3**	**Day 4**	**Day 5**
Check Oral Vocabulary	Check Retelling	Check Fluency	Check Oral Vocabulary

Success Predictor

English Language Learners
Concept map Work with students to add new words to the concept map.

Oral Vocabulary
Success Predictor

Objectives
◎ Review fact and opinion.
◎ Review homonyms.
• Review suffixes *-tion* and *-sion*.
• Review flashbacks.

Comprehension Review
↻ Fact and Opinion

Student Edition p. EI•7

Teach fact and opinion

Envision It!

Review the definitions of statements of fact and statements of opinion on p. 390. Remind students that statements of fact can be proven true or false by checking with an expert or a reference source. Statements of opinion tell about personal ideas or feelings, and cannot be proved true or false. For additional support, have students review p. EI•7 on fact and opinion.

Guide practice

Have partners find a statement of fact and a statement of opinion in *The Dinosaurs of Waterhouse Hawkins.* Ask them to decide if statements of opinion are well supported or poorly supported. Then have them tell how they could find out if the statement of fact is correct.

On their own

For additional practice with fact and opinion, use *Let's Practice It!* p. 148 on the *Teacher Resources DVD-ROM.*

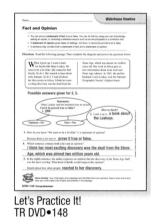

Let's Practice It!
TR DVD•148

Vocabulary Review
↻ Homonyms

Teach homonyms

Remind students to use context clues to help them understand the meaning of homonyms.

Guide practice

Review with students how to determine the meaning of the word *bow* in this sentence: *We learned how to bow in front of the Queen.*

On their own

Have partners each write three sentences that use the homonym *bow*. Encourage them to use a print or electronic dictionary if necessary. Then partners exchange sentences and determine the meaning of the word *bow* in each sentence.

Word Analysis Review
Suffixes *-tion, -sion*

Teach suffixes
Remind students of the definitions of the following: morpheme, base word, and suffix. Discuss how the verb *create* changes when the suffix *-tion* is added.

Guide practice
Display the following words: *reduction, estimation, expression* and *description.* Use the Strategy for Meaningful Word Parts to teach the word *reduction.*

ROUTINE Strategy for Meaningful Word Parts

1 **Introduce word parts** Circle the suffix *-tion* and write the base word. Explain that the final *e* is dropped when the suffix is added.

2 **Connect to meaning** Define the base word. The word *reduce* means "to become smaller." The suffix *-tion* forms nouns of action and condition.

3 **Read the word** Blend the meaningful word parts together to read *reduction. Reduction* means "the process of becoming smaller."

Routines Flip Chart

On their own
Have students use the strategy to determine the meanings of *estimation, expression,* and *description,* using knowledge of these Latin suffixes.

Literary Terms Review
Flashback

Teach flashback
Remind students that a flashback is when an event is recounted out of chronological order to show how it impacts a current situation.

Guide practice
Have students point out the flashback that describes Waterhouse's childhood. Discuss the author's purpose in using the flashback.

On their own
Have students write a short story about a real person's life. Have them include a flashback that connects to a later event in his or her life.

English Language Learners
Fact and opinion If students have difficulty distinguishing between fact and opinion, reread each statement. Ask students which part of the sentence can be proven to be true and circle that part of the sentence. If a sentence gives a judgment or belief, underline those words.

Suffixes Provide a list of other words with suffixes *-tion* and *-sion,* such as *election, distribution, confusion,* and *foundation.* Have students write the base words and guide them to use each word in a sentence.

Objectives
• Read grade-level text with fluency.

Assessment

Check words correct per minute

Fluency Make two copies of the fluency passage on p. 423k. As the student reads the text aloud, mark mistakes on your copy. Also mark where the student is at the end of one minute. To check the student's comprehension of the passage, have him or her retell what was read. To figure words correct per minute (wcpm), subtract the number of mistakes from the total number of words read in one minute.

Corrective feedback

If... students cannot read fluently at a rate of 115–122 WCPM,
then... make sure they practice with text at their independent reading level. Provide additional fluency practice by pairing nonfluent readers with fluent readers.

If... students already read at 140 WCPM,
then... have them read a book of their choice independently.

Plan to Assess Fluency

☑ **Week 1** Assess Advanced students.

☑ **Week 2** Assess Strategic Intervention students.

☑ **This week assess On-Level students.**

☐ **Week 4** Assess Strategic Intervention students.

☐ **Week 5** Assess any students you have not yet checked during this unit.

Set individual goals for students to enable them to reach the year-end goal.
• Current Goal: 115–122 WCPM
• Year-End Goal: 140 WCPM

Small Group Time

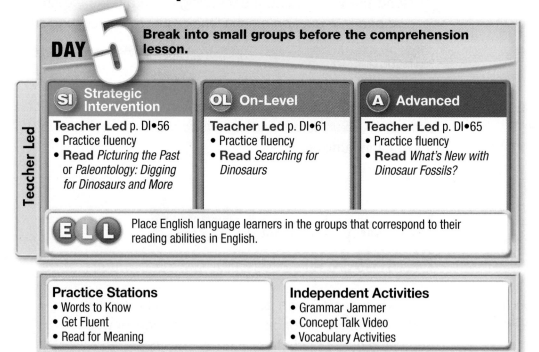

DAY 5 **Break into small groups before the comprehension lesson.**

Teacher Led

SI Strategic Intervention	**OL** On-Level	**A** Advanced
Teacher Led p. DI•56 • Practice fluency • **Read** *Picturing the Past* or *Paleontology: Digging for Dinosaurs and More*	**Teacher Led** p. DI•61 • Practice fluency • **Read** *Searching for Dinosaurs*	**Teacher Led** p. DI•65 • Practice fluency • **Read** *What's New with Dinosaur Fossils?*

ELL Place English language learners in the groups that correspond to their reading abilities in English.

Practice Stations
• Words to Know
• Get Fluent
• Read for Meaning

Independent Activities
• Grammar Jammer
• Concept Talk Video
• Vocabulary Activities

Changing the Way People Think

For more than a hundred years, people thought dinosaurs were just big and slow. Picture a T-rex with its head held high. Its tail drags on the ground. Its feet slam on the ground one after the other. Thump…Thump…Thump.

In the 1960s and 1970s, ideas began to change. It started in 1964 when a new kind of dinosaur was found. It was small, but in proportion with the others. And it had a huge claw on its foot. Not on its hand, but on its foot. How did it use a claw like that? It must have stood on one foot and kicked with the other. And to do that, it must have been fast.

A team of people discovered this dinosaur. One of the people was named John Ostrom. He was a teacher at Yale University. Another person was his student, Robert Bakker.

The two men had an idea. It seemed hard to believe. But it made sense. It fit the facts. What if all dinosaurs were fast?

Look at a bird when it walks. Its back is parallel to the ground. Maybe T-rex did not stand up straight. Maybe its tail did not drag on the ground. Maybe it ran with its back parallel to the ground. Then it could run fast.

Ostrom and Bakker were great scientists. The new picture of dinosaurs is much more accurate. It's also much more exciting.

MONITOR PROGRESS

• Fact and Opinion

Objectives
- Communicate inquiry results.
- Administer spelling test.
- Review principal parts of irregular verbs.

Research and Inquiry
Communicate

Present ideas Have students present their schedules for the imaginary seminar. They should present a few of the available seminar topics and indicate the relevant parts of the chart as they speak. At the end of the presentation, students should tell what primary and secondary sources they used.

Listening and speaking Remind students how to be good speakers and how to communicate effectively with their audience.

- Speak clearly and loudly, and vary speaking rate.
- Keep eye contact with the audience.
- As you present your chart, point to parts of it to help people interpret the information.
- Respond to questions with details from your research.

Remind students of these tips for being a good listener.

- Listen to and interpret all of a speaker's messages, both verbal and nonverbal.
- Ask questions if you don't understand a part of the chart or how the chart is designed. Make sure you can read the chart without help.
- Try to identify which parts of the chart are based on fact and which parts (time and location, for example) are imaginary.

Spelling Test
Words with Consonant Sounds /j/, /ks/, /sk/, /s/

Spelling test To administer the spelling test, refer to the directions, words, and sentences on p. 391c.

Conventions
Extra Practice

Teach Remind students that the four principal parts of a verb are the present, past, present participle, and past participle. Irregular verbs do not use *-ed* or *-d* to form the past tense or past participle. These verbs may use different forms for the past and past participle.

Guide practice Have students work with a partner to complete the sentence frames below, using the following verbs: *begin, buy, do, make, see.*

> **When did you _____ that? I _____ that yesterday.**
> **I am _____ that today.**

Daily Fix-It Use Daily Fix-It numbers 9 and 10 in the right margin.

On their own Write these sentences. Have students look back in *The Dinosaurs of Waterhouse Hawkins* to find the correct irregular verb to fill in the blanks. Remind students that irregular verbs do not use *-ed* or *-d* to form the past tense or past participle.

> **1. Waterhouse often _____ of his childhood.** (thought)
>
> **2. Waterhouse _____ open his workshop doors.** (threw)
>
> **3. How on earth had he _____ the models?** (made)
>
> **4. He had _____ foundations for his models.** (built)
>
> **5. The table was elegantly _____.** (set)

Students should complete *Let's Practice It!* p. 149 on the *Teacher Resources DVD-ROM.*

Daily Fix-It

9. Hawkins became famus for his dinosaur modles. *(famous; models)*

10. He brought dinosaurs to the public and people was fascinated. *(public,; were)*

Let's Practice It!
TR DVD•149

Objectives

- Proofread the revised draft of an advertising brochure, including principal parts of irregular verbs.
- Create and present a final draft.

Writing—Advertising Brochure
Principal Parts of Irregular Verbs

Review revising

Remind students that yesterday they revised their advertising brochures, paying particular attention to subtracting irrelevant details and using sound reasoning. Today they will proofread their advertising brochures.

MINI-LESSON

Proofread for Principal Parts of Irregular Verbs

■ **Teach** When we proofread, we look closely at our work, searching for errors in mechanics such as spelling, capitalization, punctuation, and grammar. Today we will focus on the principal parts of irregular verbs.

■ **Model** Let's look at a paragraph from the brochure we saw yesterday. Display Writing Transparency 13C. Explain that you will look for errors in the principal parts of irregular verbs. I see a problem in the second sentence. The brochure says, "Have you ever saw." But *saw* is the past tense of the irregular verb *see.* With the helping verb *have,* I need to use the past participle form of the verb. The past participle of *see* is *seen.* Explain to students that they should reread their composition several times, each time looking for a different type of error: spelling, punctuation, capitalization, and grammar.

Writing Transparency 13C, TR DVD

Proofread

Display the Proofreading Tips. Ask students to proofread their compositions, using the Proofreading Tips and paying particular attention to principal parts of irregular verbs. Circulate around the room answering students' questions. When students have edited their own work, have pairs proofread one another's work.

Proofreading Tips

✔ Be sure that all principal parts of irregular verbs are used correctly.

✔ Be sure every point on a bulleted list has a bullet.

✔ Check for correct spelling, punctuation, capitalization, and grammar. Use a grammar book for reference, if needed.

Present

Have students incorporate revisions and proofreading edits into their advertising brochure to create a final draft.

Give students two options for presenting their work: an oral presentation to the class or a written brochure. Have students find or create images to accompany what they have written. For oral presentations, students should use images large enough for the class to see. Tell them that they should try to convince the class to attend Hawkins's event. Students preparing a written brochure should consider the layout of the brochure as well as the content. Provide samples of folded brochures to show how students can layout their brochures.

ROUTINE   Quick Write for Fluency   Team Talk

1. **Talk** Pairs discuss what they learned about writing an advertising brochure.

2. **Write** Each person writes a few sentences summarizing what they learned.

3. **Share** Each partner reads the other's sentences.

Routines Flip Chart

E L L

English Language Learners
Poster Preview Prepare students for next week by using Week 4, ELL Poster 14. Read the Poster Talk-Through to introduce the concept and vocabulary. Ask students to identify and describe objects and actions in the art.

Selection Summary Send home the summary of *Mahalia Jackson,* in English and the students' home languages, if available. Students can read the summary with family members.

Preview NEXT WEEK

How does an artist use music to inspire others? Tell students that next week they will read about Mahalia Jackson.

Weekly Assessment

Use pp. 87–94 of *Weekly Tests* to check:

✔ **Word Analysis** Suffixes *-tion, -sion*

✔ ☉ **Comprehension Skill** Fact and Opinion

✔ **Review** **Comprehension Skill**
Main Idea and Details

✔ **Lesson Vocabulary**

erected	proportion
foundations	tidied
mold	workshop
occasion	

Weekly Tests

A

Advanced

OL

On-Level

SI

Strategic Intervention

Differentiated Assessment

Use pp. 73–78 of *Fresh Reads for Fluency and Comprehension* to check:

✔ ☉ **Comprehension Skill** Fact and Opinion

✔ **Review** **Comprehension Skill** Main Idea and Details

✔ **Fluency** Words Correct Per Minute

Fresh Reads for Fluency and Comprehension

Managing Assessment

Use *Assessment Handbook* for:

✔ **Weekly Assessment Blackline Masters for Monitoring Progress**

✔ **Observation Checklists**

✔ **Record-Keeping Forms**

✔ **Portfolio Assessment**

Assessment Handbook

Graveyards of the Dinosaurs
Continued from p. 389b

For a few seconds he was frozen. Then he let out a huge yell that bounced off the distant cliffs and brought his teammates running.

As the others crowded around the skeleton to examine it closely, Sereno walked away. He couldn't bear to look.

So much of what paleontologists do is pure grunt work. They spend their summers in dusty deserts, living on warm water, stale crackers, and tinned tuna, tripping over snakes and scorpions, going for weeks without a shower. Sereno was a talented but very young professor who was leading the first expedition of his life. People thought he was crazy, that his chances of finding such a rare fossil in the middle of desert were one in a million.

But, he had set out to do it anyway.

Sereno walked back to the group and took another look. It was indeed a Herrerasaurus—the most complete skeleton that had ever been found.

Small Group Time

5-Day Plan

DAY 1	• Reinforce the concept • Read Leveled Readers Concept Literacy Below Level
DAY 2	• ◉ Fact and Opinion • ◉ Predict and Set Purpose • Revisit Student Edition pp. 394–401
DAY 3	• ◉ Homonyms • Revisit Student Edition pp. 402–411
DAY 4	• Practice Retelling • Read/Revisit Student Edition pp. 416–421
DAY 5	• Reread for fluency • Reread Leveled Readers

3- or 4-Day Plan

DAY 1	• Reinforce the concept • Read Leveled Readers
DAY 2	• ◉ Fact and Opinion • ◉ Predict and Set Purpose • Revisit Student Edition pp. 394–401
DAY 3	• ◉ Homonyms • Revisit Student Edition pp. 402–411
DAY 4	• Practice Retelling • Read/Revisit Student Edition pp. 416–421 • Reread for fluency • Reread Leveled Readers

SI Strategic Intervention

DAY 1

Build Background

■ **Reinforce the Concept** Discuss the weekly question *How can paleontologists help us understand the past?* Ask students what movies they have seen that feature dinosaurs. What do they know about dinosaurs and the people who study them? This week's concept is *dinosaurs and paleontology.* Paleontologists are scientists who study plant and animal fossils for information about life in the past. Add new words to the concept map.

■ **Connect to Reading** Point out to students that paleontologists travel thousands of miles for their work. They may find fossils in remote desserts, valleys, and on mountains. The work is hard but exciting when they find a new type of dinosaur. This week you will read about paleontologists and how they learn about prehistoric life. In the Read Aloud "Graveyards of the Dinosaurs," why didn't Paul Sereno get excited when he first found the fossil in the Valley of the Moon in Argentina? *(He thought it was the fossil of a much more common lizard.)*

Objectives
• Interpret a speaker's messages (both verbal and nonverbal).

For a complete literacy instructional plan and additional practice with this week's target skills and strategies, see the **Leveled Reader Teaching Guide.**

Concept Literacy Reader

■ **Read** *Picturing the Past*

■ **Before Reading** Preview the selection with students, focusing on key concepts and vocabulary. Then have them set a purpose for reading.

■ **During Reading** Read the first two pages of the selection aloud while students track the print. Then have students finish reading the selection with a partner.

■ **After Reading** After students finish reading the selection, connect it to the weekly question *How can paleontologists help us understand the past?*

Below-Level Reader

■ **Read** *Paleontology: Digging for Dinosaurs and More*

■ **Before Reading** Have students preview the selection, using the illustrations. Then have students set a purpose for reading.

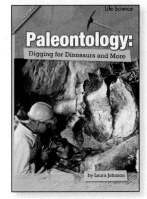

■ **During Reading** Do a choral reading of pp. 6–8. If students are able, have them read and discuss the remainder of the book with a partner. Have partners discuss the following questions:

• What do paleontologists learn from fossils? *(They learn the size of dinosaurs and how dinosaurs changed over time.)*

■ **After Reading** Have students look at and discuss the concept map. Connect the Below-Level Reader to the weekly question *How can paleontologists help us understand the past?*

MONITOR PROGRESS

If... students have difficulty reading the selection with a partner,

then... have them follow along as they listen to the Leveled Readers DVD-ROM.

If... students have are unsure of what paleontologists do,

then... reread pp. 6–7 and talk about what paleontologists specifically look for and do.

Objectives
• Interpret a speaker's messages (both verbal and nonverbal).

Small Group Time

Reinforce Comprehension

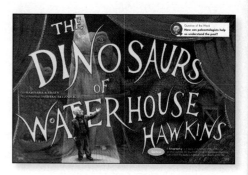

◉ Skill Fact and Opinion Review with students *Envision It!* p. El•7 on Fact and Opinion. Then use p. 390 to review the definitions of fact and opinion. Remind them that statements of fact can be proved true or false. Statements of opinion give feelings or judgments and cannot be proved true or false.

◉ Strategy Predict and Set Purpose Review the definitions of predict and set purpose. Remind students to use the selection title and illustrations to predict and set a purpose before reading. Why is it important to confirm predictions during and after reading? For additional support, refer students to *Envision It!* p. El•20.

Revisit *The Dinosaurs of Waterhouse Hawkins* on pp. 394–401. As students read, have them apply the comprehension skill and strategy to the story.

- Why is the statement "there were horse-drawn carriages in London in 1853" a fact? *(It can be proven true or false by checking historical records.)*

- Waterhouse used a skeleton of iron for his creatures. Is this a fact or an opinion? Why? *(It is a fact because it can be proved true or false from records or historical sources.)*

- The Queen believed that Waterhouse's dinosaurs were extraordinary. Why is this an opinion? *(The statement expresses a feeling and not something someone can prove true or false.)*

- Is the following sentence a fact or an opinion? Explain. *The New Year's Eve dinner party to show the iguanodon lasted eight hours. (Fact. It can be proved true or false by checking historical accounts.)*

Use the During Reading Differentiated Instruction for additional support for struggling readers.

MONITOR PROGRESS

If... students have difficulty reading along with the group,
then... have them follow along as they listen to the AudioText.

Objectives
- Establish purposes for reading selected texts based upon their own desired outcome to enhance comprehension.
- Verify facts through established methods.

Student Edition p. El•7

More Reading

Use additional Leveled Readers or other texts at students' instructional levels to reinforce this week's skills and strategies. For text suggestions, see the Leveled Reader Database or the Leveled Readers Skills Chart on pp. CL 24–CL 29.

Student Edition p. W•11

Reinforce Vocabulary

◉ **Homonyms/Context Clues** Say the word *bill* as you write it on the board.

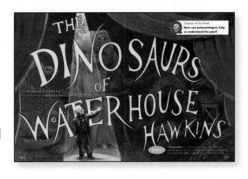

Homonyms are words with the same spelling but with different meanings and histories. For instance, the word *bill* is a homonym. When I see the word *bill*, I don't know if it means "a statement of money owed" or "the beak of a bird." However, I can use the words around *bill* as context clues to the right meaning. "The bird has a curved *bill*." The words *bird* and *curved* tell me that *bill* means the "beak of a bird."

Revisit *The Dinosaurs of Waterhouse Hawkins* on pp. 402–411. Review *Words!* on pp. W•7 and W•11.

- Point out the word *down* in the first sentence of the story. In this sentence, the carriages are moving *down*, or through, the streets, but *down* can also mean "the soft feathers of a bird."

- Look at the word *tipped* on this page. What does it mean in this context? *(Tipped means "took off their hats in greeting.")* What else can *tipped* mean? *(It can also mean "gave a small gift of money" or "knocked something over.")*

Encourage students to use context clues to figure out the meaning of any words that have more than one meaning.

Use the During Reading Differentiated Instruction for additional support for struggling readers.

More Reading

Use additional Leveled Readers or other texts at students' instructional levels to reinforce this week's skills and strategies. For text suggestions, see the Leveled Reader Database or the Leveled Readers Skills Chart on pp. CL 24–CL 29.

MONITOR PROGRESS

If... students need more practice with the lesson vocabulary, **then...** use *Envision It! Pictured Vocabulary Cards.*

Objectives
- Use the context to determine the meaning of multiple-meaning words.

Small Group Time

Practice Retelling

■ **Retell** Have students work in pairs and use the Retelling Cards to retell *Waterhouse Hawkins*. Monitor retelling and prompt students as needed. For example, ask:

• Who is the subject of this biography?

• Tell me what this person did in a few sentences.

If students struggle, model a fluent retelling.

Genre Focus

■ **Before Reading or Revisiting** "A Model Scientist" on pp. 416–421, read aloud the genre information about interviews on p. 416. A printed interview often includes the questions and the person's exact words as the answers.

Then have students preview "A Model Scientist." Ask:

• What pictures and text features do you see? *(drawings of dinosaurs; questions in bold type, answers below them)*

Then have students set a purpose for reading based on their preview.

■ **During Reading or Revisiting** Have students read along with you while tracking the print or do a choral reading of the interview. Stop to discuss any unfamiliar words, such as *prehistoric* and *paleo-artist*.

■ **After Reading or Revisiting** Have students share their reactions to the interview. Then guide them through the Reading Across Texts and Writing Across Texts activities.

• How is "A Model Scientist" similar to *The Dinosaurs of Waterhouse Hawkins*? *(Both are about scientists who build models of dinosaurs.)* How are the two works different? *(One is a biography. The other is an interview.)*

MONITOR PROGRESS

If... students have difficulty retelling the selection,
then... have them review the selection using the illustrations.

Objectives
• Synthesize ideas across two or three texts representing similar or different genres.

For a complete literacy instructional plan and additional practice with this week's target skills and strategies, see the **Leveled Reader Teaching Guide**.

Concept Literacy Reader

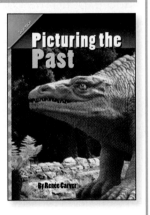

Picturing the Past
By Renee Carver

■ **Model** Model the fluency skill of appropriate phrasing for students. Ask students to listen carefully as you read aloud the first two pages of *Picturing the Past.* Have students note how you use punctuation marks to help you group words in phrases.

Fluency Routine

1. Have students reread passages from *Picturing the Past* with a partner.

2. For optimal fluency, students should reread three to four times.

3. As students read, monitor fluency and provide corrective feedback. Have students note that using punctuation to group words helps them express the meaning better than reading word by word.

See *Routines Flip Chart* for more help with fluency.

■ **Retell** Have students retell *Picturing the Past.* Prompt as necessary.

Below-Level Reader

Life Science
Paleontology:
Digging for Dinosaurs and More
by Laura Johnson

■ **Model** Ask students to listen carefully as you read aloud pp. 3–5 of *Paleontology: Digging for Dinosaurs and More,* emphasizing appropriate phrasing.

Fluency Routine

1. Have students reread passages from *Paleontology: Digging for Dinosaurs and More* with a partner or individually.

2. For optimal fluency, students should reread three to four times.

3. As students read, monitor fluency and provide corrective feedback. Encourage students to use punctuation marks to help them group words when reading.

See *Routines Flip Chart* for more help with fluency.

■ **Retell** For additional practice, have students retell *Paleontology: Digging for Dinosaurs and More* page-by-page, using the illustrations. Prompt as necessary.

• What happens in this part?

• How do the pictures help you understand the selection?

MONITOR PROGRESS

If... students have difficulty reading fluently,
then... provide additional fluency practice by pairing nonfluent readers with fluent ones.

Objectives
• Read aloud grade-level stories with fluency.

Small Group Time

Pacing Small Group Instruction

15–20 mins.

5-Day Plan

DAY 1	• Expand the concept • Read On-Level Reader
DAY 2	• Fact and Opinion • Predict and Set Purpose • Revisit Student Edition pp. 394–401
DAY 3	• Homonyms • Revisit Student Edition pp. 402–411
DAY 4	• Practice Retelling • Read/Revisit Student Edition pp. 416–421
DAY 5	• Reread for fluency • Reread On-Level Reader

3- or 4-Day Plan

DAY 1	• Expand the concept • On-Level Reader
DAY 2	• Fact and Opinion • Predict and Set Purpose • Revisit Student Edition pp. 394–401
DAY 3	• Homonyms • Revisit Student Edition pp. 402–411
DAY 4	• Practice Retelling • Read/Revisit Student Edition pp. 416–421 • Reread for fluency • Reread On-Level Reader

3-Day Plan: Eliminate the shaded box.

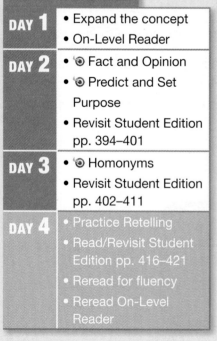

OL On-Level — DAY 1

Build Background

Expand the Concept Connect the weekly question *How can paleontologists help us understand the past?* and expand the concept. When we learn about the work of paleontologists, we appreciate their contributions to our understanding of the past. Have students add new words to the concept map.

On-Level Reader

For a complete literacy instructional plan and additional practice with this week's target skills and strategies, see the **Leveled Reader Teaching Guide.**

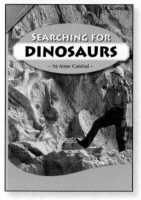

■ **Before Reading** *Searching for Dinosaurs,* have students preview the On-Level Reader by looking at the title, cover, and pictures in the book. Ask:

• What is the topic of this book? *(how scientists search for dinosaur fossils and uncover them)*

• What does the map on p. 9 show? *(areas where paleontologists have found dinosaur fossils)*

Have students create a graphic organizer like the one on p. 390 and use it to find and verify facts in *Searching for Dinosaurs.*

This book gives information about paleontologists and how they build robotic models of dinosaurs. As you read, look for facts and opinions, and record them on your graphic organizer. Think about the facts paleontologists have learned about the past.

■ **During Reading** Read aloud the first three pages of the book as students follow along. Then have them finish reading the book on their own. Remind students to add facts and opinions to their graphic organizers as they read.

■ **After Reading** Have partners compare their fact and opinion graphic organizers.

• What are three facts you learned? How do you know they are facts?

• How do the facts and opinions you recorded relate to the weekly question *How can paleontologists help us understand the past?*

Objectives
• Interpret a speaker's messages (both verbal and nonverbal).

OL On-Level   DAY **2**

Expand Comprehension

Skill Fact and Opinion Use p. 390 to review the definitions of fact and opinion. For additional review, see p. EI•7 in *Envision It!*

In the Read Aloud "Graveyards of the Dinosaurs," Paul Sereno discovered a *Herrarasaurus* skull. This is a fact because you can prove it by doing research.

Strategy Predict and Set Purpose Review the definitions of predict and set purpose.

Encourage students to continue to predict and adjust their predictions as they read. For additional support, use the Extend Thinking questions or refer students to *Envision It!* p. EI•20.

Revisit *The Dinosaurs of Waterhouse Hawkins* on pp. 394–401. Then have students apply the comprehension skill and strategy as they begin reading the selection aloud.

• Waterhouse's models of animals seemed to come alive. Why is this statement an opinion? *(It is the author's belief and not a literal fact.)*

• Is it a fact or an opinion that the Crystal Palace was an art and science museum in Queen Victoria's time? Explain your answer. *(Fact; it can be proved through research.)*

Student Edition p. EI•7

More Reading

Use additional Leveled Readers or other texts at students' instructional levels to reinforce this week's skills and strategies. For text suggestions, see the Leveled Reader Database or the Leveled Readers Skills Chart on pp. CL 24–CL 29.

Objectives
• Establish purposes for reading selected texts based upon their own desired outcome to enhance comprehension.
• Verify facts through established methods.

Student Edition p. W•11

More Reading

Use additional Leveled Readers or other texts at students' instructional levels to reinforce this week's skills and strategies. For text suggestions, see the Leveled Reader Database or the Leveled Readers Skills Chart on pp. CL 24–CL 29.

OL On-Level · **DAY 3**

Expand Vocabulary

Homonyms/Context Clues Explain that homonyms are words that are spelled the same but have different meanings and histories. Write the word *date* and then ask:

- One meaning for this word is "a sweet fruit." What is another meaning? *("an appointment to meet someone")*

- In *The Dinosaurs of Waterhouse Hawkins,* children *ducked* the horse-drawn carriages. What is this meaning of *ducked?* *("dodged out of the way")*

- What is another meaning for *duck? ("a water bird")*

- How do you know which meaning of a homonym is correct in a sentence? *(Other words in the sentence or surrounding sentences will give you context clues to the right meaning.)*

Revisit *The Dinosaurs of Waterhouse Hawkins* on pp. 402–411. Then review *Words!* on p. W•11. Read the following sentence from the selection: "Then she and Prince Albert invited the spectators to enjoy the amazing sights."

- What are some of the meanings of the homonym *sight? ("the sense of seeing; an image of something")*

- What words give you clues to the right meaning of *sight* in this sentence? *(The words "invited the spectators" and "enjoy the amazing" are clues that people are looking at something; therefore, the meaning of sight is "an image or event.")*

As students finish reading *The Dinosaurs of Waterhouse Hawkins,* encourage them to apply the strategy as they read. Have students recall the selection. Ask: Why did Waterhouse's dinosaurs create such a dramatic effect? *(He "built" complete dinosaurs; previously, only parts of dinosaurs were displayed.)*

Objectives
- Use the context to determine the meaning of multiple-meaning words.

OL On-Level

DAY 4

Practice Retelling

■ **Retell** To assess students' comprehension, use the Retelling Cards. Monitor retelling and prompt students as needed.

Genre Focus

■ **Before Reading or Revisiting** "A Model Scientist" on pp. 416–421, read aloud the genre information about interviews on p. 416. Have students preview "A Model Scientist" and set a purpose for reading. Ask:

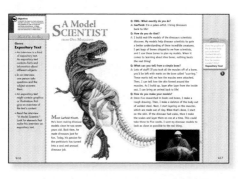

- What text features do you see that are different from those in short stories you read? *(a question-and-answer format, scientific illustrations)*

- What does a preview of the questions in bold print tell you about the selection? *(It is an interview.)*

■ **During Reading or Revisiting** Have students read along with you while tracking the print.

- What are some facts that you learn about Garfield Minott? *(He is a paleo-artist who builds models and got started at the Royal Ontario Museum.)*

- What kind of person do you think Garfield is? *(patient, enthusiastic, someone who likes to learn about dinosaurs)*

■ **After Reading or Revisiting** Have students share their reaction to the interview. Then have them work in pairs to write a one-page interview about what interests them about paleontologists. Students can take turns being the interviewer and the subject.

Objectives
- Synthesize ideas across two or three texts representing similar or different genres.

Small Group Time

On-Level Reader

■ **Model** Model the fluency skill of appropriate phrasing for students. Point out to students that punctuation cues can help them learn how to group words into appropriate phrases. Read aloud the first page the On-Level Reader *Searching for Dinosaurs,* emphasizing the way you group words according to punctuation.

SEARCHING FOR DINOSAURS
~ by Anne Cambal ~

Fluency Routine

1. Have students reread passages from *Searching for Dinosaurs* with a partner.

2. For optimal fluency, students should reread passages three to four times.

3. As students read, monitor fluency and provide corrective feedback. Have students note how to use commas, periods, and quotation marks to group words into phrases. Discuss how reading with appropriate phrasing communicates meaning better than reading word by word.

See the *Routines Flip Chart* for more help with fluency.

■ **Retell** For additional practice, have students use headings as a guide to summarize *Searching for Dinosaurs*. Prompt as necessary.

• What is the main idea of this section?

• What is the author trying to teach us?

Objectives
• Read aloud grade-level stories with fluency.

A Advanced

DAY 1

Build Background

■ **Extend the Concept** Discuss the weekly question *How can paleontologists help us understand the past?* Our knowledge of dinosaurs has changed over time as scientists continue to make new discoveries through their study of fossils. For example, think of how much we know about dinosaurs today compared with what people knew in Hawkins's time.

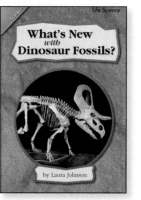

Advanced Reader

For a complete literacy instructional plan and additional practice with this week's target skills and strategies, see the **Leveled Reader Teaching Guide.**

■ **Before Reading** *What's New with Dinosaur Fossils?* tell students to recall the Read Aloud "Graveyards of the Dinosaurs." Why was Paul Sereno's discovery important to our understanding of dinosaurs? *(The skull was part of the most complete* Herrarasaurus *skeleton found up to that time.)* Today's book explores recent findings about dinosaurs.

Have students use the headings to help them predict what will be statements of fact and what will be statements of opinion. Then have students set a purpose for reading.

■ **During Reading** Have students read the Advanced Reader independently. Encourage them to think critically. For example, ask:

• Why were scientists surprised that dinosaur fossils were found in Alaska? *(They didn't know that the land had once been warm.)*

• How might birds and dinosaurs be related? *(They have some of the same bone structures, have three toes, and share the covering of feathers.)*

■ **After Reading** Have students review the concept map and explain how *What's New with Dinosaur Fossils?* helps them answer the weekly question *How can paleontologists help us understand the past?* Prompt as necessary.

• Why do scientists think dinosaurs became extinct?

• What did scientists in the past think was the reason?

■ **Now Try This** Assign "Now Try This" at the end of the Advanced Reader.

Pacing Small Group Instruction

15–20 mins.

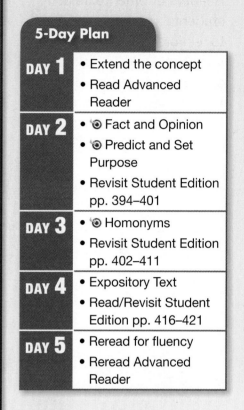

5-Day Plan

DAY 1	• Extend the concept • Read Advanced Reader
DAY 2	• Fact and Opinion • Predict and Set Purpose • Revisit Student Edition pp. 394–401
DAY 3	• Homonyms • Revisit Student Edition pp. 402–411
DAY 4	• Expository Text • Read/Revisit Student Edition pp. 416–421
DAY 5	• Reread for fluency • Reread Advanced Reader

3- or 4-Day Plan

DAY 1	• Extend the concept • Advanced Reader
DAY 2	• Fact and Opinion • Predict and Set Purpose • Revisit Student Edition pp. 394–401
DAY 3	• Homonyms • Revisit Student Edition pp. 402–411
DAY 4	• Expository Text • Read/Revisit Student Edition pp. 416–421 • Reread for fluency • Reread Advanced Reader

3-Day Plan: Eliminate the shaded box.

Small Group Time

More Reading

Use additional Leveled Readers or other texts at students' instructional levels to reinforce this week's skills and strategies. For text suggestions, see the Leveled Reader Database or the Leveled Readers Skills Chart on pp. CL 24–CL 29.

A Advanced

DAY 2

Extend Comprehension

 Skill Fact and Opinion To broaden students' understanding of fact and opinion, encourage them to look for opinions that are supported by facts.

 Strategy Predict and Set Purpose Review the definition of the strategy. Remind students to use illustrations and headings or titles to predict what the selection may be about and set a purpose for reading *The Dinosaurs of Waterhouse Hawkins.*

Revisit *The Dinosaurs of Waterhouse Hawkins* on pp. 394–401. Have students apply the comprehension skill and strategy as they read the selection.

- Which facts in *What's New with Dinosaur Fossils?* support the opinion that dinosaurs continue to fascinate people?
  Then encourage students to look for opinions supported by facts as they begin reading *The Dinosaurs of Waterhouse Hawkins.*

- Which facts support the opinion that Waterhouse loved making models of animals? *(He started making his own models as a child; he loved working with modeling materials.)*

Critical Thinking Encourage students to think critically as they read *The Dinosaurs of Waterhouse Hawkins.*

- What else do you think Hawkins could have done to show his guests the wonders of dinosaurs?

- What do you think Hawkins would say to people who didn't believe that dinosaurs were real?

Objectives
- Establish purposes for reading selected texts based upon their own desired outcome to enhance comprehension.
- Verify facts through established methods.

Advanced

DAY **3**

Extend Vocabulary

◉ **Homonyms/Context Clues** Choose and read a sentence containing a homonym, such as the following from p. 402 of *The Dinosaurs of Waterhouse Hawkins:* "With the help of his assistants, he had formed the life-size clay figures and created the *molds* from them."

- The word *mold* is a homonym. It means "a hollow shape" in this sentence. How do the context clues reveal the meaning? *(Waterhouse created a hollow shape around the clay.)*

- What is another meaning for *mold*? *(a fungus that grows in damp places)*

Revisit *The Dinosaurs of Waterhouse Hawkins* on pp. 402–411. Discuss how context clues can be helpful in reading homonyms. Remind students to use the strategy as they read *The Dinosaurs of Waterhouse Hawkins.*

Critical Thinking Have students recall what happened in the selection. Encourage them to think critically. For example, ask:

- Do you predict everyone will be as enthusiastic about the dinosaurs as Queen Victoria? Explain.

- Who might be critical of the dinosaurs?

More Reading

Use additional Leveled Readers or other texts at students' instructional levels to reinforce this week's skills and strategies. For text suggestions, see the Leveled Reader Database or the Leveled Readers Skills Chart on pp. CL 24–CL 29.

Objectives
- Use the context to determine the meaning of multiple-meaning words.

Small Group Time

Genre Focus

■ **Before Reading or Revisiting** "A Model Scientist" on pp. 416–421, read the sidebar information on interviews. Ask students to use the text features to set a purpose for reading.

■ **During Reading or Revisiting** Have students read independently. Ask students to share facts and opinions from "A Model Scientist." Draw a two-column Fact and Opinion chart on the board to record their answers.

There are both facts and opinions in the interview. Let's list some of them. *(Facts: A paleo-artist builds real-life models. Marks on bones are called "scarring." Opinions: As a child, Garfield was crazy about lizards.)*

■ **After Reading or Revisiting** Have students discuss Reading Across Texts. Then have them do Writing Across Texts independently.

Objectives
• Synthesize ideas across two or three texts representing similar or different genres.

■ **Reread for Fluency** Have students silently reread passages from the Advanced Reader *What's New with Dinosaur Fossils?* Then have them reread aloud with a partner or individually. As students read, monitor fluency and provide corrective feedback. If students read fluently on the first reading, they do not need to reread three to four times. Assess the fluency of students in this group using p. 423j.

■ **Retell** Have students summarize the main idea and key details from the Advanced Reader *What's New with Dinosaur Fossils?*

■ **Now Try This** Have students complete their projects. You may wish to review their work to see if they need additional ideas. Have them share their finished work with classmates.

Objectives
• Read aloud grade-level stories with fluency.

Support for English Language Learners

ELL — English Language Learners

The ELL lessons are organized by strands. Use them to scaffold the weekly curriculum of lessons or during small group time instruction.

Academic Language

Students will hear or read the following academic language in this week's core instruction. As students encounter the vocabulary, provide a simple definition or concrete example. Then ask students to suggest an example or synonym of the word and identify available cognates.

Skill Words	fact and opinion persuasive writing	irregular verbs word choice suffixes *(sufijos)*
Concept Words	dinosaur *(dinosaurio)* fossil *(fosil)*	paleontologist *(paleontólogo)*

*Spanish cognates in parentheses

Concept Development

How can paleontologists help us understand the past?

■ **Preteach Concept**

- **Prior Knowledge** Have students turn to pp. 388–389 in the Student Edition. Call attention to the pictures and tap into students' knowledge of dinosaurs. Can you name any dinosaurs here? What do you know about them? Have you ever seen their bones? Where can people go to see dinosaur skeletons today?

- **Discuss Concept** Elicit students' knowledge and experience of how paleontologists help us understand the past. Scientists who study fossils are called paleontologists. What are the paleontologists doing in the bottom photograph? How can the work of paleontologists help us understand things about the past? Use the visual support on the poster to enhance students' understanding of spoken language about dinosaurs and paleontologists.

- **Poster Talk-Through** Read aloud the Poster Talk-Through on ELL Poster 13 and work through the Day 1 activities.

■ **Daily Concept and Vocabulary Development** Use the daily activities on ELL Poster 13 to build concept and vocabulary knowledge.

Objectives
- Use prior knowledge and experiences to understand meanings in English.
- Learn new language structures, expressions, and basic and academic vocabulary heard during classroom instruction and interactions.

Content Objectives
- Use concept vocabulary related to paleontology.

Language Objectives
- Express ideas in response to art and discussion.
- Use visual support to understand language.

Daily Planner	
DAY 1	• **Frontload Concept** • **Preteach** Comprehension Skill, Vocabulary, Phonics/Spelling, Conventions • **Writing**
DAY 2	• **Review** Concept, Vocabulary, Comprehension Skill • **Frontload Main Selection** • **Practice** Phonics/Spelling, Conventions/Writing
DAY 3	• **Review** Concept, Comprehension Skill, Vocabulary, Conventions/Writing • **Reread Main Selection** • **Practice** Phonics/Spelling
DAY 4	• **Review Concept** • **Read ELL/ELD Readers** • **Practice** Phonics/Spelling, Conventions/Writing
DAY 5	• **Review** Concept, Vocabulary, Comprehension Skill, Phonics/Spelling, Conventions • **Reread ELL/ELD Readers** • **Writing**

*See the ELL Handbook for ELL Workshops with targeted instruction.

Concept Talk Video

Use this week's Concept Talk Video to help students build background knowledge about dinosaurs. Follow the Concept Talk Video Routine (*ELL Handbook*, p. 477).

The Dinosaurs of Waterhouse Hawkins **DI•66**

Support for English Language Learners

Language Objectives

• Understand and use basic vocabulary.

• Learn meanings of grade-level vocabulary.

Cognates

For Spanish learners, point out the similarity between the English *scientist* and the Spanish *científico.* Reinforce the concept that these languages share many words that are the same or similar.

ELL Workshops

Provide practice for students to better comprehend English vocabulary used in written classroom materials with *Learn New Words* (pp. 402–403, *ELL Handbook*).

Basic Vocabulary

■ **High-Frequency Words** Use the vocabulary routine above and the high-frequency word list on p. 451 of the *ELL Handbook* to systematically teach new-comers the first 300 sight words in English. Students who began learning ten words per week at the beginning of the year are now learning words 121–130.

Lesson Vocabulary

■ **Preteach** Introduce the Selection Vocabulary using this routine:

1. Distribute copies of this week's Word Cards (*ELL Handbook*, p. 101).

2. Display ELL Poster 13 and reread the Poster Talk-Through.

3. Using the poster illustrations, model how a word's meaning can be expressed with other similar words: The workshop was built on a concrete *foundation*, or a strong layer of support.

4. Use these sentences to reveal the meaning of the other words.

• The scientist *erected* a model dinosaur. (built)

• The scientist used a *mold* to shape the bones in the dinosaur model. (form)

• The day the museum opened was a happy *occasion*. (event)

• The *proportions* of the model dinosaur are correct. (size of each part)

• A paleontologist worked at her desk in the *workshop*. (lab)

• After work, the scientists *tidied* the workshop. (cleaned up)

Objectives

• Use prior knowledge and experiences to understand meanings in English.
• Use strategic learning techniques such as concept mapping, drawing, memorizing, comparing, contrasting, and reviewing to acquire basic and grade-level vocabulary.
• Develop basic sight vocabulary, derive meaning of environmental print, and comprehend English vocabulary and language structures used routinely in written classroom materials.

 English Language Learners

■ **Reteach** Ask questions to check and reinforce students' understanding of the vocabulary.routine to check and reinforce students' understanding of the vocabulary.

- If you *erect* a building, do you put it up or take it down? (put it up)

- Is a *foundation* under a building or on top of a building? (under a building)

- Is a birthday or a regular school day an *occasion*? (a birthday)

- What might a scientist do in a *workshop*? (study things, do experiments, work)

- After you *tidy* your room, how does it look? (neat or clean)

- Are the *proportions* of a dinosaur big or small? (big)

- Does a *mold* give color or shape to something? (shape)

■ **Writing** Place students into mixed proficiency groups. Have students use the strategies of drawing and writing to learn the grade-level lesson words. Put the Word Cards face down and have each group take a card. Assign groups to create a Three-Column Chart (*ELL Handbook*, p. 494) for the word they picked. Before students begin, model using the graphic organizer. Word: foundation; **Meaning:** the part of the building that holds it up; **Picture:** a building with an arrow pointing to the foundation; **Example:** The foundation is the bottom part of a building. Circulate to provide assistance as needed. Then have groups share their charts.

 Leveled Support

Beginning/Intermediate Have students draw pictures for their charts. Have them label the pictures.

Advanced/Advanced High Assign students to write a sentence using their word.

Language Objectives

- Use strategies such as drawings, phrases, and short sentences to acquire grade-level vocabulary.

- Understand the general meaning of spoken language.

Language Opportunity: Listening

Use the text with the vocabulary words on p. 393 as a Listening Exercise. Have students listen as you read aloud. Then have them restate the general meaning. Challenge them to use at least two of the lesson words as they tell the general meaning of the passage.

Objectives
- Use prior knowledge and experiences to understand meanings in English.
- Use strategic learning techniques such as concept mapping, drawing, memorizing, comparing, contrasting, and reviewing to acquire basic and grade-level vocabulary.

Support for English Language Learners

Content Objectives

• Monitor and adjust oral comprehension.

Language Objectives

• Discuss oral passages.

• Use a graphic organizer to take notes.

Graphic Organizer

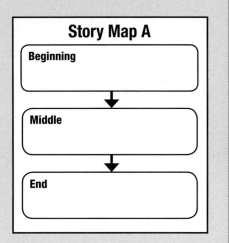

Story Map A

Beginning

↓

Middle

↓

End

ELL Teacher Tip

Ask questions to help students determine the important points of the beginning, middle, and end. For example: What did Paul Sereno want to do? Where did he go to do it? What did he find there?

ELL Workshop

Encourage students to demonstrate listening comprehension of the Read Aloud and other spoken messages. Provide *Retell or Summarize* (*ELL Handbook,* pp. 408–409) for practice.

Listening Comprehension

Finding Dinosaurs

Paul Sereno is a kind of teacher called a professor. He has found many dinosaur fossils. He found a very important dinosaur fossil. The fossil was a dinosaur called Herresaurus. Scientists called paleontologists found some bones that belonged to Herresaurus. No one had found a skull, or head bone, of this dinosaur. They needed to find more bones.

Sereno wanted to look for Herresaurus fossils. He and some other paleontologists went to a place in Argentina. People had found some Herresaurus fossils there. The group walked and walked and looked and looked.

One day, Sereno found some neck bones. Was there also a skull? Yes, there was! Sereno was so excited that he yelled. He had found a complete skeleton. He had found all the bones of Herresaurus.

Prepare for the Read Aloud The modified Read Aloud above prepares students for listening to the oral reading "Graveyards of the Dinosaurs" on p. 387b.

■ **First Listening: Listen to Understand** Write the title of the Read Aloud on the board. This is about a scientist who finds something important. What kind of fossils did he find? Afterwards, ask the question again and have students share their answers.

■ **Second Listening: Listen to Check Understanding** Using the Story Map A graphic organizer (*ELL Handbook,* p. 483), work with students to determine what happened at the beginning, middle, and end of the story. Have them record their ideas in the Story Map. Now listen again to check your ideas. Afterwards, reread the Story Map and make any changes if necessary.

Objectives

• Demonstrate comprehension of increasingly complex English by participating in shared reading, retelling or summarizing material, responding to questions, and taking notes commensurate with content area and grade level needs.

• Demonstrate listening comprehension of increasingly complex spoken English by following directions, retelling or summarizing spoken messages, responding to questions and requests, collaborating with peers, and taking notes commensurate with content and grade-level needs.

ELL *English Language Learners*

Phonics and Spelling

■ **Consonant Sounds /j/ and /s/** Distribute *ELL Handbook* p. 275.

• **Preteach** Have students point to the bridge at the top of the page. This is a bridge. Say it with me: bridge. The ending sound is /j/. Say it with me: /j/. Have students point to the jet in row 1. This is a jet. Say it with me: jet. Do you hear the /j/ sound? Repeat for the pictures in row 1 and 2.

• **Teach Spellings** Write a 2-column chart on the board with the headings _ge and _dge. List the words *bridge, cage, ridge, rage* in the columns where they belong. Have students add the words with the /j/ sound to the chart.

• **Distinguish Sounds** I will say some words. Raise your hand if the words have the /j/ sound or the /s/ sound: *sell, sale; cage, rage.* Write the words on the board and as you say a sound, have students point to the letters in the word that make that sound. Then say a word with a sound for students to write. Have them check for correct spelling to represent each sound.

Word Analysis: Suffixes *-tion* and *-sion*

■ **Suffixes *-tion* and *-sion***

Teach and Model Write *perfection.* This word is a base word and a suffix. A suffix is at the end of a word. Circle *-tion.* This is the suffix. Write *perfect + tion. Perfect* is the base word. *-tion* is the suffix. Cross out the final letter of *perfect.* Sometimes we have to change the spelling when we add a suffix. Help students to understand the difference in the words with the suffix added: the words change to nouns. Say sentences that show how the words are used in context.

■ **Practice** Write these words: *education, creation, reaction, decision, revision.* Provide practice for students at their language proficiency levels.

Beginning/Intermediate Have students circle the suffixes.

Advanced/Advanced High Have pairs write the base word and suffix for each word. Have them cross out letters in the base word that need to be dropped when adding the suffix. Then students should spell the words, monitoring their work for correct spelling.

Objectives
• Distinguish sounds and intonation patterns of English with increasing ease.
• Recognize elements of the English sound system in newly acquired vocabulary such as long and short vowels, silent letters, and consonant clusters.
• Practice producing sounds of newly acquired vocabulary such as long and short vowels, silent letters, and consonant clusters to pronounce English words in a manner that is increasingly comprehensible.

Content Objectives
• Identify suffixes *-tion* and *-sion* in words.
• Identify consonant sounds /j/ and /s/.

Language Objectives
• Apply phonics and decoding skills to vocabulary.
• Discuss meanings of words with suffixes.
• Monitor written language production.
• Learn relationships between sounds and letters of English.
• Use contextual support to grasp language structures.

Transfer Skills
English learners may benefit from extra practice distinguishing between /j/ and /ch/ sounds. Have students pronounce the sounds while placing their hands on their throat. Have them feel how the /j/ is voiced from their throat and the /ch/ sound is unvoiced and originates in their mouth.

Support for English Language Learners

Content Objectives

- Distinguish between facts and opinions.

- Identify facts and opinions to aid comprehension.

Language Objectives

- Discuss evidence for facts and opinions.

- Retell facts and opinions from a reading.

- Expand inferential skills to differentiate fact from opinion.

- Discuss facts and opinions from personal experience.

Comprehension
Fact and Opinion

■ **Preteach** A statement of fact can be proven true or false. An opinion cannot be proven true or false. *The sky is blue* is a fact. *Sunny days are best* is an opinion. Have students turn to Envision It! on p. EI•7 in the Student Edition. Read aloud the dialogue together. Have students "prove" or show that one boy is taller than the other. Can they show that the other boy is funnier? Have them use their inferential skills as they examine the illustration.

■ **Reteach** Distribute copies of the Picture It! (*ELL Handbook*, p. 102). Have students look at the image. Tell them to listen for facts while you read the paragraph aloud for the first time. For the second reading, done chorally, have students listen for opinions. Have them use their inferential skills to determine whether a statement could be proven true or false, and thus would be a fact. (Fact: T. rex was 18 feet tall and weighed 6 tons. Its teeth were sharp and pointed. They could cut through bone and meat. Opinion: T. rex was the "king" of dinosaurs. No other dinosaur can compare. People will always think of T. rex as the biggest and scariest.)

Beginning/Intermediate Reread the paragraph as students read along. Guide them as they look for facts and opinions. Have them circle terms they think indicate opinion (such as *scary*). Clarify with them *why* these words might indicate opinion.

Advanced/Advanced High Have students reread the paragraph. Have them write three facts and three opinions.

MINI-LESSON

Social Language

Tell students that people often express facts and opinions in daily life. Make a list of animals that the students are familiar with, such as *cat, dog, bird,* and so on. Have students state facts about each animal. Provide these sentence frames: It is _____. It has _____. It can _____. Then guide students in stating their opinions about these animals. Provide this sentence frame: I think that _____.

Objectives

- Express opinions, ideas, and feelings ranging from communicating single words and short phrases to participating in extended discussions on a variety of social and grade-appropriate academic topics.
- Use prereading supports such as graphic organizers, illustrations, and pretaught topic-related vocabulary and other prereading activities to enhance comprehension of written text

 **ELL** *English Language Learners*

Reading Comprehension
The Dinosaurs of Waterhouse Hawkins

Student Edition pp. 394–395

■ **Frontloading** Have students look through *The Dinosaurs of Waterhouse Hawkins,* pp. 394–411 in the Student Edition. Distribute copies of the English summary of *The Dinosaurs of Waterhouse Hawkins* (*ELL Handbook,* p. 103). Have students read the summary aloud with you. Preview the selection by having students look at the pictures.

■ **Sheltered Reading** Ask questions to guide students' comprehension. Students may need extra support to understand the complex language of this text. Read aloud when necessary. On p. 398, for example, read aloud to be sure that students understand what Waterhouse Hawkins was building and why he wanted to build it. Have students retell the information to show their understanding.

• p. 398: What was Waterhouse Hawkins building? **(dinosaurs)**

• p. 400: Which important people visited Waterhouse Hawkins' workshop? **(Queen Victoria and Prince Albert)**

• p. 404: Why did Waterhouse Hawkins have a dinner party? **(to show his dinosaurs to scientists)**

• p. 407: What did the scientists think of the dinosaurs? **(They liked them.)**

■ **Fluency: Read with Appropriate Phrasing** Remind students that reading with appropriate phrasing means to pause at a comma and stop briefly at a period. Read the last paragraph on p. 400. Point out the commas and periods and pause and stop appropriately. Have pairs reread this paragraph to each other to practice appropriate phrasing. For more practice, use the Fluency: Paired Reading Routine (*ELL Handbook,* p. 474).

■ **After Reading** Help students summarize the text with the Retelling Cards. Extend the reading with p. 423 of the Student Edition. Read the directions to students before beginning the activity and have them restate to be sure they understand. Then have then prepare a short speech using the directions and tips listed on the page.

Objectives
• Learn new language structures, expressions, and basic and academic vocabulary heard during classroom instruction and interactions.
• Use prereading supports such as graphic organizers, illustrations, and pretaught topic-related vocabulary and other prereading activities to enhance comprehension of written text.
• Use visual and contextual support and support from peers and teachers to read grade-appropriate content area text, enhance and confirm understanding, and develop vocabulary, grasp of language structures, and background knowledge needed to comprehend increasingly challenging language.

Content Objectives
• Monitor and adjust comprehension.
• Make and adjust predictions.

Language Objectives
• Read grade-level text with appropriate phrasing.
• Summarize text using visual support.
• Understand the general meaning and important details of increasingly complex spoken language.
• Follow directions.

Audio Support
Students can prepare for reading *The Dinosaurs of Waterhouse Hawkins* by using the eSelection or the AudioText CD.

Language Opportunity: Listening
The scientific language may prove challenging for some students. Have them listen as you read aloud text, such as p. 402 of the Student Edition. After you read, have students rephrase with your assistance to show that they know the general meaning. After reading the selection, read aloud pp. 416–417 of the Student Edition. Have students listen for important details about Garfield Minott and his job. They can tell those details to partners.

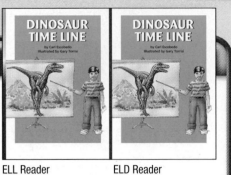

ELL Reader   ELD Reader

For additional leveled instruction, see the **ELL/ELD Reader Teaching Guide.**

Comprehension
Dinosaur Time Line

■ **Before Reading** Distribute copies of the ELL and ELD readers, *Dinosaur Time Line*, to students at their reading level. As students are able to read material with less linguistic accommodation, move them from the ELD to the ELL Reader.

• **Preview** Read the title aloud with students: This is a nonfiction poem about different kinds of dinosaurs. Invite students to look through the pictures and say what they see. Have them point out differences they see among the different dinosaurs.

• **Set a Purpose for Reading** Let's read to find out how these dinosaurs are different from each other.

■ **During Reading** Follow this Reading Routine for both reading groups.

1. Read the entire Reader aloud slowly.

2. Reread pp. 1–5, pausing to build background or model comprehension. Use the questions in the chart to check students' comprehension.

3. Reread pp. 1–5 chorally with students.

4. Repeat the steps for pp. 6–8.

■ **After Reading** Use the exercises on the inside back cover of each Reader and invite students to share their writing. In a whole-group discussion, ask students How are dinosaurs different from each other? Record their answers on the board and invite them to point to pictures in the book to support their answers.

ELD Reader   Beginning/Intermediate

• **p. 3** When was the Eoraptor alive? (230 million years ago) Point to the part of the text that gives you the answer. (header on p.3)

• **p. 4** Which dinosaur had spikes and plates? (Steogosaurus) Read aloud the sentence that tells you the answer. (Stegosaurus was its name. It had spikes and plates on its back.)

Writing Choose a dinosaur that you like. Find a sentence that tells a fact about that dinosaur. Copy the sentence. Then read it aloud to your partner.

ELL Reader   Advanced/Advanced High

• **p. 3** What two kinds of dinosaurs lived 230 million years ago? (eoraptor and saltopus) Point to the part of the text that gives you the answer. (header on p.3)

• **p. 7** What dinosaur had spikes? (stegosaurus) Read aloud the sentence that tells you the answer. (image and sentence 6)

Study Guide Distribute copies of the ELL Reader Study Guide (ELL Handbook, p. 106). Scaffold comprehension of fact and opinion by helping students write *fact* or *opinion* beside each statement. Review responses together. (See *ELL Handbook*, pp. 209–212.)

Objectives
• Use prereading supports such as graphic organizers, illustrations, and pretaught topic-related vocabulary and other prereading activities to enhance comprehension of written text.

English Language Learners

Conventions
Principal Parts of Irregular Verbs

■ **Preteach** Write on the board: *throw, catch, run, sit.* Read the words aloud with the students. Have two students come to the front of the room. Give them a small ball or other small item. Have one student throw the item and the other catch it. (Name of student 1) threw the ball. (Name of student 2) caught the ball. Write *threw* and *caught* next to their present forms on the board. When something already happened, we use the past form of the verb. Read past forms aloud with students.

■ **Practice** Write: *They throw the ball. They catch itl. They run. They sit down.* Have students speak using the grammatical structure of verbs. Verbs come after the subject. Verb tense matches the time of the action.

 Leveled LS Support

Beginning Read sentences with students. Then have them say the past form of each verb.

Intermediate Have students say the sentences in the past tense.

Advanced/Advanced High Have students use the past forms of the verbs as they say their own sentences.

■ **Reteach** Write a new present tense sentence for each of these verbs: *throw, catch, run, sit.* Guide students in changing sentences to past tense.

■ **Practice** Display a chart to show the past tense forms of more irregular verbs.

Present	Past
eat	ate
drink	drank
spend	spent
sleep	slept

 Leveled LS Support

Beginning For each verb, read the present form and have students read the past form.

Intermediate Have students say a sentence for each past tense verb.

Advanced/Advanced High Have students say write a sentence for each past tense verb.

Content Objectives
• Correctly form past tense form of irregular verbs.

Language Objectives
• Correctly pronounce irregular past tense verb forms.

• Say and write sentences with irregular past tense verbs.

• Speak using the grammatical structure of verbs.

Transfer Skills

Many English learners need extra practice with the variety of irregular verbs that also feature unfamiliar phonics elements such as *catch/caught, buy/bought,* and *can/could.* Have students prepare index cards with irregular verbs. On one side, write the present tense. On the other side, write the past tense.

Grammar Jammer

For more practice, use the Grammar Jammer: Verbs. Follow the Grammar Jammer Routine (*ELL Handbook,* p. 478).

Support for English Language Learners

Content Objectives

- Use sound reasoning when making word choices.

Language Objectives

- Write persuasive paragraphs.
- Share feedback for editing and revising.
- Expand on the learning strategy of reasoning.
- Express opinions.
- Speak using connecting words.

Mini-Lesson: Expressing Opinions

Have students discuss why people should see an exhibit of Hawkins's dinosaurs. Tell them that the idea that someone should see the dinosaurs is an opinion. Turn to p. 414 of the Student Edition and read the prompt. Tell students that advertisements express opinions. Have them express their opinions about the exhibit. Provide sentence frames: *You should see the exhibit because _____. This exhibit is the best because _____!*

ELL English Language Learners

Making Word Choices

■ **Introduce** Display the paragraph model and read it aloud. When I write, I want to choose the best words to explain my ideas. Underline the words *important* and *excited.* It was a big day for Waterhouse Hawkins when the queen visited his workshop. I used the words *important* and *excited* to help explain that.

> **Writing Model**
>
> Queen Victoria was a very important person. Waterhouse Hawkins was excited when she visited his workshop. He showed his dinosaur models to the queen.
>
> ■ **Practice** Write this incomplete paragraph on the board. Work together to choose the best words to complete the paragraph.

Queen Victoria liked Waterhouse Hawkins' dinosaurs. Waterhouse Hawkins felt very _____. He wanted to show his dinosaurs to other _____ people. He decided to give a dinner for scientists.

(proud, important) Point out that students may think of more than one word to explain how Hawkins felt. In that case, they would list the words with a connector. Have them speak to practice using connecting words with ease. *(Hawkins felt excited, happy, and proud.)*

■ **Write** Have students write a paragraph telling people why they should see an exhibit of dinosaurs by Waterhouse Hawkins. Tap into students' knowledge of reasoning. To get people to see an exhibit, they need to provide persuasive reasons and use words that will entice viewers. Have students reread their work to look for sound and convincing reasoning, adding details as necessary.

Beginning Have students circle the best word to complete each sentence and then say why that word provides the best reason to visit.

Visit the Dinosaur Museum. See the _____ (nice/amazing) dinosaurs. They are _____ (huge/big). They have razor- _____ (white/sharp) teeth.

Intermediate Provide students with the same incomplete sentences but no word choices. Have them work in pairs to choose a word to complete each sentence. Have them explain why they chose these words.

Advanced/Advanced High Have students develop their paragraphs independently. Then have pairs exchange papers and provide feedback for revising and editing. Encourage students to discuss why they chose certain words.

Objectives

- Write using newly acquired basic vocabulary and content-based grade-level vocabulary.
- Narrate, describe, and explain with increasing specificity and detail to fulfill content area writing needs as more English is acquired.

Story Exchange

Writing Project Create a shared fantasy story about an invention with the beginning, middle, and ending each written by different authors.

Purpose Enhance skills in the use of an Internet server for creating and sharing text and locating images; use applications for word processing.

Audience student, peers, younger students, teacher, family

Introduce genre and key features

In this workshop, we will cooperate to write fantasy stories about inventions gone wrong. Each member of a group will contribute a part of the story. We will use the Internet to help us share the stories as we write and then use a word processing application to revise and edit our stories.

Key Features of a Story Exchange

- use of a text-sharing application to write a story beginning and pass it to the next writer

- building of the story through successive writers, who add the middle and ending

- sharing of the revision and the completed story by all authors

Academic Vocabulary

Fantasy A fantasy is a story that could not really happen.

Teacher Tip

Explore Examples Do an online search for fantasy stories written by or for children to show as models in class. Use a projector or equivalent technology to display examples as you read them aloud. Review setting, characters, and plot with students.

English Language Learners
Build Vocabulary and Concepts Use examples of fantasies to familiarize students with key vocabulary and concepts. Read one story aloud, pointing out sentences that show setting, character, and the problem to be solved. Then have students identify these elements in a second story.

Objectives

- Understand and identify features of a story.
- Brainstorm and focus ideas for writing.

① Plan and Prewrite

MINI-LESSON

Read Like a Writer

■ **Examine Model Text** Display a brief story from the Internet on the projector. A short story is a brief narrative telling how one or more characters discover a problem and solve it. Read aloud the story and discuss how the characters solve the problem. You are going work in a group to write three parts of a fantasy story about an invention. In a fantasy, you use your imagination to create characters, a setting, or events that could not happen in real life. The story parts are a beginning that introduces the characters, setting, and an invention; a middle with problems caused by the invention; and an ending with a solution.

■ **Explore Model Text** Let's look at an example of a fantasy story about an invention gone haywire. This is the kind of story that you will write. Display and read aloud to students "Mighty Maid" on 21st Century Transparency TC6. Ask them to describe the characters, the setting, the invention, and the problem. Make sure that students understand a story builds excitement by making the problem more complicated until it is solved.

Mighty Maid

Dave looked around his room and sighed. Piles of toys, books, papers, and clothes covered the chair, floor, and bed. His mom had just told him, "Enough! Until this room is cleaned up, David Roger, you are grounded."

Dave had to admit things had gotten out of hand, but tidying up was not his thing. Dave had great ideas and loved to tinker. As he surveyed the mess, the wheels in his brain were turning. He got a fabulous idea.

"A robot maid!" he exclaimed. He rooted in a pile for a tablet of graph paper and drew a design. All day he tinkered in the basement. At last he finished. He placed his Mighty Maid in his room and punched the "sort" button. The machine should sort the piles and organize each type of thing on a different shelf. Or so Dave thought. The Mighty Maid lifted the first pile and flang it across the room.

"Whoa!" cried Dave. "I think Mighty Maid needs an adjustment." As he reached for a screw driver, Mighty Maid revved her engine and raced out the door. Dave ran after her with a sinking feeling.

She ripped into the living room and lifted Dave's old dog Snark, who was snoozing on the sofa. Just then, Dave's dad opened the front door.

"Uh oh," said Dave. He dived at the robot, but she raced out the door.

"Rogue robot!" yelled Dave. "She's got Snark!" He and his dad raced down the sidewalk after Mighty Maid and the bewildered, sleepy dog.

"What's the plan, Dave?" yelled Dad, who was gaining on the robot.

"Switch on the bottom," gasped Dave. "Click left."

Dad tackled the racing robot and hit the switch. Unluckily, Dave had confused right and left; Mighty Maid went into overdrive.

Dave raced after the robot on his bike. Dave caught up when Mighty Maid got hung up on a curb. He quickly wired the robot to the street lamp.

"Here goes nothing," he muttered, and slapped two large magnets on Mighty Maid's controls. She whirred, rattled, and stopped.

"Lucky I remembered computers and magnets don't mix," said Dave. "I guess I'll clean my room myself." Snark wagged his tail in agreement.

Unit 3 Story Exchange   21st Century Writing **TC6**

21st Century Transparency TC6, TR DVD

Brainstorm story ideas

We will write fantasy stories in which an inventor or inventors must solve the problems caused when an invention does something unexpected. Your stories will have characters, a setting, an invention that causes a problem, and a solution to the problem. Have students brainstorm ideas for an invention fantasy story they would like to write. Encourage ideas about gadgets that will do the seemingly impossible, such as complete homework, create muscles, or cause plants to grow overnight. Write students' ideas on the board. Then ask students to continue brainstorming on their own, listing additional story ideas.

Choose a story idea

Now that you have several ideas for a fantasy about an invention, you need to choose one story idea to develop. Encourage students to choose the story idea that is most intriguing to them and for which they have the most ideas for plot development.

Objectives
- Organize ideas to prepare for writing.
- Write a first draft of a story beginning.

① Plan and Prewrite
PREWRITE

MINI-LESSON

Create a Story Plan

■ Now that you have chosen your story idea, you need to create a story plan. A story plan sets up the where, when, who, and what of a story. Explain that authors begin a story by establishing the setting and describing the characters and their problem. Display 21st Century Transparency TC7 on the projector and read aloud each question. Discuss the setting, characters, and invention that apply to the model story.

Story Plan

Where and when does the story happen?	at Dave's house, in the suburbs, on a weekend
Who are the characters?	David Roger, a boy who has ideas and likes to tinker
	Dave's mom, who wants his room cleaned
	Dave's dad, who tries robot catching
	Snark, Dave's old dog
What is the invention?	Mighty Maid, a robot that cleans and organizes and seems to have a mind of its own
What goes wrong with the invention?	It doesn't work right. Instead of making things neat, it causes chaos. It "cleans up" the dog and then runs away.

Unit 3 Story Exchange   21st Century Writing **TC7**

21st Century Transparency
TC7, TR DVD

■ Have students use the table function of a word processing application to create their own chart with details of setting, character, and invention for their own story idea. As students work, circulate and answer students' questions about formatting their charts.

Corrective feedback **If...** students have trouble deciding on a story plan,
then... suggest that they skim a fantasy or science fiction story online, using the chart questions to analyze it, and then imagine themselves in a similar setting.

Draft

Organize ideas

Have students visualize the characters, setting, and action as their story opens. Then have them list details they want to include and number the listed details in a logical order. Remind students to refer to their story plan to be sure they include all the details of setting, character, and invention.

Getting started

Have students log onto the shared document site and create a file for their story. Have them consult their list and write a beginning sentence for their story. Then they can add sentences that describe the setting, characters, and the invention they create. Explain that their story beginning should build up to a problem caused by the invention.

Examine model text

Display 21st Transparency TC6 and review the first three paragraphs of "Mighty Maid." This student started with details that tell when and where the story takes place and introduces the characters Dave, his mom, and Mighty Maid. Then the story describes how the invention, a robot maid, behaves strangely. This introduces the problem.

21st Century Transparency TC6, TR DVD

Develop draft

Remind students that their story beginning will describe setting, tell what the characters are doing, and introduce the invention. Circulate as students input their story beginnings to answer any questions they have about word processing commands. The shared text site should have an interface similar to most common word processing applications.

Differentiated Instruction

 **Strategic Intervention**

Story Beginning Students who have trouble getting started with their story can discuss their characters and invention with their group, inventing personality traits and descriptive details. Encourage struggling students to make a sketch of the invention and visualize a possible opening scene.

Technology Tip

Establish Shared Files An Internet document sharing site will allow students to share and collaborate on stories, including writing and editing in real time. Multiple people can view and make changes at the same time. Enter search words *"shared docs"* to find such a site and register.

English Language Learners

Record Story Drafts You may choose to have students record their story beginning in their first language and then in English. Either assist students yourself or assign a fluent English-speaking student to assist them in writing their story beginning from the recording.

Objectives

- Write a first draft of a story middle and ending.
- Collaborate with others to improve a draft of a story.
- Write dialogue to improve a story.
- Revise a draft of a story.

 **Draft**

Drafting a story middle

Display the 21st Century Transparency TC6 with the last six lines of the story covered, so the students can't see it. Discuss with students the middle of "The Mighty Maid." Establish groups of three and give each group member a letter: A, B, C. Instruct students to access and read the story beginning of the next student: A reads B, B reads C, and C reads A. Each student is then to write the middle of that story. In a fantasy story, the problem to be solved becomes more exciting and complex. What happens might not be possible in real life, but there should be enough realistic detail for readers to feel involved. Encourage students to be imaginative and use their sense of fun as they develop their plots.

Drafting a story ending

When students have completed their story middles, uncover the final two paragraphs of 21st Century Transparency TC6 and discuss how the story ending resolves the problem. Then have students access the next student story (Story A passes to C, B to A, and C to B) and write a story ending. Remind students that their story endings should resolve the problem caused by the invention and make readers feel relieved.

③ Revise

MINI-LESSON

Using Dialogue

■ One way to improve a story is to make it more vivid by adding dialogue, or conversation between characters. Dialogue adds to the "real" feeling of a story and can make readers feel that they are present in the scene. The exact words of a character belong in quotation marks. Read these examples with students:

No dialogue	Dave explained the situation to his dad. Dad had no idea what to do if he caught up to the robot, so he asked Dave. Dave told him to turn off the switch on the bottom.
With dialogue	"Rogue robot!" yelled Dave. "She's got Snark!" "What's the plan, Dave?" yelled Dad, who was gaining on the robot. "Switch on the bottom," gasped Dave. "Click left."

■ Discuss with students how the dialogue makes the characters and action more immediate and lively.

Peer conferencing Have students work in their group to read each story aloud together. As they read, invite them to discuss ways to improve the story's beginning, middle, and ending. Then have each student work to revise the story he or she began.

Revise drafts Now we will revise our story drafts. When we revise, we incorporate suggestions from peer conferencing and try to make our stories more exciting and interesting. A good fantasy about an invention uses realistic dialogue and its action becomes more and more exciting and intense until the problem is solved.

Corrective feedback **If...** students have difficulty writing dialogue, **then...** suggest that the students in a group act out a scene, brainstorming what the characters would say. Have them pause to write down the conversation.

Academic Vocabulary

Dialogue Dialogue is the conversation of two or more people reproduced in writing.

Differentiated Instruction

SI Strategic Intervention

Focused Revision As they read the draft, help each student stay on task by asking the following questions:
• *Are the characters clear?*
• *What is happening here?*
• *Do the actions make sense within the story's context?*
• *Is the problem solved satisfactorily?*

Technology Tip

Text-Sharing in Real Time To have students in a group share their story documents, at the shared-text Internet page, enter the e-mail addresses of the group members and send them an invitation. Anyone invited can access the document together or separately and make changes or additions.

Technology Tip

The shared-text function of an Internet server may have toolbar buttons students can use to bold, underline, indent, and change font commands as they edit text.

Objectives
- Edit a revised draft of a story to correct errors in grammar, mechanics, and spelling.
- Use the Internet to search for clip art images to enhance a story.

4 Edit

MINI-LESSON

Using the Computer to Edit

■ Your computer's grammar and spelling checker will find some mistakes in your writing. The computer highlights words and usages that might be errors. It is up to you to think through what you have written and decide whether the computer is right. **Have students use the grammar and spelling checker at the text-sharing site (or on word processing application) they used to write their stories.**

■ Show the error not caught by the spelling checker in the following passage:

"Enough! Until this room is cleaned up, David Roger, your grounded."

The spelling checker does not recognize *your* as an error, although the writer should have used you're. *Change your to you're.*

■ Have students practice editing the following sentences, first applying the spelling and grammar checker and then by themselves.

The twins gazed at there invention with prid.

The frame had broke in to.

The meter world around and around when it's spring broke.

Edit Drafts Ask students to edit their story drafts. After they use the grammar and spelling checker, have them print out their story and read it sentence by sentence to check for errors in spelling, grammar, punctuation, and capitalization. Remind students that a character's spoken words are set off with quotation marks, and each new speaker's words begin a new paragraph.

(5) Publish and Present

MINI-LESSON

Incorporating Clip Art

- Display the home page of an Internet search engine on a projector. *We can use pictures to illustrate our stories. We can look for clip art images on the Internet. This search engine will help us find pictures that will make our stories more vivid and interesting.*

- *I want to find a picture of a messy room.* If it is available, choose the option for searching for images in the search engine. Type the key phrases *free clip art, messy room* into the search field. Display the results on the projector. Click on an option that is appropriate and go to the site that holds the image source.

- Have students search for appropriate images for their stories. Show students how to copy and save images onto their computer desktop. Suggest that they name each file to make it easy to identify and then store their story images in a folder so they will be easy to access when it is time to complete their story.

Corrective feedback

If... students have difficulty finding appropriate images or get too many hits,
then... have them use more specific key words for their search and enclose each phrase in quotation marks, for example change *"outer space"* to *"rocket ship in space."*

Differentiated Instruction

(A) Advanced

Concepts of Print Some students may enjoy organizing the stories into book format using a page design program. Have them consult the Help menu for instructions in creating a table of contents. Encourage them to name each section of the book creatively, for example "Out of This World Stories" for stories of inventions in space.

Technology Tip

Story documents can be saved to students' computers in DOC, PDF, HTML and other formats. They may also be stored online at the Internet server where they were created.

Teacher Tip

As students search for clip art, circulate to be sure they can distinguish free images from copyrighted ones. You may want to approve students' search terms for appropriate results.

ELL

English Language Learners
English Conventions Assist students as they edit their stories, explaining how spelling and grammar corrections should be made and the reasons for the changes. Use the appropriate lessons in the ELL Handbook to support teaching English conventions.

5 Publish and Present

Options for presenting

Offer students two options for presenting their work:

Have students print out a hard copy of their story for sharing at home with families or in the class in a reading session.	For a broader audience, students can convert their files to Portable Document Format (PDF). PDFs can be downloaded onto a class or school Web site or educational file-sharing site.

Illustrate and format

Now that we have written and revised our fantasy stories, it is time to add pictures and put the stories into a finished form. We will use commands on our shared-text Internet site (or word processing application) to place images and format text.

Help students import, resize, and place their clip art images appropriately in their stories. Then instruct students in the use of formatting tools to change font size and emphasis for the story title and captions, if needed. Finally, have students check their paragraphs for proper spacing and indentation.

Have each student print a final copy of his or her story on a color printer. Invite students to share their stories with classmates, either by reading them aloud to the class or a small group or by creating a class book. Schedule a day when interested students can read their stories to groups of younger students.

Contents

Section 1 Planning — 2

Pacing Guide

Teaching Record Chart

Section 2 Instruction — 8

Comprehension Mini-Lessons
- Sequence
- Main Idea and Details
- Fact and Opinion
- Predict and Set Purpose (includes ANCHOR CHART)

Using Multiple Strategies

Glossary of Literacy Terms

Section 3 Matching Books and Readers — 24

Leveled Readers Skills Chart

What Good Readers Do

Conversation Starters: Asking Good Questions

Connecting Science and Social Studies

Section 4 Building Community — 42

Planning Teacher Study Groups

Trial Lessons

Books for Teachers

Pacing Guide

This chart shows the instructional sequence from *Scott Foresman Reading Street* for Grade 5. You can use this pacing guide as is to ensure you are following a comprehensive scope and sequence. Or, you can adjust the sequence to match your calendar, curriculum map, or testing schedule.

Grade 5

READING	UNIT 1 Week 1	Week 2	Week 3	Week 4	Week 5 REVIEW WEEK	UNIT 2 Week 1	Week 2
Comprehension Skill	Character and Plot	Cause and Effect	Theme and Setting	Fact and Opinion	Cause and Effect	Compare and Contrast	Sequence
Comprehension Strategy	Monitor and Clarify	Summarize	Inferring	Questioning	Text Structure	Visualize	Inferring
Vocabulary Strategy/Skill	Context Clues/ Homographs	Context Clues/ Homonyms	Dictionary/ Glossary/ Unknown Words	Context Clues/ Antonyms	Context Clues/ Multiple-Meaning Words	Context Clues/ Unfamiliar Words	Dictionary/ Glossary/ Unknown Words
Fluency	Expression	Rate	Expression	Phrasing/ Punctuation	Accuracy	Expression	Accuracy
Spelling/ Word Work	Short Vowel VCCV, VCV	Long Vowel VCV	Long Vowel Digraphs	Adding -ed, -ing	Contractions	Digraphs *th, sh, ch, ph*	Irregular Plurals

	UNIT 4 Week 1	Week 2	Week 3	Week 4	Week 5 REVIEW WEEK	UNIT 5 Week 1	Week 2
Comprehension Skill	Draw Conclusions	Generalize	Graphic Sources	Generalize	Draw Conclusions	Character and Plot	Graphic Sources
Comprehension Strategy	Questioning	Predict and Set Purpose	Important Ideas	Story Structure	Visualize	Background Knowledge	Inferring
Vocabulary Skill/ Strategy	Word Structure/ Endings	Context Clues/ Unfamiliar Words	Context Clues/ Synonyms	Context Clues/ Unfamiliar Words	Word Structure/ Suffixes	Word Structure/Greek and Latin Roots	Dictionary/ Glossary/ Unknown Words
Fluency	Phrasing	Accuracy	Rate	Expression	Phrasing	Expression	Expression
Spelling/ Word Work	Words from Many Cultures	Prefixes *sub-, over-, out-, under-, super-*	Homophones	Suffixes *-ible, -able*	Negative Prefixes	Multisyllabic Words	Related Words

> *Are you the adventurous type? Want to use some of your own ideas and materials in your teaching? But you worry you might be leaving out some critical instruction kids need?* **Customize Literacy** *can help.*

REVIEW WEEK

REVIEW WEEK

 **UNIT 3**

Week 3	Week 4	Week 5	Week 1	Week 2	Week 3	Week 4	Week 5
Compare and Contrast	Author's Purpose	Author's Purpose	Sequence	Main Idea/Details	Fact and Opinion	Main Idea/Details	Graphic Sources
Story Structure	Monitor and Clarify	Background Knowledge	Summarize	Visualize	Predict and Set Purpose	Text Structure	Important Ideas
Word Structure/Greek and Latin Roots	Context Clues/Unfamiliar Words	Word Structure/Endings -s, -ed, -ing	Context Clues/Multiple-Meaning Words	Word Structure/Greek and Latin Roots	Context Clues/Homonyms	Context Clues/Antonyms	Word Structure/Prefixes
Expression	Phrasing	Rate	Expression	Rate	Phrasing	Rate	Accuracy
Vowel Sounds with *r*	Final Syllables -en, -an, -el, -le, -il	Final Syllables -er, -ar, -or	Words with schwa	Compound Words	Consonant Sounds /j/, /ks/, /sk/, /s/	One Consonant or Two	Prefixes *un-, de-, dis-*

REVIEW WEEK

REVIEW WEEK

UNIT 6

Week 3	Week 4	Week 5	Week 1	Week 2	Week 3	Week 4	Week 5
Author's Purpose	Cause and Effect	Generalize	Draw Conclusions	Main Idea/Details	Compare and Contrast	Fact and Opinion	Sequence
Monitor and Clarify	Summarize	Questioning	Important Ideas	Text Structure	Story Structure	Predict and Set Purpose	Background Knowledge
Context Clues/Multiple-Meaning Words	Context Clues/Unfamiliar Words	Word Structure/Prefixes	Dictionary/Glossary/Unknown Words	Word Structure/Endings	Word Structure/Suffixes	Word Structure/Unfamiliar Words	Context Clues/Homographs
Accuracy	Phrasing	Rate	Accuracy	Phrasing/Punctuation Clues	Rate	Phrasing	Expression
Greek Word Parts	Latin Roots	Greek Word Parts	Suffixes -ous, -sion, -ion, -ation	Final Syllable -ant, -ent, -ance, -ence	Latin Roots	Related Words	Easily Confused Words

Pacing Guide

Grade 5

Unit 1 / Review Week / Unit 2

LANGUAGE ARTS	UNIT 1					UNIT 2	
	Week 1	Week 2	Week 3	Week 4	Week 5	Week 1	Week 2
Speaking and Listening	Interview	Storytelling	How-to Demonstration	Sportscast	Job Ad	Talk Show	Informational Speech
Grammar	Four Kinds of Sentences	Subjects and Predicates	Independent and Dependent Clauses	Compound and Complex Sentences	Common, Proper, and Collective Nouns	Regular and Irregular Plural Nouns	Possessive Nouns
Weekly Writing	Directions	Tall Tale	Invitation	Newsletter Article	Expository Composition	Description	Informal Letter
Trait of the Week	Organization	Voice	Focus/Ideas	Word Choice	Organization/ Paragraphs	Sentences	Voice
Writing	Podcast/Personal Narrative						

Unit 4 / Review Week / Unit 5

LANGUAGE ARTS	UNIT 4					UNIT 5	
	Week 1	Week 2	Week 3	Week 4	Week 5	Week 1	Week 2
Speaking and Listening	How-to Demonstration	Persuasive Speech	Description	Give Advice	Interview	Dramatization	Newscast
Grammar	Subject and Object Pronouns	Pronouns and Antecedents	Possessive Pronouns	Indefinite and Reflexive Pronouns	Using *Who* and *Whom*	Contractions and Negatives	Adjectives and Articles
Weekly Writing	Picture Book	Friendly Letter	Formal Letter	Narrative Poetry	Autobio-graphical Sketch	Rhyming Poem	Notes
Trait of the Week	Focus/Ideas	Sentences	Conventions	Word Choice	Voice	Word Choice	Focus/Ideas
Writing	E-Pen Pals/Cause-and-Effect Essay						

REVIEW WEEK

UNIT 3

Week 3	Week 4	Week 5
Readers' Theater	Panel Discussion	Documentary
Action and Linking Verbs	Main and Helping Verbs	Subject-Verb Agreement
Poem	Personal Narrative	Historical Fiction
Organization/ Poetic Structure	Word Choice	Word Choice

E-Newsletter/Comic Book Graphic Novel

Week 1	Week 2	Week 3	Week 4	Week 5
Play Review	Newscast	Introducing a Special Person	Give Directions	Advertisement
Past, Present, and Future Tenses	Principal Parts of Regular Verbs	Principal Parts of Irregular Verbs	Troublesome Verbs	Prepositions and Prepositional Phrases
Play	Persuasive Speech	Ad Brochure	Description	Expository Text
Word Choice	Focus/Ideas	Word Choice	Word Choice	Organization

Story Exchange/Compare and Contrast Essay

REVIEW WEEK

UNIT 6

Week 3	Week 4	Week 5
Storytelling	Discussion	Debate
This, That, These, and *Those*	Comparative and Superlative Adjectives	Adverbs
Biographical Sketch	Letter to the Editor	Summary
Sentences	Voice	Focus/Ideas

Interview/Persuasive Essay

Week 1	Week 2	Week 3	Week 4	Week 5
Debate	Interview	Storytelling	Newscast	Readers' Theater
Modifiers	Conjunctions	Commas	Quotations and Quotation Marks	Punctuation
Journal Entry	Mystery	Parody	Review	Personal Narrative
Voice	Focus/Ideas	Voice	Organization/ Paragraphs	Voice

Photo Description/Research Report

Teaching Record Chart

This chart shows the critical comprehension skills and strategies you need to cover. Check off each one as you provide instruction.

Reading/Comprehension	DATES OF INSTRUCTION		
Compare and contrast the themes or moral lessons of several works of fiction from various cultures.			
Describe the phenomena explained in origin myths from various cultures.			
Explain the effect of a historical event or movement on the theme of a work of literature.			
Analyze how poets use sound effects (e.g., alliteration, internal rhyme, onomatopoeia, rhyme scheme) to reinforce meaning in poems.			
Analyze the similarities and differences between an original text and its dramatic adaptation.			
Describe incidents that advance the story or novel, explaining how each incident gives rise to or foreshadows future events.			
Explain the roles and functions of characters in various plots, including their relationships and conflicts.			
Explain the different forms of third-person points of view in stories.			
Identify the literary language and devices used in biographies and autobiographies, including how authors present major events in a person's life.			
Evaluate the impact of sensory details, imagery, and figurative language in literary text.			
Read independently for a sustained period of time and summarize or paraphrase what the reading was about, maintaining meaning and logical order (e.g., generate a reading log or journal; participate in book talks).			
Draw conclusions from the information presented by an author and evaluate how well the author's purpose was achieved.			
Summarize the main ideas and supporting details in a text in ways that maintain meaning and logical order.			

> Tired of using slips of paper or stickies to make sure you teach everything you need to? Need an easier way to keep track of what you have taught, and what you still need to cover? **Customize Literacy** can help.

Reading/Comprehension	DATES OF INSTRUCTION		
Determine the facts in a text and verify them through established methods.			
Analyze how the organizational pattern of a text (e.g., cause-and-effect, compare-and-contrast, sequential order, logical order, classification schemes) influences the relationships among the ideas.			
Use multiple text features and graphics to gain an overview of the contents of text and to locate information.			
Synthesize and make logical connections between ideas within a text and across two or three texts representing similar or different genres.			
Identify the author's viewpoint or position and explain the basic relationships among ideas (e.g., parallelism, comparison, causality) in the argument.			
Recognize exaggerated, contradictory, or misleading statements in text.			
Interpret details from procedural text to complete a task, solve a problem, or perform procedures.			
Interpret factual or quantitative information presented in maps, charts, illustrations, graphs, time lines, tables, and diagrams.			
Establish purposes for reading a text based on what students hope to accomplish by reading the text.			
Ask literal, interpretive, and evaluative questions of a text.			
Monitor and adjust comprehension using a variety of strategies.			
Make inferences about a text and use evidence from the text to support understanding.			
Summarize and paraphrase information in a text, maintaining meaning and logical order.			
Make connections between and among texts.			

Student Edition p. EI•13

Sequence

Objectives:

- Students identify sequence relationships and events, including those that occur simultaneously and in flashbacks.
- Students put events in correct chronological order.

What is it? **Sequence** means the order in which things happen. Sequence can also mean the steps we follow to make or do something. Understanding sequence, or time relationships, is important in understanding certain genres, such as historical fiction and biography. Social studies and science texts use sequence to describe events and processes. At Grade 5, when clue words are not used to explicitly point out sequence, readers need to think about the order in which events occur.

How Good Readers Use the Skill Students experience time relationships every day. Teachers can build on these experiences and help students connect them to reading. At first, students understand sequence as what happens first, next, and last in a selection. Students can then move on to use clue words to decipher more complicated sequence relationships, such as flashbacks and simultaneous events.

Texts for Teaching

Student Edition
- *Hold the Flag High,* 5.1, pages 208–219
- *The Fabulous Perpetual Motion Machine,* 5.1, pages 330–343
- *Sweet Music in Harlem,* 5.2, pages 440–457

Leveled Readers
- See pages 24–29 for a list of Leveled Readers.

Mini-Lesson 1

Teach the Skill
Use the **Envision It!** lesson on page EI•13 to visually review sequence.

Remind students that:
- **sequence** means the order in which things happen. It can also be the steps we take to do or make something.
- **clue words** such as *first*, *last*, and *after* can help students figure out order.

Practice
Write the following sentences in random order on the board and have students put them in sequential order using clue words such as *first*, *next*, *then*, and so on. Students might use other words that indicate time as well, such as *last night* or *Monday*.

I made supper for everyone.
I got out a jar of sauce and a box of pasta.
I boiled the pasta and heated up the sauce.
I scooped ice cream for everyone.
We all did the dishes.

If... students have difficulty identifying sequence relationships, **then...** use just two sentence and work with them to decide which action would come first.

Apply
As students read the assigned text, have them complete a sequence graphic organizer to order events.

Writing
Students can write about an activity or event using clue words.

ini-Lesson 2

Teach the Skill

Use the **Envision It!** lesson on page EI•13 to visually review sequence.

Remind students that:

- **sequence** means the order in which things happen. It can also be the steps we take to do or make something.
- **clue words** such as *first*, *last*, and *after* can help students figure out order.
- not all selections that are in time order have clue words.
- clue words such as *while*, *meanwhile*, and *during* signal events that are happening simultaneously.

Practice

Read aloud the following passage and have students listen for three events that happen in sequence and two events that happen simultaneously. Remind students that they may need to use their common sense and prior knowledge to determine sequence, as every event may not include a clue word.

Last night the kids made supper for everyone. I got the ingredients out of the fridge and lined them up. Meanwhile, Jarod set the table. I started the water boiling for pasta. This would take longer than heating the sauce. While the pasta boiled and the sauce bubbled, Jarod and I made a salad. After dinner, Jarod and I washed the dishes. As a treat, Dad took everyone out for dessert.

If... students have difficulty identifying sequence relationships,
then... chunk the text and have them point out clue words that identify events in each chunk.

Apply

As students read the assigned text, have them complete a sequence graphic organizer.

Writing

Using appropriate clue words, students can write about two events that happen at the same time.

ini-Lesson 3

Teach the Skill

Use the **Envision It!** lesson on page EI•13 to visually review sequence.

Remind students that:

- **sequence** means the order in which things happen. It can also be the steps we take to do or make something.
- not all selections that are in time order have clue words.
- clue words such as *while*, *meanwhile*, and *during* signal events that are happening simultaneously.
- sometimes events are told out of order and readers must look at verb tenses for clues to sequence.

Practice

Read aloud the following passage and have students listen for the order of events. Record their responses.

The story we read today brought another incident to mind. I was just eight when I got my first guitar, but this was still years after I had been taking piano lessons. I started those lessons shortly after turning five. The guitar sat in my closet until one day when my piano teacher brought her guitar to my lesson. We played a duet! I started playing the guitar that day and haven't stopped.

If... students have difficulty identifying sequence relationships,
then... provide the graphic organizer for additional practice.

Apply

As students read the assigned text, have them complete a sequence graphic organizer.

Writing

Students can use what they learned about clue words to revise descriptions or personal narratives.

Instruction

Student Edition p. EI•12

Main Idea and Details

What is it? The **main ideas** of a piece of writing are what the piece is mostly about. At Grade 5, students are reading nonfiction that may have several main ideas and they are finding the main ideas of an article or a longer passage. They see parallels between main idea and theme. Sometimes a main idea is stated in a single sentence within a paragraph or article; at other times, readers must infer the main ideas and put them in their own words. Students learn to locate details that support the main idea.

How Good Readers Use the Skill Identifying and stating main ideas is a critical skill for readers because it helps them determine the important information in a text. At first, students think about what the selection is mostly about. They go on to select a statement of main idea, from a choice of statements or from the selection itself. They begin to identify supporting details as pieces of information that enlarge on the main idea, help clarify the main idea, or give examples. Older readers are able to identify main ideas, stated or implied, and are able to frame main ideas in their own words.

Texts for Teaching

Student Edition
- *Leonardo's Horse,* 5.1, pages 360–377
- *Mahalia Jackson,* 5.1, pages 430–437
- *The Mystery of Saint Matthew Island,* 5.2, pages 350–359

Leveled Readers
- See pages 24–29 for a list of Leveled Readers.

Objectives:
- Students identify main ideas in nonfiction passages and articles.
- Students use a graphic organizer to record ideas.
- Students express main ideas in their own words in ways that maintain meaning.
- Students give details to support main ideas.

Mini-Lesson 1

Teach the Skill
Use the **Envision It!** lesson on page EI•12 to visually review main idea.

Remind students that:
- the **topic** is what a paragraph or article is about.
- the **main ideas** are the most important ideas of the topic.
- **details** tell more about the main ideas.

Practice
Read the following and have students identify the topic (Franklin D. Roosevelt) and the stated main idea. Discuss with students how all the other sentences are supporting details.

Franklin D. Roosevelt was a well-known President of the United States. He helped our country get through the Great Depression. Many people had lost their jobs and did not have enough money. As President, he began the New Deal program to make new jobs. These jobs put many people back to work. Roosevelt was also in charge of the way the United States fought in World War II.

If... students have difficulty identifying the stated main idea,
then... have students choose between two sentences, one of which states the main idea.

Apply
As students read the assigned text, have them first identify the topic and then the main idea.

Writing
Students can list topics they would like to write or read about.

Instruction

Mini-Lesson 2

Teach the Skill
Use the **Envision It!** lesson on page EI•12 to visually review main idea.

Remind students that:
- the **main ideas** are the most important ideas of the topic.
- the **main idea** is often stated in a paragraph or article.
- **details** tell more about the main ideas.

Practice
Supply students with a nonfiction article that has subheads. Model using a main idea/supporting details chart to organize the information in each section of the text. Think aloud as you figure out the main idea. For example:

The subhead tells me what this section will be about. I will look for a sentence that states a main idea—it's often the first or last sentence in a paragraph or section. Some of these details are interesting, but not that important. Which details support the main idea?

If... students have difficulty identifying main ideas and details, **then...** provide a main idea and have students locate details for it and explain how they tell more about the main idea

Apply
As students read the assigned text, have them use a main idea/supporting details chart to organize information. They can use it to identify or state the main ideas of the article.

Writing
Give students a main idea and have them write a paragraph about it.

Mini-Lesson 3

Teach the Skill
Use the **Envision It!** lesson on page EI•12 to visually review main idea.

Remind students that:
- the **main ideas** are the most important ideas of the topic.
- the **main idea** may be implied in a paragraph or article and not stated directly.
- **details** tell more about the main ideas.

Practice
Supply students with a nonfiction article. (If it has subheads, you might choose one with fanciful rather than instructional subheads.) Choose a piece with an implied main idea. Reread a section aloud and use a main idea/details chart. Then think aloud as you figure out the main idea. For example:

I don't see a sentence that states the main idea. When I look at the chart I made, it tells me what this section is all about. I will use my own words to write a sentence that tells what this section is all about. Write a sentence of the main idea and then ask: What do you think? Does this make sense? Do the details support my main idea? Or do I need to rewrite it?

If... students have difficulty writing a main idea statement, **then...** tell them to finish this sentence: *The most imporant idea is that* _____.

Apply
As students read the assigned text, have them use a main idea/details chart to organize information.

Writing
Students can put the main idea of the selection in their own words.

Fact and Opinion

Student Edition p. EI•7

What is it? A **statement of fact** tells something that can be proved true or false. A **statement of opinion** tells a person's ideas or feelings and cannot be proved true or false. At Grade 5, students are explaining the difference between facts and opinions and identifying them in their reading. They are judging the validity of opinions.

How Good Readers Use the Skill Students meet statements of facts and opinions throughout their day. We want to teach them how to distinguish the two and understand ways to check the veracity of factual statements and be able to judge statements of opinion thoughtfully. Evaluating statements of fact and statements of opinion boosts students' comprehension and helps them avoid being misled.

Texts for Teaching

Student Edition
- *Satchel Paige*, 5.1, pages 116–129
- *The Dinosaurs of Waterhouse Hawkins*, 5.1, pages 394–411
- *The* Hindenburg, 5.2, pages 408–423

Leveled Readers
- See pages 24–29 for a list of Leveled Readers.

Objectives:
- Students define *fact* and *opinion*.
- Students use clue words to identify statements as fact or opinion.
- Students understand that statements of fact can be proved true or false and statements of opinion can be supported or explained.

Mini-Lesson 1

Teach the Skill
Use the **Envision It!** lesson on page EI•7 to visually review fact and opinion.

Remind students that:
- a statement of **fact** tells something that can be proved true or false.
- a statement of **opinion** tells a person's ideas or feelings and cannot be proved true or false.

Practice
Use a commercial or an ad that contains both facts and opinions and help students distinguish between them. (**Fact:** *The milk for this cheese comes from cows that eat only grass.* **Opinion:** *Grass-fed cows are happy cows.*) Model identifying the statements by asking and answering questions: Can I prove this statement? If this is a fact, how could I check to see if it is really true? If this is an opinion, does it seem thoughtful? Provide other ads and have students identify statements of facts and opinions and support their ideas.

If... students have difficulty distinguishing statements of fact, **then...** suggest ways to check a statement, such as check an encyclopedia, the internet, or an expert.

Apply
As students read, have them be alert for statements of fact and opinion.

Writing
Students can collect ads and underline facts and circle opinions.

Mini-Lesson 2

Teach the Skill

Use the **Envision It!** lesson on page EI•7 to visually review fact and opinion.

Remind students that:

- a statement of **fact** tells something that can be proved true or false.
- a statement of **opinion** tells a person's ideas or feelings and cannot be proved true or false.
- **clue words** and phrases such as *best, in my opinion, I believe, I think,* and so on can signal an opinion.
- some sentences contain both facts and opinions.

Practice

Tell students that they can use clue words to help them separate fact and opinion. Write these sentences on the board. Have students determine which phrases are statements of fact and which are statements of opinion and tell why they think as they do. Encourage students to think of how they could verify statements of fact.

Charlotte's Web, my favorite book, was first published in 1952. Everyone should read it.

The Taj Mahal in Agra, India, is India's most popular tourist attraction.

Jackie Joyner-Kersee, one of the greatest female athletes of all time, competed while suffering from asthma.

If... students have difficulty distinguishing fact and opinion, **then...** point out the facts and talk about how they could be proved true or false.

Apply

As students read, have them look for statements of fact and opinion.

Writing

Students can write sentences that contain both a fact and an opinion.

Mini-Lesson 3

Teach the Skill

Use the **Envision It!** lesson on page EI•7 to visually review fact and opinion.

Remind students that:

- a statement of **fact** tells something that can be proved true or false.
- a statement of **opinion** tells a person's ideas or feelings and cannot be proved true or false.
- **clue words** and and phrases such as *best, in my opinion, I believe, I think,* and so on can signal an opinion.
- some sentences contain both facts and opinions.
- opinions can be faulty or valid.

Practice

Remind students that statements of opinion may be based on bad information or poor logic. Students need to use their common sense, information in the text, and their prior knowledge to judge statements of opinions. Model reading a letter to the editor. Think aloud as you read each sentence to decide whether it is fact or opinion and then judge the validity of each. You could take notes on a chart like the following.

Fact or Opinion?	How to Check It Out	Valid or Faulty?
Opinion: Homework should be abolished.	Ask experts like teachers or principals.	Faulty: No support for statement. Also, some homework is useful.

If... students have difficulty evaluating facts and opinions, **then...** model your thinking and ask the student what he or she thinks.

Apply

As students read, have them look for opinions and ask themselves if they are faulty or valid.

Writing

Students can write sentences with a supported, valid opinion.

Instruction

Objectives:

- Students use text features and the author's language to preview and identify genre, topic, and subject.
- Students use text features to activate background knowledge.
- Students set own purpose for reading.
- Students use details from text to make and confirm predictions.
- Students ask questions to help them preview, set purpose, and predict.

Texts for Teaching

Student Edition

- *The Dinosaurs of Waterhouse Hawkins*, 5.1, pages 394–411
- *Tripping Over the Lunch Lady*, 5.2, pages 52–67
- *The* Hindenburg, 5.2, pages 408–423

Leveled Readers

- See pages 24–29 for a list of Leveled Readers.

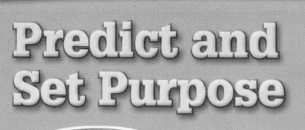

Predict and Set Purpose

Mini-Lesson

Student Edition p. EI•20

Understand the Strategy

To predict means to tell what you think might happen next in a story or what the author may tell you next. Predicting goes hand-in-hand with previewing, which involves looking at text features and language to get an overview of a piece of writing. Before reading, previewing and predicting helps readers access what they already know about the topic and **set a purpose** to guide reading.

Teach

Use the **Envision It!** lesson on page EI•20 to visually review predict and set purpose with students.

Remind students that making predictions helps them better understand what they read. Model predicting and setting purpose using the tips below.

Before You Read
Look at pictures, graphic features, headings, and other details to determine genre.
Think about what you already know about this topic, subject, characters, or author.
Ask: Why will I read this? Predict what you think the selection will be about.

As You Read
Is there new information that makes you want to revise a prediction?
What do you think will happen next? Make a new prediction.
What information do you think the author will tell you next?

After You Read
Look back at the selection. How close were your predictions?
Do you want to read more by the same author? about the same topic?

Practice

Give students a passage of either fiction or nonfiction and have them preview, set a purpose for reading, and then make predictions. Discuss what details they used to make a prediction. Then have them read to check it.

If... students have difficulty making predictions,
then... model the process using text clues and personal experience.

Apply

Encourage students to predict whenever they read. You might provide a T-Chart they can use to write down and then confirm predictions.

Anchor Chart

Anchor charts help students make their thinking visible and permanent. With an anchor chart, the group can clarify their thinking about how to use a strategy. Here is a sample chart for predict and set purpose.

Predict and Set Purpose

1. Before you read anything, preview. Look at everything to see if you will be reading fiction or nonfiction. (You can usually tell this pretty quickly.)

2. Read a little to see whether you need to read fast or slow.

3. Think about what you already know about the topic or the subject or the author. Usually there is something you can connect to.

4. Make some predictions.
What will this story be about?
What will the author tell me about?

5. Set a purpose for reading. Here are a few purposes.
I love these characters. I will read to see what they do in this story.
I want to read to find out more about castles.

6. Check your predictions. Were you close?

Anchor Chart

7. Make new predictions based on what you have read. Read on to check these.

Using Multiple Strategies

Good readers use multiple strategies as they read. You can encourage students to read strategically through good classroom questioning. Use questions such as these to help students apply strategies during reading.

Answer Questions

- Who or what is this question about?

- Where can you look to find the answer to this question?

Ask Questions

- What do you want to know about _____?

- What questions do you have about the _____ in this selection? Use the words *who, what, when, where, why,* and *how* to ask your questions.

- Do you have any questions after reading?

Graphic Organizers

- What kind of graphic organizer could you use to help you keep track of the information in this selection?

Monitor and Clarify

- Does the story or article make sense?

- What don't you understand about what you read?

- Do you need to reread, review, read on, or check a reference source?

- Do you need to read more slowly or more quickly?

- What is a _____? Where could you look to find out?

Predict/Confirm Predictions

- What do you think this story or article will be about? Why do you think as you do?

- What do you think you will learn from this selection?

- Do the text features help you predict what will happen?

- Based on what has happened so far, what do you think will happen next?

- Is this what you thought would happen?

- How does _____ change what you thought would happen?

Preview

- What do the photographs, illustrations, or graphic sources tell about the selection?

- What do you want to find out? What do you want to learn?

Background Knowledge

- What do you already know about _____?
- Have you read stories or articles by this author before?
- How is this selection like others that you have read?
- What does this remind you of?
- How does your background knowledge help you understand _____?
- Did the text match what you already knew? What new information did you learn?

Story Structure

- Who are the characters in this story? the setting?
- What is the problem in this story? How does the problem get solved?
- What is the point of this story?

Summarize

- What two or three important ideas have you read so far?
- How do the text features relate to the important ideas?
- Is there a graphic organizer that can help you organize the information before you summarize?

Text Structure

- How has the author organized the writing?
- What clues tell you that the text is structured _____?

Visualize

- When you read this, what do you picture in your mind?
- What do you hear, see, or smell?
- What do you think _____ looks like? Why do you think as you do?

" You know explicit strategy instruction is a must! But you also want students to use strategies every time they read. **Customize Literacy** shows you how to help them do this. "

Glossary of Literacy Terms

This glossary lists academic language terms that are related to literacy.
They are provided for your information and professional use.

A

alliteration	the repetition of a consonant sound in a group of words, especially in poetry
allusion	a word or phrase that refers to something else the reader already knows from history, experience, or reading
animal fantasy	a story about animals that talk and act like people
answer questions	a reading strategy in which readers use the text and prior knowledge to answer questions about what they are reading
antonym	a word that means the opposite of another word
ask questions	a reading strategy in which readers ask themselves questions about the text to help make sense of what they read
author's point of view	the author's opinion on the subject he or she is writing about
author's purpose	the reason the author wrote the text
autobiography	the story of a real person's life written by that person

B

background knowledge	the information and experience that a reader brings to a text
biography	the story of a real person's life written by another person

C

cause	why something happens
character	a person, an animal, or a personified object in a story
chronological order	events in a selection, presented in the order in which they occurred
classify and categorize	put things, such as pictures or words, into groups
climax	the point in a story at which conflict is confronted
compare	tell how things are the same
comprehension	understanding of text being read—the ultimate goal of reading
comprehension strategy	a conscious plan used by a reader to gain understanding of text. Comprehension strategies may be used before, during, or after reading.
conclusion	a decision or opinion arrived at after thinking about facts and details and using prior knowledge
conflict	the problem or struggle in a story
context clue	the words, phrases, or sentences near an unfamiliar word that give the reader clues to the word's meaning
contrast	tell how things are different

Instruction

details	small pieces of information
dialect	form of a language spoken in a certain region or by a certain group of people that differs from the standard form of that language
dialogue	written conversation
diary	a day-to-day record of one's activities and thoughts
draw conclusions	arrive at decisions or opinions after thinking about facts and details and using prior knowledge

D

effect	what happens as the result of a cause
etymology	an explanation of the origin and history of a word and its meaning
exaggeration	a statement that makes something seem larger or greater than it actually is
expository text	text that contains facts and information. Also called *informational text*.

E

fable	a story, usually with animal characters, that is written to teach a moral, or lesson
fact	piece of information that can be proved to be true
fairy tale	a folk story with magical characters and events
fantasy	a story that could not really happen
fiction	writing that tells about imaginary people, things, and events
figurative language	the use of language that gives words a meaning beyond their usual definitions in order to add beauty or force
flashback	an interruption in the sequence of events of a narrative to include an event that happened earlier
folk tale	a story that has been passed down by word of mouth
foreshadowing	the use of hints or clues about what will happen later in a story

F

generalize	make a broad statement or rule after examining particular facts
graphic organizer	a drawing, chart, or web that illustrates concepts or shows how ideas relate to each other. Readers use graphic organizers to help them keep track of and understand important information and ideas as they read. Story maps, word webs, Venn diagrams, and KWL charts are graphic organizers.
graphic source	a chart, diagram, or map within a text that adds to readers' understanding of the text

G

H

historical fiction	realistic fiction that takes place in the past. It is an imaginary story based on historical events and characters.
humor	writing or speech that has a funny or amusing quality
hyperbole	an exaggerated statement not meant to be taken literally, such as *I'm so hungry I could eat a horse.*

I

idiom	a phrase whose meaning differs from the ordinary meaning of the words. *A stone's throw* is an idiom meaning "a short distance."
imagery	the use of language to create beautiful or forceful pictures in the reader's mind
inference	conclusion reached on the basis of evidence and reasoning
inform	give knowledge, facts, or news to someone
informational text	writing that contains facts and information. Also called *expository text.*
interview	a face-to-face conversation in which someone responds to questions
irony	a way of speaking or writing in which the ordinary meaning of the words is the opposite of what the speaker or writer is thinking; a contrast between what is expected and what actually happens

J

jargon	the language of a special group or profession

L

legend	a story coming down from the past about the great deeds of a hero. Although a legend may be based on historical people and events, it is not regarded as historically true.
literary elements	the characters, setting, plot, and theme of a narrative text

main idea	the big idea that tells what a paragraph or a selection is mainly about; the most important idea of a text	**M**
metacognition	an awareness of one's own thinking processes and the ability to monitor and direct them to a desired goal. Good readers use metacognition to monitor their reading and adjust their reading strategies.	
metaphor	a comparison that does not use *like* or *as*, such as *a heart of stone*	
meter	the pattern of beats or accents in poetry	
monitor and clarify	a comprehension strategy by which readers actively think about understanding their reading and know when they understand and when they do not. Readers use appropriate strategies to make sense of difficult words, ideas, or passages.	
mood	the atmosphere or feeling of a written work	
moral	the lesson or teaching of a fable or story	
motive	the reason a character in a narrative does or says something	
mystery	a story about mysterious events that are not explained until the end, so as to keep the reader in suspense	
myth	a story that attempts to explain something in nature	
narrative	a story, made up or true, that someone tells or narrates	**N**
narrator	the character in a selection who tells the story	
nonfiction	writing that tells about real things, real people, and real events	
onomatopoeia	the use of words that sound like their meanings, such as *buzz* and *hum*	**O**
opinion	someone's judgment, belief, or way of thinking	
oral vocabulary	the words needed for speaking and listening	
outcome	the resolution of the conflict in a story	
paraphrase	retell the meaning of a passage in one's own words	**P**
personification	a figure of speech in which human traits or actions are given to animals or inanimate objects, as in *The sunbeam danced on the waves.*	
persuade	convince someone to do or to believe something	
photo essay	a collection of photographs on one theme, accompanied by text	
play	a story that is written to be acted out for an audience	

Instruction

P

plot	a series of related events at the beginning, middle, and end of a story; the action of a story
poem	an expressive, imaginative piece of writing often arranged in lines having rhythm and rhyme. In a poem, the patterns made by the sounds of the words have special importance.
pourquoi tale	a type of folk story that explains why things in nature came to be. *Pourquoi* is a French word meaning "why."
predict	tell what a selection might be about or what might happen in a text. Readers use text features and information to predict. They confirm or revise their predictions as they read.
preview	look over a text before reading it
prior knowledge	the information and experience that a reader brings to a text. Readers use prior knowledge to help them understand what they read.
prop	an item, such as an object, picture, or chart, used in a performance or presentation

R

reading vocabulary	the words we recognize or use in print
realistic fiction	a story about imaginary people and events that could happen in real life
repetition	the repeated use of some aspect of language
resolution	the point in a story where the conflict is resolved
rhyme	to end in the same sound(s)
rhythm	a pattern of strong beats in speech or writing, especially poetry
rising action	the buildup of conflicts and complications in a story

S

science fiction	a story based on science that often tells what life in the future might be like
semantic map	a graphic organizer, often a web, used to display words or concepts that are meaningfully related
sensory language	the use of words that help the reader understand how things look, sound, smell, taste, or feel
sequence	the order of events in a selection or the order of the steps in which something is completed
sequence words	clue words such as *first, next, then,* and *finally* that signal the order of events in a selection

setting	where and when a story takes place
simile	a comparison that uses *like* or *as*, as in *as busy as a bee*
speech	a public talk to a group of people made for a specific purpose
stanza	a group of lines in a poem
steps in a process	the order of the steps in which something is completed
story map	a graphic organizer used to record the literary elements and the sequence of events in a narrative text
story structure	how the characters, setting, and events of a story are organized into a plot
summarize	give the most important ideas of what was read. Readers summarize important information in the selection to keep track of what they are reading.
supporting detail	piece of information that tells about the main idea
symbolism	the use of one thing to suggest something else; often the use of something concrete to stand for an abstract idea

S

tall tale	a humorous story that uses exaggeration to describe impossible happenings
text structure	the organization of a piece of nonfiction writing. Text structures of informational text include cause/effect, chronological, compare/contrast, description, problem/solution, proposition/support, and ask/answer questions.
theme	the big idea or author's message in a story
think aloud	an instructional strategy in which a teacher verbalizes his or her thinking to model the process of comprehension or the application of a skill
tone	author's attitude toward the subject or toward the reader
topic	the subject of a discussion, conversation, or piece of text

T

visualize	picture in one's mind what is happening in the text. Visualizing helps readers imagine the things they read about.

V

Instruction

Leveled Readers Skills Chart

Scott Foresman Reading Street provides more than six hundred leveled readers.
Each one is designed to:

- Practice critical skills and strategies
- Build fluency
- Build vocabulary and concepts
- Develop a lifelong love of reading

Grade 5

Title	Level*	DRA Level	Genre	Comprehension Strategy
Jenna and the High Dive	N	30	Realistic Fiction	Monitor and Clarify
Dangerous Storms	N	30	Expository Nonfiction	Summarize
Our Village	N	30	Historical Fiction	Inferring
Rube Foster and the Chicago American Giants	N	30	Nonfiction	Questioning
The Golden Spike	O	34	Expository Nonfiction	Text Structure
The Ocean's Treasures	O	34	Expository Nonfiction	Visualize
From Slave to Soldier	O	34	Historical Fiction	Inferring
China: Today and Yesterday	O	34	Expository Nonfiction	Story Structure
A Visit to the Navajo Nation	O	34	Expository Nonfiction	Monitor and Clarify
Paul Revere's Ride	P	38	Narrative Nonfiction	Background Knowledge
George Ferris's Wheel	P	38	Expository Nonfiction	Summarize
The Designs of Da Vinci	P	38	Biography	Visualize
Paleontology: Digging for Dinosaurs and More	P	38	Nonfiction	Predict and Set Purpose
The Root of the Blues	P	38	Narrative Nonfiction	Text Structure
The Magic of Makeup	P	38	Expository Nonfiction	Important Ideas
The Long Trip Home	Q	40	Realistic Fiction	Monitor and Clarify
Storm Chasing Challenges	Q	40	Expository Nonfiction	Summarize
Toby's California Vacation	Q	40	Realistic Fiction	Inferring
Famous Women in Sports	Q	40	Biography	Questioning
Playing the Game	Q	40	Realistic Fiction	Questioning
The Land of Plenty	Q	40	Historical Fiction	Predict and Set Purpose
Surviving the Elements	Q	40	Expository Nonfiction	Important Ideas
Moving	Q	40	Realistic Fiction	Story Structure
Let the Games Begin	Q	40	Expository Nonfiction	Visualize
Giant Pumpkin on the Loose	Q	40	Fiction	Background Knowledge
A Railroad Over the Sierra	R	40	Expository Nonfiction	Text Structure
Sea Life	R	40	Expository Nonfiction	Visualize
A Spy in Disguise	R	40	Nonfiction	Inferring
Abuela's Gift	R	40	Realistic Fiction	Story Structure
Helping Others	R	40	Nonfiction	Monitor and Clarify

* Suggested Guided Reading Level. Use your knowledge of students' abilities to adjust levels as needed.

The chart here and on the next few pages lists titles of leveled readers appropriate for students in Grade 5. Use the chart to find titles that meet your students' interest and instructional needs. The books in this list were leveled using the criteria suggested in *Matching Books to Readers* and *Leveled Books for Readers, Grades 3–6* by Irene C. Fountas and Gay Su Pinnell. For more on leveling, see the *Reading Street Leveled Readers Leveling Guide.*

Target Comprehension Skill	Additional Comprehension Instruction	Vocabulary
Character and Plot	Graphic Sources	Homographs/Context Clues
Cause and Effect	Draw Conclusions	Context Clues/Homonyms
Setting and Theme	Author's Purpose	Dictionary/Glossary/Unfamiliar Words
Fact and Opinion	Generalize	Context Clues/Antonyms
Cause and Effect	Graphic Sources	Context Clues/Multiple Meanings
Compare and Contrast	Graphic Sources	Unfamiliar Words/Context Clues
Sequence	Draw Conclusions	Dictionary/Glossary/Unfamiliar Words
Compare and Contrast	Draw Conclusions	Word Structure/Greek and Latin Roots
Author's Purpose	Main Idea and Details	Context Clues/Unfamiliar Words
Author's Purpose	Draw Conclusions	Word Structure/Endings
Sequence	Generalize	Context Clues/Multiple Meanings
Main Idea and Details	Compare and Contrast	Word Structure/Greek and Latin Roots
Fact and Opinion	Cause and Effect	Context Clues/Homonyms
Main Idea and Details	Author's Purpose	Context Clues/Antonyms
Graphic Sources	Main Idea and Details	Word Structure/Prefixes
Character and Plot	Problem and Solution	Word Structure/Suffixes
Cause and Effect	Draw Conclusions	Context Clues/Homonyms
Setting and Theme	Generalize	Dictionary/Glossary/Unfamiliar Words
Fact and Opinion	Compare and Contrast	Context Clues/Antonyms
Draw Conclusions	Theme	Word Structure/Endings
Generalize	Plot	Context Clues/Unfamiliar Words
Graphic Sources	Main Idea and Details	Context Clues/Synonyms
Generalize	Theme	Context Clues/Unfamiliar Words
Draw Conclusions	Graphic Sources	Word Structure/Suffixes
Character and Plot	Author's Purpose	Word Structure/Greek and Latin Roots
Cause and Effect	Draw Conclusions	Context Clues/Multiple Meanings
Compare and Contrast	Main Idea and Details	Unfamiliar Words/Context Clues
Sequence	Generalize	Dictionary/Glossary/Unfamiliar Words
Compare and Contrast	Theme	Word Structure/Greek and Latin Roots
Author's Purpose	Main Idea and Details	Context Clues/Unfamiliar Words

Matching Books & Readers

Leveled Readers Skills Chart Continued

Grade 5

Title	Level*	DRA Level	Genre	Comprehension Strategy
Titanic: The "Unsinkable" Ship	R	40	Narrative Nonfiction	Inferring
Aim High: Astronaut Training	R	40	Expository Nonfiction	Monitor and Clarify
The Inside Story of Earth	R	40	Expository Nonfiction	Summarize
The California Gold Rush	R	40	Expository Nonfiction	Questioning
A Happy Accident	R	40	Realistic Fiction	Important Ideas
Paul Revere/American Revolutionary War	S	40	Narrative Nonfiction	Background Knowledge
The Search to Build a Perpetual Motion Machine	S	40	Expository Nonfiction	Summarize
The Italian Renaissance and Its Artists	S	40	Expository Nonfiction	Visualize
Searching for Dinosaurs	S	40	Expository Nonfiction	Predict and Set Purpose
Blues Legends	S	40	Biography	Text Structure
Computers in Filmmaking	S	40	Nonfiction	Important Ideas
Saving an American Symbol	S	40	Expository Nonfiction	Text Structure
Ancient Gold from the Ancient World	S	40	Expository Nonfiction	Story Structure
The Flight Over the Ocean	S	40	Narrative Nonfiction	Predict and Set Purpose
Jazz, Jazz, Jazz	S	40	Narrative Nonfiction	Background Knowledge
Journey to the New World	T	50	Historical Fiction	Questioning
Wilma Rudolph: Running to Win	T	50	Biography	Predict and Set Purpose
Changing for Survival: Bird Adaptations	T	50	Expository Nonfiction	Important Ideas
The New Kid at School	T	50	Narrative Nonfiction	Story Structure
Strange Sports with Weird Gear	T	50	Expository Nonfiction	Visualize
Bill Lucks Out	T	50	Realistic Fiction	Background Knowledge
Explore with Science	U	50	Expository Nonfiction	Inferring
Sailing the Stars	U	50	Expository Nonfiction	Monitor and Clarify
The Journey Through the Earth	U	50	Science Fiction	Summarize
The United States Moves West	U	50	Expository Nonfiction	Questioning
Driven to Change	U	50	Expository Nonfiction	Important Ideas
The Kudzu Invasion	U	50	Expository Nonfiction	Text Structure
The Signs	V	50	Realistic Fiction	Monitor and Clarify
Weather Forecasting	V	50	Expository Nonfiction	Summarize
The Medicine Harvest	V	50	Historical Fiction	Inferring

* Suggested Guided Reading Level. Use your knowledge of students' abilities to adjust levels as needed.

"You know the theory behind leveled books: they let you match books with the interest and instructional levels of your students. You can find the right reader for every student with this chart."

Target Comprehension Skill	Additional Comprehension Instruction	Vocabulary
Graphic Sources	Cause and Effect	Dictionary/Glossary/Unfamiliar Words
Author's Purpose	Graphic Sources	Context Clues/Multiple Meanings
Cause and Effect	Fact and Opinion	Context Clues/Unfamiliar Words
Generalize	Main Idea and Details	Word Structure/Prefixes
Draw Conclusions	Graphic Sources	Dictionary/Glossary/Unfamiliar Words
Author's Purpose	Cause and Effect	Word Structure/Endings
Sequence	Draw Conclusions	Context Clues/Multiple Meanings
Main Idea and Details	Generalize	Word Structure/Greek and Latin Roots
Fact and Opinion	Compare and Contrast	Context Clues/Homonyms
Main Idea and Details	Author's Purpose	Context Clues/Antonyms
Graphic Sources	Main Idea and Details	Word Structure/Prefixes
Main Idea and Details	Cause and Effect	Word Structure/Endings
Compare and Contrast	Draw Conclusions	Word Structure/Suffixes
Fact and Opinion	Graphic Sources	Context Clues/Unfamiliar Words
Sequence	Fact and Opinion	Context Clues/Homographs
Draw Conclusions	Plot	Word Structure/Endings
Generalize	Author's Purpose	Context Clues/Unfamiliar Words
Graphic Sources	Main Idea and Details	Context Clues/Synonyms
Generalize	Cause and Effect	Context Clues/Unfamiliar Words
Draw Conclusions	Compare and Contrast	Word Structure/Suffixes
Character and Plot	Cause and Effect	Word Structure/Greek and Latin Roots
Graphic Sources	Cause and Effect	Dictionary/Glossary/Unfamiliar Words
Author's Purpose	Sequence	Context Clues /Multiple Meanings
Cause and Effect	Character and Plot	Context Clues/Unfamiliar Words
Generalize	Fact and Opinion	Word Structure/Prefixes
Draw Conclusions	Main Idea and Details	Dictionary/Glossary/Unfamiliar Words
Main Idea and Details	Generalize	Word Structure/Endings
Character and Plot	Author's Purpose	Homographs/Context Clues
Cause and Effect	Author's Purpose	Context Clues/Homonyms
Theme and Setting	Draw Conclusions	Dictionary/Glossary/Unfamiliar Words

Matching Books & Readers

Leveled Readers Skills Chart Continued

Grade 5 Title	Level*	DRA Level	Genre	Comprehension Strategy
The Journey of African American Athletes	V	50	Biography	Questioning
The Land of Opportunity	V	50	Narrative Nonfiction	Summarize
Our Essential Oceans	V	50	Expository Nonfiction	Visualize
The Golden Journey	V	50	Historical Fiction	Story Structure
Stop That Train!	V	50	Narrative Nonfiction	Predict and Set Purpose
Grandma Betty's Banjo	V	50	Realistic Fiction	Background Knowledge
The Most Dangerous Woman in America	W	60	Nonfiction	Inferring
Moving to Mali	W	60	Realistic Fiction	Story Structure
The Talker	W	60	Nonfiction	Questioning
The National Guard: Today's Minutemen	W	60	Expository Nonfiction	Background Knowledge
Philo and His Invention	W	60	Nonfiction	Summarize
Art's Inspiration	W	60	Expository Nonfiction	Visualize
What's New With Dinosaur Fossils?	W	60	Expository Nonfiction	Predict and Set Purpose
The Blues Evolution	X	60	Narrative Nonfiction	Text Structure
Special Effects in Hollywood	X	60	Expository Nonfiction	Important Ideas
Cheaper, Faster, and Better	X	60	Expository Nonfiction	Questioning
Operation Inspiration	X	60	Realistic Fiction	Predict and Set Purpose
Can Humans Make a Home in Outer Space?	X	60	Expository Nonfiction	Important Ideas
Nathaniel Comes to Town	X	60	Realistic Fiction	Story Structure
What Makes Great Athletes?	X	60	Expository Nonfiction	Visualize
The Sandwich Brigade	X	60	Realistic Fiction	Background Knowledge
Space Travel Inventions	X	60	Expository Nonfiction	Inferring
Astronauts and Cosmonauts	Y	60	Expository Nonfiction	Monitor and Clarify
The Shaping of the Continents	Y	60	Expository Nonfiction	Summarize
From Territory to Statehood	Y	60	Expository Nonfiction	Questioning
How the Wolves Saved Yellowstone	Y	60	Expository Nonfiction	Important Ideas
Mixed-Up Vegetables	Y	60	Expository Nonfiction	Text Structure
Precious Goods: From Salt to Silk	Y	60	Expository Nonfiction	Story Structure
Traveling by Plane	Y	60	Narrative Nonfiction	Predict and Set Purpose
Unexpected Music	Y	60	Expository Nonfiction	Background Knowledge

* Suggested Guided Reading Level. Use your knowledge of students' abilities to adjust levels as needed.

" You know the theory behind leveled books: they let you match books with the interest and instructional levels of your students. You can find the right reader for every student with this chart. "

Target Comprehension Skill	Additional Comprehension Instruction	Vocabulary
Fact and Opinion	Fact and Opinion	Context Clues/Antonyms
Cause and Effect	Generalize	Context Clues/Multiple Meanings
Compare and Contrast	Author's Purpose	Unfamiliar Words/Context Clues
Compare and Contrast	Character	Word Structure/Suffixes
Fact and Opinion	Generalize	Context Clues/Unfamiliar Words
Sequence	Compare and Contrast	Context Clues/Homographs
Sequence	Graphic Sources	Dictionary/Glossary/Unfamiliar Words
Compare and Contrast	Character and Setting	Word Structure/Greek and Latin Roots
Fact and Opinion	Main Idea and Details	Context Clues/Unfamiliar Words
Author's Purpose	Main Idea and Details	Word Structure/Endings
Sequence	Generalize	Context Clues/Multiple Meanings
Main Idea and Details	Draw Conclusions	Word Structure/Greek and Latin Roots
Fact and Opinion	Draw Conclusions	Context Clues/Homonyms
Main Idea and Details	Cause and Effect	Context Clues/Antonyms
Graphic Sources	Sequence	Word Structure/Prefixes
Draw Conclusions	Cause and Effect	Word Structure/Endings
Generalize	Compare and Contrast	Context Clues/Unfamiliar Words
Graphic Sources	Main Idea and Details	Context Clues/Synonyms
Generalize	Theme and Plot	Context Clues/Unfamiliar Words
Draw Conclusions	Sequence	Word Structure/Suffixes
Character and Plot	Theme	Word Structure/Greek and Latin Roots
Graphic Sources	Generalize	Dictionary/Glossary/Unfamiliar Words
Author's Purpose	Compare and Contrast	Context Clues/Multiple Meanings
Cause and Effect	Graphic Sources	Context Clues/Unfamiliar Words
Generalize	Sequence	Word Structure/Prefixes
Draw Conclusions	Author's Purpose	Dictionary/Glossary/Unfamiliar Words
Main Idea and Details	Compare and Contrast	Word Structure Endings
Compare and Contrast	Draw Conclusions	Word Structure/Suffixes
Fact and Opinion	Setting	Context Clues/Unfamiliar Words
Sequence	Draw Conclusions	Context Clues/Homographs

Matching Books & Readers

What Good Readers Do

You can use the characteristics and behaviors of good readers to help all your students read better. But what are these characteristics and behaviors? And how can you use them to foster good reading behaviors for all your students? Here are some helpful tips.

Good Readers enjoy reading! They have favorite books, authors, and genres. Good readers often have a preference about where and when they read. They talk about books and recommend their favorites.

Develop this behavior by giving students opportunities to respond in different ways to what they read. Get them talking about what they read, and why they like or dislike it.

This behavior is important because book sharing alerts you to students who are somewhat passive about reading or have limited literacy experiences. Book sharing also helps you when you select books for the class.

Good Readers select books they can read.

Develop this behavior by providing a range of three or four texts appropriate for the student and then letting the student choose.

This behavior is important because students gain control over reading when they can choose from books they can read. This helps them become more independent in the classroom.

Good Readers read independently for longer periods of time.

Develop this behavior by taking note of the level of support students need during guided reading. Use this information to gauge independent reading time accordingly.

This behavior is important because students become better readers when they spend time reading many texts at their independent level.

Good Readers use text features to help them preview and set purposes.

Develop this behavior by having students use the title and illustrations in fiction texts or the title, contents, headings, and other graphic features in nonfiction texts to make predictions about what they will be reading.

This behavior is important because previewing actually makes reading easier! Looking at features and sampling the text enables readers to predict and set expectations for reading.

66 **Want to improve student performance by fostering good reading behaviors? Customize Literacy can help.** 99

Good Readers predict and ask questions before and while they read.

Develop this behavior by asking questions. After reading a passage, ask students what they think will happen next in a fiction text. Have them ask a question they think will be answered in a nonfiction text and read on to see if it is.

This behavior is important because when students predict and ask questions as they read, they are engaged. They have a purpose for reading and a basis for monitoring their comprehension.

Good Readers read meaningful phrases aloud with appropriate expression.

Develop this behavior by giving students lots of opportunities to read orally. As they read, note students' phrasing, intonation, and attention to punctuation and give help as needed.

This behavior is important because reading fluently in longer, meaningful phrases supports comprehension and ease in reading longer, more complex texts.

Good Readers read aloud at an appropriate reading rate with a high percent of accuracy.

Develop this behavior by timing students' oral reading to calculate their reading rates. You can also record students' miscues to determine a percent of accuracy. This will help identify problems.

This behavior is important because when students read fluently texts that are "just right," they find reading more enjoyable. A fluent reader is able to focus more on constructing meaning and is more likely to develop a positive attitude toward reading.

Matching Books & Readers

Good Readers use effective strategies and sources of information to figure out unknown words.

Develop this behavior by teaching specific strategies for figuring out unknown words, such as sounding out clusters of letters, using context, reading on, and using references.

This behavior is important because when readers have a variety of strategies to use, they are more able to decode and self-correct quickly. Readers who do these things view themselves as good readers.

CH-
QU-
ST-

Good Readers construct meaning as they read and then share or demonstrate their understanding.

Develop this behavior by having students retell what they read or write a summary of what they read in their own words.

This behavior is important because the ability to retell or write a summary is essential for success in reading. It shows how well a student has constructed meaning.

Good Readers locate and use what is explicitly stated in a text.

Develop this behavior by asking questions that require students to go back into the text to find explicitly stated information.

This behavior is important because the ability to recall, locate, and use specific information stated in a text enables readers to respond to literal questions as well as support opinions and justify their responses.

Good Readers make connections.

Develop this behavior by asking questions to help students make connections: *What does this remind you of? Have you ever read or experienced anything like this?*

This behavior is important because making connections helps readers understand and appreciate a text. Making connections to self, the world, and other texts supports higher-level thinking.

Good Readers interpret what they read by making inferences.

Develop this behavior by asking questions to help students tell or write about what they think was implied in the text: *Why do you think that happened? What helped you come to that conclusion?*

This behavior is important because the ability to go beyond the literal meaning of a text enables readers to gain a deeper understanding. When students make inferences, they use background knowledge, their personal knowledge, and the text to grasp the meaning of what is implied by the author.

Good Readers determine importance and evaluate what they read.

Develop this behavior by always having students identify what they think is the most important message, event, or information in a text.

This behavior is important because readers must be able to sort out important from interesting information. The ability to establish and/or use criteria and provide support when making judgments is an important critical thinking skill.

Good Readers support their responses using information from a text and/or their own background knowledge.

Develop this behavior by always asking students to give the reason(s) they identified an event, message, or idea as most important.

This behavior is important because the ability to justify one's response is important for all learners. It enables others to know the basis for a decision and provides an opening for further discussion.

Conversation Starters

Asking Good Questions When students read interesting and thought-provoking books, they want to share! You can encourage students to think critically about what they read. Use questions such as the following to assess comprehension as well as evoke good class/group discussions.

Author's Purpose

- Why did the author write this piece?

- How does figuring out the author's purpose help you decide how to read the text?

Compare and Contrast

- What clue words show the author is comparing and/or contrasting in this article?

- How are the fictional characters and events in this story like and/or different from real people and events you know of?

Fact and Opinion

- What clue word or words signal that this is a statement of opinion?

- How could this statement of fact be proved true or false?

Cause and Effect

- Why did these events happen? How might they have been different if the causes had been different?

- Are there several causes that result in a single effect?

- Is there a single cause that has several effects?

Draw Conclusions

- Based on what you have read, seen, or experienced, what can you conclude about this event in the selection?

- This story seems to be a fantasy. Why might you conclude this?

- What words help you draw conclusions about the relationship between the characters?

Generalize

- What generalization can you make about the story or the characters in it? What examples lead to that generalization?

- What details, facts, and logic does the author use to support this generalization?

- Is this a valid or a faulty generalization? Explain your ideas.

Graphic Sources

- How does the author use graphic sources (chart, maps, illustrations, time lines, and so on) to support ideas and opinions?

- This selection has many graphic sources. Which one or ones best help you understand the events or ideas in the selection? Why?

Literary Elements: Character, Setting, Plot, Theme

- Describe the main character at the beginning of the story and at the end of the story. How and why does this change take place?

- How is the setting important to the story? How might the story be different if its time or its place were different?

- What does the main character want at the beginning of the story? How does the main character go about trying to achieve this?

- A plot has a conflict, but the conflict isn't always between two characters. What is the conflict in this story? How is it resolved?

- In a few sentences, what is the plot of the story?

- What is the theme of the story? Use details from the story to support your statement.

Main Idea and Details

- What is the main idea of this paragraph or article? What are some details?

- The author makes this particular statement in the article. What details does the author provide to support that statement?

Sequence

- How is the sequence of events important in the text?

- Is the order of events important in this story? Why or why not?

- Based on what has already happened, what will most likely happen next?

Connecting Science and Social Studies

Scott Foresman Reading Street Leveled Readers are perfect for covering, supporting, or enriching science and social studies content. Using these books ensures that all students can access important concepts.

Grade 5 Leveled Readers

Science

Earth and Space Science

Nonfiction Books

- *Aim High: Astronaut Training*
- *Astronauts and Cosmonauts*
- *Can Humans Make a Home in Outer Space?*
- *Cheaper, Faster, and Better*
- *Dangerous Storms*
- *Explore with Science*
- *The Inside Story of Earth*
- *Sailing the Stars*
- *The Shaping of the Continents*
- *Space Travel Inventions*
- *Storm Chasing Challenges*
- *Traveling by Plane*
- *Weather Forecasting*

Fiction Books

- *The Journey Through the Earth*
- *The Signs*

Life Science

Nonfiction Books

- *Changing for Survival: Bird Adaptations*
- *Driven to Change*
- *How the Wolves Saved Yellowstone*
- *The Kudzu Invasion*
- *Mixed-Up Vegetables*
- *Our Essential Oceans*
- *Paleontology: Digging for Dinosaurs and More*
- *Sea Life*
- *Searching for Dinosaurs*
- *Surviving the Elements: Animals and Their Environments*
- *What's New with Dinosaur Fossils?*

Fiction Books

- *The Long Trip Home*
- *Toby's California Vacation*

Physical Science

Nonfiction Books

- *George Ferris's Wheel*
- *The Magic of Makeup: Going Behind the Mask*
- *Philo and His Invention*
- *The Search to Build a Perpetual Motion Machine*

Fiction Books

- *A Happy Accident*
- *Jenna and the High Dive*

Grade 5 Leveled Readers

Social Studies

Citizenship

Nonfiction Books

- Helping Others
- The National Guard: Today's Minutemen
- The New Kid at School

Fiction Books

- Bill Lucks Out
- Giant Pumpkin on the Loose
- The Sandwich Brigade

Culture

Nonfiction Books

- Art's Inspiration
- China: Today and Yesterday
- Computers in Filmmaking: Very Special Effects
- The Root of the Blues
- Special Effects in Hollywood
- Strange Sports with Weird Gear
- The Talker
- Unexpected Music
- A Visit to the Navajo Nation

Fiction Books

- Abuela's Gift
- Grandma Betty's Banjo
- The Medicine Harvest
- Moving
- Moving to Mali

Culture

- Nathaniel Comes to Town
- Operation Inspiration
- Our Village
- Playing the Game

Economics

Nonfiction Books

- Ancient Gold from the Ancient World
- The Oceans' Treasures
- Precious Goods: From Salt to Silk

History

Nonfiction Books

- The Blues Evolution
- The California Gold Rush
- The Flight Over the Ocean: Yesterday and Today
- From Territory to Statehood
- The Golden Spike
- The Italian Renaissance and Its Artists
- Jazz, Jazz, Jazz
- The Land of Opportunity
- Let the Games Begin: History of the Olympics
- The Most Dangerous Woman in America

History

- Paul Revere and the American Revolutionary War
- Paul Revere's Ride
- A Railroad Over the Sierra
- Rube Foster and the Chicago American Giants
- Saving an American Symbol
- A Spy in Disguise
- Stop That Train!
- Titanic: The "Unsinkable" Ship
- The United States Moves West
- What Makes Great Athletes?

Fiction Books

- From Slave to Soldier
- The Golden Journey
- Journey to the New World
- The Land of Plenty

More Great Titles

Biography

- Blues Legends
- The Designs of Da Vinci
- Famous Women in Sports
- The Journey of African American Athletes
- Wilma Rudolph: Running to Win

Connecting Science and Social Studies

Need more choices? Look back to Grade 4.

Grade 4 Leveled Readers

Science

Earth and Space Science

Nonfiction Books
- *Danger: The World Is Getting Hot!*
- *Darkness Into Light*
- *Day for Night*
- *Earth's Closest Neighbor*
- *Let's Explore Antarctica!*
- *Looking For Changes*
- *The Mysteries of Space*
- *One Giant Leap*
- *Orbiting the Sun*
- *Putting a Stop to Wildfires*
- *Severe Weather: Storms*
- *Storm Chasers*
- *Wondrously Wild Weather*

Fiction Books
- *Exploring the Moon*
- *Flash Flood*
- *Life on Mars: The Real Story*
- *Stuart's Moon Suit*
- *Surviving Hurricane Andrew*
- *To the Moon!*

Life Science

Nonfiction Books
- *Birds Take Flight*
- *Come Learn About Dolphins*
- *Dolphins: Mammals of the Sea*
- *Florida Everglades: Its Plants and Animals*
- *The Gray Whale*
- *How Does Echolocation Work?*
- *Migration Relocation*
- *Mini Microbes*
- *Mysterious Monsters*
- *Plants and Animals in Antarctica*
- *Saving Trees Using Science*
- *Sharing Our Planet*
- *What in the World Is That?*

Life Science

Fiction Books
- *The Missing Iguana Mystery*
- *Protecting Wild Animals*
- *The Salamander Stumper*
- *Top Hat Tompkins, the Detective*

Grade 4 Leveled Readers

Social Studies

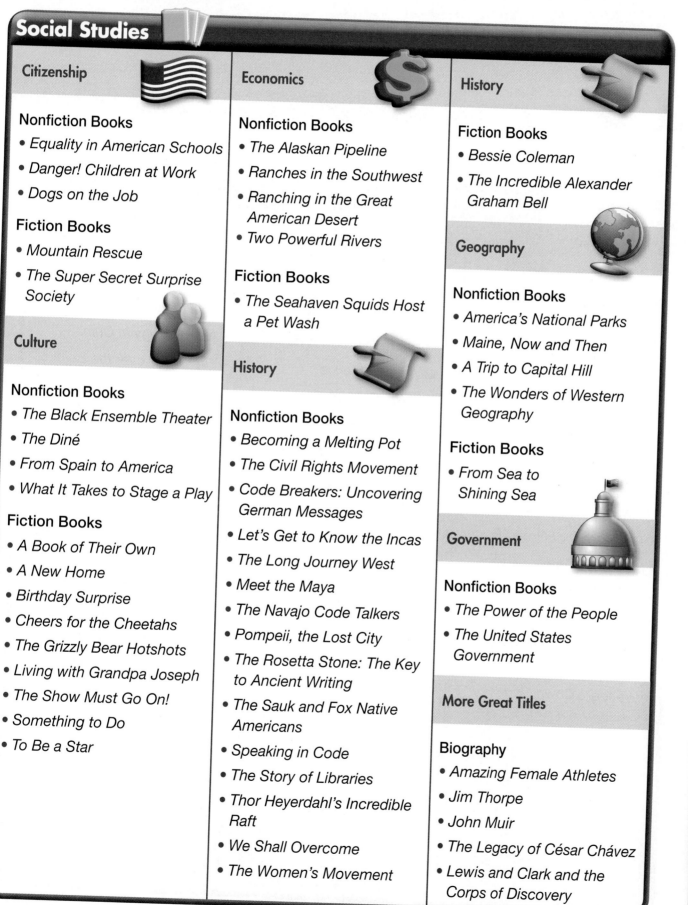

Citizenship

Nonfiction Books
- *Equality in American Schools*
- *Danger! Children at Work*
- *Dogs on the Job*

Fiction Books
- *Mountain Rescue*
- *The Super Secret Surprise Society*

Culture

Nonfiction Books
- *The Black Ensemble Theater*
- *The Diné*
- *From Spain to America*
- *What It Takes to Stage a Play*

Fiction Books
- *A Book of Their Own*
- *A New Home*
- *Birthday Surprise*
- *Cheers for the Cheetahs*
- *The Grizzly Bear Hotshots*
- *Living with Grandpa Joseph*
- *The Show Must Go On!*
- *Something to Do*
- *To Be a Star*

Economics

Nonfiction Books
- *The Alaskan Pipeline*
- *Ranches in the Southwest*
- *Ranching in the Great American Desert*
- *Two Powerful Rivers*

Fiction Books
- *The Seahaven Squids Host a Pet Wash*

History

Nonfiction Books
- *Becoming a Melting Pot*
- *The Civil Rights Movement*
- *Code Breakers: Uncovering German Messages*
- *Let's Get to Know the Incas*
- *The Long Journey West*
- *Meet the Maya*
- *The Navajo Code Talkers*
- *Pompeii, the Lost City*
- *The Rosetta Stone: The Key to Ancient Writing*
- *The Sauk and Fox Native Americans*
- *Speaking in Code*
- *The Story of Libraries*
- *Thor Heyerdahl's Incredible Raft*
- *We Shall Overcome*
- *The Women's Movement*

History

Fiction Books
- *Bessie Coleman*
- *The Incredible Alexander Graham Bell*

Geography

Nonfiction Books
- *America's National Parks*
- *Maine, Now and Then*
- *A Trip to Capital Hill*
- *The Wonders of Western Geography*

Fiction Books
- *From Sea to Shining Sea*

Government

Nonfiction Books
- *The Power of the People*
- *The United States Government*

More Great Titles

Biography
- *Amazing Female Athletes*
- *Jim Thorpe*
- *John Muir*
- *The Legacy of César Chávez*
- *Lewis and Clark and the Corps of Discovery*

Connecting Science and Social Studies

Need more choices? Look ahead to Grade 6.

Grade 6 Leveled Readers

Science

Earth and Space Science

Nonfiction Books

- *Earth and Its Place in Space*
- *Electricity*
- *Elements in Our Universe*
- *Exploring Mars*
- *Exploring the World Below*
- *Global Warming*
- *The Hidden Worlds of Caves*
- *The History of Green Power*
- *It's About Time!*
- *Living Greener*
- *Riches from Our Earth*
- *Swimming Safely in the Ocean*
- *Wonders Down Under*

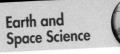

Earth and Space Science

Fiction Books

- *The Domes on Mars*
- *Moon Kids, Earth Kids*
- *Moonman Markie*
- *The Rip Current Rescue*
- *Rock Canyon Challenge*
- *Sea's Visit: A Tale From Nigeria*
- *Tom Rides Out the Quake*

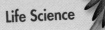

Life Science

Nonfiction Books

- *Animals of the Arctic*
- *Archaeology in China*
- *The Battle over the Rain Forests*
- *A Biome of the World: The Taiga*
- *The Debate over Zoos: Captive or Free?*
- *Ecosystems of Rain Forests*
- *Faithful Four-Footed Friends*
- *The Great Apes*
- *Life in the Arctic Circle*
- *Speaking for Wolves*
- *The Price of Knowledge: The Interaction of Animals and Scientists*
- *Saving Feathered Friends*

Fiction Books

- *Egg Watching*
- *Twilight of the Wolves*
- *The Very Special Gift*

Grade 6 Leveled Readers

Social Studies

Citizenship

Fiction Books

• The Best Community Service Project Ever

Culture

Nonfiction Books

• Armchair Archaeology
• Cuban Americans
• From China to America: My Story
• Living and Growing in China
• Tribes of the Amazon Rain Forest
• Viva America! Cubans in the United States

Fiction Books

• Adams's Hippo Lesson
• Chess Is for Fun
• How Anansi Captured the Story of the Rain
• Jeff and Jack
• Jenna the Scatterbrain
• Lady Red Rose and the Woods
• Monkey Tales
• Our New Life in the Big City
• Pedro's Flute
• Sally's Summer with Her Grandparents
• A Small-Town Summer
• When Julie Got Lost

History

Nonfiction Books

• Ancient Greece, Modern Culture
• Ancient Life Along the Nile
• The Aztec Empire
• The Chinese Struggle to America: An Immigration History
• Colonization and Native Peoples
• Defying Death and Time: Mummies
• Discovering Classical Athens
• The Freedoms of Speech and Assembly in the United States
• Greetings from the Four Corners!
• How Did Ancient Greece Become So Great?
• Immigrants of Yesterday and Today
• A Migrant Music: Jazz
• The Movements of Citizens
• Pulling Down the Walls: The Struggle of African American Performers
• The Race to the Bottom of the World
• Restless Humanity
• Robert Abbott's Dream: The Chicago Defender and the Great Migration
• The Secrets of the Past
• Spanish Conquests of the Americas
• The Struggle for Higher Education

History

• Uncovering the Secrets of Ancient Egypt

Fiction Books

• The Doaks of Montana
• From Youngsters to Old Timers
• Grizzled Bill's New Life
• Lucky Chuck and His Least Favorite Cousin
• The Noble Boy and the Brick Maker
• Sir Tom
• Sleepyville Wakes Up
• Timmy Finds His Home

Geography

Nonfiction Books

• The Mining Debate
• Mystery of the Ancient Pueblo
• The Quests for Gold

Fiction Books

• The Adventures in Matunaland

More Great Titles

Biography

• 20th Century African American Singers
• From Oscar Micheaux to the Oscars
• Inventors at Work

Planning Teacher Study Groups

Adventurous teachers often have good ideas for lessons. A teacher study group is a great way to share ideas and get feedback on the best way to connect content and students. Working with other teachers can provide you with the support and motivation you need to implement new teaching strategies. A teacher study group offers many opportunities to collaborate, support each other's work, share insights, and get feedback.

Think About It

A weekly or monthly teacher study group can help support you in developing your expertise in the classroom. You and a group of like-minded teachers can form your own study group. What can this group accomplish?

- Read and discuss professional articles by researchers in the field of education.

- Meet to share teaching tips, collaborate on multi-grade lessons, and share resources.

- Develop lessons to try out new teaching strategies. Meet to share experiences and discuss how to further improve your teaching approach.

Let's Meet!

Forming a study group is easy. Just follow these four steps:

1. **Decide on the size of the group.** A small group has the advantage of making each member feel accountable, but make sure that all people have the ability to make the same commitment!

2. **Choose teachers to invite to join your group.** Think about who you want to invite. Should they all teach the same grade? Can you invite teachers from other schools? Remember that the more diverse the group, the more it benefits from new perspectives.

3. **Set goals for the group.** In order to succeed, know what you want the group to do. Meet to set goals. Rank goals in order of importance and refer often to the goals to keep the group on track.

4. **Make logistical decisions.** This is often the most difficult. Decide where and when you will meet. Consider an online meeting place where group members can post discussion questions and replies if people are not able to meet.

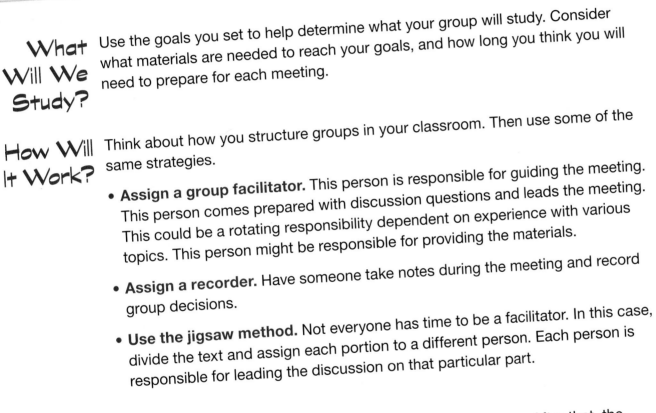

What Will We Study? Use the goals you set to help determine what your group will study. Consider what materials are needed to reach your goals, and how long you think you will need to prepare for each meeting.

How Will It Work? Think about how you structure groups in your classroom. Then use some of the same strategies.

- **Assign a group facilitator.** This person is responsible for guiding the meeting. This person comes prepared with discussion questions and leads the meeting. This could be a rotating responsibility dependent on experience with various topics. This person might be responsible for providing the materials.

- **Assign a recorder.** Have someone take notes during the meeting and record group decisions.

- **Use the jigsaw method.** Not everyone has time to be a facilitator. In this case, divide the text and assign each portion to a different person. Each person is responsible for leading the discussion on that particular part.

Meet Again Make a commitment to meet for a minimum number of times. After that, the group can reevaluate and decide whether or not to continue.

Have some great teaching tips to share? Want to exchange ideas with your colleagues? Build your own professional community of teachers. **Customize Literacy** *gets you started.*

Building Community

Trial Lessons

Use your colleagues' experiences to help as you think about new ways to connect content and students. Use the following plan to create a mini-lesson. It should last twenty minutes. Get the support of your colleagues as you try something new and then reflect on what happened.

Be Creative!

As you develop a plan for a mini-lesson, use these four words to guide planning: *purpose*, *text*, *resources*, and *routine*.

- **Purpose:** Decide on a skill or strategy to teach. Define your purpose for teaching the lesson.

- **Text:** Develop a list of the materials you could use. Ask your colleagues for suggestions.

- **Resources:** Make a list of the available resources, and consider how to use those resources most effectively. Consider using the leveled readers listed on pages CL24–CL29 and CL36–CL41 of Customize Literacy.

- **Routine:** Choose an instructional routine to structure your mini-lesson. See the mini-lessons in Customize Literacy for suggestions.

Try It!

Try out your lesson! Consider audio- or videotaping the lesson for later review. You may wish to invite a colleague to sit in as you teach. Make notes on how the lesson went.

How Did It Go?

Use the self-evaluation checklist on page CL45 as you reflect on your trial lesson. This provides a framework for later discussion.

Discuss, Reflect, Repeat

Solicit feedback from your teacher study group. Explain the lesson and share your reflections. Ask for suggestions on ways to improve the lesson. Take some time to reflect on the feedback. Modify your lesson to reflect what you have learned. Then try teaching the lesson again.

Checklist for Teacher Self-Evaluation

How Well Did I ...

	Very Well	Satisfactory	Not Very Well
Plan the lesson?			
Select the appropriate level of text?			
Introduce the lesson and explain its objectives?			
Review previously taught skills?			
Directly explain the new skills being taught?			
Model the new skills?			
Break the material down into small steps?			
Integrate guided practice into the lesson?			
Monitor guided practice for student understanding?			
Provide feedback on independent practice?			
Maintain an appropriate pace?			
Assess student understanding of the material?			
Stress the importance of applying the skill as they read?			
Maintain students' interest?			
Ask questions?			
Handle student questions and responses?			
Respond to the range of abilities?			

Building Community

Books for Teachers

Students aren't the only ones who need to read to grow. Here is a brief list of books that you may find useful to fill your reading teacher basket and learn new things.

A Professional Bibliography

Afflerbach, P. "Teaching Reading Self-Assessment Strategies." *Comprehension Instruction: Research-Based Best Practices.* The Guilford Press, 2002.

Bear, D. R., M. Invernizzi, S. Templeton, and F. Johnston. *Words Their Way.* Merrill Prentice Hall, 2004.

Beck, I. L. and M. G. McKeown. *Improving Comprehension with Questioning the Author: A Fresh and Expanded View of a Powerful Approach.* Scholastic, 2006.

Beck, I., M. G. McKeown, and L. Kucan. *Bringing Words to Life: Robust Vocabulary Instruction.* The Guilford Press, 2002.

Blachowicz, C. and P. Fisher. "Vocabulary Instruction." *Handbook of Reading Research,* vol. III. Lawrence Erlbaum Associates, 2000.

Blachowicz, C. and D. Ogle. *Reading Comprehension: Strategies for Independent Learners.* The Guilford Press, 2008.

Block, C. C. and M. Pressley. "Best Practices in Comprehension Instruction." *Best Practices in Literacy Instruction.* The Guilford Press, 2003.

Daniels, H. *Literature Circles.* 2nd ed. Stenhouse Publishers, 2002.

Dickson, S. V., D. C. Simmons, and E. J. Kame'enui. "Text Organization: Instructional and Curricular Basics and Implications." *What Reading Research Tells Us About Children with Diverse Learning Needs: Bases and Basics.* Lawrence Erlbaum Associates, 1998.

Diller, D. *Making the Most of Small Groups: Differentiation for All.* Stenhouse Publishers, 2007.

Duke, N. and P. D. Pearson. "Effective Practices for Developing Reading Comprehension." *What Research Has to Say About Reading Instruction,* 3rd ed. Newark, DE: International Reading Association, 2002.

Fillmore, L. W. and C. E. Snow. *What Teachers Need to Know About Language.* Office of Educational Research and Improvement, U.S. Department of Education, 2000.

Fountas, I. C. and G. S. Pinnell. *Guiding Readers and Writers Grades 3–6: Teaching Comprehension, Genre, and Content Literacy.* Heinemann, 2001.

Guthrie, J. and E. Anderson. "Engagement in Reading: Processes of Motivated Strategic, Knowledgeable, Social Readers." *Engaged Reading: Processes, Practices, and Policy Implications.* Teachers College Press, 1999.

Harvey, S. and A. Goudvis. *Strategies That Work: Teaching Comprehension to Enhance Understanding.* 2nd ed. Stenhouse Publishers, 2007.

Keene, E. O. and S. Zimmerman. *Mosaic of Thought.* 2nd ed. Heinemann, 2007.

Leu Jr., D. J. "The New Literacies: Research on Reading Instruction with the Internet and Other Digital Technologies." *What Research Has to Say About Reading Instruction,* 3rd ed. International Reading Association, 2002.

McKeown, M. G. and I. L. Beck. "Direct and Rich Vocabulary Instruction." *Vocabulary Instruction: Research to Practice.* The Guilford Press, 2004.

McTighe, J. and K. O'Conner. "Seven Practices for Effective Learning." *Educational Leadership,* vol. 63, no. 3 (November 2005).

Nagy, W. E. *Teaching Vocabulary to Improve Reading Comprehension.* International Reading Association, 1998.

National Reading Panel. *Teaching Children to Read.* National Institute of Child Health and Human Development, 1999.

Ogle, D. and C. Blachowicz. "Beyond Literature Circles: Helping Students Comprehend Information Texts." *Comprehension Instruction: Research-Based Practices.* The Guilford Press, 2001.

Pressley, M. *Reading Instruction That Works: The Case for Balanced Teaching,* 3rd ed. The Guilford Press, 2005.

Stahl, S. A. "What Do We Know About Fluency?" *The Voice of Evidence in Reading Research.* Paul H. Brookes, 2004.

Taylor, B. M., P. D. Pearson, D. S. Peterson, and M. C. Rodriguez. "The CIERA School Change Framework: An Evidence-Based Approach to Professional Development and School Reading Improvement." *Reading Research Quarterly,* vol. 40, no. 1 (January/February/March 2005).

Valencia, S. W. and M. Y. Lipson. "Thematic Instruction: A Quest for Challenging Ideas and Meaningful Learning." *Literature-Based Instruction: Reshaping the Curriculum.* Christopher-Gordon Publishers, 1998.

Building Community

Perpetual Motion Machine

Amazing Words Oral Vocabulary Routine

DAY 1

theory

1. **Introduce** A *theory* is an explanation based on observation and reasoning.
2. **Demonstrate** It is my *theory* that people feel better after helping others.
3. **Apply** Have students share a *theory* about something they've observed.

DAY 2

vehicle

1. **Introduce** A *vehicle* is a device for carrying people or things.
2. **Demonstrate** A ship is a type of ocean *vehicle.*
3. **Apply** Ask students to identify other kinds of *vehicles* and the purpose of each.

enterprise

1. **Introduce** An *enterprise* is an important, difficult, or dangerous plan to be tried.
2. **Demonstrate** A trip into the desert is a daring *enterprise.*
3. **Apply** Have students identify which is an *enterprise:* a trip to the zoo or a trek through the Amazon.

DAY 3

design

1. **Introduce** A *design* is a sketch, drawing, or plan that serves as a pattern from which to work.
2. **Demonstrate** The *design* showed how to build the machine. The architect completed the *design* for the new house.
3. **Apply** Have students talk about when it's important to have a *design.*

DAY 4

entrepreneur

1. **Introduce** An *entrepreneur* is someone who organizes and manages a business.
2. **Demonstrate** An *entrepreneur* opened two new coffee shops and a bookstore in our town.
3. **Apply** Ask students to discuss the type of business they would open if they were *entrepreneurs.*

Leonardo's Horse

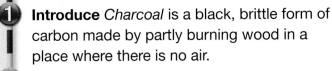 **Amazing Words** Oral Vocabulary Routine

DAY 1

charcoal

1 **Introduce** *Charcoal* is a black, brittle form of carbon made by partly burning wood in a place where there is no air.

2 **Demonstrate** We use *charcoal* when we cook on the grill.

3 **Apply** Have students discuss other uses for *charcoal* besides grilling outdoors.

canvas

1 **Introduce** *Canvas* is a strong, heavy cloth made from cotton and used for making tents, sails, and artists' paintings.

2 **Demonstrate** The beautiful *canvas* was hanging in the art museum.

3 **Apply** Discuss with students famous paintings they have seen that are painted on *canvas*.

DAY 2

marble

1 **Introduce** *Marble* is a hard rock formed from limestone by heat and pressure. Marble comes from all over the world, and some of the fanciest comes from Italy.

2 **Demonstrate** The statue in Mrs. Jackson's garden is made from Italian *marble*.

3 **Apply** Have students talk about places where they've seen *marble* used in art or in building.

DAY 3

projector

1 **Introduce** A *projector* is a device used to project an image on a screen.

2 **Demonstrate** My teacher used a *projector* so the whole class could see the transparency.

3 **Apply** Have students brainstorm a list of things that might be shown on a *projector*.

DAY 4

muse

1 **Introduce** *Muse* means to think in a dreamy way.

2 **Demonstrate** I used to *muse* about being a player in the NFL.

3 **Apply** Have students share things that they *muse* about.

inspire

1 **Introduce** *Inspire* means to fill others with thoughts of hope.

2 **Demonstrate** I hope to *inspire* others with my speech about doing your best.

3 **Apply** Ask students how they might *inspire* people.

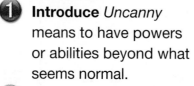
Waterhouse Hawkins

Amazing Words Oral Vocabulary Routine

DAY 1

fossils

1 Introduce *Fossils* are the hardened remains of things that lived in a former age.

2 Demonstrate The arch-aeologist found *fossils* of leaves during the excavation.

3 Apply Ask students what kinds of *fossils* they've heard about or found themselves.

uncanny

1 Introduce *Uncanny* means to have powers or abilities beyond what seems normal.

2 Demonstrate Dogs have an *uncanny* sense of smell.

3 Apply Discuss other examples of things that are *uncanny*.

sandstone

1 Introduce *Sandstone* is a kind of stone that is made mostly of sand.

2 Demonstrate As he walked along the beach, Zach picked up interesting pieces of *sandstone*.

3 Apply Discuss with students other types of stone that they have heard about or seen.

DAY 2

model

1 Introduce A *model* is a small copy of something.

2 Demonstrate Barack made a *model* of the White House for his history project.

3 Apply Have students identify a model of something in the classroom or school.

DAY 3

illustration

1 Introduce An *illustration* is a picture, diagram, or map used to explain or decorate something.

2 Demonstrate My science book has an *illustration* of how the heart works.

3 Apply Ask students what they would include if they were to make an *illustration* of the classroom, school, or neighborhood.

DAY 4

archaic

1 Introduce *Archaic* refers to something from an earlier time, out-of-date, or ancient.

2 Demonstrate Dinosaurs are *archaic* because they lived millions of years ago. Because technology changes so quickly, computers become *archaic* within a few years.

3 Apply Have students give examples of other things that are *archaic*.

UNIT 3

Acknowledgments

Acknowledgments

Text

Grateful acknowledgment is made to the following for copyrighted material:

26: From *Red Kayak* by Priscilla Cummings, copyright © 2004 by Priscilla Cummings Frece. Used by permission of Dutton Children's Books, A Division of Penguin Young Readers Group, A Member of Penguin Group (USA) Inc., 345 Hudson Street, New York, NY 10014. All rights reserved.

56: From *Thunder Rose*, Text Copyright © 2003 by Jerdine Nolen, illustrations copyright © 2003 by Kadir Nelson, reprinted by permission of Harcourt, Inc. This material may not be reproduced in any form or by any means without the prior written permission of the publisher.

78: *Measuring Tornadoes* (originally titled *Storm Chasers*) by Trudi Strain Trueit. Copyright © 2002 Franklin Watts, a Division of Scholastic, Inc. All rights reserved. Used by permission of Franklin Watts, an imprint of Scholastic Library Publishing, Inc.

88: From *Island of the Blue Dolphins* by Scott O'Dell. Copyright © 1960, renewed 1988 by Scott O'Dell. Reprinted by permission of Houghton Mifflin Company and McIntosh and Otis, Inc. All rights reserved.

104: "7 Survival Questions," by Buck Tilton. Used with permission of Buck Tilton and *Boys' Life*, April 2001, published by the Boy Scouts of America.

116: From *Satchel Paige* by Lesa Cline-Ransome, paintings by James E. Ransome. Text copyright © 2000 Lesa Cline-Ransome. Illustrations copyright © 2000 James E. Ransome. Reprinted with the permission of Simon & Schuster Books for Young Readers, an imprint of Simon & Schuster Children's Publishing Division.

146: From *Ten Mile Day: and the Building of the Transcontinental Railroad* written and illustrated by Mary Ann Fraser, 1993.

170: "The Microscope" by Maxine W. Kumin. Copyright © 1968 by Maxine W. Kumin. Used by permission of The Anderson Literary Agency Inc.

172: "Full Day" from *Come With Me: Poems For A Journey* by Naomi Shihab Nye. Text copyright © 2000 by Naomi Shihab Nye, Greenwillow Books. Used by permission of HarperCollins Publishers.

182: "At the Beach," from *Salsa Stories* by Lulu Delacre. Copyright © 2000 Lulu Delacre. Reprinted by permission of Scholastic, Inc.;

198: "The Eagle and the Bat" from *The Sound of Flutes and Other Indian Legends* by Richard Erdoes and illustrated by Paul Goble, copyright © 1976 by Richard Erdoes. Illustrations copyright © 1976 by Paul Goble. Used by permission of Random House Children's Books, a division of Random House, Inc.

208: "Hold the Flag High" by Catherine Clinton. Text copyright © 2005 by Catherine Clinton. Illustrated by Shane W. Evans. Illustrations copyright © 2005 by Shane W. Evans. Used by permission of HarperCollins Publishers.

236: "The Ch'i-lin Purse" from *The Ch'i-lin Purse* by Linda Fang. Copyright © 1963 by Linda Fang. Reprinted by permission of Farrar, Straus and Giroux, LLC.

490

264: Salina Bookshelf, Inc. *A Summer's Trade* by Deborah W. Trotter. Copyright © 2007 by Deborah W. Trotter. Illustrations copyright © 2007 by Irving Toddy. Used by permission of Salina Bookshelf, Inc. A note about *A Summer's Trade:* Native North American languages are spoken by about 380,000 Americans according to the 2000 census. The Navajo Nation has a population of nearly 300,000 with 178,000 speakers of the Navajo language making it the most widely spoken Native American language. The Navajo language is taught in colleges, high schools and elementary schools in the southwest. In 2008 the state of New Mexico became the first state to adopt a textbook: *Bizaad Bínáhoo'aah: Rediscovering the Navajo Language* that teaches a Native American language. The book is a model and inspiration for other threatened languages. Having young people see their language taken seriously and packaged as something valuable can have a very important impact on teaching the Navajo language to future generations of students. The Window Rock Immersion School (Diné bi Olta) in Ft. Defiance Arizona is one example of a school where Diné students learn to read, write and speak their Navajo language.

294: Illustrations from *The Midnight Ride of Paul Revere* by Henry Wadsworth Longfellow, graved and painted by Christopher Bing, © 2001 Christopher Bing. Reproduced with permission of the publisher, Handprint Books, Inc.

318: "For Peace Sake" by Cedric McClester, 1990. Reproduced with permission of the author. For more poems by Cedric McClester go to Poetry.com.

320: "Two People I Want to Be Like" from *If Only I Could Tell You* by Eve Merriam. Copyright © 1983 Eve Merriam. Used by permission of Marian Reiner.

321: "Strangers" from *Good Luck Gold and Other Poems* by Janet S. Wong. Copyright © 1994 by Janet S. Wong. Reprinted with the permission of Margaret K. McElderry Books, an imprint of Simon & Schuster Children's Publishing Division. All rights reserved.

360: *Leonardo's Horse* by Jean Fritz and illustrated by Hudson Talbott. Text Copyright © 2001 by Jean Fritz. Illustrations Copyright © 2001 Hudson Talbott. Published by arrangement with G. P. Putnam's Sons, a division of Penguin Young Readers Group, a member of Penguin Group (USA) Inc. All rights reserved.

394: From *The Dinosaurs of Waterhouse Hawkins* by Barbara Kerley Kelly, illustrated by Brian Selznick. Text copyright © 2001 by Barbara Kerley Kelly. Illustrations copyright © 2001 by Brian Selznick. Reprinted by permission of Scholastic, Inc.

416: "A Model Scientist" adapted from *OWL* Magazine, May 1996 OWL. Used by permission of Bayard Presse Canada Inc.

430: "Mahalia Jackson" from *The Blues Singers* by Julius Lester. © 2001 Julius Lester. Illustrated by Lisa Cohen. Reprinted by permission of Hyperion Books for Children.

442: From *Perfect Harmony: A Musical Journey With The Boys Choir of Harlem* by Charles Smith, Jr., Copyright © 2002 by Charles Smith, Jr. Reprinted by permission of Hyperion Books for Children. All rights reserved.

454: From *Special Effects in Film and Television* by Jake Hamilton. © 1998 Dorling Kindersley. Reprinted by permission.

468: Extract from *A Trick of the Eye* by Brian Sibley © Brian Sibley, 2000. Reproduced by permission of Sheil Land Associates Ltd.

474: "Chemistry 101" from *Carver: A Life In Poems* by Marilyn Nelson, 2001. Permission granted by Boyds Mills Press, Inc.

475: "The Bronze Horse" by Beverly McLoughland, *Cricket*, November 1990. Used by permission of the author.

476: "The Termites" from *Insectlopedia*, copyright © 1998 by Douglas Florian, reprinted by permission of Harcourt, Inc. This material may not be reproduced in any form or by any means without the prior written permission of the publisher.

Note: Every effort has been made to locate the copyright owner of material reproduced on this component. Omissions brought to our attention will be corrected in subsequent editions.

491

Acknowledgments

Illustrations

Cover: Greg Newbold, **EI2–EI25** Dan Santat; **26–39** Ron Mazellan; **56–58** Darryl Ligasan; **88–100** E.B. Lewis; **104–106** Maryjo Koch; **170–172** Greg Newbold; **182–194** Michael Steirnagle; **198** Amanda Hall; **236–249** Ed Young; **254** Chi Chung; **330–343** Gerardo Suzan; **416–420** Phil Wilson; **W2–W15** Dean MacAdam.

Photographs

Every effort has been made to secure permission and provide appropriate credit for photographic material. The publisher deeply regrets any omission and pledges to correct errors called to its attention in subsequent editions.

Unless otherwise acknowledged, all photographs are the property of Pearson Education, Inc.

Photo locators denoted as follows: Top (T), Center (C), Bottom (B), Left (L), Right (R), Background (Bkgd)

18 (C) ©Charles Marion Russell/Getty Images, ©Rob Howard/Corbis; **20** (BL) ©Bob Daemmrich/PhotoEdit, (B) ©Robert W. Ginn/PhotoEdit, (BC) ©i2i Images /Jupiter Images; **24** (T) ©Ian Edelstein/Alamy Images, (C) ©izmostock/Alamy Images, (C) ©Matthias Kulka/zefa/Corbis; **46** (B) Getty Images; **50** (B) ©Eric Nguyen/Corbis, (BL) ©Galen Rowell/Corbis, (BC) Jupiter Images; **54** (T) ©Dennis Kirkland/Jaynes Gallery/Alamy Images, (C) ©Mark & Audrey Gibson/PhotoLibrary Group, Ltd., (B) ©Tomas Van Houtryve/Corbis; **78** (Bkgd) ©International Stock Photography/Taxi/Getty Images; **79** (TL, CL) ©Jim Reed/Corbis; **82** (B) ©Ron Sanford/Corbis; **83** (CC) ©Brian Finke/Getty Images, (BR) ©Mischa Photo Ltd/Getty Images; **86** (B) ©Heather Angel/Natural Visions/Alamy Images, (C) ©Radius Images/Jupiter Images, (T) ©W. Perry Conway/Corbis; **110** (BL) ©Stefan Zaklin/epa/Corbis, (B) ©Dimitri Lundt/Corbis; **111** (BR) ©AP Photo; **114** (T) ©Bananastock /Jupiter Images, (B) ©Cut and Deal Ltd/Alamy, (C) ©Kim Karpeles/Alamy Images; **117** (TC) Legends Archive; **134** (TL) ©Focus On Sport/Getty Images, (T) ©Stockbyte; **135** (B) ©DK Images; **136** (TL) ©Bettmann/Corbis; **137** (BC) ©Focus On Sport/Getty Images; **140** (BC) ©AbleStock/Index Open, (B) Corbis; **141** (BR) ©AP Photo; **144** (C) ©allOver photography/Alamy Images, (B) ©Mike Goldwater/Alamy Images, (T) ©TMI/Alamy Images; **162** (BR) ©Carl & Ann Purcell/Corbis; **163** (TC) ©Scott T. Smith/Corbis; **164** (CR) ©Topham/The Image Works, Inc., (B) Corbis; **165** (CR) ©Huntington Library/SuperStock; **176** (B) ©David Young-Wolff/PhotoEdit, (BC) ©John Neubauer/PhotoEdit; **177** (BR) Tom Carter/PhotoEdit; **180** (C) ©ImageState/Alamy Images, (T) ©Michael Gilday/Alamy Images, (B) Jupiter Images; **181** ©Roland Seitre/Peter Arnold, Inc.; **202** (B) ©Duomo/Corbis, (BC) ©Joe Rosenthal/Corbis; **203** (BC) ©Transtock/Corbis; **206** (C) ©image100/Corbis, (T) ©Joan Comalat/PhotoLibrary Group, Ltd., (B) PhotoLibrary; **224** ©Walter B. McKenzie/Getty Images; 225 ©Corbis; **230** (B) ©Jim Cummins/Corbis, (BL) ©Louise Gubb/Corbis; **231** (TR) ©Dennis Hallinan/Jupiter Images; **234** (C) ©Jose Luis Pelaez Inc./Jupiter Images, (B) ©Mark & Audrey Gibson/PhotoLibrary Group, Ltd., (T) ©Misty Bedwell/Design Pics/Corbis; **258** (BL) ©SW Productions/Brand X/Corbis;

492

259 (BR) ©Moodboard Micro/Corbis; **262** (B) ©Christoph von Haussen/PhotoLibrary Group, Ltd., (T) ©Jean J. Trome Talbot/PhotoLibrary, (C) PhotoLibrary; **280** (BL) ©Mark Wilson/Pool/epa/Corbis, (B) ©Michael Newman/PhotoEdit; **281** (BR) ©Kevin Lamarque/Corbis; **290** (BR) ©Hans Neleman/Getty Images; **291** (TR, BR, BL) ©Hans Neleman/Getty Images; **292** (B) ©Jon Feingersh/Blend Images/Getty Images, (C) ©Jorgen Larsson/Nordic Photos/Getty Images, (T) ©Randy Faris /Jupiter Images; **318** (C) ©Images/Corbis; **320** (C) ©Images/Corbis; **322** (B) ©Brownie Harris/Corbis, (C) ©Richard Cummins/Corbis, ©The Gallery Collection/Corbis; **324** (BL) ©Rick Friedman/Corbis, (B) JLP/Jose Luis Pelaez/Corbis; **325** (BR) ©Bettmann/Corbis; **328** (T) ©David P. Hall/Corbis, (C) ©Randy Faris/Corbis, (B) Getty Images; **349** (B) ©Neil Guegan/Getty Images; **350** (B) Jupiter Images; **354** (B) ©Jeff Greenberg/PhotoEdit; **355** (TR) ©Bill Bachmann/Alamy Images, (CR) Mark Wilson/Getty Images; **358** (B) ©Gary Cralle/Getty Images, (C) ©ian nolan/Alamy Images, (T) ©Steve Chenn/Corbis; **360** (Bkgd) ©Randall Fung/Corbis; **388** (B) ©IIHS/AP Images; **389** (TR) ©Layne Kennedy/Corbis, (CR) De Agostini Picture Library/Getty Images; **392** (T) ©Joel Sartore/National Geographic/Getty Images, (C) ©Martin Poole/Getty Images, (B) ©Neil Beckerman/Getty Images; **417** (BR) ©Kevin Kelly; **424** (B) ©Chad Ehlers/Stock Connection/Jupiter Images, (BL) Tim Pannell/Corbis; **425** (BR) Catherine Karnow/Corbis; **428** (C) ©Alex Segre/Alamy Images, (B) ©Ian Shaw/Alamy Images, (T) Getty Images; **443** (TR) The Boys Choir of Harlem, Inc.; **448** (CL) ©Buddy Mays/Corbis, (BC) ©Image Source Limited, (B) ©Jeff Greenberg/Alamy Images; **452** (B) ©Kevin O'Hara/PhotoLibrary Group, Ltd., (C) ©Margaret O'Grady/PhotoLibrary Group, Ltd., (T) ©Martin Sundberg/Photolibrary; **454** (C) ©Jim Henson's Creature Shop/DK Images; **455** (R) ©Millennium FX Ltd/DK Images; **456** (B) ©Mike Valentine (BSC)/DK Images; **457** (TL, BR) ©Millennium FX Ltd/DK Images; **458** (TR, R, CL, BC) ©Millennium FX Ltd/DK Images; **459** (TL) ©Millennium FX Ltd/DK Images; **460** (TL) ©Millennium FX Ltd/DK Images, (R) ©Turbo Squid, Inc.; **461** (TC, CR, CC, BR) ©Millennium FX Ltd/DK Images; **462** (TC, B) ©Millennium FX Ltd/DK Images; **463** (TR) ©Paramount/Everett Collection, Inc.; **468** (C) ©American Artist; **469** (CR) Getty Images; **470** (TR, CL) ©American Artist, (BL) ©Matthias Kulka/Corbis; **474** (Bkgd) ©Steve Drake/Solus Photography/Veer, Inc., (TR) Getty Images; **475** (Bkgd) ©Stuart McClymont/Getty Images; **476** (Bkgd) ©Walter Bibikow/Index Stock Imagery; **477** (Bkgd) ©Pete Turner/Getty Images; **478** ©Peter Steiner/Alamy; **479** Getty Images; **480** (BL) ©FogStock/Index Open, (TR) Getty Images; **481** ©Everett Johnson/Index Open; **482** Digital Vision; **483** (T) ©Elmer Frederick Fischer/Corbis, (BR) Tracy Morgan/©DK Images; **485** (L) Getty Images, (R) Image Source/Getty Images; **486** ©Patrik Giardino/Corbis; **487** Getty Images; **488** (R) ©PhotoLibrary/Index Open, (L) ©Tetra Images/Alamy; **489** (R) ©Blend Images/Alamy, (L) Paul Springett/©DK Images; **490** (L) ©Image Source, (R) Susanna Price/©DK Images; **491** Getty Images.

493

Teacher's Edition

Text

KWL Strategy: The KWL Interactive Reading Strategy was developed and is used by permission of Donna Ogle, National-Louis University, Skokie, Illinois, co-author of *Reading Today and Tomorrow,* Holt, Rinehart & Winston Publishers, 1988. (See also the *Reading Teacher,* February 1986, pp. 564–570.)

Understanding by Design quotes: Wiggins, G. & McTighe, J. (2005). *Understanding by Design.* Alexandria, VA: Association for Supervision and Curriculum Development.

Illustrations

Cover Greg Newbold

Running Head Linda Bronson

Photographs

Every effort has been made to secure permission and provide appropriate credit for photographic material. The publisher deeply regrets any omission and pledges to correct errors called to its attention in subsequent editions.

Unless otherwise acknowledged, all photographs are the property of Pearson Education, Inc.

Teacher Resources

Looking for Teacher Resources and other important information?

In the **First Stop** on Reading Street

- **Dear Fifth Grade Teacher**
- **Research into Practice on Reading Street**
- **Guide to Reading Street**
- **Assessment on Reading Street**
- **Customize Writing on Reading Street**
- **Differentiate Instruction on Reading Street**
- **ELL on Reading Street**
- **Customize Literacy on Reading Street**
- **Digital Products on Reading Street**
- **Teacher Resources for Grade 5**
- **Index**

Teacher Resources

Looking for Teacher Resources and other important information?

In the **First Stop** on Reading Street

- **Dear Fifth Grade Teacher**

- **Research into Practice on Reading Street**

- **Guide to Reading Street**

- **Assessment on Reading Street**

- **Customize Writing on Reading Street**

- **Differentiate Instruction on Reading Street**

- **ELL on Reading Street**

- **Customize Literacy on Reading Street**

- **Digital Products on Reading Street**

- **Teacher Resources for Grade 5**

- **Index**